LOCOMOTIVES
OF THE
GREAT SOUTHERN & WESTERN RAILWAY

by
Jeremy Clements, Michael McMahon & Alan O'Rourke

All rights reserved. No part of this publication may be reproduced, stored in a retrieval system or transmitted in any form by any means, electronic, mechanical, photocopying, scanning, recording or otherwise, without the prior written permission of the copyright owners.

First Edition; First Impression

Published by and copyright of: Jeremy Clements, Michael McMahon, Alan O'Rourke 2020

Designer: Kevin Robertson, Newbury, England

Printer: Lettertec Ireland Ltd, Springhill House, Springhill Business Park, Carrigtwohill, Co Cork T45 NX81, Ireland

ISBN 978-1-5272-7028-2

Sole distributor: Collon Publishing, Collon House, Ardee Street, Collon, Co Louth, A92 YT29, Ireland

Email: collonpublishing@gmail.com

While every effort has been made to trace the copyright holders of the photographs used in this work, many of the illustrations in private collections or from digitised sources bore no clues regarding the photographer's identity and/ or valid contact details.

Front main: Of the seventeen 4-6-0s introduced by the Great Southern & Western Railway, the last was unquestionably the best. JR Bazin's Type XXII [22] Class 500 No 500 was theoretically a mixed traffic machine with 5' 8½" driving wheels but it proved competent on all categories of main line work, including the Dublin-Cork "Enterprise" express. Bazin was friendly with Richard Maunsell but whether the latter had a direct hand in the design process is unknown. It is certain though that No 500 was the first design in these islands to follow the 2-cylinder outside Walschaerts long-lap valve gear configuration so effectively refined by Maunsell in his improvement of the Southern Railway's H15, N15 and S15 family. The genre would be pursued by the LMS (Stanier Black 5) in the 1930s and by the LNER (Thompson B1) in the 1940s.

Front lower: McDonnell's initial policy was to use 2-4-0s for passenger services on the Dublin-Cork trunk route. His first new locomotives, as opposed to renewal or rebuilding of earlier machines, were the ten examples of Type X [10] introduced in 1873. No 68 was built in May 1876 and worked until 1928. Within two years, 4-4-0s were entering service resulting in relegation of 2-4-0s to secondary passenger services.

Front endpaper: No 312 (Type XVII [17] Class 309) ready to leave Cork with a Dublin Kingsbridge express prior to World War 1. The 1355-yard long Glanmire tunnel commences about 20 yards beyond the platform end with a gradient of 1 in 78 and a final stretch at 1 in 64. It was an unwelcome challenge at the start of the journey as the tunnel was "wet" leading to perennially greasy rail conditions, hence the presence of a pilot locomotive. In this case, assistance was provided by an unidentified member of 0-6-0 Type XXXV [35] Class 101 which would be detached at Rathpeacon, 4 miles out from Cork. The 1864-gallon Type A tender (authors' classification) attached to the 0-6-0 is in original condition but equipped with Aspinall's unique two pipe vacuum brake system. The 4-4-0 is coupled to a Type B 2730-gallon tender, also in original condition.

Frontispiece: A fine model of one of McDonnell's 2-4-0 locomotives, RNC Type X [10], scale 1.5 inches : 1 foot, built in the period 1872-1880 by D MacNamara. This side is painted while the other is polished metal. The model belonged to John Aspinall who presented it to the Institution of Mechanical Engineers in 1899. Being a contemporary model, this may be assumed to be an accurate representation of the full GSWR livery style in the latter part of the 19th Century. Body colour is reported to have been close to olive green during that period so presumably the shade has darkened over the intervening 140 years.
Reproduced by permission of Institution of Mechanical Engineers

Rear endpaper: At Waterford (Abbey Junction) in GSR days, Type XIX [19] Class 333 No 336 leaves Waterford bound for New Ross with a mixed train comprising a non-corridor Composite coach, a 6-wheel passenger brake van, a selection of wagons and a goods brake. Equipped with 5' 8½" driving wheels, this was the mixed traffic version of the Coey 4-4-0s, and much favoured on workings to Rosslare. The fence in the left foreground marked the boundary between the Dublin & South Eastern Railway and GSWR territory. Out of sight to the left was the other company's locomotive area including shed and turntable, plus a 2-road carriage shed.

Rear cover: The GSWR's family of 0-4-4Ts was a distinctive and successful group of locomotives that saw service from 1869 to 1945. Type XLVI [46] No 35 was a conventional rigid-framed design and a derivation of Type XLV [45], the world's first Single Fairlie.

Locomotives of the Great Southern & Western Railway

Contents

Introduction		4
Locomotive identification		6
Locomotive number keys		11
Chapter 1	Company history	22
Chapter 2	Design and construction	33
Chapter 3	Locomotive works and commercial manufacturers	59
Chapter 4	Passenger tender locomotives	73
Chapter 5	Goods tender locomotives	112
Chapter 6	Tank locomotives	143
Chapter 7	Acquired companies' locomotives	173
Chapter 8	Locomotives of the Waterford, Limerick & Western Railway	193
Chapter 9	Tenders	240
Chapter 10	Amalgamation	262

Appendix:-

A	Influences on locomotive design policy	268
B	McDonnell at the North Eastern Railway	273
C	Accident reports	274
D	Locomotive names	276
E	The Gallant 44	279
	Bibliography	281
	Index	282

Introduction

The need for a comprehensive survey of the Great Southern & Western Railway's motive power was recognised in early 2004, at commencement of the project that culminated in *Locomotives of the GSR* (Colourpoint Publishing, 2008). Explanation of factors that affected evolution post-1925 required delving into earlier history. It became readily apparent that while a detailed review of the Great Southern Railways had not previously reached the public domain, much of the Great Southern & Western Railway's locomotive story was even more obscure.

It was truly remarkable that so little attention had been paid in published works to the locomotives of two companies that successively over one hundred years formed by the definition of route mileage the largest railway undertaking on the island of Ireland. Four years' exploration of the GSR's story underlined the need for a prequel to catalogue the 80 years that witnessed establishment and consolidation of the locomotive fleet of the Great Southern & Western Railway. It was therefore decided in 2011 that if the task was not tackled then, it probably never would be and an important segment of Irish transport history would slip from the collective memory to be lost for ever.

As with the earlier work, the studious endeavours of the late RN Clements and the extensive archives that he left in the care of the Irish Railway Record Society have provided a vital information source. However, for all their thoroughness it became evident that RNC's records were inadequate concerning factors that were more remote in time. With realisation that authoritative confirmation required a wider cast of the net, research through archival material held in Britain has formed a major element of this project. Over half of the locomotive fleet at the time of McDonnell's appointment had been built by British commercial manufacturers. Further, it is evident that the design practices of Beyer Peacock and the London & North Western Railway exerted influence before the GSWR emerged as a significant producer of locomotives in its own right. From the mid-1870s, Inchicore was overshadowed by the facilities of the larger British railway companies in terms of size but developed as more than their match in modernity and competence.

With respect to the smaller companies taken over and absorbed into the GSWR, their fleets were mainly acquired from British commercial manufacturers, with a minority (also originating in Britain) purchased second-hand from other Irish companies. The largest contingent was provided by the Waterford, Limerick & Western Railway. Allowing for certain rebuilding exercises whose ancestry remains uncertain, it could be argued that its motive power fleet owed its origins almost entirely to British commercial practice, reinforced by two migrant locomotive superintendents from the Great Western Railway.

These factors have made this work an international effort. More corporate records are accessible than in RNC's day and custodians are happily willing to co-operate with serious enquirers. However, even with this support, research is costly and time-consuming. For all practical purposes it can only be pursued diligently and thoroughly by a UK resident prepared to explore the dark and dusty corners. Investigations yielded a harvest of General Arrangement drawings but sadly the years have taken their toll and most are unsuitable for reproduction. Nevertheless, information so gathered has proved enormously valuable in amplification or modification of previously recorded "facts". Where differences cannot be resolved, alternative views are provided to allow the reader the final judgement. Further, there are instances where previously documented information has required re-evaluation, necessitating corrective comments.

Establishment of location has been straightforward with the archives for prominent names such as Beyer Peacock and Sharp Stewart but the search process has been frustrated in other cases. Three manufacturers that were significant for the GSWR and its absorbed railways illustrate this point. The records of Bury, Curtis & Kennedy were apparently deposited at the Field Columbian Museum, Chicago, Illinois in the 1890s. Attempts to trace their subsequent fate have led to dead ends; "historian" Clement Stretton (a name that carries a health warning) is linked with this transaction. The fate of the records of Avonside Engine Co and its antecedents is more definite for they were destroyed in a fire in 1870. Following the liquidation of Fairbairn in 1899, the company records were also destroyed. With such important sources irrecoverable, gaps in this account are inevitable. Chapter 3 lists the custodians and who is taking care of what for the benefit of others tempted to pursue this path.

It would be rash to pretend that this work provides the definitive account in all quarters but the authors have run out of places in which to search. Nevertheless they are hopeful that this publication will prompt enquiry and elicit valuable information from previously unidentified sources. They undertake to use their best endeavours to circulate any such information that might emerge post-publication in support of the mission to place in the public domain a comprehensive record of the Locomotives of the Great Southern & Western Railway.

--- o O o ---

Chapter 3 and the Bibliography illustrate the scale and scope of the search among established sources

Locomotives of the Great Southern & Western Railway

but two deserve particular recognition. As with the earlier work, the voluminous archives of RN Clements have played a central role in the creation of this survey. The second is *Irish Steam Loco Register* by JWP Rowledge (Irish Traction Group 1993), a monumental work which at first sight appears dauntingly complex but with a little familiarity provides an easily interpreted and user-friendly guide through the heterogeneous mysteries of Irish motive power. It is the cornerstone for any historical investigation of the Irish locomotive scene.

Very much in the spirit of Rowledge, creation of a logical means of navigating the confusing collection of numbers, types, classes and wheel arrangements has formed an important part of the project. Early GSWR locomotives and all of those contributed by the smaller companies were never formally classified and the numbers of similar machines did not always run sequentially. Running numbers were commonly recycled as with 35 which between 1847 and 1959 adorned locomotives: a 2-2-2 (1847-1869); an 0-4-4T (1875-1892); a 2-4-2T (1894-1959). As an aid to penetrating the maze, the reader is advised to study the section on Locomotive Identification below and to commence any search by reference to the Locomotive Number Keys: GSWR and minor constituents on pages 12 to 20 and Waterford, Limerick & Western Railway on pages 198 to 200.

Once again, Charles Friel has generously allowed a full search of his photographic archive and permitted use of suitable material for reproduction. The authors gratefully acknowledge the support and advice of Kevin Robertson who undertook the layout and design of this work.

Jeremy Clements, County Meath.

Michael McMahon, County Louth

Alan O'Rourke, Sheffield, England

December 2020

The GSWR's network immediately prior to absorption into the Great Southern Railway (note not Railways) in November 1924.

Locomotive Identification

The original intention of the Great Southern & Western Railway had been to identify locomotives by name alone and several were so treated. Names known to have been used were *Antelope, Buffalo, Camel, Dromedary, Grouse, Leopard, Lion, Pheasant, Stag, Urus*, although this list might not be complete. The engine numbers that succeeded these names have not been recorded. It has been suggested that the distinction between mammals and birds might indicate that the former applied to the first passenger engines and the two bird names to the first two goods engines, but this is speculative. The limitations were soon recognised and they were removed marking the first identification principle as throughout its existence, the GSWR was parsimonious in the use of names.

In substituting numbers, the second identification principle was enunciated through the allocation of separate blocks to differentiate between passenger and goods locomotives. Accordingly, numbers 1 to 40 were used for passenger engines (all single drivers) with goods engines (four-coupled) starting from 41 upwards. As traffic expanded, this proved too restrictive so goods locomotives were reallocated numbers in the series starting at 100. Use of different number blocks for passenger and goods engines continued for many years, albeit with exceptions. However, the re-identification of locomotive No 41 as No 100 marked the commencement of a complex, confusing and occasionally misleading pattern of changes that discourages definitive analysis of the company's fleet in the years prior to 1870. Nos 1 to 40 were the *only* engines of the early period to retain their original identities throughout their careers.

RN Clements summarised with blunt succinctness the GSWR's locomotive numbering system as "chaotic", although it gradually became more readily understandable as McDonnell's re-organisational efforts started to bear fruit. To isolate any particular machine for study and to follow the audit trail of changes in form and identity, careful reference to the Locomotive Number Key at the end of this section is strongly recommended. The same caveat applies to the locomotives of the Waterford, Limerick & Western Railway and its constituents, where the history is also confusing, albeit with a significantly smaller fleet. A separate Locomotive Number Key for that concern appears in Chapter 8.

Some locomotives were rebuilt in processes that could substantially change their form while retaining the same number. To demonstrate how this added to complexity, the history of locomotives that bore the number 27 is summarised:

1. Circumstantial evidence suggests that the 20 locomotives built by Bury were ordered as 2-2-0s but were changed to 2-2-2s after trials with that manufacturer's first two (Nos 21 & 22), following their delivery.

2. Built by Bury as a 2-2-2, delivered for service in October 1846.

3. Rebuilt as a "hybrid" type in January 1867 with new boiler and converted to 2-4-0 (still regarded as a passenger locomotive). Last ran in this condition in April 1870.

4. Rebuilt April 1870 (details unknown but still a 2-4-0) and renumbered 62 in August 1870; last ran December 1888 although other records state broken up October 1888.

5. New locomotive in form of 0-4-4T created in January 1871 but officially described as a renewal. Initially identified only as locomotive No X, it was later numbered 27, possibly on entering service or shortly thereafter; withdrawn 1899.

6. New locomotive built November 1900 as 4-4-2T; withdrawn March 1953.

Surviving records have been cross-checked to verify dates and details but this process highlighted anomalies that cannot be definitely resolved. The terms "renewal" and "rebuild" appear have been applied indiscriminately without differentiating between, say, the straightforward matter of a new boiler and more complicated replacement of frames and driving wheels leading to changes in wheel arrangement and/ or diameters.

Also, in several cases the records conflict regarding dates at the end of a locomotive's career. Sub-paragraph 4. in the sequence above concerning locomotives bearing the number 27 suggests that the engine was still working after it had been officially broken up. Where such inconsistencies occur, possible explanations include:

a. Sometimes locomotives stopped working and were technically withdrawn, but lingered on in a "half-life" only to be unexpectedly restored for limited service. Ex-GSWR 4-4-0 No 301 underwent this treatment as late as 1961.

b. A locomotive based at a remote location might be officially withdrawn in Inchicore's records while local authorities deemed it fit enough to continue on restricted duties. A good example was Sharp 2-2-2 No 15 which was recorded standing derelict at Tralee 18 months after its official withdrawal date, while actually remaining in unofficial use as the Castleisland branch relief engine.

c. There was uncertainty over what the term "broken up" actually meant. For example, it could constitute removal and re-cycling of certain parts that might be conveniently replaced if the engine was required later for further service, as opposed to complete dismantling or cutting up. Inchicore was adept at recovering usable parts for use in "new" construction.

    d. Confusion between date(s) that define taken out of service/ withdrawal/ stopped working/ broken up/ sold for scrap/ the officially recorded date in the six-monthly accounting cycle.

    e. Management miscommunication and clerical error.

A further source of confusion stems from disposal of withdrawn locomotives to scrap merchants. Faced with material and monetary shortages from the time of his appointment, McDonnell was notably reluctant to release components that might be recycled for further use in a renewal or rebuilding exercise. Instances have been noted where, despite sale of a locomotive for scrap, key components appear to have been retained for possible re-use. The likelihood is that in these circumstances, disposal involved a worn-out boiler, most of the superstructure and possibly the frames. wheels, cylinders, motion and tender stood a better chance of survival for further use. This would explain apparent contradictions where locomotives were sold but apparently also served as donors of parts for the next generation.

Inchicore occasionally assigned locomotives for departmental duties or placed those near the end of their lives on a duplicate list. Occasional references have been found regarding these lists but no reliable information concerning which engines were so demarcated has been traced. The date sequences in some instances show that an ageing locomotive could stay in service with the same number as that of a new arrival. This phenomenon on other railways resulted in the older engine being distinguished with the addition of a letter prefix or suffix. Apparently, the GSWR relied on the verbal distinction between "old" No xxx and "new" No xxx, which seemed adequate for contemporary needs but is of no value over a century later.

The dominant character in the story of GSWR locomotives was Alexander McDonnell who joined the company as Locomotive Superintendent in 1864. An early step in his reform programme was to renumber the entire fleet (except Nos 1 to 40), and to allow room for future construction and expansion. This was conducted in the autumn of that year in what is known as the October 1864 renumbering scheme. There were some changes after that date which required careful checking but the "October 1864 number" (see Tables on pages 18 and 19) formed the backbone for all subsequent number applications. It continued under the auspices of the Great Southern Railways as formed in 1924/ 5 and was expanded to accommodate the fleets of the Dublin & South Eastern, Midland Great Western, Cork Bandon & South Coast, and the smaller railways.

In this work, the 1864 number forms the core of individual identification despite early locomotives having previously carried other numbers. Class or type identification presents a further challenge as prior to McDonnell there was no formal system in place.

The principle source of data for this work has been, as with *Locomotives of the GSR*, the copiously detailed archives of RN Clements (RNC). The issue of grouping locomotives of the same type was solved by his adoption of a Roman-numerical system of classification. The authors have continued with this discipline to facilitate cross-reference between their own manuscripts and RNC's notes. Also, it was impossible to conceive of a better means of charting a course through a minefield of jumbled data and conflicting historical records. Each locomotive type or class is primarily identified by the RNC's Roman-numeric system and where a recognised GSWR system does not exist, a particular group of locomotives are referred to as Type V, Type IX etc in the relevant commentaries. With later construction that came under the GSWR classification system, the Class designation is added by way of suffix.

The Roman-numeric discipline has been employed for these reasons but as the manner in which this ancient system functions might be unfamiliar, the modern equivalent has been added as a suffix, thus:

Nine = IX = IX [9] = Type IX [9]

Twenty-one = XXI = XXI [21] = Type XXI [21]
                                                                 Class 400

Thirty-five = XXXV = XXXV [35] = Type XXXV [35]
                                                                  Class 101

Forty-six = XLVI = XLVI [46] = Type XLVI [46]

This discipline has been maintained throughout in the Locomotive Key set out below from 2-2-2 No 1 (Type I [1]) to the last locomotive of GSWR design origin, 4-6-0 No 502 (Type XXII [22] Class 500). The highest identification under RNC's Type system relates to locomotives Nos 216/ 7(later 248/ 9) which are Type LXXIII [73]. The system is cumbersome but linked with the Locomotive Numbers Keys provides a more practicable index, as was the case with the Number/ Class Key in *Locomotives of the GSR*. As with the earlier publication, a conventional index was attempted but space is a constraint; a detailed record would add enormously to the size and weight of the work whereas a brief summary would be superficial and purposeless.

Information taken from the RNC archives plus that found in other files in the care of the Irish Railway Record Society, and numerous published works have been distilled into the Locomotive Key. RNC went to considerable effort to reconcile annual fleet totals but his analyses aided by JWP Rowledge remains incomplete, suggesting that the subject was left open in the hope that more information might come to light. The authors have not followed this search string as with the passage of time, anything of a conclusive nature is unlikely now to be uncovered and, in any event, might not be authoritative, given the ambiguity in allocation of locomotive numbers described above.

The search for information in other quarters has borne fruit in adding archival sources that were probably denied RNC. One record at the authors' disposal is the "Riley Book". This was an official GSWR booklet printed in 1874 (manually updated to December 1877) to serve as a summary of the motive power fleet and as a record of locomotive mileages. It was up-dated on a six-monthly basis with changes to the fleet composition annotated by hand. It has not been possible to confirm Mr Riley's position in the motive power hierarchy but he was obviously a senior officer and well-informed. The Riley Book is thus an invaluable resumé of GSWR locomotives at a time when McDonnell's herculean work in fleet overhaul was yielding significant progress.

Another informative document, found in the UK, is a survey report prepared at Swindon in 1874 on the motive power of the Waterford & Limerick Railway. The obvious intent was that it should form part of a due diligence assessment to determine whether the Great Western Railway should launch a takeover bid. As an internal management document in support of a board-level decision concerning a significant potential investment, it bears a high level of both credibility and objectivity.

Locomotive Classification Systems

The Roman-numeric system of Type identification devised by RN Clements is used throughout as a standard method of identification, supported by the GSWR's classification methodology. The latter would seem to have been introduced in the early 1880s with the evolution of McDonnell's 0-6-0s into a recognised locomotive group of substantial proportions. The early principle of number blocks 1 to 40 for passenger engines and 41 upwards for goods was revised and expanded in the 1864 renumbering scheme to accommodate the greater number of engines then in service and planned. The new scheme allowed numbers 1 to 99 for passenger engines and 100 upwards for goods.

By 1866, the highest number in use was 146. The first 0-6-0s of what was to become Class 101 entered service that year as rebuilds of older goods engines and took their numbers (103, 113 etc upwards). The first batch of new locomotives were four from Beyer Peacock introduced in 1867 which were allocated Nos 147-50. Thereafter, additions either took numbers of withdrawn older goods locomotives or were given numbers in the sequence 151 upwards. At some stage in this process, it was decided to identify each class using the lowest running number then in use. For the standard 0-6-0s this was then No 101 built 1882 as the 78th of the class so it appears that the system dates from that year or soon after. The number 100 seems to have been tacitly added to the passenger locomotive block.

From then it became practice to christen types by the number of the prototype which was usually, but not always, the lowest borne by that class. Thus No 2 was the prototype of 4-4-0 Class 2 built 1877; conversely, No 93 built 1885 was the prototype of what became 4-4-0 Class 60 (locomotive No 60 was built in 1891). Withdrawal of the eponymous prototype did not result in re-christening of the class (although this did apply in certain cases following the 1924 Amalgamation). As the GSWR locomotive contingent was the largest in the newly formed Great Southern Railways, these locomotives retained their numbers and the system was extended to accommodate renumbering of the other companies' locomotives (the "GSR system").

On succeeding Watson in 1921, JR Bazin introduced an alpha-numeric classification system which closely followed that devised by Ivatt for use by the English Great Northern Railway. It cannot be established whether this method had an official title; for the purposes of this work, it is referred to as the "Bazin system". The principle was a letter prefix that denoted wheel arrangement and a numeric suffix that denoted relative power (the lower the number, the higher the power output, based on tractive effort). With the Amalgamation, the core principle was retained but it was expanded and recast to include locomotives taken over from the other companies at which time it became officially the "Inchicore system". In practice, neither the Bazin nor the Inchicore alpha-numeric classifications seem to have been much used although references do appear in some GSR files. Pre-Amalgamation application that has been traced appears in the chart reproduced on Page 21.

This work relies solely on RNC's Roman-numeric system and, where appropriate, the GSWR Classes. For cross-reference purposes, the later systems are set out in the table opposite:

RNC Type	Wheel Arrangement	GSWR Class	GSWR (Bazin) Class	GSR Class	Inchicore Class
XII [12]	4-4-0	2	D11	2	D19
X [10]	2-4-0	21	G2	21	G4
LIX [59]	4-4-2T	27	C1	27	C4
LV [55]/ LVI [56]	2-4-2T	33/ 35	F2	33	F6
LVII [57]/ LXI [61]	4-4-2T	37/ 317	C3	37	C7
LII [52]	0-4-4BT	47	K3	47	E3
XIII [13]	4-4-0	52	D10	52	D17
XIV [14]	4-4-0	60	D8	60	D13/ D14
XLVIII [48]	0-6-0T	90	J13	90	J30
XLVIII [48]	0-6-0ST	91	J12	91	J29
XLVIII [48]	0-6-4T	92	H2	92	H2
LIV [54]	0-6-0T	99/ 100	J13	99	J30
XXXV [35]	0-6-0	101	J7	101	J15
LIII [53]	0-6-0T	201	J4	201	J11
LVIII [58]	0-6-0T	201	J4	201	J11
LX [60]	0-6-0T	201	J4	201	J11
LI [51]	0-6-4T	203	H1	203	H1
LI [51]	0-6-0T	204	J5	204	J12
LXII [62]/ XL [40]	0-6-2T/ 0-6-0	211/ 213	J1/ I1	211/ 213	J3/ I1
XXXV [35]-W	0-6-0	222	J9	222	J25
XVI [16]-W	0-4-0ST	228	M2	228	n/a
XXXI [31]-W	0-6-0	233	J8	235	J22
XLIII [43]	0-6-0	257	J2	257	J4
XXIX [29]-W	2-4-2T	266	F1	267 & 491	F4/ F5
XXXIII [33]-W	4-4-2T	269	C2	269	C5
XXVIII [28]-W	2-4-0	263	G1	276	G3
XXA [20A]-W	0-4-4T	279	K1	279	E1
XXXII [32]-W	0-4-4T	294/ 295	K2	295	E2
XXXIV [34]-W	4-4-0	296	D9	296	D15
LXVI [66]	0-6-0ST	299	J11	299	J28
XV [15]	4-4-0	301	D6	301	D11
XVI [16]	4-4-0	305	D7	305	D12
XVII [17]	4-4-0	309/ 310	D4/ D5	309/ 310	D10/ D3
XVIII [18]	4-4-0	321/ 332	D4	321/ 332	D2/ D3 /D4
XIX [19]	4-4-0	333	D1/ D2	333/ 338	D2/ D4 /D4A/ D3
XX [20]	4-4-0	341	D3	341	D1
XXXVII [37]/ XLII [42]	0-6-0	351 (249)	J3	351	J9
XXXVIII [38]	0-6-0 later 2-6-0	355	E1	355	K3
XXXIX [39]	4-6-0	362	B3	362	B3
XLI [41]	2-6-0	368	E2	368	K4
XXI [21]	4-6-0	400	B2	400/ 402	B2/ B2a
XXII [22]	4-6-0	500	B1	500	B1
LXV [65]	4-8-0T	900	A1	900	A1

The following were known only by their names:

RNC Type	Wheel Arrangement	GSWR Class	GSWR (Bazin) Class	GSR Class	Inchicore Class
LXVII [67]	0-6-0T	Erin	J10	[300]	J27
XLVII [47]	0-4-2T	Fairy	L1	Sprite	L4
XLVII [47]	0-4-2T	Sprite	L2	Sprite	L5/ L4
LXIX [69]	0-4-0T	Imp	M1	Imp	M1/ M2
XLIX [49]	0-6-0T	Jumbo	J6	Jumbo	J13
LXIV [64]	0-4-2ST	Sambo	L3	Sambo	L2

EA Watson introduced the GSWR's second 4-6-0 design with his Type XXI [21] Class 400. No 407 is seen here in original 4-cylinder form prior to its rebuilding in 2-cylinder form in 1930 on a Down mail working on the approaches to Cork tunnel.

A late photograph taken in CIE days of Type XXII [22] No 500, at Inchicore shed. In contrast to Class 400, the three members of this 2-cylinder 4-6-0 class underwent no significant modifications except for experimental work carried out by the GSR on No 500 itself in the 1920s. Apart from the livery, this locomotive is in original condition, and coupled to one of the two Type F tenders introduced in 1926 together with 4-6-0 Nos 501/ 2. The tender carries a side ladder, a souvenir from CIE's oil-burning period in the late 1940s. *City Photographic Services per Charles Friel Collection*

The last, the largest, and the best GSWR 4-4-0 was the solitary Type XX [20] Nos 341 *Sir William Goulding*. Strangely camera-shy during its foreshortened 15-year career, illustrations of it at work are hard to find. This locomotive, usually attributed as a Coey/ Maunsell joint design; many regarded its withdrawal as premature. The principal beneficiary of this locomotive was probably Maunsell in addressing the conflicting constraints of high power output and weight limitations in larger inside-cylinder 4-4-0s. This experience would be put to good use later in his career with the South Eastern & Chatham and (English) Southern railways.

Locomotive Number Keys

GSWR Key: the Legend

1864 No.	The number carried and retained by the locomotive as at October 1864 OR The new number allocated through the numbering scheme of October 1864 OR The number carried by locomotives built post-1864 that conformed with the discipline and principles of the October 1864 scheme through to Nos 502 and 901, the last locomotives built to pure GSWR design. Locomotive numbers entered in brackets [ ] were either allocated but never carried before withdrawal or are numbers believed possibly to have been carried for a short period before replacement by another.
RNC Type	The Roman-numeric system of class/ type identification adopted by RN Clements with the modern numeric equivalent suffixed in brackets [ ].
GSWR Class	This is the GSWR classification system introduced by McDonnell, usually but not always based on the lowest running number carried by members of the type. Engines of pre-McDonnell vintage were not formally classified in this fashion, hence the "n/a" entries.
Built	The year, and sometimes the month, in which the locomotive was built new, or the date a locomotive re-entered service after rebuilding or renewal.
Wheel Arrangement	The standard Whyte notification.
Withdrawn	The date the locomotive was taken out of service for sale, dismantling, or rebuild/ renewal subject to the qualifications noted above.

This Key comprises a list of all the numbers carried by locomotives built at Inchicore or supplied by commercial manufacturers plus details sufficient to distinguish between different locomotive types that carried the same number during the company's 80-year history. It also contains summary details of the number exchanges conducted under the 1864 Scheme, and also of the interim letter-based identification system, where such details are known.

Locomotives of the Great Southern & Western Railway

1864 No	RNC Type	GSWR Class	Built	W.A.	W' drawn	1864 No	RNC Type	GSWR Class	Built	W.A.	W' drawn
1	I [1]	n/a	Feb 1846	2-2-2	1865	15	I [1]	n/a	Dec 1847	2-2-2	Jun 1876
	I [1]	n/a	Sep 1866	2-4-0	1871		XII [12]	2	Oct 1880	4-4-0	Sep 1951
	VIII [8]	n/a	Feb 1871	2-4-0	Jun 1887	16	I [1]	n/a	Dec 1847	2-2-2	1865
	XIII [13]	52	Mar 1890	4-4-0	Jun 1955		I [1]	n/a	Apr 1866	2-4-0	Mar 1872
2	I [1]	n/a	Feb 1846	2-2-2	Dec 1873		VIII [8]	n/a	Jan 1873	2-4-0	Nov 1885
	XII [12]	2	May 1877	4-4-0	Mar 1953		XIII [13]	52	Dec 1886	4-4-0	Oct 1959
3	I [1]	n/a	Feb 1846	2-2-2	1865	17	I [1]	n/a	Jan 1848	2-2-2	Dec 1868
	VIII [8]	n/a	May 1869	2-4-0	Oct 1887		VIII [8]	n/a	Jun 1872	2-4-0	1909
	XIII [13]	52	Mar 1890	4-4-0	Nov 1957	18	I [1]	n/a	Jan 1848	2-2-2	1865
4	I [1]	n/a	Feb 1846	2-2-2	1865		I [1]	n/a	1868	2-4-0	1871
	I [1]	n/a	Oct 1867	2-4-0	1871 or 1872		VIII [8]	n/a	Dec 1871	2-4-0	Apr 1888
	VIII [8]	n/a	Mar 1872	2-4-0	Apr 1888		XIII [13]	52	Jun 1888	4-4-0	Oct 1959
	XIII [13]	52	Apr 1888	4-4-0	Mar 1957	19	I [1]	n/a	Mar 1848	2-2-2	1870
5	I [1]	n/a	Apr 1846	2-2-2	Jun 1875		VIII [8]	n/a	Jul 1872	2-4-0	Jan 1891
	XII [12]	2	Jun 1877	4-4-0	1949	20	I [1]	n/a	Mar 1848	2-2-2	1868
6	I [1]	n/a	Apr 1846	2-2-2	Dec 1872		VIII [8]	n/a	Feb 1870	2-4-0	Oct 1888
	XII [12]	2	Aug 1877	4-4-0	Jul 1952		XIII [13]	52	Jun 1890	4-4-0	Aug 1959
7	I [1]	n/a	Apr 1846	2-2-2	Dec 1874	21	II [2]	n/a	Aug 1845	2-2-2	Jun 1873
	XII [12]	2	Sep 1877	4-4-0	May 1953		X [10]	21	Jun 1873	2-4-0	1928
8	I [1]	n/a	Jul 1846	2-2-2	Jan 1874	22	II [2]	n/a	Aug 1845	2-2-2	Jun 1873
	XII [12]	2	Jul 1880	4-4-0	1945		X [10]	21	Jul 1873	2-4-0	1928
9	I [1]	n/a	Aug 1846	2-2-2	1865	23	II [2]	n/a	Jul 1846	2-2-2	Jun 1872
	I [1]	n/a	Oct 1866	2-4-0	1870 or 1871		X [10]	21	Oct 1873	2-4-0	1912
	VIII [8]	n/a	Oct 1874	2-4-0	May 1884	24	II [2]	n/a	Jul 1846	2-2-2	Dec 1872
	XIII [13]	52	Dec 1886	4-4-0	Oct 1955		X [10]	21	Sep 1873	2-4-0	1924
10	I [1]	n/a	Aug 1846	2-2-2	Dec 1874	25	II [2]	n/a	Aug 1846	2-2-2	Dec 1872
	XII [12]	2	Jul 1880	4-4-0	Feb 1952		X [10]	21	Oct 1873	2-4-0	1924
11	I [1]	n/a	Feb 1847	2-2-2	1865	26	II [2]	n/a	Aug 1846	2-2-2	Dec 1872
	I [1]	n/a	1865	2-4-0	1871 or 1872		X [10]	21	Nov 1873	2-4-0	1928
	VIII [8]	n/a	Mar 1872	2-4-0	Jun 1888	27	II [2]	n/a	Oct 1846	2-2-2	Apr 1870
	XIII [13]	52	Apr 1888	4-4-0	1949		IX [9]	n/a	Apr 1870	2-4-0	Dec 1888
12	I [1]	n/a	Feb 1847	2-2-2	1865		XLVI [46]	n/a	Jan 1871	0-4-4T	1899
	VIII [8]	n/a	Jun 1869	2-4-0	Jan 1889		LIX [59]	27	Nov 1900	4-4-2T	Mar 1953
	XIII [13]	52	May 1890	4-4-0	1949	28	II [2]	n/a	Oct 1846	2-2-2	Dec 1873
13	I [1]	n/a	Nov 1847	2-2-2	Dec 1874		L [50]	28	May 1879	0-4-4T	1906
	XII [12]	2	Oct 1880	4-4-0	Jun 1953	29	II [2]	n/a	Oct 1846	2-2-2	Dec 1872
14	I [1]	n/a	Nov 1847	2-2-2	1865		L [50]	28	May 1879	0-4-4T	1907
	I [1]	n/a	Jan 1868	2-4-0	1871 or 1872	30	II [2]	n/a	Apr 1847	2-2-2	Apr 1871
	VIII [8]	n/a	Nov 1872	2-4-0	Mar 1887		IX [9]	n/a	Apr 1871	2-4-0	Jun 1890
	XIII [13]	52	May 1888	4-4-0	Mar 1951		XLVI [46]	n/a	Mar 1871	0-4-4T	1899
							LIX [59]	27	Dec 1900	4-4-2T	May 1950

Locomotive Number Keys

1864 No	RNC Type	GSWR Class	Built	W.A.	W' drawn
31	II [2]	n/a	May 1847	2-2-2	Jun 1870
	XLVI [46]	n/a	Jun 1870	0-4-4T	Apr 1896
	LIX [59]	27	Dec 1900	4-4-2T	May 1953
32	II [2]	n/a	May 1847	2-2-2	Dec 1876
	XLVI [46]	n/a	Jun 1870	0-4-4T	Aug 1896
	LIX [59]	27	Jun 1901	4-4-2T	Mar 1951
33	II [2]	n/a	Jun 1847	2-2-2	1865
	VII [7]	n/a	Mar 1869	2-4-0	Jun 1887
	XLV [45]	n/a	Dec 1869	0-4-4SF	1890
	LV [55]	33	Dec 1892	2-4-2T	Aug 1957
34	II [2]	n/a	Jun 1847	2-2-2	Dec 1867
	XLV [45]	n/a	May 1870	0-4-4SF	1892
	LV [55]	33	Dec 1892	2-4-2T	Dec 1957
35	II [2]	n/a	Jun 1847	2-2-2	Dec 1869
	XLVI [46]	n/a	Oct 1875	0-4-4T	Oct 1892
	LVI [56]	33	Feb 1894	2-4-2T	Oct 1959
36	II [2]	n/a	Jul 1847	2-2-2	Dec 1875
	XLVI [46]	n/a	Oct 1875	0-4-4T	Nov 1892
	LVI [56]	33	Apr 1894	2-4-2T	Dec 1957
37	II [2]	n/a	Jan 1848	2-2-2	Dec 1873
	XLVI [46]	n/a	Nov 1875	0-4-4T	Mar 1893
	LVII [57]	37/ 317	Jul 1894	4-4-2T	Dec 1954
38	II [2]	n/a	Jan 1848	2-2-2	Jun 1871
	XLVI [46]	n/a	Dec 1875	0-4-4T	Mar 1893
	LVII [57]	37/ 317	Oct 1894	4-4-2T	Aug 1950
39	II [2]	n/a	Jan 1848	2-2-2	Dec 1868
	L [50]	28	Jun 1879	0-4-4T	1916
40	II [2]	n/a	Feb 1848	2-2-2	1875
	L [50]	28	Jul 1879	0-4-4T	1936
41	XXIII [23]	n/a	Aug 1845	0-4-2	Dec 1873
	III [3]	n/a	Aug 1855	2-4-0	Aug 1870
	VIII [8]	n/a	Aug 1871	2-4-0	Dec 1888
	LV [55]	33	Dec 1892	2-4-2T	Dec 1957
42	XXIII [23]	n/a	Sep 1845	0-4-2	Dec 1880
	III [3]	n/a	Aug 1855	2-4-0	Dec 1870
	VIII [8]	n/a	Sep 1871	2-4-0	Jun 1887
	LV [55]	33	Mar 1893	2-4-2T	1964
43	XXIII [23]	n/a	Sep 1847	0-4-2	Jun 1871
	IV [4]	n/a	Jul 1853	2-2-2	Dec 1873
	XII [12]	2	Jul 1878	4-4-0	1945
44	XXIII [23]	n/a	Sep 1847	0-4-2	Dec 1865
	VI [6]	n/a	Dec 1859	2-2-2	Jun 1878
	XII [12]	2	Jul 1878	4-4-0	Jul 1950
45	XXIV [24]	n/a	Dec 1847	0-4-2	Dec 1870
	V [5]	n/a	Mar 1858	2-2-2	Dec 1878
	XII [12]	2	Oct 1878	4-4-0	1945
46	XXIV [24]	n/a	Dec 1847	0-4-2	1868
	V [5]	n/a	Apr 1858	2-2-2	Jun 1878
	XII [12]	2	Nov 1878	4-4-0	1935
47	XXIV [24]	n/a	Dec 1847	0-4-2	Jun 1871
	V [5]	n/a	Apr 1858	2-2-2	Jun 1876
	LII [52]	47	May 1883	0-4-4T	1945
48	XXIV [24]	n/a	Jan 1848	0-4-2	Dec 1875
	VI [6]	n/a	Dec 1859	2-2-2	Jul 1881
	LII [52]	47	Jul 1883	0-4-4T	1930
49	XXIV [24]	n/a	Jan 1848	0-4-2	Dec 1874
	VI [6]	n/a	Dec 1859	2-2-2	May 1882
	LII [52]	47	Aug 1883	0-4-4T	1945
50	XXIV [24]	n/a	Jan 1848	0-4-2	Dec 1876
	VI [6]	n/a	Aug 1861	2-2-2	Dec 1878
	LII [52]	47	Sep 1883	0-4-4T	1911
51	XXV [25]	n/a	1849	0-4-2	1867
	VI [6]	n/a	Aug 1861	2-2-2	Jan 1882
	LII [52]	47	Apr 1884	0-4-4T	1934
52	XXV [25]	n/a	1849	0-4-2	1867
	VI [6]	n/a	Oct 1861	2-2-2	Dec 1882
	XIII [13]	52	Nov 1883	4-4-0	1949
53	XXVI [26]	n/a	1850	0-4-2	June 1865
	VI [6]	n/a	Oct 1862	2-2-2	Jun 1882
	XIII [13]	52	Dec 1883	4-4-0	1925
54	XXVI [26]	n/a	1850	0-4-2	1865
	VI [6]	n/a	Dec 1862	2-2-2	Dec 1878
	XIII [13]	52	Dec 1883	4-4-0	Oct 1959
55	XXVI [26]	n/a	1850	0-4-2	Jul 1869
	VI [6]	n/a	Jan 1863	2-2-2	Jan 1882
	XIII [13]	52	Feb 1884	4-4-0	Jun 1955
56	XXVI [26]	n/a	1850	0-4-2	1868
	VII [7]	n/a	Nov 1868	2-4-0	1887
	XIII [13]	52	Sep 1888	4-4-0	1951
57	XXVIII [28]	n/a	Sep 1852	0-4-2	Jun 1873
	VII [7]	n/a	Dec 1868	2-4-0	1887
	XIII [13]	52	Oct 1888	4-4-0	1957
58	XXVIII [28]	n/a	1852	0-4-2	1865
	VII [7]	n/a	Feb 1869	2-4-0	Jun 1887
	XIII [13]	52	Oct 1888	4-4-0	Sep 1953
59	IV [4]	n/a	Jul 1853	2-2-2	Dec 1873
	VII [7]	n/a	Mar 1869	2-4-0	Jun 1887
	XIII [13]	52	Oct 1888	4-4-0	Apr 1955
60	XXXIII [33]	n/a	Apr 1854	0-6-0	Jun 1874
	VII [7]	n/a	Oct 1870	2-4-0	Feb 1891
	XIV [14]	60	Oct 1891	4-4-0	1957
61	XXXIII [33]	n/a	May 1854	0-6-0	Jun 1876
	VII [7]	n/a	Nov 1870	2-4-0	May 1891
	XIV [14]	60	Nov 1891	4-4-0	Jun 1955
62	XXX [30]	n/a	Oct 1854	0-4-2	Jan 1882
	IX [9]	n/a	Apr 1870	2-4-0	Dec 1888
	XIV [14]	60	Dec 1891	4-4-0	Dec 1959

Locomotives of the Great Southern & Western Railway

1864 No	RNC Type	GSWR Class	Built	W.A.	W' drawn	1864 No	RNC Type	GSWR Class	Built	W.A.	W' drawn
63	XXX [30]	n/a	Nov 1854	0-4-2	Jun 1879	85	XXXI [31]	n/a	Feb 1861	0-4-2	Mar 1879
	IX [9]	n/a	Apr 1871	2-4-0	Jun 1890		XIV [14]	60	1886	4-4-0	Aug 1959
	XIV [14]	60	Dec 1891	4-4-0	Jun 1955	86	XXXI [31]	n/a	Mar 1861	0-4-2	Jul 1882
64	XXIX [29]	n/a	Jul 1855	2-4-0	Dec 1873		XIV [14]	60	1886	4-4-0	Aug 1957
	XI [11]	n/a	Jul 1875	2-4-0	1894	87	XXXI [31]	n/a	Mar 1861	0-4-2	Oct 1881
	XIV [14]	60	Oct 1895	4-4-0	Aug 1959		XIV [14]	60	1886	4-4-0	Mar 1957
65	XXIX [29]	n/a	Jul 1855	2-4-0	Dec 1873	88	VI [6]	n/a	Aug 1861	2-2-2	Dec 1878
	XI [11]	n/a	Aug 1875	2-4-0	1894		XIV [14]	60	1886	4-4-0	Mar 1957
	XIV [14]	60	Oct 1895	4-4-0	Aug-59	89	VI [6]	n/a	Aug 1861	2-2-2	Jan 1882
66	XXIX [29]	n/a	Jul 1855	2-4-0	Nov 1873		XIV [14]	60	1886	4-4-0	Feb 1960
	X [10]	21	Mar 1876	2-4-0	1928	90	VI [6]	n/a	Oct 1861	2-2-2	Dec 1882
67	XXXIV [34]	n/a	Feb 1856	0-6-0	Dec 1878		XLVIII [48]	90	Sep 1875	0-6-4T/ 0-6-0T	Oct 1959
	X [10]	21	Mar 1876	2-4-0	1928	91	XXXI [31]	n/a	Mar 1862	0-4-2	Dec 1880
68	XXXIV [34]	n/a	Mar 1856	0-6-0	Jun 1873		XLVIII [48]	91	Apr 1881	0-6-4T/ 0-6-0ST	1930
	X [10]	21	May 1876	2-4-0	1928	92	XXXI [31]	n/a	Apr 1862	0-4-2	Aug 1881
69	XXXIV [34]	n/a	Apr 1856	0-6-0	Dec 1874		XLVIII [48]	92	Jun 1881	0-6-4T	1945
	X [10]	21	Jun 1876	2-4-0	1911	93	XXXI [31]	n/a	April 1862	0-4-2	Jan 1884
70	III [3]	n/a	Jul 1855	2-4-0	Aug 1870		XIV [14]	60	Jun 1885	4-4-0	Oct 1959
	LII [52]	47	Jun 1884	0-4-4T	1934 or 1940	94	VI [6]	n/a	Oct 1862	2-2-2	Jun 1882
71	III [3]	n/a	Aug 1855	2-4-0	Dec 1870		XIV [14]	60	Aug 1885	4-4-0	Aug 1959
	LII [52]	47	Dec 1884	0-4-4T	1907	95	VI [6]	n/a	Dec 1862	2-2-2	Dec 1878
72	XXXIV [34]	n/a	Oct 1856	0-6-0/ 0-6-0T	Mar 1879		XIV [14]	60	Oct 1885	4-4-0	Jun 1955
	LII [52]	47	Dec 1884	0-4-4T	1940	96	VI [6]	n/a	Jan 1863	2-2-2	Jan 1882
73	XXXIV [34]	n/a	Oct 1856	0-6-0/ 0-6-0T	Dec 1874		XIV [14]	60	Nov 1885	4-4-0	Oct 1959
	LII [52]	47	Jun 1887	0-4-4T	1928	97	XXXII [32]	n/a	May 1863	0-4-2	Jun 1883
74	XXXIV [34]	n/a	Dec 1856	0-6-0	Dec 1877		XIII [13]	52	Feb 1887	4-4-0	1930
	LII [52]	47	Jun 1887	0-4-4T	1930	98	XXXII [32]	n/a	Jul 1863	0-4-2/ 0-6-0	Dec 1884
75	XXVII [27]	n/a	1856	0-4-2	1913		XIII [13]	52	Feb 1887	4-4-0	Dec 1954
	LII [52]	47	Sep 1887	0-4-4T	1931	99	XXXII [32]	n/a	Aug 1863	0-4-2/ 0-6-0	Jul 1881
76	VI [6]	n/a	Dec 1859	2-2-2	Jun 1878		LIV [54]	99	Dec 1890	0-6-0T	1930
	LII [52]	47	Sep 1887	0-4-4T	1931	100	XXIII [23]	n/a	Aug 1845	0-4-2	Dec 1873
77	V [5]	n/a	Mar 1858	2-2-2	Dec 1878	[100]	XXXII [32]	n/a	Apr 1865	0-4-2	Jun 1884
	LII [52]	47	Sep 1886	0-4-4T	1931	[100]	L [50]	47	Jul 1879	0-4-4T	Temp No
78	V [5]	n/a	Apr 1858	2-2-2	Jun 1878		LIV [54]	99	Jan 1891	0-6-0T	Oct 1959
	LII [52]	47	Sep 1886	0-4-4T	1945	101	XXIII [23]	n/a	Sep 1845	0-4-2	Dec 1880
79	V [5]	n/a	Apr 1858	2-2-2	Jun 1876	[101]	XXXII [32]	n/a	May 1865	0-4-2	Dec 1884
	LII [52]	47	Oct 1886	0-4-4T	1923		XXXV [35]	101	Sep 1882	0-6-0	1962
80	VI [6]	n/a	Dec 1859	2-2-2	Jul 1881	102	XXIII [23]	n/a	Sep 1847	0-4-2	Jun 1871
	LII [52]	47	Oct 1886	0-4-4T	1931	[102]	XXXII [32]	n/a	May 1865	0-4-2	Jun 1886
81	VI [6]	n/a	Dec 1859	2-2-2	May 1882		XXXV [35]	101	Jan 1873	0-6-0	1962
	LII [52]	47	Aug 1884	0-4-4T	1934	103	XXIII [23]	n/a	Sep 1847	0-4-2	Dec 1865
82	XXXI [31]	n/a	Aug 1860	0-4-2	Dec 1880		XXXV [35]	101	Aug 1867	0-6-0	1886
	LII [52]	47	Sep 1884	0-4-4T	1906		XXXV [35]	101	Aug 1889	0-6-0	Jul 1957
83	XXXI [31]	n/a	Aug 1860	0-4-2	Dec 1880	104	XXIV [24]	n/a	Dec 1847	0-4-2	Dec 1870
	LII [52]	47	Sep 1884	0-4-4T	1928		XXXV [35]	101	Jan 1873	0-6-0	1965
84	XXXI [31]	n/a	Oct 1860	0-4-2	Jun 1883	105	XXIV [24]	n/a	Dec 1847	0-4-2	1868
	LII [52]	47	Dec 1884	0-4-4T	1908		XXXV [35]	101	May 1868	0-6-0	1895
							XXXV [35]	101	Jun 1896	0-6-0	1963

Locomotive Number Keys

1864 No	RNC Type	GSWR Class	Built	W.A.	W' drawn	1864 No	RNC Type	GSWR Class	Built	W.A.	W' drawn
106	XXIV [24]	n/a	Dec 1847	0-4-2	Jun 1871	128	XXXI [31]	n/a	Mar 1861	0-4-2	Jul 1882
	XXXV [35]	101	Jan 1874	0-6-0	1964		XXXV [35]	101	Mar 1882	0-6-0	1963
107	XXIV [24]	n/a	Jan 1848	0-4-2	Dec 1875	129	XXXI [31]	n/a	Mar 1861	0-4-2	Oct 1881
	XXXV [35]	101	Feb 1881	0-6-0	Dec 1957		XXXV [35]	101	Sep 1889	0-6-0	1940
108	XXIV [24]	n/a	Jan 1848	0-4-2	Dec 1874	130	XXXI [31]	n/a	Mar 1862	0-4-2	Dec 1880
	XXXV [35]	101	Feb 1875	0-6-0	Oct 1959		XXXV [35]	101	Dec 1882	0-6-0	1965
109	XXIV [24]	n/a	Jan 1848	0-4-2	Dec 1876	131	XXXI [31]	n/a	Apr 1862	0-4-2	Aug 1881
	XXXV [35]	101	Jan 1877	0-6-0	1964		XXXV [35]	101	Dec 1882	0-6-0	1963
110	XXV [25]	n/a	1849	0-4-2	1867	132	XXXI [31]	n/a	Apr 1862	0-4-2	Jan 1884
	XXXV [35]	101	Jul 1868	0-6-0	1890		XXXV [35]	101	Dec 1888	0-6-0	1965
	XXXV [35]	101	Dec 1890	0-6-0	1963	133	XXXII [32]	n/a	May 1863	0-4-2	Jun 1883
111	XXV [25]	n/a	1849	0-4-2	1867		XXXV [35]	101	Jun 1885	0-6-0	1963
	XXXV [35]	101	Sep 1867	0-6-0	1888	134	XXXII [32]	n/a	Jul 1863	0-4-2	Dec 1884
	XXXV [35]	101	Mar 1891	0-6-0	1963		XXXV [35]	101	Jun 1885	0-6-0	1961
112	XXVI [26]	n/a	1850	0-4-2	Jun 1865	135	XXXII [32]	n/a	Aug 1863	0-4-2	Jul 1881
	XXXV [35]	101	Jun 1866	0-6-0	Sep 1929		XXXV [35]	101	Sep 1885	0-6-0	Dec 1957
113	XXVI [26]	n/a	1850	0-4-2	1865	136	XXXII [32]	n/a	Apr 1865	0-4-2	Jun 1884
	XXXV [35]	101	Dec 1866	0-6-0	1930		XXXV [35]	101	Dec 1888	0-6-0	1962
114	XXVI [26]	n/a	1850	0-4-2	Jul 1869	137	XXXII [32]	n/a	May 1865	0-4-2	Dec 1884
	XXXV [35]	101	Aug 1869	0-6-0	1885		XXXV [35]	101	Dec 1888	0-6-0	Nov 1960
	XXXV [35]	101	Aug 1889	0-6-0	Mar 1961	138	XXXII [32]	n/a	May 1865	0-4-2	Jun 1886
115	XXVI [26]	n/a	1850	0-4-2	1868		XXXV [35]	101	Dec 1888	0-6-0	1962
	XXXV [35]	101	Oct 1869	0-6-0	1929	139	XXXIII [33]	n/a	Apr 1854	0-6-0	Jun 1874
116	XXVII [27]	n/a	1856	0-4-2/ 0-4-2ST	1913		XXXV [35]	101	Apr 1881	0-6-0	Mar 1961
	XXXV [35]	101	Aug 1896	0-6-0	1964	140	XXXIII [33]	n/a	May 1854	0-6-0	Jun 1876
117	XXVIII [28]	n/a	Sep 1852	0-4-2	Jun 1873		XXXV [35]	101	May 1881	0-6-0	Mar 1961
	XXXV [35]	101	Mar 1874	0-6-0	1930	141	XXXIV [34]	n/a	Feb 1856	0-6-0	Dec 1878
118	XXVIII [28]	n/a	1852	0-4-2	1865		XXXV [35]	101	May 1881	0-6-0	Oct 1959
	XXXV [35]	101	May 1867	0-6-0	1890	142	XXXIV [34]	n/a	Mar 1856	0-6-0	Jun 1873
	XXXV [35]	101	May 1891	0-6-0	1966		XXXV [35]	101	Mar 1875	0-6-0	1928
119	XXIX [29]	n/a	Jul 1855	2-4-0	Dec 1873	143	XXXIV [34]	n/a	Apr 1856	0-6-0	Dec 1874
	XXXV [35]	101	Jan 1877	0-6-0	1962		XXXV [35]	101	Dec 1877	0-6-0	Nov 1960
120	XXIX [29]	n/a	Jul 1855	2-4-0	Dec 1873	144	XXXIV [34]	n/a	Oct 1856	0-6-0/ 0-6-0T	Mar 1879
	XXXV [35]	101	Feb 1877	0-6-0	Jun 1955		XXXV [35]	101	Feb 1878	0-6-0	Oct 1954
121	XXIX [29]	n/a	Jul 1855	2-4-0	Nov 1873	145	XXXIV [34]	n/a	Oct 1856	0-6-0/ 0-6-0T	Dec 1874
	XXXV [35]	101	Feb 1877	0-6-0	1963		XXXV [35]	101	Feb 1878	0-6-0	1926
122	XXX [30]	n/a	Oct 1854	0-4-2	Jan 1882	146	XXXIV [34]	n/a	Dec 1856	0-6-0	Dec 1877
	XXXV [35]	101	Sep 1882	0-6-0	1963		XXXV [35]	101	Feb 1878	0-6-0	Jun 1955
123	XXX [30]	n/a	Nov 1854	0-4-2	Jun 1879	147	XXXV [35]	101	May 1867	0-6-0	1888
	XXXV [35]	101	Jul 1881	0-6-0	1963		XXXV [35]	101	May 1891	0-6-0	Mar 1956
124	XXXI [31]	n/a	Aug 1860	0-4-2	Dec 1880	148	XXXV [35]	101	Jun 1867	0-6-0	Jun 1953
	XXXV [35]	101	Sep 1881	0-6-0	1965	149	XXXV [35]	101	Jun 1867	0-6-0	1887
125	XXXI [31]	n/a	Aug 1860	0-4-2	Dec 1880		XXXV [35]	101	Oct 1889	0-6-0	1962
	XXXV [35]	101	Oct 1881	0-6-0	1965	150	XXXV [35]	101	Jul 1867	0-6-0	Dec 1957
126	XXXI [31]	n/a	Oct 1860	0-4-2	Jun 1883	151	XXXV [35]	101	Mar 1868	0-6-0	1965
	XXXV [35]	101	Nov 1881	0-6-0	Oct 1959	152	XXXV [35]	101	Mar 1868	0-6-0	Oct 1959
127	XXXI [31]	n/a	Feb 1861	0-4-2	Mar 1879	153	XXXV [35]	101	Mar 1868	0-6-0	Nov 1954
	XXXV [35]	101	Feb 1882	0-6-0	1963	154	XXXV [35]	101	Mar 1868	0-6-0	Jan 1962

Locomotives of the Great Southern & Western Railway

1864 No.	RNC Type	GSWR Class	Built	W.A.	W' drawn
155	XXXV [35]	101	Feb 1871	0-6-0	1930
156	XXXV [35]	101	Apr 1871	0-6-0	Mar 1961
157	XXXV [35]	101	Mar 1872	0-6-0	1963
158	XXXV [35]	101	Apr 1872	0-6-0	Dec 1957
159	XXXV [35]	101	Sep 1871	0-6-0	1949
160	XXXV [35]	101	Oct 1871	0-6-0	Jun 1955
161	XXXV [35]	101	Oct 1871	0-6-0	1963
162	XXXV [35]	101	Dec 1871	0-6-0	1963
163	XXXV [35]	101	Jul 1872	0-6-0	Jun 1955
164	XXXV [35]	101	Aug 1872	0-6-0	1963
165	XXXV [35]	101	Aug 1872	0-6-0	1945
166	XXXV [35]	101	Aug 1872	0-6-0	1963
167	XXXV [35]	101	Mar 1873	0-6-0	Feb 1960
168	XXXV [35]	101	Apr 1873	0-6-0	1962
169	XXXV [35]	101	Mar 1874	0-6-0	1928
170	XXXV [35]	101	Apr 1874	0-6-0	1963
171	XXXV [35]	101	Jul 1874	0-6-0	Mar 1961
172	XXXV [35]	101	Aug 1874	0-6-0	1964
173	XXXV [35]	101	Sep 1874	0-6-0	1933
174	XXXV [35]	101	Nov 1874	0-6-0	Feb 1953
175	XXXV [35]	101	Aug 1873	0-6-0	Mar 1956
176	XXXV [35]	101	Aug 1873	0-6-0	Oct 1959
177	XXXV [35]	101	Dec 1873	0-6-0	1927
178	XXXV [35]	101	Dec 1873	0-6-0	1926
179	XXXV [35]	101	Apr 1875	0-6-0	1963
180	XXXV [35]	101	May 1875	0-6-0	1928
181	XXXV [35]	101	Aug 1879	0-6-0	Oct 1959
182	XXXV [35]	101	Sep 1879	0-6-0	1962
183	XXXV [35]	101	Jan 1880	0-6-0	1965
184	XXXV [35]	101	Feb 1880	0-6-0	1963
185	XXXV [35]	101	Aug 1879	0-6-0	Dec 1959
186	XXXV [35]	101	Nov 1879	0-6-0	1964
187	XXXV [35]	101	Mar 1882	0-6-0	1957
188	XXXV [35]	101	Jul 1882	0-6-0	Oct 1959
189	XXXV [35]	101	May 1881	0-6-0	1923
190	XXXV [35]	101	May 1881	0-6-0	1963
191	XXXV [35]	101	Oct 1885	0-6-0	1962
192	XXXV [35]	101	Sep 1898	0-6-0	Mar 1956
193	XXXV [35]	101	Sep 1898	0-6-0	1963
194	XXXV [35]	101	Nov 1898	0-6-0	Oct 1959
195	XXXV [35]	101	Dec 1898	0-6-0	1965
196	XXXV [35]	101	May 1899	0-6-0	Mar 1961
197	XXXV [35]	101	Jun 1899	0-6-0	Mar 1961
198	XXXV [35]	101	Jun 1899	0-6-0	1965
199	XXXV [35]	101	Nov 1899	0-6-0	Sep 1954
200	XXXVI [36]	200	Feb 1903	0-6-0	
	XXXV [35]	101		0-6-0	Nov 1960
201	XLIX [49]	201	Sep 1876	0-6-4T	May 1910
	LVIII [58]	201	Dec 1895	0-6-0T	1963
202	XLIX [49]	201	Sep 1876	0-6-4T/ 0-6-0T	Mar 1957
	LVIII [58]	201	Dec 1895	0-6-0T	Nov 1955
203	LI [51]	203	Dec 1879	0-6-4T	1940
204	LI [51]	203	Dec 1879	0-6-4T/ 0-6-0T	1952
205	LI [51]	203	Apr 1880	0-6-4T	1928
206	LI [51]	203	May 1880	0-6-4T	1928
207	LIII [53]	207	Dec 1887	0-6-0T	Oct 1959
208	LIII [53]	207	Dec 1887	0-6-0T	Oct 1959
209	LIII [53]	207	Dec 1887	0-6-0T	Mar 1949
210	LIII [53]	207	Dec 1887	0-6-0T	Oct 1959
211	LXII [62]	211	Dec 1903	0-6-2T	1907
	XL [40]	211	1907	0-6-0	1949
212	LXII [62]	212	Dec 1903	0-6-2T	1907
	XL [40]	211	1907	0-6-0	1951
213	LXII [62]	211/ 213	Dec 1903	0-6-2T	Jan 1953
214	LXII [62]	211/ 213	Dec 1903	0-6-2T	1949
215-216	VACANT				
217	LX [60]	217	1901	0-6-0T	Mar 1961
218	LX [60]	217	1901	0-6-0T	Oct 1959
219	LX [60]	217	1901	0-6-0T	Aug 1955
220	LX [60]	217	1901	0-6-0T	Oct 1959
221-222	VACANT				
223	XXXVI [36]	200	Feb 1903	0-6-0	
	XXXV [35]	101		0-6-0	Nov 1960
224-228	VACANT				
229	XXXVI [36]	200	Mar 1903	0-6-0	
	XXXV [35]	101		0-6-0	1960
230-231	VACANT				
232	XXXVI [36]	200	Mar 1903	0-6-0	
	XXXV [35]	101		0-6-0	1963
233-239	VACANT				
240	XXXVI [36]	200	Oct 1902	0-6-0	
	XXXV [35]	101		0-6-0	Dec 1957
241	XXXVI [36]	200	Dec 1902	0-6-0	
	XXXV [35]	101		0-6-0	Aug 1957
242	XXXVI [36]	200	Dec 1902	0-6-0	
	XXXV [35]	101		0-6-0	Mar 1957
243	XXXVI [36]	200	Jan 1903		
	XXXV [35]	101		0-6-0	Nov 1955
244-248	VACANT				
249	XLII [42]	351	Apr 1912	0-6-0	1963
250	XLII [42]	351	May 1912	0-6-0	1963
251	XLII [42]	351	May 1912	0-6-0	1964
252	XLII [42]	351	Jun 1912	0-6-0	Mar 1961
253	XXXVI [36]	200	1903	0-6-0	
	XXXV [35]	101		0-6-0	1963

Locomotive Number Keys

1864 No	RNC Type	GSWR Class	Built	W.A.	W' drawn	1864 No	RNC Type	GSWR Class	Built	W.A.	W' drawn
254	XXXVI [36]	200	1903	0-6-0		335	XIX [19]	333	Jun 1907	4-4-0	Jun 1955
	XXXV [35]	101		0-6-0	Mar 1961	336	XIX [19]	333	Jun 1907	4-4-0	Apr 1957
255	XXXVI [36]	200	1903	0-6-0		337	XIX [19]	333	Jun 1908	4-4-0	Jun 1955
	XXXV [35]	101	1903	0-6-0	1964	338	XIX [19]	333	Jun 1908	4-4-0	Oct 1959
256	XXXVI [36]	200	1903	0-6-0		339	XIX [19]	333	Jun 1908	4-4-0	Dec 1959
	XXXV [35]	101		0-6-0	Oct 1959	340	XIX [19]	333	Jun 1908	4-4-0	Dec 1955
257	XLIII [43]	257	Oct 1913	0-6-0	Nov 1960	341	XX [20]	341	May 1913	4-4-0	1928
258	XLIII [43]	257	Oct 1913	0-6-0	1963	342-50	VACANT				
259	XLIII [43]	257	Nov 1913	0-6-0	Oct 1959	351	XXXVII [37]	351	Nov 1903	0-6-0	1964
260	XLIII [43]	257	Nov 1913	0-6-0	1962	352	XXXVII [37]	351	Dec 1903	0-6-0	Jun 1955
261	XLIII [43]	257	Nov 1914	0-6-0	1965	353	XXXVII [37]	351	Dec 1903	0-6-0	1931
262	XLIII [43]	257	Nov 1914	0-6-0	1965	354	XXXVII [37]	351	Dec 1903	0-6-0	1962
263	XLIII [43]	257	Dec 1914	0-6-0	1962	355	XXXVIII [38]	355	Nov 1903	0-6-0/ 2-6-0	1928
264	XLIII [43]	257	Dec 1914	0-6-0	May 1960	356	XXXVIII [38]	355	Nov 1903	0-6-0/ 2-6-0	Mar 1957
265-300	VACANT					357	XXXVIII [38]	355	Dec 1903	0-6-0/ 2-6-0	Feb 1960
301	XV [15]	301	Apr 1900	4-4-0	1960	358	XXXVIII [38]	355	Dec 1903	0-6-0/ 2-6-0	Mar 1957
302	XV [15]	301	Apr 1900	4-4-0	Aug 1957	359	XXXVIII [38]	355	Dec 1903	0-6-0/ 2-6-0	Dec 1959
303	XV [15]	301	Jun 1900	4-4-0	Oct 1959	360	XXXVIII [38]	355	Dec 1903	0-6-0/ 2-6-0	Jun 1955
304	XV [15]	301	Jun 1900	4-4-0	Nov 1959	361	XXXVIII [38]	355	Dec 1903	0-6-0/ 2-6-0	Oct 1959
305	XVI [16]	305	Mar 1902	4-4-0	Apr 1957	362	XXXIX [39]	362	Dec 1905	4-6-0	1928
306	XVI [16]	305	Jun 1902	4-4-0	Oct 1959	363	XXXIX [39]	362	Dec 1905	4-6-0	1928
307	XVI [16]	305	Jun 1902	4-4-0	Oct 1959	364	XXXIX [39]	362	Dec 1905	4-6-0	1928
308	XVI [16]	305	Jun 1902	4-4-0	Aug 1931	365	XXXIX [39]	362	Dec 1905	4-6-0	1928
309	XVII [17]	309	Jun 1903	4-4-0	Oct 1959	366	XXXIX [39]	362	Jun 1907	4-6-0	1931
310	XVII [17]	309	Jun 1903	4-4-0	Nov 1957	367	XXXIX [39]	362	Jun 1907	4-6-0	1928
311	XVII [17]	309	Jun 1903	4-4-0	Oct 1959	368	XLI [41]	368	Sep 1909	2-6-0	1928
312	XVII [17]	309	Jun 1903	4-4-0	Oct 1959	369	XLI [41]	368	Sep 1909	2-6-0	Mar 1957
313	XVII [17]	309	Jun 1903	4-4-0	Dec 1957	370	XLI [41]	368	Sep 1909	2-6-0	Mar 1957
314	XVII [17]	309	Jun 1903	4-4-0	Dec 1957	371	XLI [41]	368	Sep 1909	2-6-0	1928
315/ 6	VACANT					372-399	VACANT				
317	LXI [61]	31/ 317	Jun 1901	4-4-2T	Apr 1955	400	XXI [21]	400	Aug 1916	4-6-0	1929
318	LXI [61]	31/ 317	Jun 1901	4-4-2T	May 1953	401	XXI [21]	400	Apr 1921	4-6-0	Mar 1961
319	LXI [61]	31/ 317	Jun 1901	4-4-2T	1950	402	XXI [21]	400	Aug 1921	4-6-0	Mar 1961
320	LXI [61]	31/ 317	Jun 1901	4-4-2T	Dec 1954	403	XXI [21]	400	Jun 1923	4-6-0	1959
321	XVIII [18]	321	Dec 1904	4-4-0	1957	404	XXI [21]	400	Jun 1923	4-6-0	1930
322	XVIII [18]	321	Jan 1905	4-4-0	Feb 1960	405	XXI [21]	400	Jun 1923	4-6-0	Sep 1955
323	XVIII [18]	321	Jan 1905	4-4-0	Jun 1955	406	XXI [21]	400	Nov 1921	4-6-0	Mar 1957
324	XVIII [18]	321	Feb 1905	4-4-0	1928	407	XXI [21]	400	Jun 1923	4-6-0	Mar 1955
325	XVIII [18]	321	May 1905	4-4-0	1928	408	XXI [21]	400	Jun 1923	4-6-0	1930
326	XVIII [18]	321	Jun 1905	4-4-0	1927	409	XXI [21]	400	Jun 1923	4-6-0	Mar 1958
327	XVIII [18]	321	Jun 1905	4-4-0	Oct 1959	410-499	VACANT				
328	XVIII [18]	321	Jun 1905	4-4-0	Aug 1959	500	XXII [22]	500	Apr 1924	4-6-0	Jun 1955
329	XVIII [18]	321	Nov 1906	4-4-0	Feb 1960	501-899	VACANT				
330	XVIII [18]	321	Dec 1906	4-4-0	Mar 1957	Sambo	LXIV [64]	Sambo	Jun 1914	0-4-2ST	1962
331	XVIII [18]	321	Oct 1906	4-4-0	Aug 1959	900	LXV [65]	900	Sep 1915	4-8-0T	1928
332	XVIII [18]	321	Oct 1906	4-4-0	Oct 1959	Sprite (1st)	XLIV [44]	76/ Sprite	1857	0-2-4T	1871-2
333	XIX [19]	333	Jun 1907	4-4-0	Aug 1955	Sprite (2nd)	XLVII [47]	Sprite	Jan 1873	0-4-2T	1927
334	XIX [19]	333	Jun 1907	4-4-0	Jun 1955	Fairy	XLVII [47]	Sprite	Dec 1894	0-4-2T	1927
						No.1	LXIII [63]	Railmotor	Aug 1904	0-2-2VBT	1915

Locomotives of the Great Southern & Western Railway

The Key on pages 12-17 refers **ONLY** to locomotives of GSWR origin and does **NOT** include the following:

Cork & Youghal Railway (refer pages 174/ 5): Nos 61 to 70, later Nos 71 to 80

Regarding later transactions, numbers between 211 to 300 were used for the following locomotives:

Waterford, Dungarvan & Lismore Railway (refer pages 175-8): Nos 211-7, later 244-9

Waterford, Limerick & Western Railway (refer Chapter 8): Nos 221-239, 260 to 298

Fishguard & Rosslare Railways & Harbours Company (refer pages 179/ 180); No 300 & other unnumbered

Waterford & Central Ireland Railway (refer pages 181-190) Nos 250-259

Tralee & Fenit Pier & Harbour Commissioners (pages 190/ 1) sold one locomotive to the GSWR – No 299

Following withdrawal of acquired locomotives, some of these numbers were re-used by GSWR-origin engines as recorded in the Key.

The 1864 Renumbering Programme

As mentioned above in Locomotive Identification, Inchicore instituted a renumbering programme for sixty-eight locomotives excluding the forty 2-2-2s in Types I [1] and II [2] in their original condition. Most were carried out in October 1864 but a few followed in successive years. Details are included in the relevant Locomotive Type histories but are also summarised below in the numerical order of both the original and the 1864 identification systems.

Former No	Date changed	Type	1864 Scheme No	Former No	Date changed	Type	1864 Scheme No	Former No	Date changed	Type	1864 Scheme No
27	Aug 1870	IX [9]	62	58	Oct 1864	XXVIII [28]	118	81	Oct 1864	VI [6]	49
30	May 1871	IX [9]	63	59	Oct 1864	IV [4]	43	82	Oct 1864	XXXI [31]	124
31	Nov 1868	VII [7]	56	60	Oct 1864	XXXIII [33]	139	83	Oct 1864	XXXI [31]	125
32	Feb 1869	VII [7]	58	61	Oct 1864	XXXIII [33]	140	84	Oct 1864	XXXI [31]	126
33	Mar 1869	VII [7]	59	62	Oct 1864	XXX [30]	122	85	Oct 1864	XXXI [31]	127
34	Dec 1868	VII [7]	57	63	Oct 1864	XXX [30]	123	86	Oct 1864	XXXI [31]	128
41	Oct 1864	XXIII [23]	100	64	Oct 1864	XXIX [29]	119	87	Oct 1864	XXXI [31]	129
42	Oct 1864	XXIII [23]	101	65	Oct 1864	XXIX [29]	120	88	Oct 1864	VI [6]	50
43	Oct 1864	XXIII [23]	102	66	Oct 1864	XXIX [29]	121	89	Oct 1864	VI [6]	51
44	Oct 1864	XXIII [23]	103	67	Oct 1864	XXXIV [34]	141	90	Oct 1864	VI [6]	52
45	Oct 1864	XXIV [24]	104	68	Oct 1864	XXXIV [34]	142	91	Oct 1864	XXXI [31]	130
46	Oct 1864	XXIV [24]	105	69	Oct 1864	XXXIV [34]	143	92	Oct 1864	XXXI [31]	131
47	Oct 1864	XXIV [24]	106	70	Oct 1864	III [3]	41	93	Oct 1864	XXXI [31]	132
48	Oct 1864	XXIV [24]	107	71	Oct 1864	III [3]	42	94	Oct 1864	VI [6]	53
49	Oct 1864	XXIV [24]	108	72	Oct 1864	XXXIV [34]	144	95	Oct 1864	VI [6]	54
50	Oct 1864	XXIV [24]	109	73	Oct 1864	XXXIV [34]	145	96	Oct 1864	VI [6]	55
51	Oct 1864	XXV [25]	110	74	Oct 1864	XXXIV [34]	146	97	Oct 1864	XXXII [32]	133
52	Oct 1864	XXV [25]	111	75	Oct 1864	XXVII [27]	116	98	Oct 1864	XXXII [32]	134
53	Oct 1864	XXVI [26]	112	76	Oct 1864	VI [6]	44	99	Oct 1864	XXXII [32]	135
54	Oct 1864	XXVI [26]	113	77	Oct 1864	V [5]	45	[100]	Apr 1865	XXXII [32]	136
55	Oct 1864	XXVI [26]	114	78	Oct 1864	V [5]	46	[101]	May 1865	XXXII [32]	137
56	Oct 1864	XXVI [26]	115	79	Oct 1864	V [5]	47	[102]	May 1865	XXXII [32]	138
57	Oct 1864	XXVIII [28]	117	80	Oct 1864	VI [6]	48				

1864 Scheme No	Date changed	Type	Former No	1864 Scheme No	Date changed	Type	Former No	1864 Scheme No	Date changed	Type	Former No
41	Oct 1864	III [3]	70	102	Oct 1864	XXIII [23]	43	125	Oct 1864	XXXI [31]	83
42	Oct 1864	III [3]	71	103	Oct 1864	XXIII [23]	44	126	Oct 1864	XXXI [31]	84
43	Oct 1864	IV [4]	59	104	Oct 1864	XXIV [24]	45	127	Oct 1864	XXXI [31]	85
44	Oct 1864	VI [6]	76	105	Oct 1864	XXIV [24]	46	128	Oct 1864	XXXI [31]	86
45	Oct 1864	V [5]	77	106	Oct 1864	XXIV [24]	47	129	Oct 1864	XXXI [31]	87
46	Oct 1864	V [5]	78	107	Oct 1864	XXIV [24]	48	130	Oct 1864	XXXI [31]	91
47	Oct 1864	V [5]	79	108	Oct 1864	XXIV [24]	49	131	Oct 1864	XXXI [31]	92
48	Oct 1864	VI [6]	80	109	Oct 1864	XXIV [24]	50	132	Oct 1864	XXXI [31]	93
49	Oct 1864	VI [6]	81	110	Oct 1864	XXV [25]	51	133	Oct 1864	XXXII [32]	97
50	Oct 1864	VI [6]	88	111	Oct 1864	XXV [25]	52	134	Oct 1864	XXXII [32]	98
51	Oct 1864	VI [6]	89	112	Oct 1864	XXVI [26]	53	135	Oct 1864	XXXII [32]	99
52	Oct 1864	VI [6]	90	113	Oct 1864	XXVI [26]	54	136	Apr 1865	XXXII [32]	[100]
53	Oct 1864	VI [6]	94	114	Oct 1864	XXVI [26]	55	137	May 1865	XXXII [32]	[101]
54	Oct 1864	VI [6]	95	115	Oct 1864	XXVI [26]	56	138	May 1865	XXXII [32]	[102]
55	Oct 1864	VI [6]	96	116	Oct 1864	XXVII [27]	75	139	Oct 1864	XXXIII [33]	60
56	Nov 1868	VII [7]	31	117	Oct 1864	XXVIII [28]	57	140	Oct 1864	XXXIII [33]	61
57	Dec 1868	VII [7]	34	118	Oct 1864	XXVIII [28]	58	141	Oct 1864	XXXIV [34]	67
58	Feb 1869	VII [7]	32	119	Oct 1864	XXIX [29]	64	142	Oct 1864	XXXIV [34]	68
59	Mar 1869	VII [7]	33	120	Oct 1864	XXIX [29]	65	143	Oct 1864	XXXIV [34]	69
62	Aug 1870	IX [9]	27	121	Oct 1864	XXIX [29]	66	144	Oct 1864	XXXIV [34]	72
63	May 1871	IX [9]	30	122	Oct 1864	XXX [30]	62	145	Oct 1864	XXXIV [34]	73
100	Oct 1864	XXIII [23]	41	123	Oct 1864	XXX [30]	63	146	Oct 1864	XXXIV [34]	74
101	Oct 1864	XXIII [23]	42	124	Oct 1864	XXXI [31]	82				

GSWR interim letter-based identification system

The first tank locomotive built at Inchicore was Type XLV [45] Single Fairlie 0-4-4T with running No 33, completed in December 1869. During construction, and possibly for a period after entering service, it was identified solely as P (just as its companion completed May 1870 was Q, later No 34). The purpose of these designations is unknown but possibly they were an accounting convenience prior to selection of suitable running numbers from vacancies within the locomotive stock list. Locomotive No P is the earliest identified example of this system but its origins may have pre-dated December 1869 as the logical starting place for such a methodology would have been A, B, C etc.

Between 1869 and 1875, apparently random applications of designation by letter have been identified, as follows: -

Letter	Type	Running No	Built	Letter	Type	Running No	Built
P	XLV [45]	33	Dec 1869	U	VII [7]	61	Nov 1870
L	VIII [8]	20	Feb 1870	X	XLVI [46]	27	Jan 1871
Q	XLV [45]	34	May 1870	Y	XLVI [46]	30	Mar 1871
N	XLVI [46]	31	Jun 1870	C	XLVIII [48]	90	Sep 1875
O	XLVI [46]	32	Jun 1870	C2	XLVIII [48]	91	Apr 1881
T	VII [7]	60	Oct 1870	C3	XLVIII [48]	92	Jun 1881

The system was revived for some of 0-4-4T Type LII [52] Class 47 during construction: -

Letter	Running No	Built
A	47	May 1883
B	48	Jul 1883
C	49	Aug 1883
D	50	Sep 1883

Letters between A and R were also adopted for all sixteen newly-built members of 4-4-0 Type XIII [13] Class 52 during construction. The remaining four (Nos 56 to 59) were officially renewals of earlier engines (see overleaf).

Locomotives of the Great Southern & Western Railway

Letter	Running No	Built	Letter	Running No	Built
A	52	Nov 1883	K	4	Apr 1888
B	53	Dec 1883	L	11	Apr 1888
C	54	Dec 1883	M	14	May 1888
D	55	Feb 1884	N	18	Jun 1888
E	9	Dec 1886	O	1	Mar 1890
F	16	Dec 1886	P	3	Mar 1890
G	97	Feb 1887	Q	12	May 1890
H	98	Feb 1887	R	20	Jun 1890

GSWR numbers: Acquired Companies' Locomotives

Engines absorbed from companies taken over or purchased from third parties were renumbered in the GSWR fleet list:

GSWR No	Acq'd Coy	Acq'd No	RNC Type	W.A.	2nd GSWR No	GSWR No	Acq'd Coy	Acq'd No	RNC Type	W.A.
61	CYR	1	LXX [70]	2-4-0ST	71 § $	[250]	WCIR	1	IX [9]-WKR	0-4-2
62	CYR	2	LXX [70]	2-4-0ST	72 §	[251]	WCIR	2	II [2] - WKR	2-4-0
63	CYR	3	LXX [70]	2-4-0ST	73 §	252	WCIR	4	X [10]-WKR	0-4-2
64	CYR	4	LXX [70]	2-4-0ST	74 §	[253]	WCIR	6	V [5]-WKR	2-4-0
65	CYR	5	LXX [70]	2-4-0ST	75 §	[254]	WCIR	7	V [5]-WKR	2-4-0
66	CYR	9	LXX [70]	2-4-0ST	76 §	[255]	WCIR	8	VI [6]-WKR	2-4-0
67	CYR	10	LXX [70]	2-4-0ST	77 §	[256]	WCIR	9	VI [6]-WKR	2-4-0
68	CYR	6	LXXI [71]	2-4-0ST	78 §	257	WCIR	10	VII [7]-WKR	0-4-2
69	CYR	7	LXXI [71]	2-4-0ST	79 §	258	WCIR	11	VII [7]-WKR	0-4-2
70	CYR	8	LXXI [71]	2-4-0ST	80 §	[259]	WCIR	12	VIII [8]-WKR	0-4-2T
90	CR	None	XLVIII [48]	0-6-4T	n/a ±	299	TFHC	Shamrock	LXVI [66]	0-6-0ST
211	WDLR	1	LXXII [72]	0-4-2	244 #	[300]	FRRHC	Erin	LXVII [67]	0-6-0ST
212	WDLR	2	LXXII [72]	0-4-2	245 #	Cambria	FRRHC	Cambria	LXVIII [68]	0-4-0ST
213	WDLR	3	LXXII [72]	0-4-2	246 #	Imp	DBST	2	LXIX[69]	0-4-0T
214	WDLR	4	LXXII [72]	0-4-2	247 #					
[215]	WDLR	5	LXX [70]	2-4-0ST	n/a $					
216	WDLR	6	LXXIII [73]	0-4-2	248 #					
217	WDLR	7	LXXIII [73]	0-4-2	249 #					

§   First GSWR numbered applied January 1866; renumbered by GSWR October 1870
\#   First GSWR numbered applied 1898; renumbered by GSWR 1901
±   Locomotive built at Inchicore for this railway; identified as "C" during construction but apparently ran unnumbered while on Castleisland Railway; renumbered 90 in GSWR list on takeover on 31st August 1879
$ This locomotive was originally CYR No 1, later GSWR No 61 and then GSWR No 71; it was sold to WDLR in January 1883 becoming their No 5; condemned shortly before takeover by GSWR, it was nevertheless allocated No 215, but not carried as locomotive was broken up shortly afterwards

Key to initials:
CR = Castleisland Railway; CYR = Cork & Youghal Railway; DBST = Dublin & Blessington Steam Tramway; FRRHC = Fishguard & Rosslare Railways & Harbours Company; TFHC = Tralee & Fenit Pier & Harbour Commissioners; WCIR = Waterford & Central Ireland Railway; WDLR = Waterford, Dungarvan & Lismore Railway

Waterford Limerick & Western Railway

With the takeover of the WLWR in 1901, acquired locomotives were allocated numbers in the following blocks 221 to 239 and 260 to 298 in the GSWR stock list. GSWR numbers in brackets [ ] were allocated but the respective locomotives were withdrawn before they could be applied.

GSWR No	WLWR No	RNC Type	W.A.	GSWR No	WLWR No	RNC Type	W.A.
221	1	XXIII [23] - W	0-6-0ST	266/ 267	13/ 14	XXIX [29] - W	2-4-2T
222	2	XXXV [35] - W	0-6-0	268	15	XXX [30] - W	0-4-4T
[223]	4	XIV [14] - W	0-4-2	269 to 271	16 to 18	XXXIII [33] - W	4-4-2T
224/ 225	5/ 6	XIVA [14A] - W	0-6-0	[272]	19	XX [20] - W	0-4-2
226	7	XVIIA [17A] - W	0-6-0	273	20	XXVIII [28] - W	2-4-0

Locomotives of the Great Southern & Western Railway

227	24	XXVII [27] - W	0-6-0
228	29	XVI [16] - W	0-4-0ST
[229]	34	XXI [21] - W	0-6-0T
230/ 231	40/ 41	XXII [22] - W	0-6-0
[232]	42	XXIV [24] - W	0-4-2WT
233 to 236	45/ 46/ 49/ 50	XXXI [31] - W	0-6-0
237 to 239	56 to 58	XXXV [35] - W	0-6-0
260	3	XXX [30] - W	0-4-2T
[261]	8	XIX [19] - W	2-4-0
262	9	XXV [25] - W	4-4-0
263	10	XXVIII [28] - W	2-4-0
[264]	11	IV [4] - W	2-4-0
274	21	XXXIII [33] - W	4-4-2T
275/ 276	22/ 23	XXVIII [28] - W	2-4-0
[277]	25	XIX [19] - W	2-4-0
278	26	XX [20] -W	0-4-2
279	27	XXA [20A] - W	0-4-4T
[280]	28	XV [15] - W	2-2-2
281 to 283	30 to 32	XIX [19] - W	2-4-0
[284]	33	XX [20] - W	0-4-2
285 to 289	35 to 39	XIX [19] - W	2-4-0
290 to 293	43/ 44/ 47/ 48	XXVIII [28] - W	2-4-0
294/ 295	51/ 52	XXXII [32] - W	0-4-4T
296 to 298	53 to 55	XXXIV [34] - W	4-4-0

The logic and simplicity of the Bazin alpha-numeric system enabled it to be summarised together with individual locomotive identities on a single sheet. The principles were retained for the expanded and recast "Inchicore" Class system that embraced the fleets of all the other companies absorbed into the Great Southern Railways at the Amalgamation. The chart is undated but includes 4-6-0 Nos 403-5/ 407-9 delivered June 1923 and dimensions for a planned 4-6-0 yet to be identified as No 500. This implies that is was prepared in the second half of that year.

Chapter 1
Company history

As an independent entity, the Great Southern & Western Railway (GSWR) had a life span from incorporation on 6th August 1844 until its absorption on 12th November 1924 into the Great Southern Railway (Railways from 1st January 1925). The development, consolidation and operation of the GSWR fell neatly into three distinct phases that chronologically-speaking broadly synchronised with the principal evolutionary stages of the company's motive power fleet over 80 years.

The first 15-16 years were marked by rapid and mainly successful expansion southwards from Dublin that resulted in coverage of all but the south-eastern seaboard which was served by what later became the aptly named Dublin & South Eastern Railway (DSER). While ambitions as reflected by the word "Southern" in the GSWR title were essentially fulfilled, the "Western" element remained unrealised, by virtue of a discontented contingent within the company board. This engendered a breakaway venture that culminated with incorporation in July 1845 of the Midland Great Western Railway (MGWR). Nonetheless, by the mid-1860s the core network was in place that enabled the GSWR to establish itself as the largest company in terms of route mileage.

The forty years to the end of the 19th century saw continued growth but on a more parochial level through the addition of feeder lines. These later ventures differed in that finance and construction was no longer the sole responsibility of the GSWR's proprietors. They were either satellite companies in which the GSWR held part of the capital, or independent initiatives that failed and were taken over at a discounted cost, or, where social needs dictated, were funded by governmental support. Growth in this fashion continued in the 20th Century but at a more restrained pace.

Establishment of the railway

Prior to 1825, rail facilities were confined to short tramways that served docks and collieries but the opening of the Stockton & Darlington Railway on 27th September 1825 stimulated interest in fully fledged systems. Early ambitions identified the potential offered by connections between population centres and trading hubs in the southern parts of Ireland. The ports of Dublin, Cork and Waterford were well placed

Type XXXV [35] Class 101 was designed for goods work but regularly appeared on rural branch passenger services as with No 133 which has arrived at Valencia Harbour (as described in the 1901 GSWR timetable) from Farranfore. This locomotive was built in June 1885, reboilered in 1904 and withdrawn in 1963. This undated view could be drawn from GSWR, GSR or CIE eras. The gentleman to the right had apparently met the train to collect some parcels, including a box of bananas; his load is a reminder of the realities of rural Irish life in earlier times.

Branch line passenger economics were an early factor in McDonnell's motive power planning and experiments were conducted with combined locomotive and coach units as the forerunners to later steam- and diesel-powered railcars. The concept suffered from shortage of power and/ or inadequate passenger accommodation. Type XLVIII [48] 0-6-4T Class 92 No 92 was the longest-lived of the genre. It served exclusively for many years as "the cab" i.e. the Dublin, Kingsbridge-Inchicore staff shuttle. Combined locomotive and carriage units had no lasting impact on the GSWR's public passenger services. In this view, No 92 is at Inchicore with a rake of rundown 6-wheel coaches that were probably serving out their time on workmen's train duties.

to handle trade with Britain and continental Europe while the opening of the Grand Canal in April 1804 had improved Limerick's access to those markets. Nevertheless, land transportation between those centres, and with other important towns, remained primitive and slow thus leading to consideration of the new steam-powered technology. As early as 1826, the speed advantage over canal transport was instrumental in passage of a parliamentary Act for a rail connection between Limerick and Waterford. A survey resulted in a preferred route by way of Tipperary and Clonmel but the project failed through shortage of capital, a recurrent factor that shaped much of Ireland's later transport development. The next major initiative, a canal between Dublin and Kingstown (now Dun Laoghaire) to ease pressure upon the former's docks, also failed for lack of funds but a competing project did proceed as the Dublin & Kingstown Railway (DKR), albeit helped by a government loan. The immediate success of the DKR, opened on 17th December 1834, galvanised public interest and Acts passed in 1836 authorised two further railways: the Ulster (opened 12th August 1839), and the Dublin & Drogheda (opened 15th March 1844).

Three Acts passed for other railway projects in 1837 failed through funding difficulties and also because of uncertainty over the pattern of railway development.

This was under review by a Royal Commission which had started its work in October 1836, producing its first report on 11th March 1837. This body's analysis of the Irish economy, and of the condition of existing canals and roads, concluded that longer railway routes were unlikely to be remunerative. Nevertheless, it was felt that two trunk lines connecting Dublin with the north-west and with the south-west were justified, together with some key branch lines. Reflecting doubts over viability, it was recommended in 1839 that railways should be treated as public works, subject to governmental supervision, and funded in large part by a public sector loan of £2,500,000. Enthusiasm for these ideas was not endorsed in London, where a precedent was feared that would conflict with the preference for *laissez-faire* practices in railway investment. This assessment ignored the disparity in wealth levels between Ireland and Britain.

An alternative scheme for the south-western route was then proposed by London-based financiers that anticipated public sector support through the local rating structure. While this idea also failed, it excited the interest of parties behind the London & Birmingham Railway (LBR). This influential group was alert to new trading opportunities across the Irish Sea that would rely on the ports of Liverpool and Holyhead. More visionary than practicable was the notion of an east-west route across the country to link with trans-Atlantic liner services that would operate from locations such as Berehaven (in Bantry Bay, Co Cork) or Valencia Harbour. Other prospective ports similarly identified were Galway in 1835 and Foynes in 1853.

LBR interests in the Irish market were paralleled by those of the Great Western Railway (GWR) which focussed on access to Waterford and Cork. In the event, pressures on the GWR's resources in Britain prevented that company from matching the commitment and support extended by the LBR camp. A further factor was the interest of an influential Dublin-based investor group which in 1842 tried but failed to resuscitate the grandly titled Great Leinster & Munster Railway (GLMR). This had been authorised by Act of Parliament in 1836 to connect Dublin with Kilkenny. Investor support had fallen well short of the enthusiasm generated for the GLMR project but there remained an appetite for rail connections between Dublin and the south.

Dublin investors led by Peter Purcell, a wealthy landowner and stage coach operator developed an entirely fresh plan to link Dublin with Galway, Limerick and other population centres under the auspices of a new venture to be titled the "Great Southern & Western Railway". Critically, Purcell enlisted the interest of the LBR camp, and the services of John Macneill, an eminent engineer. The latter had surveyed the north-western route for the Royal Commission, and was well connected with influential parties in London who had backed construction of the LBR. These factors placed the project in better shape than its predecessors, and was aided in its ambitions by Sir Robert Peel, Prime Minister since 1841. He favoured the concept of a single railway company to serve most of Ireland, not for any socially-orientated purpose but in anticipation of a profitable investment opportunity on a scale not possible through more modest enterprises. Further, he believed that governmental control and influence would be more easily exercised over a single company than over several.

Planning proceeded rapidly. The Royal Commission's recommendations were set aside and new routes were surveyed. With powerful support from the government, the Bill to construct a line from Dublin to Cashel (then the main town in Co Tipperary) and a branch to Carlow had an easy passage through parliament and became law on 6th August 1844. A second Act the following year authorised an alternative route to that recommended by the Royal Commission. This followed a more westerly course that bypassed Cashel in favour of Charleville and Mallow. A branch from Cherryville Junction near Kildare to Carlow would partially fulfil the objectives of the defunct GLMR.

The first sod was ceremonially cut by the Duke of Leinster near Lucan in January 1845 and with invested capital of £1,300,000, construction proceeded speedily. The first contracts were let to William McCormick and William Dargan for the Dublin-Hazlehatch and Hazelhatch-Sallins sections respectively. By June it was possible for dignitaries to travel a short distance in ballast wagons. Preference was given to completion of the Carlow branch before venturing southwest beyond Kildare. As joint contractors, McCormick and Dargan rapidly completed the Sallins-Carlow section which commenced operations on 4th August 1846, the date on which Kingsbridge Station, Dublin officially opened. To place this date in chronological context, the opening dates of other major Dublin stations were: Westland Row December 1834; Amiens Street November 1844; the Broadstone June 1847; and Harcourt Street February 1859. Commencement of services within two years of the original Act's passage was an impressive achievement, despite difficulties imposed by unusually adverse weather, by delays in obtaining title to requisite land in the Dublin area, and by industrial disputes. Initial Dublin-Carlow services comprised two trains a day in each direction, taking 2½ hours for the 56-mile journey. Difficulties were experienced in delays caused by the Post Office's failure to deliver mails to the termini promptly, a foretaste of the postal service's role in the fashioning of Irish railway timetables. Carlow quickly became an important point of connection with road coach services to Cork, Kilkenny, Clonmel and Waterford. As more rolling stock became available, trains were doubled to four each way per day, with a slight easing in journey times.

The GSWR's network expansion was significantly influenced by poor maintenance of the road system in the first half of the 19th Century. For the minority of the population wealthy enough to travel in their own carriages, or by horse or stage coach services, these conditions prolonged journey times. For the majority, mobility was limited to the distance that could be walked in a day plus the availability of suitable shelter at night. Many communities were thus isolated from their neighbours where distance between them exceeded ten miles.

Carlo Bianconi, an Italian entrepreneur migrated to Ireland aged 16 years in 1802 and started as an itinerant pedlar of engravings. In 1815, he initiated a service of horse-drawn "cars", effectively open wagons fitted with seats, to provide faster travel between Clonmel, Cahir and Carrick-on-Suir. These settlements were sufficiently distant from each other to prevent those lacking their own transport from making return journeys within the day. Bianconi's system made public transport available to the "middle

GSWR tank locomotives tended to be a hardy, long-lived breed. No 27, the first of Type LIX [59] Class 27 was introduced in 1900 and worked until March 1953. There were four members of this class and they were mainly used on Cork suburban services. No 27 is awaiting departure from Cork (Glanmire Road) on a service to Youghal or Cobh. The house behind the locomotive provided overnight accommodation for locomotive crews on lodging turns. The bedroom whose window is between the locomotive's dome and chimney was regularly occupied by one of the authors on his photographic safaris, providing an excellent vantage point from which to observe comings and goings. *Kelland*

classes", based on a modest tariff albeit too expensive for labourers. Nicknamed "Bians", the service expanded to serve territory that the GSWR aspired to penetrate but focussed on cross-country routes rather than the main arterial routes that radiated from Dublin. Roads were subject to much improvement at this time and through careful route selection, good quality cars and horses plus competent management, Bianconi's services soon out-grew the competition. By 1861, Bians were covering an aggregate daily mileage of 4,000.

Bianconi recognised that he could not compete directly with the new railway and so re-fashioned his business as a feeder, serving places that the railway would never reach. This alignment with the new technology ensured commercial continuity while relieving railway companies of the obligation to contemplate investment in areas of marginal commercial potential. With no heir to continue the business, Bianconi broke up his empire in 1866, selling it in parcels to his agents. Despite this fragmentation, the Bian system remained integral to rural transportation in the south and west until arrival of the motor omnibus.

In April 1845 contracts were let for extension of the main line, and passenger services comprising two trains per day commenced on 26th June 1847 to Maryborough (now Portlaoise). This work was helped by a loan of £500,000 from the government specifically to provide unemployment relief to the distressed local population. Construction proceeded rapidly, reaching Ballybrophy in September 1847 and Thurles the following March. A single contract for the entire 78 miles of route from Thurles to Cork was given to Dargan who by then had established a formidable reputation as a railway engineer. The line opened to Limerick Junction on 3rd July 1848.

The Act of 1845 had authorised a branch to Limerick in addition to re-direction of the main route to Mallow. The latter changes were not well received further south, being regarded as an unnecessary delay in completion of the Cork connection. A revival of the failed 1826 Bill led to the successful creation of the Waterford & Limerick Railway (WLR) on 21st July 1845. With insufficient traffic to support two routes, an arrangement was reached whereby the GSWR would concentrate on completing the line to Cork

Ennis in 1931 and 0-4-4T Type LII [52] No 51 has paused with a local Athenry-Limerick service and is taking on water. Built in April 1884, this locomotive would remain in service for another three years. The whole ensemble has the distinct flavour of the previous century.

while the WLR would provide the link to Limerick City (22 miles). The GSWR was granted the right to work trains over this section but never exercised these powers during the WLR's independent existence. The WLR and GSWR main lines crossed at Limerick Junction, located in the county of Tipperary and Ireland's most famous railway intersection, usually known to railway men simply as "The Junction." For further details of the WLR and its services, see below and Chapter 8. A further Act was also passed in 1845 for an extension as far as Cork (Victoria), locally known as Blackpool and the southern terminus from 1849 until 1855. In 1846, a further Act authorised a mile and a half extension from Blackpool through Glanmire Tunnel to the site that has since served as Cork's principal station.

The mainline from Limerick Junction to Mallow, which penetrated hilly country, opened on 19th March 1849. Beyond Mallow the terrain was even less favourable, necessitating heavy civil engineering works including substantial stone bridges, embankments, cuttings and the ten-arched viaduct over the River Blackwater. A directors' special train reached the temporary Blackpool terminus on 18th October 1849, having covered 164 miles from Dublin in 5½ hours. Ordinary service trains (two per day each way) commenced on 29th October 1849 and operated at a more leisurely pace. The Mail train covered the journey in seven hours whereas the third class all stations "Parliamentary" took twelve. There was also a separate Cork-Limerick Junction service.

As the GSWR's initial intention had been to connect Dublin with Limerick, Edward Bury, an early locomotive supplier, had recommended establishment of a locomotive works in Tipperary i.e. approximately central to a network that would connect these two centres with Cork. As there would be an interval before the railway extended that far, land was purchased for the purpose outside the Dublin city boundary at Inchicore and locomotive construction commenced there around 1852.

The GSWR approached Limerick from two directions. From the north, it sponsored a secondary line via Nenagh; from the south its protégé, the Cork & Limerick Direct Railway (CLDR), built a line from Charleville to Patrickswell. However, both these routes depended on smaller lines in the hands of the WLR for access to Limerick (the Limerick & Castleconnell Railway and the Limerick & Foynes Railway respectively). Only after the 1901 takeover did the GSWR have its own routes to Limerick, although through the CLDR it did obtain its own goods station on the south side of that city.

Concurrent with these developments, moves were afoot in 1845 to connect Wexford with central Ireland which scheme enjoyed the backing of the GWR. One proposal contemplated a coastal route between Wexford and Dublin while another took the form of the Wexford, Carlow & Dublin Junction Railway (WCDJR), both of which would have enticed traffic away from the GSWR. The GWR was partly motivated by mounting a competitive challenge to the afore-mentioned alliance between the Dublin investors and the LBR (from 1846, the London & North Western Railway). However, the GWR's involvement at investor-support level soon dissolved leaving the WCDJR and the GLMR holding enabling Acts but virtually no tangible assets. The solution was to merge the two companies into the Irish South Eastern Railway (ISER), in which the GSWR held a 50% stake. The new company's activities were restricted to the provision of an important connection between Carlow and Kilkenny, construction of which proceeded rapidly. The Carlow-Bagenalstown section opened in July 1848, and was extended to Kilkenny in November 1850. Services, always using GSWR locomotives and stock, worked the final two miles over Waterford & Kilkenny Railway metals from Lavistown Junction. The ISER was fully absorbed into the GSWR on 1st July 1863.

The Royal Commission of 1838 had opined that the west of Ireland would be best served by continued reliance on canals but this view yielded within two years to a logical but abortive scheme to link Dublin with Galway by way of Sallins, Edenderry, Clara, Athlone, Ballinasloe and Loughrea. Some years later, an investor group published a scheme for a separate railway to connect Dublin with Mullingar and Athlone, plus a branch to Longford. Some of the promoters were also GSWR directors and their actions were considered to conflict with the GSWR's objectives. A major board dispute erupted resulting in those who favoured the Mullingar venture departing to establish the MGWR.

These developments threatened curtailment of the GSWR's "western" aspirations but a separate dispute within the MGWR camp led to some of those directors leaving to set up the Irish Great Western Railway (IGWR). The GSWR welcomed this prodigal group back into its fold by agreeing to support to IGWR's venture to build a line from Portarlington on the Dublin-Cork route north-westerly to Athlone and then on to Galway. Bills for the MGWR and IGWR, in large part competing for the same territory, were presented in 1845 and internecine arguments followed over the next two years in both Houses of Parliament at Westminster. By 1847, with appalling famine conditions afflicting country areas, the appetite for further dispute had abated. The MGWR's route to Galway was approved while the GSWR, in face of prevailing economic pressures, agreed to build a branch from Portarlington to Tullamore, completed in October 1854. Nevertheless, there remained an intent to reach the important regional centre of Athlone.

Already strained relations took a turn for the worse over the matter of the Grand Canal. This major artery had been officially opened in 1804, after 47 years of construction, to link the River Liffey in Dublin with Shannon Harbour on the River Shannon in Kings County (now Co Offaly). The canal which connected Sallins, Prosperous, Edenderry, Tullamore and Pollagh was eighty-one miles long, and had several

Moderately loaded 4-4-0 Type XV [15] Class 301 No 304 at the West Cabin on approach to Waterford, where the three lines *via* Dungarvan, Clonmel and Kilkenny converged. Built for Dublin-Cork express services, the performance of this four-strong class was soon found wanting and were relegated to secondary services, often in the Waterford area.

Type XIII [13] Class 52 No 59 (built 1888, withdrawn 1955) at Tullow on 17 June 1939 with a branch service bound for Sallins. Corridor Brake 3rd coach No 1087 (Inchicore 1923 with seating for 32) in two tone GSR livery as applied to bogie stock between 1929 and 1934. Any first class passengers would be confined to the 6-wheel Composite behind. *WA Camwell*

feeder routes. The capacity of canals to handle substantial freight volumes formed a significant part of railway planning, and helped explain why the GSWR's early locomotive policy was heavily slanted towards passenger traffic. Both the GSWR and MGWR regarded ownership of the Grand Canal as complementary to their plans and had been negotiating to purchase the enterprise jointly. The MGWR's route to Athlone had been expensive to complete, especially in legal costs, and that company was alive to the threat of an incursion by the GSWR through extension onwards from Tullamore. Accordingly, the MGWR withdrew from these negotiations and sought to purchase the canal in its own right with intent to penetrate GSWR territory as far as Waterford. Another legal dispute followed, eventually resulting in reduction of the MGWR's plans to a seven-year lease of the canal.

In 1857, Parliament scrutinised bills from the MGWR and the GSWR. Among its decisions, it granted the latter powers to extend its Tullamore branch to Athlone. In this case, the company may have been lucky enough for its interest to line up with government policy. Athlone was a garrison town and a second rail link was attractive to the British authorities.

Years of heated dispute ensued over competing plans to extend westward into central Ireland, principally focussed on access to Athlone. Eventually, recognising the futility of fruitless dispute and mounting legal expense, differences were submitted for arbitration. The agreement of July 1860 tidied up several issues but most significantly segmented central Ireland into spheres of influence by means of a dividing line running Dublin-Edenderry-Athlone and then along the River Shannon. To the north and west lay MGWR territory while the GSWR held the south and east. A few months after the agreement with the MGWR was ratified, the GSWR opened a short but useful line between the two companies' stations in Athlone. This was the first physical link between the two systems. The GSWR's Athlone line was commercially unsuccessful although it did serve as a diversionary route to the MGWR main line after 1925. While Irish railway expansion sometimes generated dispute between promoters of alternative schemes, the Athlone case was unusual in leading to competing routes reaching the same location as was more often the case in Britain. An over-capitalised and unnecessarily dense British network eroded the industry's long-term commercial viability, whereas in Ireland a sparsely funded system had to contend with slim traffic volumes emanating from a depopulated, and in many areas impoverished, country.

More positively, Killarney was an established tourist resort long before railways reached the far southwest and a line from Mallow was approved in the form of the Killarney Junction Railway (KJR) as early as 1846. The KJR was a satellite of the GSWR which subscribed most of the capital, and which worked the route from its opening on 15th July 1853. Dargan engineered the route which was cheap to construct, apart from crossing the Quagmire River near

Headford. Further delays were caused by local famine conditions. Nevertheless, profit levels enabled a capital reduction, a rarity in those days. It was one of the first railways in Ireland to inaugurate a telegraph line (concurrent with its opening), and the first to open a railway hotel, the famous Great Southern at Killarney on 11th July 1854.

The KJR was the major investor in the Tralee & Killarney Railway (TKR), another Dargan creation, which opened in July 1859 using locomotives and rolling stock provided by the GSWR. The GSWR was well represented on the boards of the KJR and TKR and both companies were fully absorbed in May 1860. The Mallow-Tralee route, operated as a secondary mainline, saw a wide variety of motive power but is perhaps most associated with the famous Kerry Bogies, of which more anon.

Consolidation

Establishment of the GSWR's mainline network had been reasonably swift but further additions risked the law of diminishing returns, as cogently exemplified by the bruising Athlone saga. In contrast, the successful Killarney connection was geographically ideal to exploit indigenous and tourist-based traffic flows between Kerry, Cork and Waterford. Further, the financial burden had been relieved by the engagement of funding partners, a device that aided post-1860 expansion.

Over the following 40 years, new investment was more conservative, in part enforced by the need to renew and improve existing infrastructure. The company had shown foresight in laying its original track with the heaviest rails available, which then had a projected life expectancy of decades. However, increases in train weights and speeds were more rapid than originally expected, and necessitated earlier than planned replacement of rails. There had been initial reliance on timber overbridges and many were falling due for replacement by metal or stone structures. Livestock had become an important source of revenue but fresh regulations in 1870 governing their protection in transit had enforced the acquisition of more than 300 roofed cattle wagons. Following the accident on the Great Northern Railway of Ireland at Armagh on 12th June 1889, the Regulation of Railways Act required installation of block signalling and interlocking on all lines, and the equipping of all passenger trains with continuous brakes. Expenditure of this nature was obligatory and operationally desirable, but did not improve direct revenue.

From the 1860s onwards, it was policy to share establishment costs with other parties who in some cases also bore a measure of the operating

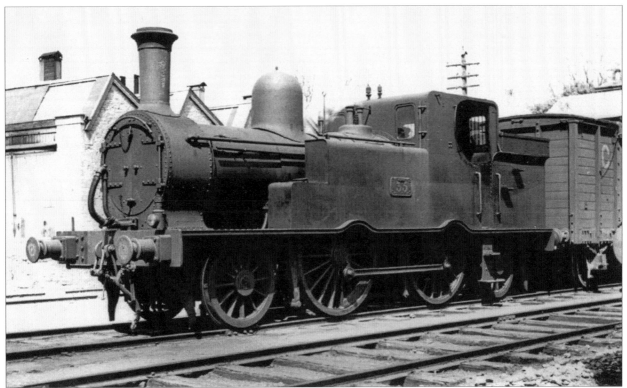

2-4-2T Type LVI [56] Class 33 No 35 (built 1894, withdrawn 1959) was busily engaged at Birr on 2 May 1938. The cut-away front upper section of the side tanks reduced running weight at the expense of 120 gallons less water capacity. Also, there is an addition or modification to the number plate on the tank side but precisely what this states cannot be discerned. *WA Camwell*

Other network expansion 1854 to 1893			
Section	Miles	Opened	Built by company:
Portarlington-Athlone	39¼	1854-1860 ‡	GSWR
Ballybrophy-Roscrea-Birr	22	1857-8	Roscrea & Parsonstown Junction #
Bagenalstown-Palace East	24	1858-70	Bagenalstown & Wexford#; Waterford, New Ross & Wexford Junction §
Cork-Youghal	26¾	1859-60	Cork & Youghal #
Cobh (Queenstown) branch	5¾	1862	Cork & Youghal #
Mallow-Fermoy	16¾	1860	GSWR
Charleville-Patrickswell	18½	1862	Cork & Limerick Direct #
Roscrea-Nenagh-Birdhill	32¼	1863-4	GSWR
Birr-Portumna Bridge	12	1868	Parsonstown & Portumna Bridge ¶
Gortatlea-Castleisland	4½	1875	Castleisland #
Islandbridge Junction-Glasnevin Junction	2¾	1877	GSWR
Clara-Banagher	18¼	1884	Clara & Banagher #
Sallins -Tullow	34¾	1885-6	GSWR
Farranfore-Valencia	39½	1885-93	GSWR
Banteer-Newmarket	8¾	1889	Kanturk & Newmarket #
Fermoy-Mitchelstown	12	1891	Fermoy & Mitchelstown #
Headford Junction-Kenmare	19¾	1893	GSWR

‡ Completion of link to MGWR station in Athlone
# Later absorbed by GSWR
¶ Closed 1878; later abandoned and its materials appropriated by local populace for its own use: "The Stolen Railway"
§ Purchased jointly by the GSWR and the Dublin Wicklow & Wexford Railway, and divided between them

expenses. A significant move on 2nd September 1877 saw completion of a line between Islandbridge Junction and Glasnevin Junction, and connection with the Liffey branch of the MGWR, which allowed access to the Dublin quays. Rather than presaging any burying of the hatchet, this project was instigated by the LNWR which saw the GSWR network as a valuable feeder to its port facilities. The greater share of the cost was borne by the LNWR with the GSWR's contribution limited to £50,000.

The table above summarises the expansion of the GSWR in the years 1854 to 1893 beyond its main lines linking Dublin, Cork, Kilkenny and Tralee.

Network expansion increased route mileage from 350 in 1860 to 604 in 1900, the longest of any Irish railway company. Annual gross revenue was typically 25% or more of the total for the Irish railway sector. Apart from hiccoughs during trade recessions in the 1860s and 1880s, earnings achieved a constant year-on-year growth and exceeded £1 million in 1900. Management policy favoured restraint in expenditure, with emphasis on value-for-money. By the standards of the time, staff were reasonably well rewarded and the company was in many respects a benign employer. Additional remuneration was paid for work demands beyond the norm, a superannuation scheme was introduced for footplate personnel in 1873, and a pension scheme for salaried staff in 1879. By these criteria, the GSWR could be regarded as Ireland's premier railway company.

Perhaps the least satisfactory element was the company's relationships with its neighbours. Failure to reach Galway compounded by the MGWR's obstreperous attitude resulted in disputes where the possible prizes did not justify the cost and effort. The rental of the GSWR's Limerick Junction facilities to the WLR, was a constant source of controversy. The GSWR preferred to direct goods traffic over its own rails via Nenagh or by way of the Cork & Limerick Direct Railway, rather than use the Limerick-Limerick Junction section. The WLR retaliated by hampering the passage of GSWR originating traffic bound for Ennis, and over the later extension northwards to Sligo.

Another company with which the GSWR was often at loggerheads was the Waterford & Central Ireland Railway (WCIR), mainly concerning disputes over the exchange of traffic at Maryborough and Kilkenny. Originally formed as the Waterford & Kilkenny Railway (WKR), this company worked and later absorbed the Kilkenny Junction Railway, which proceeded north to join the GSWR at Maryborough. The WKR renamed itself the Waterford & Central Ireland Railway in 1868, to reflect its ambitious

Christmas 1931 found Type XII [12] Class 2 No 15 at Mitchelstown, at the end of the 12-mile branch from Fermoy with a modestly loaded mixed train and in the company of a fine collection of enamelled tin advertising signs. This view demonstrates the versatility of the Kerry bogie, found here trespassing in deepest Co Cork. *AW Croughton*

intention to connect Waterford with Mullingar. By tapping into the wealthy agricultural market of the Irish midlands it was hoped that the dismal financial performance of the erstwhile WKR could be improved. However the northern extension, built by the Central Ireland Railway (later absorbed by the WCIR), reached only as far as Mountmellick in Queens County (Co Laois from 1922). Bitter operating disputes with the WLR at Waterford at one stage required Board of Trade arbitration, and the WCIR had a long history of poor management and financial problems. In keeping with the practice of purchasing assets at discounted prices, the GSWR paid only £17 10s for every £100 of WCIR ordinary stock in 1900. However, the GWR had invested capital in the WCIR/ CIR and significantly this was repaid at par as a token of the GSWR's improving relations with the English company.

Into the 20th Century

The Waterford & Limerick Railway had fulfilled its title by opening its main line between those two centres between 1848 and 1853. It subsequently absorbed a number of smaller companies so that by 1895 it operated a route mileage of 350, making it Ireland's fourth largest railway system and the biggest without a terminus in Dublin, Belfast or Cork. From Limerick, its trains ran west to Tralee, north to Sligo and with branches to Fenit, Foynes, Killaloe and Thurles-Clonmel. Assisted by a government grant of £146,000 under the Light Railways Act (Ireland) 1889, the company's last expansion was construction of a 46½-mile line northwards from Claremorris to connect with the MGWR Dublin-Sligo line at Collooney. By running over MGWR metals northward from there, the WLR linked Limerick with Sligo over a distance of 146 miles and in recognition of this growth, the WLR added "& Western" to its name on 1st January 1896. This route mainly served thinly-populated and impoverished areas that generated modest returns.

The WLR had maintained close links with the Great Western Railway and an important revenue source was traffic through Waterford that connected with the GWR's New Milford steamship service. The English company granted the WLR generous rebates on the cross-channel traffic and on at least one occasion had investigated takeover of the Irish company. However, in the closing years of the 19th Century, the GWR chose to switch allegiance to the GSWR whose larger network and superior access to major conurbations offered better revenue potential. Further, the GSWR and GWR became joint owners of the Fishguard & Rosslare Railways & Harbours Co (F&RR&HC). The establishment of this strong allegiance meant significant loss of revenue for the WLWR forcing its absorption by the GSWR with effect from 1st January 1901. This was GSWR's only corporate acquisition during the 20th Century, a transaction opposed by various bodies, particularly the MGWR which had uneasily observed the WLR/ WLWR's northward incursion into its territory. By this circuitous path did the GSWR eventually partially fulfil the "Western" element of its original territorial ambitions.

Type XII [12] Class 2 No 8 (built 1880, withdrawn 1945) with an Up passenger working at Limerick Junction. The upper part of the tower to the important Limerick water softening plant is behind the first coach. The GSWR's gasometer can also be seen in the background. *Lens of Sutton*

Thus with acquisition of the WCIR and WLWR systems, the GSWR system expanded significantly in the period 1898-1901. Through partnership with the GWR in the F&RR&HC, the takeover of that company's Irish lines in 1898 added 106 more route miles (the Wexford-Rosslare-Waterford-Dungarvan-Fermoy section). Other 20th Century additions to the system were short but important lines that linked existing railways in Cork (The Cork City Railway), in the Dublin area, the Cashel Branch, and branches to Wolfhill, Castlecomer and Deerpark collieries.

The new century saw hopes for continued good fortune realised through a policy of building larger locomotives plus the introduction of modern passenger stock. Sadly, fulfilment was not realised for reasons both within and beyond the company's control. As explored in the next chapter, several of the new motive power designs failed to meet expectations and before these issues could be thoroughly addressed, political events commencing with the outbreak of the Great War in 1914 imposed external constraints. Operational responsibility from 1st January 1917 until 31st December 1919 was vested in a governmental body, the Irish Railway Executive Committee. Wartime demands placed some strain on the GSWR although the Irish gauge excluded the requisition of motive power and rolling stock for overseas service. The greater impact was exerted by the succeeding War of Independence, and then the Irish Civil War. Particularly during the later conflict, the railway as a prime target for sabotage and other malign activity suffered extensive damage to locomotives, rolling stock and infrastructure with severe repercussions for operational viability.

The signing of the Anglo-Irish treaty on 6th December 1921 heralded establishment of the Irish Free State exactly 12 months later and the future of the railway sector was high on a list of pressing issues for the new nation. In April 1922, the government convened the Railways Commission to investigate, and to recommend a revised ownership structure for the industry. This marked commencement of convoluted negotiations that ultimately concluded with the Amalgamation of 1924/ 5 whereby all railway companies of any consequence that operated solely within the new Irish Free State were grouped into the Great Southern Railways.

Chapter 2
Design and construction

The pattern of motive power development on the Great Southern & Western Railway followed a similar pattern to that of the major British pre-Grouping companies. The company formed an integral part of the railway industry of these islands as evidenced by the number of senior engineering personnel whose careers included transfers back and forth across the Irish Sea. The story can be neatly categorised into three distinct periods.

Period I (1844 to 1863)

Design and supply of locomotives initially seems to have been left in the hands of English manufacturers and it was not until March 1847 that three candidates were interviewed for the position of Locomotive Superintendent. The successful candidate was John Dewrance, an employee since October 1845 (in what role is not known). He had earlier worked for the Liverpool & Manchester Railway, was reputed to be connected with the Stephensons and claimed to have been involved in the erection of *Rocket*. The other applicants were William Robertson from Drogheda-based engineers Thomas Grendon & Co, and Robert Anderson from the Edinburgh & Glasgow Railway.

Immediately upon his appointment, Dewrance was despatched to William Fairbairn & Sons at Millwall, London, apparently for training in locomotive construction. Dewrance's employment terms were generous with a salary of £300 pa plus housing on preferential terms but short-lived as staff reductions and pay cuts were instituted in August 1847. The Board considered he was over-rewarded in relation to his experience and ability, and his services were soon terminated. He took up an appointment with the Midland Great Western Railway later that year. These events suggest that Dewrance played no active role in design and construction during his short tenure and following his departure, the role of Locomotive Superintendent was abolished.

George Miller was appointed Chief Engineer in 1847 and his duties were formally expanded when he became directly responsible for all aspects of engineering two years later. Miller had gained broad experience prior to joining the GSWR, having been an engineer with the London & Birmingham followed by a similar appointment with the London & Greenwich railways, and then resident engineer during construction of the Jamaica Railway. For 16 years, he played a leading role in the GSWR's development and was influential in the formative years of the Irish system at large. The GSWR was not alone in vesting control of both civil and mechanical engineering disciplines in the hands of one officer to achieve economies but it was a sometimes less than successful arrangement.

With Miller's abilities slanted more toward the civil side, John Wakefield was appointed in 1848 as his assistant with direct responsibility for locomotives. Wakefield had previously worked for the Stephensons and had been the fireman aboard *Rocket* at the opening of the Liverpool & Manchester Railway. Further, he claimed to have lifted the body of the unfortunate Huskisson from the track during the opening ceremony. He was an energetic individual and a good leader but lacked formal training. Apparently he could cope with the fleet when new but as repairs fell due, his technical shortcomings were exposed. Also, the design of 0-4-2 Type XXXII [32] attributed to him was publicly compared by Zerah Colborn in *Locomotive Engineering and the Mechanism of Railways* with contemporary 0-4-2s built by Beyer Peacock for the Smyrna & Cassaba Railway, Turkey. Colburn judged the steaming capacity, valve gear, and the mounting of cylinders on the frames to be inferior. This publication did not appear until 1871 but it seems that this judgement was made known to the GSWR hierarchy some years previously.

Miller died of typhus at his residence, St Johns, Islandbridge on 4th January 1864 aged 51 years. He had apparently fallen ill the previous month through driving the engine of a train conveying "passengers of importance" in bad weather. Following his death, the directors reversed their policy and split responsibilities for civil and mechanical engineering. WH Stephenson of the Ulster Railway was appointed general engineer but his tenure was short as he resigned in September. His responsibilities were then divided between Valentine Browne at Dublin and Charles Napier at Cork.

Improvements in management of mechanical engineering had become an issue for the Board which had decided in December 1858 "to allow young gentlemen in possession of an engineering diploma from Trinity College, Dublin to attend at Inchicore works". Miller's death opened the way for appointment of university-trained managers and the policy decision to reinstate the position of Locomotive Superintendent was then enacted with the appointment of McDonnell. Wakefield had evidently acknowledged his limitations by choosing not to apply for the newly established post. He resigned in May 1865 to join the Dublin, Wicklow & Wexford Railway. In locomotive terms, the most significant

McDonnell is best remembered for his classic 0-6-0 Type XXXV [35] Class 101 (or J15 for those in the United Kingdom). A total of 107 were built between 1866 and 1899 and the story of their construction and variations is understandably complex. Twelve of a slightly enlarged version appeared in 1902 as Type XXXVI [36] Class 200 which provided the template for further modification of Class 101 and later all were included within the latter designation.

No 170 was receiving plenty of attention from cleaners and shed staff in an era when corporate pride linked with plenty of staff on low incomes made it practicable to lavish attention on the appearance of even modest goods engines. This locomotive entered service in April 1874 and worked until 1963. It was twice reboilered (a 4' 4" version in 1917 and a type Z superheated in 1941) but it retained its original frames over its 89-year working life. Many of the long service members of this class kept their 19th Century frames throughout which amply reflects the quality of engineering standards that McDonnell fostered at Inchicore.
Ken Nunn Collection

aspect of the Miller/ Wakefield period had been initiation of construction at Inchicore.

There is uncertainty about the nature of the GSWR's first locomotives. Two passenger and two goods locomotives were delivered by Bury, Curtis & Kennedy in August 1845 and the chronology suggests that they were four-wheelers (2-2-0s and 0-4-0s) in keeping with that manufacturer's established policy. They initially ran trials on the Dublin & Drogheda Railway but no more were delivered for another eleven months. During this period it appears that they were modified to become 2-2-2s and 0-4-2s. The relevant factors are reviewed in the commentaries on locomotive Types II [2] and XXIII [23].

Twenty-two locomotives had been ordered from Bury (twenty passenger plus two goods) but during the 1845-6 hiatus, twenty 2-2-2s built by Sharp Stewart started to arrive. While the Burys were apparently subject to modification as deliveries proceeded, the Sharps were a standard design by that company and they proved an excellent investment. After working for around a quarter of a century, several remained sufficiently sound either for renewal as 2-4-0s or for their key components to be recycled into other new construction. Recorded career mileages as single drivers were impressive as exemplified with No 10 which notched up 480,000 miles in a career lasting a little more than 28 years.

The policy that 2-2-2s should predominate was based on the assumption that passengers would exceed goods traffic, and this was largely the case for 20 years. The GSWR in the main served an agricultural economy so tonnages moved by rail would have been modest. Livestock was traditionally driven on the hoof to market and to the ports while the canal system continued to compete effectively for freight.

Thus, revenue-earning services were handled by "second generation" six-wheeled tender locomotives

Design and construction

(2-2-2s for passenger services and 0-4-2s for goods trains). Later deliveries included introduction of 2-4-0s, possibly in more of a mixed traffic role. Following the Bury/ Sharp purchases and the concomitant standardisation, fleet expansion became piecemeal with acquisitions in small batches from other commercial manufacturers. Locomotives of the 2-4-0 and 0-4-2 wheel arrangements bought from other manufacturers enjoyed generally satisfactory careers:- Fairbairn (three engines around 29 years), Rothwell (four engines around 15 years), and Grendon (two around 16 years). The MGWR did rather better with their Grendon products lasting approximately 23 years.

Inchicore's entrée into locomotive construction in the years 1852-4 comprised a single 2-2-2, four 0-4-2s and a pair of 0-6-0s. The first two wheel arrangements were a continuation of established motive power practice but the six-coupled machines were reportedly intended to be 0-6-0Ts, to work as bankers on the incline out of Cork. They were either completed as planned and modified soon afterwards, or they were converted during construction. As tank engines they would have preceded what actually became GSWR tank construction by around 15 years. Unfortunately, it cannot be determined which locomotives were involved but Type XXXIII [33] 0-6-0 Nos 60/ 1 (1864 Nos 139/ 40) were the most probable candidates.

Passenger	No.	Builder	Original (pre-1864
Built			Running Nos)
1846-8	20	Sharp Stewart	1-20
1845-8	20	Bury	21-40
1853	1	Inchicore	9
1855	2	Fairbairn	70, 71
1858	3	Inchicore	70-79
1859-63	9	Inchicore	76, 80, 81, 88-90, 94-6
Total	55		

All 2-2-2s except No 70,71 which were 2-4-0s.

Diversity was evident in the composition of the locomotive fleet up to 1865:

Except for acquisitions through purchase of other companies, after 1856 and until 1903 the GSWR relied solely on Inchicore to cover its motive power needs except for twenty members of 0-6-0 Type XXXV [35] Class 101 supplied by Beyer Peacock (twelve) and Sharp, Stewart (eight).

Goods	W.A.	No.	Builder	Original (pre-1864
Built				Running Nos)
1845	0-4-2	2	Bury	41, 42
1847/ 8	0-4-2	8	Bury	43-50
1849	0-4-2	2	Grendon	51, 52
1850	0-4-2	4	Rothwell	53-6
1852	0-4-2	2	Inchicore	57, 58
1854	0-4-2	2	Inchicore	62, 63
1854	0-6-0	2	Inchicore	60, 61
1855	2-4-0	3	Inchicore	64-6
1856	0-4-2	1	Fairbairn	75
1856	0-6-0	6	Inchicore	67-9, 72-4
1860-2	0-4-2	9	Inchicore	82-7, 91-3
1863-5	0-4-2	6	Inchicore	97-102
Total		47		

Little is known of the pattern of train working in this period but some fragmentary records survive. Thus, a Sunday excursion in September 1850 departed Dublin for Cork consisting of 16 carriages, carrying 700 passengers. Two locomotives were used, possibly three to start the train at Dublin and also the next day at Cork for the return journey.

On 6th November 1859, the famous American Mail service was inaugurated, leaving Dublin at 11.20 am in appalling weather. The 165½-mile run to Cork took 4½ hours including four stops for water. Passengers and mails left Penrose Quay in Cork by steamer for Queenstown. However, the effort was all in vain as the Cunard vessel had been badly delayed and arrived at Queenstown a day late.

Well into Period II, schedules remained relatively relaxed. Up until 1884, the down Day Mail left Dublin at 9.00 am, taking five hours to reach Cork. The return working left Cork at 12.30 pm and took 5 hours 10 minutes with seven stops including one at Inchicore for ticket collection. With a train weight of around 76 tons, the average speed was in the region of 38 mph.

With an ample supply of single drivers, it is speculated that multiple use of motive power on heavier trains was a regular occurrence. This practice was certainly characteristic of those English companies that had relied on first generation four-wheeled locomotives. Although possibly short on power, acceptably long working careers show that they gave good value. Conversion of some Sharp

McDonnell's first new passenger design (as opposed to reconstruction/ renewal of older machines) was 2-4-0 Type X [10] Class 21 of which six were introduced in 1873. Reputed to have been influenced by the London & North Western's 2-4-0 "Newton", they were employed when new on Dublin-Cork expresses. Four more appeared in 1876 of which No 66 was the first. In due course supplanted by 4-4-0s they found plenty of work on secondary passenger duties and the ten members of the class were withdrawn between 1911 and 1928.

Stewart 2-2-2s to 2-4-0s in 1865-8 formed part of a complex rebuilding programme, details of which appear in the relevant Type/ Class histories. Modifications involving changes in wheel arrangement were not unusual, this being a period when many railways found it expedient to undertake quite radical conversions.

Possibly reflecting Wakefield's time on the exposed footplates of the Liverpool & Manchester Railway, he oversaw the installation of cabs on several locomotives. These were primitive shelters but it was unusual to provide such comfort at that time. However, cab design showed minimal advance in later years as some GSWR locomotives provided little more than Spartan protection right through to steam's replacement.

Period II (1864 to 1895)

This period saw re-organisation and expansion of motive power construction, aided by significant investment that transformed Inchicore into a modern, fully-fledged engineering establishment. Many of the locomotives built during these years formed the backbone of a fleet that would serve the GSWR network well beyond cessation of the company as an independent concern. Over 31 years the position of Locomotive Superintendent was occupied by three engineers of distinction:

1864 to 1882   Alexander McDonnell
1882 to 1886   John AF Aspinall
1886 to 1896   Henry A Ivatt

The decision to recruit Trinity College graduates bore fruit in the appointment of McDonnell. Born in Dublin in 1829, he acquired an MA there in 1851 and from then until 1858 was a pupil with Messrs Liddell & Gordon, railway construction contractors operating in England and Wales. He then became Locomotive Superintendent of the Newport, Abergavenny & Hereford Railway (of which more anon) at the age of 28, shortly before that company was absorbed into the West Midland Railway. He moved to Eastern Europe in 1862 to establish the locomotive department of the Danube & Black Sea Railway before returning to Ireland to join the GSWR on 1st March 1864. Not then regarded primarily as a locomotive designer, he is believed to have consulted extensively with commercial manufacturers about the company's needs.

On arrival at Inchicore, McDonnell was dismayed with the fleet's condition. Early tasks were

Design and construction

Although McDonnell's first use of locomotive bogies was in the pair of unusual Type XLV [45] 0-4-4 Single Fairlies of 1869/70, a more profound and lasting impact was through his 4-4-0 Type XII [12] of May 1877. No 2 was the prototype of the famous "Kerry Bogies", Ireland's first eight-wheeled tender locomotives and among the first 4-4-0s in these islands. The class was ordered originally to work the curvaceous north Kerry route where the wheelbase of 2-4-0s, then the company's principal express locomotives, was found to be too rigid. These pioneer 4-4-0s were the first of a long line of that wheel arrangement and progressive enlargements followed under Aspinall in the guise of Types XIII [13] and XIV [14], classes 52 and 60 respectively. These three types exuded an air of old-world grace and elegance. They were also long-lived as all but one of Class 2 lasted to 1945 and later; the prototype ceased work in March 1953, an obvious museum candidate in a more enlightened era.

preparation of locomotive diagrams and a survey which confirmed his first impression that there were too many different types at work. The sturdy construction of the early 2-2-2s was fortunate as there had been no scheduled maintenance regime, repairs being effected only as a consequence of component failure. Some fireboxes had been replaced but all the boilers were original.

Further, trackwork was in terrible condition having suffered from inadequate maintenance. Unusual 90 lb per yard bridge iron rails, the best available when laid from 1846 onwards, were becoming crystalline. Ahrons states there were no fishplates but specially wide sleepers were laid at rail joints which were often poorly packed accentuating problems. Where the old rails on the main line had broken into a sufficient number of pieces they were used to fill odd gaps on branch lines. Odd lengths of 3, 6 & 7 feet were abundant so passengers and locomotives had to withstand severe and frequent jolting. By the 1870s, it was considered fortunate if an express engine covered a Dublin-Cork return working without breaking a spring, despite their strong construction with twenty ½ inch leaves. By 1880, many miles had been re-laid with steel rails in chairs.

Wheels were originally made of cast iron, an alloy with many useful qualities but with a tendency to become brittle. To reduce breakages, McDonnell apparently tried wheels of either all wrought iron construction or a combination of wrought iron hubs with cast iron spokes and rims. The most viable solution seems to have been to rely on cast iron with thicker tyres or rims. Most of the pre-1864 goods locomotives had 5' 0" diameter driving wheels but in the early days of McDonnell's 0-6-0 construction programme, an engine could be in service with driving wheels from differing sources, built up to a notional 5' 1¼". In due course, the Inchicore standard diameter (when new) evolved into 5' 2" for goods locomotives. At the time, poor quality materials constituted a serious constraint for the industry which was solved through advances in the Bessemer process that yielded good quality steel at commercially attractive prices.

McDonnell faced a mammoth task but found among his subordinates the able John Carter Park whom in 1865 he appointed as Works Manager (not to be confused with James Crawford Park of the GNR[I]). Park had earlier worked at Longsight under John Ramsbottom, making this a significant early appointment of an ex-London & North Western Railway employee. Coupled with McDonnell's previous associations with Crewe, the Premier Line's design practices were influential in the GSWR's 19th Century locomotive history.

McDonnell's early years were marked by a policy of make-do-and-mend to extend the working lives of ageing equipment. The complex changes during this period are summarised through the GSWR Locomotive Key and through details of individual renewals that appear in the respective locomotive histories. Recycling, which was necessary to contain capital and maintenance expenditure, would have reinforced appreciation of standardisation's virtues. The extent of component recovery is best illustrated by the story of Sharp Stewart 2-2-2 Type I [1] No 16. Working career mileage records survive for eight members of this Type (Nos 2, 5-8, 10, 13, 15). From these it is calculated that annual totals averaged around 17,200 over careers lasting 27-29 years as 2-2-2s. No 16 was an early withdrawal, taken out of service in 1865 for rebuild as a 2-4-0. This process was completed the following year, the locomotive having previously run an estimated 310,000 miles as a 2-2-2. Six other locomotives were included in this programme (Nos 1, 4, 9, 11, 14, 18), probably selected because of their poor boiler condition. Seven "new" 2-4-0s were thus created over two years that employed the following components recovered from the 2-2-2s:

Frame sets (modified): three
Cylinder pairs: six
Motion sets: seven
Leading axles: two
Crank axles: four
Pairs of leading wheels: three
Pairs of driving wheels: three
Driving wheel pairs converted to trailing drivers: two
Pairs of leading tyres: two

"New" 2-4-0 No 16 entered service with frames, cylinders, motion, all wheels and axles, and leading

The most distinctive of all the GSWR tank engines were the 0-4-4Ts which were effective on passenger work. Their ancestry was unusual in that they derived from the pair of 0-4-4T Single Fairlies built at Inchicore in 1869/ 70. Robert Fairlie demanded extortionate reimbursement for use of his patented system of articulation. The GSWR settled for a substantially reduced sum and McDonnell continued to produce the type, with the crucial difference that the driving wheels were set within a rigid frame. Type 52 [LII] Class 47 No 83 was built in September 1884 and remained in original condition until withdrawal in 1928, having sustained damage in the Civil War.

Design and construction

The GSWR favoured the 2-4-2T wheel arrangement for some lighter branch line duties as with Type LV [55] Class 33 No 41. This locomotive, seen beside Thurles signal cabin, is still fitted fore and aft with Aspinall's unique two-pipe vacuum brake system which was eventually displaced about 1922. Built in December 1892, this engine remained in original condition until withdrawal in December 1957. *Real Photographs*

wheel tyres recovered from withdrawn 2-2-2s. These components would have accounted for about one-third the cost of a new build. With other recycled parts such as axleboxes, springs etc probably about 50% of the material cost was covered in this fashion. As they became life-expired, components were replaced: crank axle (October 1867); leading tyres (August 1868); cylinders (September 1870); leading axle (October 1871); frames, axles, wheels and tyres (January 1873); and finally motion (June 1878). Thus eight years after entering service, the main recycled elements were eventually replaced; the original 1847-vintage tender was probably retained throughout. By this process, No 16 evolved from its "hybrid" condition (RNC's description) into a member of 2-4-0 Type VIII. It last ran in June 1884 and was formally withdrawn in November 1885

Three 2-4-0s (Nos 1, 4, 16) received modified frames; those with No 16 survived 5½ years and travelled 138,000 miles. With hindsight, re-use of components might not have been cost-justified but McDonnell probably had little choice, given prevailing motive power shortages and depleted financial resources. A parallel programme was conducted to modernise elements of the goods fleet by withdrawing four-coupled locomotives and re-using key components in the construction of 0-6-0s through the hybrid process. This programme is described in the preamble to Type XXXV [35] Class 101.

On a more modest scale a report survives that details the recycling of quite minor components that probably started life with 2-2-2s of Type I [1] and were used in construction of two 0-4-4Ts built in 1887 that lasted until 1928/ 30. These components are listed in the commentary for Type LII [52]. Their retention plus the operation of Inchicore's foundry suggests that by then, virtually every piece of redundant metal was put to further use.

The LNWR was a valuable ally in the GSWR's network expansion and it is probable that McDonnell sought advice from Crewe. He enjoyed a pre-existing relationship with LNWR by virtue of his earlier appointment as Locomotive Superintendent of the Newport, Abergavenny & Hereford Railway, a company then central to the LNWR's aspirations to expand into South Wales. That plan remained unfulfilled as the NAHR became part of the West Midland Railway in 1860 and was in turn absorbed into the Great Western in 1863. Nevertheless, these contacts appear to have been exploited when McDonnell commenced new construction.

Although the balance of evidence suggests that drawings and specific advice were provided by Beyer

4-4-2T Type LIX [59] Class 27 No 31 was built for suburban passenger duties in December 1900 and worked until May 1953. This view provides good detail of the GSWR design of the flat-faced "oven-door" smokebox front. The date is post-1922 as the Aspinall double-pipe vacuum brake has been removed. *Real Photographs*

Peacock in the case of the 0-6-0 construction programme, Crewe was then the industry leader in standardisation and mass production techniques. This must have fashioned much of McDonnell's thinking about improved productivity and efficiency. While other companies (like the GSWR) operated fragmented fleets, John Ramsbottom in 1858 had introduced 0-6-0 Class Dx which by 1872 totalled 857 plus 86 built for the Lancashire & Yorkshire Railway. Numerically the largest class ever built in these islands, the Dx must have profoundly impressed McDonnell when considering the varied collection in his charge.

Immediate demands stemmed from heavier trains and from the incidence of rail fractures which discouraged use of locomotives with leading driving wheels on faster services. A batch of mixed traffic 0-4-2s was under construction when McDonnell arrived but he preferred the 2-4-0 type. Crewe's influence was prominent in Type 10 Class 21 of 1873 which bore resemblance to Ramsbottom's "Newton" class of the same year. Arrival of Class 21 in significant numbers spelled the end for earlier wheel arrangements; the last 2-2-2 was withdrawn in 1882 and the 0-4-2 type became extinct in 1886. The Newtons were the first of the LNWR's extended family of 2-4-0s, a genre that demonstrated an extraordinary capacity for punishment as hard-driving crews thrashed them up and down the West Coast Main Line with heavy loads. It is probable that Class 21 would have met most of the GSWR's less demanding needs for some years, were it not for the curvaceous nature of the Kerry and associated branches. Here the 2-4-0 wheel base was found too rigid necessitating change to an otherwise satisfactory design.

The GSWR was not alone in facing this conundrum. In 1871, the North British Railway had pioneered the eventually ubiquitous inside-cylindered 4-4-0 with its No 224 (the Tay Bridge engine nicknamed "the diver" following its recovery), and six years later McDonnell copied this initiative with his Class 2 "Kerry Bogies". These were the first 4-4-0s in Ireland and among the first of this wheelbase in these islands. (The LNWR did not have a 4-4-0 type until the "Black Prince" class in 1897 where the "bogies" were effectively double radial trucks).

Design and construction

The GSWR's 0-6-0Ts were mainly concentrated in the south at Cork and Limerick. They were used principally on banking, shunting and trip working, and were frequently seen on the street lines of the Cork City Railway. No 220 of Type LX [60] Class 201 was built in 1901 and worked until October 1959.

Following front end weight problems with 0-6-0/ 2-6-0 Type XXXVIII [38], Coey attempted in 1905-7 to compensate by building the GSWR's first 4-6-0 in the form of Type XXXIX [39] Class 362. This was the largest design in service in Ireland when introduced and a source of pride to the GSWR. However, these engines were unduly light at the front end and very poor riding resulted. Five were withdrawn in 1928 and the last survivor went in 1931.

With this new technology, McDonnell pursued an innovative course away from and in advance of Crewe. While the Kerry Bogies were early examples of what became a universal type, the other bogie-based design, which actually pre-dated the 4-4-0s, was a most unusual venture. A key reason why tender locomotives always formed the majority of the fleet was poor water quality in many areas. Nevertheless, McDonnell introduced tank engines in 1869, and the first two were of historic significance being 0-4-4T Single Fairlies. They were first of this variant of the Fairlie principle built anywhere, and the only examples of the Double/ Single/ Mason genre to have inside cylinders. With bogie technology in its infancy, exploitation of the recently patented Fairlie concept was imaginative. As explained in the Type XLV [45] history, no more were built beyond the initial pair but further rigid framed 0-4-4Ts of similar outward appearance followed. Even with this more conventional format, the 0-4-4Ts broke new ground as together with 4-4-0 Class 2, they were the first locomotives in these islands to be equipped with swing-link bogies.

McDonnell's commitment to standardisation in new building commenced with Beyer Peacock-built Type XXXV [35] Class 101 No 147 in 1867 (the first "pure" class member as opposed to the hybrid creations). A total of 107 had been built by 1899 (including eight withdrawn and replaced prior to that date). The table below compares leading dimensions of six key designs introduced over a 16-year period. While Class 101 stands out as a more muscular creation against its younger brethren, the dimensional constancy demonstrated the point that there was minimal advantage in unnecessary tinkering with a fundamentally sound concept.

McDonnell was responsible for other designs but these were smaller locomotives or built for specific purposes in small batches; they injected variety but their roles were peripheral to the main story. However in the small locomotive group, one venture dating from 1875 revealed exploration of operating economics through a vehicle that combined a small 0-6-4T (Type XLVIII [48]) and a carriage as an early steam railcar.

Mention was made earlier of the embedded interdependence between the Irish and British elements of the locomotive construction sector. Aspinall and Ivatt fully embraced the essential logic of their predecessor's policy, evidently perceiving little gain through divergence. After their time in Ireland, both moved on to become locomotive superintendents of major English companies and through their presence, Inchicore's pioneering work probably exerted greater influence on British practice than is commonly acknowledged.

Locomotive fuel

In 1856, the company chairman told a shareholders meeting that it was the aim of all concerned with the railway to consume a greater quantity of coal i.e. in substitution for more expensive coke that the railway was legally required to burn in minimisation of smoke emission. At the time, experiments were being conducted in fuel substitution in England, the results of which were closely monitored. This would appear to be the first occasion on which high fuel costs came under formal scrutiny, a subject that was repeatedly to exercise the locomotive superintendent over following years. By the next year coal and coke was being regularly mixed and at least two patented forms of firebars were being trialled.

Type	XXXV [35]	XLVI [46]	X [10]	XII [12]	L [50]	LII [52]
GSWR Class	101	n/a	21	2	28	47
No built	107	8	10	12	4	20
Introduced	1867	1870	1873	1877	1879	1883
Wheel Arrangement	0-6-0	0-4-4T	2-4-0	4-4-0	0-4-4T	0-4-4T
Boiler pressure lb/ sq in	140	140	140	150	140	150
Cylinders	17" x 24"	15" x 20"	16" x 20"	16" x 20"	16" x 20"	16" x 20"
Driving wheels	5' 0"	5' 8.5"	5' 8.5"	5' 8.5"	5' 8.5"	5' 8.5"
Leading/ bogie wheels	n/a	3' 8"	3' 8"	3' 0"	3' 8.5"	3' 9"
Tubes sq ft	856	770	770	770	677	677
Firebox sq ft	96	74	83.8	83.8	78	78
Grate sq ft	17.5	15	16	16	15	15

Design and construction

The GSWR relied mainly on good quality coal imported from south Wales which allowed the use of moderately-sized grates, a policy that raised problems when the GSR/ CIE was forced to use poorer quality fuel in the 1940s. Nonetheless, Coey was alive to modern trends in boilers and these developments could improve performance. He tried both tapered boilers and Belpaire fireboxes, although never concurrently on the same locomotive. Type XVIII [18] Class 321 No 322 which carried a tapered boiler from new was at Adelaide, Belfast in 1911 while engaged in exchange trials with the GNR(I).The GSWR habitually used good quality Welsh coal, but the dross in the tender suggests that performance assessment with sub-standard fuels formed part of the tests. *Paddy Mallon*

Eight 4-4-0s of Type XIX [19] Class 333 were built in two groups of four in 1907 and 1908 with 5' 8½' driving wheels for use on Cork-Rosslare services. The first four were plagued with hot journals on the front bogie so to alleviate the problem the second batch were built with outside-framed bogies which resulted in a slight increase in weight. The second bogie design was a case of over-engineering as minor changes to the axle boxes and introduction of a different lubricant solved the problem in 1909. No 339 was at Bray in the 1930s on an Up mail working from Wexford, during a period of motive power shortage on the ex-DSER section. *Rex Conway*

McDonnell's multi-facetted concern with efficiency led to structured investigation of alternative fuels and a summary of his work demonstrates his characteristic thoroughness. Ireland's small coal deposits are poor quality and unsuitable for steam locomotives so imports from Britain were essential. Welsh coal with its superior calorific value was preferred but more expensive at the pithead before cost of transportation was added. On arrival at Dublin port, it was shipped in lighters by the Grand Canal Co from Ringsend to the wharf adjacent to Inchicore at the rate of 5d per ton. It was then moved by horse-drawn wagons over a quarter-mile long narrow gauge tramway to the GSWR's store. This cumbersome process was avoided by completion of the line from Islandbridge Junction to Glasnevin Junction in 1877 which allowed rail transit from the quay to Inchicore. This reduced losses from pilferage but could not circumvent the impact of miners' and dockers' strikes, or of shipping delays thus necessitating substantial reserve stocks. The cost of coal was a major factor in operating viability as around 1870, annual consumption was 40,000 tons. In search of cheaper alternatives, McDonnell arranged in August 1871 for around 100 tons of Irish-mined anthracite to be acquired for competitive testing. No results have been traced but these efforts were apparently unsuccessful as in 1872 he focussed on experiments with native turf. A locomotive (believed to be a member of Class 101) ran 347 miles on a light goods train at a consumption rate of 73.9 lb per mile. A similar locomotive hauling a slightly heavier load over a matching distance consumed Welsh coal at the rate of 36.1 lb per mile. In another test, an engine hauling fourteen carriages over 320 miles at an average speed of 29 mph consumed turf at the rate of 51.6 lb per mile. The same engine with an average load of 6.4 carriages then covered 663 miles at an average speed 30 mph and burned Welsh coal at the rate of 20.3 lb per mile. In a third trial over 684 miles with a similar load and average speed, the comparison was 48.9 lb per mile for turf and 22-23 lb with coal. It was concluded that

This photograph taken at Mallow is of a special working from Cobh to Kingsbridge and Dún Laoghaire. It reveals an unsuccessful measure to overcome difficulties encountered with 4-6-0 Type XXI [21] Class 400 in its original 4-cylinder form. Funding was not available for repeat of the 2-cylinder conversion that had transformed No 402's performance in 1927. Lacklustre performance was in part attributed to poorly designed steam passages so in 1930, a cheaper solution was attempted with revised steam pipes. By means of a tee-junction on either side of the smokebox, steam was distributed rearward to the outside cylinders and forward to the inside cylinders. This clumsy and somewhat crude layout does not seem to have wrought much improvement. No 407 (which was the last to remain in 4-cylinder form, being converted in 1938) is pilot to No 403 which has also received the outside steam pipe arrangement.

The programme to convert 0-6-0 Type XXXVIII [38] Class 355 to inside-cylindered moguls was completed in 1908. In this form they proved competent machines which led Coey to produce four more in September 1909 as 2-6-0 Type XLIV [41] Class 368. This quartet differed in having a revised wheelbase of 5' 9" + 7' 3" + 8' 9" as compared with 5' 0" + 8' 0" + 9' 0" of the earlier conversions. Also Class 368 introduced (saturated) Belpaire boilers to the GSWR which added 6 sq ft to the firebox heating surface. Images suitable for reproduction of Class 368 in original form are rare. This is a view of Class 368 No 370 in GSR days by which time it had been fitted with a GSR Type Q superheated boiler and piston valves. *Real Photographs*

in combustion terms, 100 tons of turf equated 43 to 47 tons of coal.

McDonnell clearly believed that the concept had potential as he obtained board approval in February 1873 for expenditure of £300 per month for extended experiments to ascertain cost and value. Special peat-making machinery was manufactured by Messrs Courtney Stephens & Bailey and a processing facility was set up at a rather inferior bog at Mountrath, Co Laois. The machinery was powered by withdrawn Bury 2-2-2 No 22. The facility produced compressed sods which were used in some locomotives and in the Siemens regenerative gas furnace at Inchicore which was used for heating large forgings for the steam hammer. The peat proved more successful in the furnace than with locomotives; strikes which were occurring in the South Wales coalfields at the time lent urgency to these experiments. Peat production at Mountrath continued until 1875 when it was concluded that the experiment was not viable and the facility was dismantled.

Management succession

JC Park resigned in 1873 to become Locomotive Superintendent of the North London Railway in succession to William Adams. He was replaced at Inchicore by Robert Findlay who did not stay long before moving to the Belfast & Northern Counties Railway. Looking for a suitable replacement, McDonnell approached Crewe where Ramsbottom had been succeeded in 1871 by FW Webb, an individual who enjoyed a fearsome reputation among subordinates. He was less well known as an accomplished inventor and industrialist who maintained cordial relationships among his peers in other companies. Partly based on his pre-existing relationship with Crewe, McDonnell was offered the services of John Aspinall, one of Webb's best ex-apprentices who had spent time in the USA studying railroad practice. Further, he was well versed in Crewe's prominence in production line technology (long before the name of Henry Ford became synonymous with the concept) so had skills from which Inchicore could benefit. He became Works Manager in 1875, at the age of 24 years. McDonnell might have preferred someone more experienced but Webb was one whose opinions were better left unchallenged.

Webb's judgement proved sound, helping to establish a pattern of management succession that helped create Inchicore's golden years. Harmony in leadership was further consolidated through

The penultimate tank locomotive built under GSWR auspices in 1914 was 0-4-2T Type LXIV [64] *Sambo*, the Inchicore works shunter, otherwise known as the "Premises Pilot". It was cobbled together out of sundry spare parts and probably included components recovered from the first *Sambo* of 1885-vintage that was withdrawn the previous year. *Sambo* was a determined survivor, outliving Inchicore's closure to steam by becoming pilot at the ex-GNR Amiens Street shed before withdrawal in 1962. This view shows the wagon works at Inchicore, probably in the 1950s. The wagons being shunted by *Sambo* were strongly constructed of pressed steel to a design by Oliver Bulleid.

recruitment of Henry A Ivatt as Running Superintendent, Cork in October 1877. This was at Aspinall's instigation who apparently asked Webb to release Ivatt, a close friend. Both had been born in 1851 and they had worked together as apprentices at Crewe, although as he had started his career slightly earlier, Aspinall was the more senior. Ivatt was in charge of locomotive affairs at Chester when he agreed to join the GSWR. Having helped out McDonnell in making Aspinall available, Webb was apparently not too pleased to lose a second valued subordinate in this manner.

By 1877, weekly train miles had risen from the 6,000 of 1847 to 50,000 and the GSWR was acknowledged as the leading Irish railway company. McDonnell had done well to provide the equipment to cope with this traffic expansion which had required expenditure of £47,000 (a vast sum in those days) on buildings and tools at Inchicore. He was now also in charge of carriage and wagon matters and the complex (works and running sheds) had a payroll of some 1200 personnel.

Efficiency improvements had made new construction price-competitive. Analysis confirmed that Inchicore could build a locomotive for £2,300 while a British manufacturer would charge £2,750 for a similar machine. The differential was partly accounted for by the need to accommodate the 5' 3" gauge and by shipping costs but the result vindicated McDonnell's policy of self-sufficiency. The carriage shops were by then producing a new coach or van every two weeks while the wagon shops, equipped with its own smithy, was building four vehicles a week. McDonnell had initiated, and Aspinall sustained, efforts to improve standards by advancing the quality and accuracy of machine tools, and by harnessing this equipment in developing new manufacturing techniques. These capacities were adopted to great advantage in recovering scrap metal from withdrawn locomotives and in recycling this material into reusable strip and bar.

McDonnell's concern about the GSWR's vulnerability vis-à-vis imported fuel supplies and the search for viable local alternatives formed part of the self-sufficiency objective. The iron foundry, which cost £1,668 to establish in 1871, had by 1873 accounted for a reduction of £1,059 in manufacturing expenses. That same year, a plate-bending machine was acquired specifically for the production of locomotive chimneys in preference to the previous building-up process. Whether a similarly impressive pay-back was achieved with this equipment is unknown but it typified the efficiency drive.

This was a time of significant development in steel manufacture. By 1870, steel had largely replaced iron in wheel tyres and in 1875 the purchase of iron rails ceased. The advantages offered by steel replacements must have been considerable as the price was roughly double, and the company still carried substantial un-used stock of the iron variety. Aspirations for engineering independence still allowed for adoption of other people's ideas as with piston rings which in 1870 led to a summons from Ramsbottom for patent infringement. The outcome does not seem to have been recorded but a lesson was learned as the company was later paying Webb £2-10s annually for every injector built to his patent. A home-grown development that did not risk legal impediment was introduction of rectangular cast iron number plates in 1873, signalling permanence in locomotive identities and little chance of reversion to the confusing changes of the previous decade.

McDonnell was a superb leader who enjoyed the full support of the board In pursuing progressive policies. He was popular with the workforce for being firm and decisive while showing genuine concern for their well-being. His interest in personnel welfare was apparent in the provision of dining and reading rooms at Inchicore. Morale was further boosted by extensive celebrations held on 8th August 1879 to mark construction of the 144th new locomotive built there and the 100th during McDonnell's tenure. Over 2,000 people attended a day of sporting events and hospitality at the company's expense, while 400 notables plus the directors sat down to dinner followed by dancing until midnight. The old locomotive order was nearing elimination and the theme was recognition of achievement by the Locomotive Superintendent's team.

This period was not without difficulties. The matter of continuous brakes, as discussed in Appendix A, was a thorny issue between McDonnell and the board. There were also growing concerns about the quality of materials from outside suppliers at a time when the science of metallurgy was still in primitive form. Boiler tubes were a major worry as quality had declined seriously. Bury 2-2-2 No 27 had run almost 300,000 miles with its original tubes which on removal proved sufficiently sound for re-use. On the other hand, much younger boilers were requiring tube replacement within unsatisfactorily short periods. McDonnell compared notes with Martin Atock on the MGWR who shared these concerns, and the pair then collaborated on investigating causes and applying remedial action. This was a welcome change from the persistent strife that had sullied relationships in the two companies' costly competition over network expansion.

Inchicore was kept abreast of British railway developments through Aspinall's active participation in mechanical and civil engineering bodies thus ensuring that the GSWR was in no way a technical backwater beyond the barrier of the Irish sea. There was active consideration of branch line economics where the "extravagance" of the 5' 3" gauge might be relieved by narrower alternatives. Aspinall's approach derived from an interest in transportation efficiency rather than the operation of railway traffic, a subtle yet vital distinction that continued to escape the understanding of many railway managers well beyond the GSWR's demise. His trademark attention to detail had revealed that the locomotive used on Castleisland Railway had run 110,000 miles in five and a half years up to 1880 at a total repair cost of £175 which equated with 0.384d per mile, compared with the average of 1.351d per mile for main line locomotives. It was this type of analysis that supported his contention that standard gauge light railways were preferable to narrow gauge systems. He pointed out that the latter offered only minor savings in land and that other capital expenses (e.g. construction cost of a coach) yielded little advantage.

The background circumstances do not seem to have been recorded but McDonnell applied for the position of Locomotive Superintendent with the Midland Railway in June 1873. He was unsuccessful but the GSWR directors became aware of the matter as his salary was promptly raised to £900 pa (it had been £600 pa in 1869) and he was given a free house, an improvement in his circumstances that seemed just recognition for his achievements.

Even so, his resignation in 1882 was unexpected but he had no hesitation in recommending 32-year old Aspinall as his successor. The board might have raised collective eyebrows but his promotion was duly confirmed, effective from the following year, as was also the transfer of Ivatt from Cork to become Works Manager. Aspinall's tenure in charge was short as he departed in 1886 to become Locomotive Superintendent of the Lancashire & Yorkshire Railway. This was a return to Crewe's universe as the LYR and LNWR attempted to merge more than once, eventually achieving that goal in 1922. Ivatt stepped into Aspinall's shoes.

McDonnell's precepts remained a constant throughout Period II. Aspinall as Works Manager had played a crucial role in Inchicore's improvements. He then oversaw introduction of 4-4-0 Types XIII [13] & XIV [14] (Classes 52 & 60), effectively enlargements of the Kerry Bogies but no other new types. Class 52 was built to work Dublin-Cork mail trains and found to have superior riding qualities over the preceding 2-4-0s in working trains at an average speed of nearly 40 mph. With a need to work still heavier and

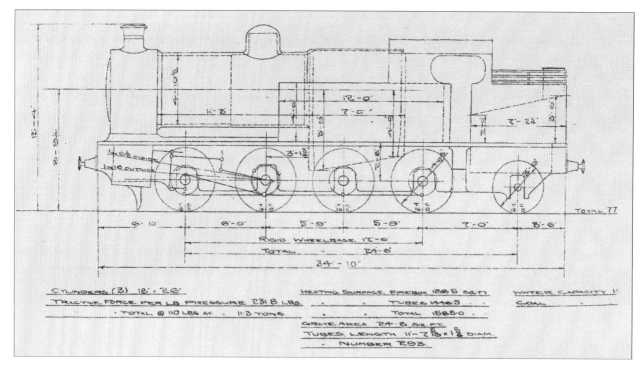

Perhaps influenced by Robinson's 3-cylinder 0-8-4T Class 8H heavy shunter of 1908 for the Great Central Railway, Maunsell proposed an 0-8-2T for use at North Wall yards in Dublin. A key objective was to achieve even torque through the use of three cylinders but difficulties were encountered in working out clearances for the centre valve motion. Before this could be resolved, Maunsell had departed to the South Eastern & Chatham Railway leaving only this drawing of the proposed design.

faster trains, Class 60 was introduced as an enlargement of Class 52. Class 101 0-6-0s are commonly regarded as the epitome of Irish locomotive longevity but these two classes were well built and tough; Class 52 averaged 64 years in service while Class 60 managed 70 years!

Aspinall was in frequent contact with Crewe at this time and Webb spared no effort in advocating the use of his compound system. With his customary attention to detail, Aspinall conducted a comparison and estimated building costs for the first four of Class 60 at £2,000 each against £2,250 for a compound. The board was content to opt for the cheaper version, undoubtedly to the GSWR's all-round benefit.

Nevertheless, compound steam remained a topic that could not be ignored. Aspinall's investigations had been ruled out on grounds of cost but Ivatt, who also maintained cordial relations with Webb, decided that experiments were justified. In 1890 he instructed Works Manager, Robert Coey, to proceed with the conversion of an 0-6-0. Class 101 No 165 was selected and at work from March 1891. This engine showed sufficient potential for a second guinea pig, 4-4-0 Class 60 No 93, to receive similar treatment in 1894. Both engines had been built with a pair of inside 18" x 24" cylinders but now an 18" diameter high pressure cylinder was set alongside its 26" diameter low pressure companion; boiler pressure remained unchanged at 150 lb/ sq in.

The 0-6-0 was fitted with an automatic flap valve devised by Worsdell (of the North Eastern Railway) whereby boiler steam was cut off from the low pressure cylinder immediately after starting and the locomotive worked constantly in compound mode thereafter. The 4-4-0 differed in having a change valve controlled by the driver which enabled the engine to work either as a simple or as a compound. In practical terms, this facility was of limited value as the size of the larger cylinder would place unreasonable demands on the boiler if worked over any distance in simple mode. The option was possibly useful when climbing gradients at the commencement of journeys, as near Inchicore and at Cork.

Mystery attaches to the belief that experience with the 0-6-0 provided sufficient grounds for the experiment to be extended. Ernest E Joynt (Chief Draughtsman at Inchicore under Coey, Maunsell and Watson) later described No 165, a regular on a goods working to Nenagh, as "undesired and unloved". The engine was noted for its asthmatic, irregular blast essentially attributed to the exertion of greater thrust by the high pressure cylinder than its

Design and construction

Watson showed no interest in continuing development work on his predecessor's proposed 0-8-2T, opting instead for a 2-cylinder 4-8-0T. Type LXV [65] No 900, his first expression of the large engine concept was introduced in 1915. Largely a synthesis of existing components from Coey-era designs, its ungainly appearance reflected a poorly thought-out design that suffered from unsatisfactory weight distribution. This photograph was taken at Inchicore 26 May 1924, just four years before withdrawal. *Ken Nunn*

Railway		GSWR	MR	GNRI
Locomotives Nos		93/ 165	1000	Class V
Cylinder volumes (cu in):	High pressure	6,107	7,372	6,083
	Low pressure	12,742	29,487	29,487
% High pressure/ low pressure		48%	25%	21%

low pressure counterpart, resulting in a pronounced pounding effect. Comparison with more modern, successful compound designs (Midland [UK] and Great Northern railways) suggests that the low pressure cylinder capacity was inadequate. The limitations imposed on a locomotive with two inside cylinders would have prohibited use of a larger low pressure diameter.

The engine was reputed to be heavier on coal and water, and less powerful than ordinary members of Class 101. Joynt believed that the exposed position of the low pressure cylinder added to the gross unevenness of the beat as the airflow meant that the vessel acted both as a steam cylinder and as a surface condenser. Ahrons reported that the 0-6-0 did better in terms of fuel and water consumption which suggests that overall the performance of the 4-4-0 was even more disappointing.

Ivatt insisted that the modifications should be limited to the cylinder configuration to measure the precise degree of change emanating from the compound system. This approach may have been too restrictive e.g. an increase in the boiler working pressure might have shown off the compound arrangement to greater advantage. In any event, No 165 sustained a cracked cylinder block in 1896 which led to its reversion to normal condition; 4-4-0 No 93 reverted when undergoing major repairs in 1901. Such was Inchicore's determined attachment to standardisation that both compounds, with their differing components, needed to show significant advantage for the system to receive serious consideration. Compound steam was never pursued again by the GSWR.

Ivatt's main contribution was the introduction of 22 tank locomotives in three wheel arrangements as

Three generations of GSWR locomotives together at Inchicore shed. At the front is 0-6-4T Type LI [51] Class 203 No 205, (built April 1880, withdrawn 1928) with tapered boiler 4-4-0 Type XVI [16] Class 305 No 306 (as built 1902), withdrawn October 1959) immediately behind. An unidentified 4-6-0 Type XXI [21] Class 400 in as-built condition is at the rear.

Type	Class	W.A.	Number	Built	Withdrawn
LIII/ LVIII/ LX	201/ 207/217	0-6-0T	10	1887-1901	1949-63
LV/ LVI	33/35	2-4-2T	6	1892-4	1957-64
LVII/ LXI	37/317	4-4-2T	6	1894/ 1901	1950-55

shown in the table above.

Standardisation and keen attention to detail were keystones to McDonnell's policy, which Aspinall and Ivatt sustained. An example which might be regarded as trivial concerned sleepers that were cut at Inchicore's sawmill. Aspinall, who adopted the procedure of "enquire/ decide/ apply" in addressing technical issues had discovered that a variety of saw blades were in use. He conducted a detailed survey to establish which saw tooth dimension was most effective, and then ensured that only this pattern was used.

Of far greater consequence was the concern shared by McDonnell and Aspinall over continuous braking systems for passenger trains. Development work commenced on this important matter but the board appeared reluctant to sanction the requisite expenditure. Aspinall persisted, his efforts leading to evolution of an effective braking system as recounted in Appendix A.

The three individuals who oversaw Period II progress (and their successors) emphasise the degree to which Irish and English practice was interwoven. Between 1864 and 1924, the GSWR had seven Locomotive Superintendents and the pattern of their later careers reinforces the point.

With the exceptions of McDonnell and Watson (the latter died soon after moving to England), their post-

Name	Leaving year	Later appointment
A McDonnell	1882	Locomotive Superintendent, North Eastern Railway
JAF Aspinall	1886	Locomotive Superintendent, Lancashire & Yorkshire Railway
HA Ivatt	1896	Locomotive Superintendent, Great Northern Railway (England)
R Coey	1911	Retired through ill-health
REL Maunsell	1913	Locomotive Superintendent, South Eastern & Chatham Railway
EA Watson	1921	General Manager & Engineer-in-Chief, Beyer Peacock, Manchester
JR Bazin	1924	Joined from GNR (England); became Locomotive Superintendent, Great Southern Railways

Design and construction

In 1900, Type XIII [13] Class 52 No 56 was derailed at the south end of Limerick Junction station in front of the South cabin and a photographer was on call to record the event. No 56's tender and train have been drawn back and sister engine No 4 has been recruited to help in the rerailing process. The photographs reveal points of interest in the "furniture" of the railway in those days while the second is particularly useful in displaying No 56's cab detail.

GSWR careers were successful. McDonnell was fated to be considered a failure at the NER although his reputation seems to have been unfairly tarnished. These factors have received little publicity and while more relevant to NER history, summarised details are provided in Appendix B.

Progression to Locomotive Superintendent by way of Works Manager had proven effective during Period II and this become an established path accepted by Board and management. Such rigidity risked a paradigm that apparently contributed to less harmonious management succession in the 20th Century.

Period III (1896 to 1924)

It was a general rule of thumb that steam locomotives should enjoy 30-40 years of useful working life, hopefully without need for rebuilding. As matters transpired, many Period II locomotives were required to work for substantially longer periods as the mainstay for many operations in Great Southern days, and the early years of Córas Iompair Eireann. This situation stood testimony to the quality of Period II designs of which comparatively few failed to exceed 30 years' service. Deteriorating economic and trading conditions in the 20th Century also enforced longevity, as did the GSWR's failure to sustain progress in design practice.

Coey who had been Works Manager since 1886 succeeded Ivatt ten years later and initially continued construction of his predecessors' designs, principally 0-6-0 Class 101 of which the last twelve introduced improvements, and 4-4-2T Classes 27 & 37 which had a clear familial relationship with earlier tank classes. Coey was responsible for a diminutive 0-2-2 as the driving unit of Type LXIII [63][Steam Rail Motor No 1 built in 1904. Based on units built by Drummond for the London & South Western Railway, it proved unsuccessful. The locomotive section was scrapped in 1912 while the coach section worked a little longer.

With traffic expanding, 1900 brought change with passenger 4-4-0 Type XV [15] Class 301 which was visually of the new era. The search for larger motive power units was exercising locomotive engineers generally and the GSWR was an active participant in this trend. Contemporary conventional views held that larger boilers and/or compound steam would provide the answer. However, Churchward on the Great Western identified that optimal shape was critical in maximising water volume adjacent to the

Another unfortunate incident, on this occasion with more serious consequences, resulted in Type LII [52] Class 47 No 80 becoming embedded in a timber-bodied Brake 3rd coach. The location and date is not recorded but the rear view of the bunker is informative. Tender-/ bunker-first running in Ireland was unusual so most photographs are of the front three-quarter or side-on variety. This view reveals placement of the tank filler centrally towards the rear of the bunker, a design feature applied by Inchicore to side, back and well tank locomotives.

firebox front, the boiler's hottest point. Coey recognised the advantages by fitting some 4-4-0s with tapered boilers but refrained from adding Belpaire fireboxes. Disadvantage lay in higher construction cost and post-Coey policy reversed the combination by using Belpaire fireboxes with parallel boilers. These essays demonstrated that Inchicore was alive to modern trends in boiler although it was not until 4-6-0 No 500 that valve design (travel: 6 3/16" and lap: 1½") caught up with GWR standards.

By 1907, there were 26 Coey large-wheeled 4-4-0s in four separate classes and eight of a smaller-wheeled mixed traffic version in service. They were conventional in design, allowing for the tapered boiler variation, and showed progressive increases in size and weight. Frame strength seems to have been a problem with some re-framed (and others withdrawn) in the 1920s. Considering that the first re-framing of a Class 101 took place with a 49-year old engine, it was evident that 20th Century construction was not so robust and that larger locomotives fell foul of conflicting demands in size, weight and power output.

Difficulties arose from attempts to replace Type XXXV [35] Class 101. In 1903, the year that construction of 101s finally ceased, an enlarged 0-6-0 appeared in Type XXXVII [37] Class 351. Entirely traditional, these engines were adequate, but undistinguished. Also in 1903, North British supplied seven larger 0-6-0s of Type XXXVIII [38] Class 355 weighing over 49 tons. They were front-end heavy and by 1908 all had been converted into ungainly-looking 2-6-0s. In 1905, the first of the six-strong 4-6-0 Type XXXIX [39] Class 362 appeared from Inchicore to much fanfare as the largest locomotives in Ireland. They proved a poor imitation of English inside-cylinder 4-6-0s being front-end light resulting in appalling riding qualities, and a proneness to derail. Their lives were short, varying between 21 and 24 years, which in the Irish context often reflected a sub-standard design. Coey's final attempt at a larger goods type was 2-6-0 Type: XLI [41] Class 368 of 1909, of which two survived for only 19 years.

In summary, Coey's work did not meet emerging 20th Century demands and his construction policy was a reversal of the standardisation principles championed by McDonnell. Best exemplified by the multiplication of Class 101, the practice continued in the next century but with the key difference that modest batches usually entailed a different class, as with the 6' 7" 4-4-0s.

As built, there were variances in cylinder dimensions and heating surfaces while the all-up weight rose by over 5 tons between classes 301 and 321. McDonnell's approach had proven cost effective but

Class	Total	Construction
301	4	1900
305	4	1902
309	6	1903
321	12	1904-6

if Coey's efforts pursued an optimal solution, this was not attained judging by the complex modifications applied to Class 321 by the GSWR, and by its successor.

Coey had enjoyed a harmonious relationship with Richard Maunsell, Works Manager, and following his retirement through ill health in 1911, better might have been expected. Unfortunately, Maunsell's tenure was short although he did complete the interesting 4-4-0 No 341. This solitary locomotive is usually attributed as a Coey/ Maunsell design but its thoroughly modern features suggest that it was largely inspired by the latter. With superheated Belpaire boiler, piston valves and inside Walschaerts valve gear it was competent and much admired. However, the civil engineer was unenthusiastic about its 60-ton weight and 19-ton axle loading. It remained a singleton, unloved by the authorities and destined for a short career, amid popular protest. The main beneficiaries were to be the English South Eastern & Chatham and Southern railways where Maunsell's Inchicore experiences were put to good use with 4-4-0 classes D1, E1 and L1.

Maunsell's attempt at a replacement for Class 101 was 0-6-0 Class 257. In the vein of No 341, these eight locomotives were built with superheaters and piston valves, and later acquired Belpaire fireboxes. Despite their competence they were inexplicably overlooked by the GSR in two failed attempts to find a replacement for ageing 101s. Two of Class 257 earned the sad distinction of being the last steam locomotives in service with Córas Iompair Eireann, just out-living their English Maunsell 0-6-0 counterparts (Southern Railway Class Q).

The GSWR's bias toward tender locomotives remained pronounced in the 20th Century. The last tank engines for general service had been 4-4-2T Types LIX [59] & LXI [61] Classes 27 & 317 completed in 1901. Two years later four of 0-6-2T Type LXI [61] Class 211 were completed by North British to work the Drumcondra link line. They were found to be overweight leading to the rebuilding of two as 0-6-0s. Weight difficulties experienced with these engines and with 0-6-0 Type XXXVIII [38] Class 355 raises questions over the quality of communication between Inchicore and North British over design specification. The manufacturer successfully supplied a wide variety of locomotives to numerous overseas railways which suggests that the fault lay with Inchicore.

Shed scene at Waterford. The timber building to the extreme left was for the Waterford & Limerick Railway and the more substantial building with the sheer legs in front was for the Waterford & Kilkenny Railway. The locomotive to the left is a GSWR Type XXXV [35] Class 101 with its oven(!) doors open, which is rarely pictured.

Thereafter only two specialised tank types appeared, but there was an interesting proposal that did not get beyond the drawing board. Maunsell attempted the design of a 3-cylinder 0-8-2T heavy shunter to work the North Wall yards in Dublin. The concept seems to have been inspired by Robinson's 0-8-4T Wath "Daisy" heavy shunters of the Great Central Railway but difficulties were encountered in finding space for the inside motion. Before this problem could be solved, Maunsell departed for Ashford. His only Irish tank engine was unnumbered 0-4-2ST Type LXIV [64] *Sambo*, cobbled together largely out of spare parts as the replacement Inchicore works shunter.

Maunsell's departure ended Inchicore's typically harmonious working environment. Following precedent, he was succeeded by EA Watson who had been appointed Works Manager in 1911. A native of Clones, Co Monaghan, Watson had spent much of his early career in the USA before becoming Assistant Works Manager, Swindon. He arrived at Inchicore with a "large engine" mentality, and a reverence for Great Western motive power policy. Nevertheless, there was a question mark over his abilities as a practical locomotive engineer. A competent leader might have succeeded despite such deficiencies but Watson had an abrasive management style, exacerbated by vociferously opiniated political views that were contrary to prevailing popular sentiment.

Watson's personal unpopularity and arrogance militated against his endeavours at modernisation. In rejection of Maunsell's initiatives he ignored the projected 0-8-2T and opted for a 2-cylinder 4-8-0T heavy shunter, using standard components. This became the GSWR's final tank engine design but poor weight distribution resulted in a proneness to derail leading to this locomotive being considered a failure. Watson's successor, Bazin, produced another example in late 1924 with detail differences that proved no more successful.

However, the heavy shunter's problems were overshadowed by the dismal reputation of the ten-strong 4-cylinder Class 400 4-6-0s. Built to eliminate the need for double-heading 4-4-0s on the Dublin-Cork route, No 400 failed to out-perform Maunsell's No 341 which had been built for the same purpose. The 400s were to prove as controversial as their accredited designer, earning disdain among the company's personnel, and independent observers; correction of the class's shortcomings was protracted. This phase of their history is beyond the scope of this work but is described in detail in *Locomotives of the GSR* (Clements and McMahon, Colourpoint Books 2008).

Eighty-five locomotives were constructed to modern designs from 1900 and while opinions will vary, in the authors' view 49 could be considered as failing to meet expectations. This assessment is borne out by

Design and construction

Class	Wheel arrangement	Running Numbers	Assessment	No. of Locos	Sub-standard as built
211	0-6-2T	211/ 2	Rebuilt as 0-6-0 after four years	2	2
213	0-6-2T	213/ 4	Overweight	2	2
257	0-6-0	257 to 264	Competent	8	4
301	4-4-0	301-4	Inadequate	4	4
305	4-4-0	305-8	Satisfactory	4	
309	4-4-0	309-314	Satisfactory	6	
321	4-4-0	321-332	Weak frames	12	12
333	4-4-0	333-340	Satisfactory	8	
341	4-4-0	341	Competent	1	
351	0-6-0	249-252, 351-354	Satisfactory but poor valve design	8	
355	0-6-0	355-361	Soon rebuilt as 2-6-0s	7	7
362	4-6-0	362-7	Poor performers; rough riding	6	6
368	2-6-0	368-371	Satisfactory	4	
400	4-6-0	400-9	Poor	10	10
500	4-6-0	500	Excellent	1	
900	4-8-0	900/ 1	Poor	2	2
			Total	85	49

this group being divided into 16 classes. An average of a little more than three per class indicates that none were regarded as sufficiently sound for multiplication in significant numbers. The assessment is shown in the above table.

It was a sad conclusion to the company's locomotive history, especially in view of Inchicore's fine reputation. Nonetheless, substantial redemption lay in JR Bazin's only design for the GSWR which appeared in 1924 as "mixed traffic" 2-cylinder 4-6-0 No 500. This locomotive, conceptually similar to Maunsell's contemporary English 2-cylinder 4-6-0s, displayed all round competence to a degree that the 4-cylinder 4-6-0s signally lacked.

The GSR completed only two more Class 500s, a decision based on economic rather than technical grounds as by then the Woolwich Moguls, derived from Maunsell's 2-6-0 Class N for the South Eastern & Chatham Railway, were entering service. This was a modern, capable design that was superior to the pre-Maunsell GSWR classes that typified late 19th Century practice. They enjoyed a wider route availability than the 4-6-0s, and their purchase in 1924 at bargain basement prices, initiated by Morton on the Midland Great Western Railway, stymied further construction of Class 500 beyond the pair built in 1926.

GSWR Locomotive liveries

Determination of the early policy has not been possible but photographs provide some clues. A view of 2-4-0 Type VIII [8] No 20 (see photograph in Type history) suggests a darkish body colour for boiler, cab sheets and tender, with single light coloured lining. Reverse curves were applied to right-angled corners. This style also appears on 4-4-0 Type XII [12] No 43, 4-4-0 Type XIV [14] No 63, and 4-4-2T Type LXI [61] No 31 (see Type histories).

Variations were evident with Type XXXV [35] Class 101 No 119 (see Type history). Its condition reveals similar styling to that described above except that the boiler bands appear to be double-lined with another colour in between. The body colour is either dark green or black; perhaps it was practice for goods engines to be in the latter colour. With 2-4-0 Type XI [11] No 64, what appears to be double or triple lining can just be discerned on the cab panels; the tender appears undecorated.

Painting was probably the last task in construction of the MacNamara model (see Frontispiece) so it may be assumed that this accurately depicts the livery in 1880, subject to the caveat concerning ageing. While paint could be reasonably stable, varnishes were not always so resilient which might account for colour change. However, this provides the best contemporary evidence before the revisions introduced by Coey.

Ernest Carter (*Britain's Railway Liveries* – Burke, London 1952) stated that about 1890 the livery for 2-4-0 Class No 64 was dark green body colour with open-work splashers picked out in yellow and crimson. No source was quoted and while green seems to have been generally accepted as the main colour, the shade does not accord with information overleaf.

Type XVIII [18] Class 321 No 322 was selected to undergo exchange trials with a 4-4-0 QL Class No 113 of the Great Northern Railway in March 1911 (both engines were built in 1904). As with the earlier view of this engine, the location is Adelaide, Belfast. Particular effort was made to ensure that the GSWR's representative was in pristine condition, as is apparent in these views that provide useful information on lining detail. On magnification, it is evident that the cab side sheets have been painted in straw/ cream on the inside. Note that the straw colour has been lined.

The Locomotive for November 1898 refers specifically to 4-4-0 Type XIV [14] Class 60 as having medium olive green bodywork with a black panel stripe bordered along each edge with a light green line and inside this a fine vermilion line. Boiler lagging bands were black with a fine red line and then a light green line on each side. Buffer beams were red with black borders, black buffer sockets and blue shaded yellow locomotive numbers. Cabside number plates consisted of bright cast iron figures on a black background. The inside cab sheets were painted straw colour. This livery's date of introduction and the extent of its application is unknown. The photograph of Type XLVIII [48] No 92 (see Type history) shows a light coloured body which could be olive green.

Coey apparently considered the olive green-based livery too elaborate. *The Locomotive* reported in 1900 that new 4-4-0s of Type XV [15] Nos 301-4 were delivered in black with a broad vermilion line edged with white and a fine vermilion inner line. This style was supposedly the official livery until the Great War, at least for passenger locomotives. However there is no evidence of white in the coloured illustration dated 1905 of 4-4-0 Type XVIII [18] No 321 below. The illustration depicting 4-6-0 Type XXXIX [39] also endorses the thick and thin vermillion treatment but there is little clear indication of white lines. Coloured illustrations from this period are rare so in view of their source, they should regarded as bearing authority. Two official photographs in workshop grey

4-4-0 Type XVIII [18] Class 321.

19th Century Locomotive purchases

Prior to 1901, there were comparatively few locomotive acquisitions from companies taken over by the GSWR and their details appear in Chapter 7. For the most part, these engines served acceptably long careers with the GSWR, except for those from the Waterford & Central Ireland Railway. This was a troubled concern that was reflected in the condition of its motive power, leading to truncated careers under GSWR ownership. The companies so acquired were all minor concerns and their locomotive contributions had no significant impact upon GSWR practice.

Waterford, Limerick & Western Railway

Taken over in 1901, this was the largest company acquired by the GSWR. The Locomotive Superintendent was John George Robinson who had been recruited from the GWR in 1884 as Assistant Locomotive Superintendent. He took charge of the company's Limerick works four years later and proceeded to re-stock and modernise the fleet. By 1901, the WLWR owned 58 locomotives of which exactly half were to his designs plus six earlier machines rebuilt under his direction. He had close ties to the GWR (his elder brother James A Robinson rose to become Northern Division Locomotive Superintendent at Wolverhampton) and that company's ornate finishes in the Dean era might have influenced his views on how an engine should appear. Definitely the famous Robinson style (including early manifestations of his trademark chimney) was evident in contrast to the functional yet antiquated appearance of contemporary GSWR locomotives. Despite efforts at rationalisation, the WLWR fleet harboured complexity reminiscent of the early GSWR.

At the time of the takeover, Robinson was already on his way to succeed Harry Pollitt at the Great Central Railway so exerted no direct influence on Inchicore practice, neither then nor later when his superheater generated widespread interest. Nevertheless, acquisition of the WLWR fleet must have invoked comparisons with the style and finish of the contemporary Inchicore product thereby influencing Coey's design approach. In service, many of the WLWR locomotives put in useful careers with the GSWR and several worked into CIE days. The last survivor was withdrawn in 1959.

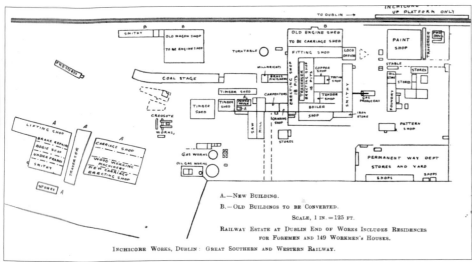

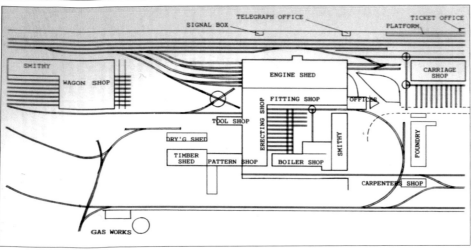

Schematic layout of Inchicore's facilities and layout in 1879. *The Engineer.*

Design and construction

This colour plate of Type XXXIX [39] No 365 was published in December 1906, 12 months after this class was introdu
therefore provides a contemporary record of the GSWR's livery policy. The only white appears to be to the upper edg
running plate valance (although the undated photograph of No 364 in Chapter 5 suggests the *lower* edging). White lin
elsewhere might have been considered too ornate for a goods locomotive. Nevertheless, the amount of vermillion lin
(axleboxes, wheel bosses, running plate edge) would have kept craftsmen engaged for some time. On a point of deta
engine's leaf springs appear also to have been painted red.

(0-6-2T Type LXII [62] No 213 and 4-8-0 Type LXV [65] in the relevant Type histories) depict elaborate lining although it seems doubtful whether these locomotives were so decorated for ordinary service.

Under wartime conditions, lined black was abandoned in favour of all-over unlined austerity grey. This looked quite smart when new but lost its lustre under the accumulation of grime. It gradually became universal and was continued by the Great Southern Railways after 1925.

An exception to the grey regime was the treatment accorded No 400 when built in 1916 and the colour plate should be considered authoritative in view of the source. Similar treatment was given to the

Gauge 0 model of No 404 built by Bassett L display on the company's stand at the 1924 Empire Exhibition at Wembley. This might b interpreted as an expression of intent conse upon restoration of the GSWR's fortunes as independent company. This model is now in of the Fry Model Railway Museum at Malal Dublin.

The three colour illustrations set out on this preceding page appeared in the following is *The Railway Magazine*:- Locomotive No 32 Volume XVI, 1905; No 365 – Volume XIX, 1 400 – Volume XXXIX, 1916. They are repro here by permission of Mortons Media Grou

4-6-0 Type XXI [21] No

19th Century Locomotive purchases

Prior to 1901, there were comparatively few locomotive acquisitions from companies taken over by the GSWR and their details appear in Chapter 7. For the most part, these engines served acceptably long careers with the GSWR, except for those from the Waterford & Central Ireland Railway. This was a troubled concern that was reflected in the condition of its motive power, leading to truncated careers under GSWR ownership. The companies so acquired were all minor concerns and their locomotive contributions had no significant impact upon GSWR practice.

Waterford, Limerick & Western Railway

Taken over in 1901, this was the largest company acquired by the GSWR. The Locomotive Superintendent was John George Robinson who had been recruited from the GWR in 1884 as Assistant Locomotive Superintendent. He took charge of the company's Limerick works four years later and proceeded to re-stock and modernise the fleet. By 1901, the WLWR owned 58 locomotives of which exactly half were to his designs plus six earlier machines rebuilt under his direction. He had close ties to the GWR (his elder brother James A Robinson rose to become Northern Division Locomotive Superintendent at Wolverhampton) and that company's ornate finishes in the Dean era might have influenced his views on how an engine should appear. Definitely the famous Robinson style (including early manifestations of his trademark chimney) was evident in contrast to the functional yet antiquated appearance of contemporary GSWR locomotives. Despite efforts at rationalisation, the WLWR fleet harboured complexity reminiscent of the early GSWR.

At the time of the takeover, Robinson was already on his way to succeed Harry Pollitt at the Great Central Railway so exerted no direct influence on Inchicore practice, neither then nor later when his superheater generated widespread interest. Nevertheless, acquisition of the WLWR fleet must have invoked comparisons with the style and finish of the contemporary Inchicore product thereby influencing Coey's design approach. In service, many of the WLWR locomotives put in useful careers with the GSWR and several worked into CIE days. The last survivor was withdrawn in 1959.

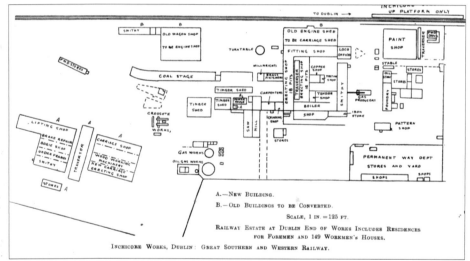
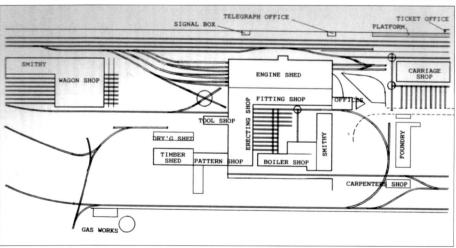

Schematic layout of Inchicore's facilities and layout in 1879. *The Engineer.*

Design and construction

This colour plate of Type XXXIX [39] No 365 was published in December 1906, 12 months after this class was introduced and therefore provides a contemporary record of the GSWR's livery policy. The only white appears to be to the upper edging of the running plate valance (although the undated photograph of No 364 in Chapter 5 suggests the *lower* edging). White lining elsewhere might have been considered too ornate for a goods locomotive. Nevertheless, the amount of vermillion lining applied (axleboxes, wheel bosses, running plate edge) would have kept craftsmen engaged for some time. On a point of detail, the engine's leaf springs appear also to have been painted red.

(0-6-2T Type LXII [62] No 213 and 4-8-0 Type LXV [65] in the relevant Type histories) depict elaborate lining although it seems doubtful whether these locomotives were so decorated for ordinary service.

Under wartime conditions, lined black was abandoned in favour of all-over unlined austerity grey. This looked quite smart when new but lost its lustre under the accumulation of grime. It gradually became universal and was continued by the Great Southern Railways after 1925.

An exception to the grey regime was the treatment accorded No 400 when built in 1916 and the colour plate should be considered authoritative in view of the source. Similar treatment was given to the Gauge 0 model of No 404 built by Bassett Lowke for display on the company's stand at the 1924 British Empire Exhibition at Wembley. This might be interpreted as an expression of intent consequent upon restoration of the GSWR's fortunes as an independent company. This model is now in the care of the Fry Model Railway Museum at Malahide, Co Dublin.

The three colour illustrations set out on this and the preceding page appeared in the following issues of *The Railway Magazine*:- Locomotive No 321 – Volume XVI, 1905; No 365 – Volume XIX, 1906; No 400 – Volume XXXIX, 1916. They are reproduced here by permission of Mortons Media Group Ltd.

4-6-0 Type XXI [21] No 400.

Chapter 3
Locomotive works and commercial manufacturers

Having declined to follow Edward Bury's advice concerning a locomotive works in the Tipperary area, the GSWR acquired approximately 87 acres of land for this purpose at Inchicore, then outside the Dublin city boundary.

Locomotive construction commenced with three locomotives in 1852-3 but in the absence of a technically qualified locomotive superintendent, it is questionable how adequate were the works facilities at that stage. It seems probable that the process was more a matter of assembly, reliant heavily upon bought-in components. For example, Grendon of Drogheda which had supplied a pair of 0-4-2s in 1849, would continue to manufacture key parts such as cylinders until about 1874.

In parallel with reorganisation of motive power affairs, McDonnell's impact on Inchicore's operational and physical infrastructure was profound. His pre-GSWR experience in railway construction and later in the establishment of a locomotive department in eastern Europe qualified him to expand and up-grade the facilities he had inherited. His initiative, sustained by his successors, resulted in creation of the most comprehensively equipped locomotive works in Ireland, earning it a redoubtable reputation for quality and efficiency.

With self-sufficiency as the underlying objective, the ability to manufacture cylinders from 1874 onwards is testimony to progress made. An article in the *Railway Magazine* for October 1913 described the complex that had been developed. Although not large by the standards of Crewe and Derby, Inchicore's facilities matched those of the better-equipped English locomotive workshops, and achieved high quality standards. At that time, the works serviced 283 locomotives, 885 passenger vehicles and 7,852 goods wagons. The Locomotive Superintendent was also responsible for all personnel working directly with locomotives, carriages and wagons throughout the system, and for maintenance of stationary plant, power cranes, capstans and other mechanical appliances. The 1913 article stated that Inchicore "is well worthy to be reckoned among the great railway shops of the United Kingdom" (i.e. before Irish Independence). As developed, it was definitely the most handsome with its crenelated stonework designed by Sancton Wood, architect.

Inchicore's facilities included construction and heavy repair shops for locomotives, carriages and wagons plus smithies, paint shop, sawmill and timber store, gas works, general stores, offices etc. Uniquely among Irish railway workshops there was an iron

Inchicore from the Dublin-Cork mainline looking towards Kingsbridge. The handsome works building is to the right matched by what could be the most elegant signal cabin in these islands. *CH Hewison*

The works looking south with Type XXI [21] Class 400, possibly No 403, approaching with an Up express service. The train's stock is typically mixed including the fourth coach which is a Pullman. *CH Hewison*

foundry, although like other companies more complex steel castings were supplied by outside specialists. In 1913, the works shared the distinction with Swindon of having a smithy that used steam stamps. These provided greater accuracy than was possible with the more common drop stamps.

The complex also included running and carriage sheds, plus extensive sidings bordering the Cork mainline. The works employed approximately 1,400 men and boys. Engineering tasks were undertaken for other departments, except for the Permanent Way establishment which employed around 200 people and which was housed on the site but operated as a separate unit. The company's central stores employed another 100 personnel to cater for the needs of the entire system. An exception to this comprehensive range of activities was signal equipment which was serviced at Thurles.

Housing was provided for around 500 employees on the site which was also home to a large institute, dining hall and library. Those not enjoying the benefits of accommodation used the nearby Dublin United Tramways Company terminus which connected with the city centre, or travelled the 1¾ miles from Dublin Kingsbridge by a shuttle service of staff trains.

By comparison, Limerick works was a modest establishment as befitted the smaller locomotive fleet of the WLWR. The company relied almost entirely on motive power supplied by commercial manufacturers in Britain although facilities did allow extensive repairs and locomotive rebuilding. JG Robinson, Locomotive Superintendent, was committed to improving efficiency and engineering standards. He insisted on maximum standardisation of components, regardless of the source of supply and he exercised firm influence on the quality and style of the locomotives for which he was responsible.

Commercial manufacturers

As with other railway companies which commenced operations in the 1840s, the GSWR bought its first locomotives from established manufacturers, usually to their standard designs modified for the different gauge. The 2-2-2s and 0-4-2s from Bury, Curtis & Kennedy had that company's trademark bar frames and domed haycock fireboxes. The Sharp 2-2-2s were part of family of some 600 generally similar machines, supplied to British and overseas railways in the period 1837-57 including several other early Irish railways.

Through McDonnell's investment programme, the GSWR's self-sufficiency meant that the only machines provided by commercial manufacturers from 1864 until 1903 were twenty members of Class 101:- twelve from Beyer Peacock between 1867 and 1881, and eight from Sharp Stewart between 1872 and 1879. In the 20th Century, the GSWR turned to Neilson Reid, the North British Locomotive Company and Armstrong Whitworth for supply of small batches.

Panoramic view of Inchicore locomotive depot. *CH Hewison*

During the 19th Century, the GSWR absorbed a number of minor railway companies of which the following owned their own locomotives:

Castleisland Railway (CR)
Cork & Youghal Railway (CYR)
Waterford & Central Ireland Railway (WCIR) previously Waterford & Kilkenny Railway (WKR)
Waterford, Dungarvan & Lismore Railway (WDLR)
Waterford & Wexford Railway (WWR)

All obtained all their motive power from outside builders, except for the solitary Castleisland engine (an Inchicore product). In the main, commercial manufacturers supplied locomotives derived from their standard products, modified for the Irish gauge, which reduced purchase price per engine and eased the supply of spares. These were important factors for small, impecunious companies with minimal repair capacity. The only locomotive-owning railway company taken over in the 20th Century was the Waterford, Limerick & Western Railway which transaction accounted for the single largest fleet expansion. The locomotives acquired had been supplied by British manufacturers.

In theory, records of the main locomotive building firms (general arrangement drawings; order books; line drawings used in promotional material; and official works photos) should be available from keepers of the relevant archives. In practice, survival of such records is variable. Where builders' records no longer survive, alternative drawings are sometimes available by way of contemporary engineering journals, or the collections of societies, or through studies by individual historians. Identified archival sources have been exhaustively canvassed. The locomotives concerned are summarised below while fuller information is contained in the locomotive histories (Chapters 4 to 9). Brief information is also provided concerning the relevant manufacturers. Details of the whereabouts, where known, of the relative archives appear in italics at the conclusion of each manufacturer's section.

Sir WG Armstrong Whitworth & Co Ltd, Newcastle-upon-Tyne

This was a major manufacturer engaged in production of armaments, ships, motorcars and aircraft. In 1919, its Scotswood factory was converted to steam locomotive manufacture, using modern equipment. Between then and 1937, when the works reverted to armaments production, a total of 1,464 locomotives were built of which about 1,000 were exported. Two batches of three members of 4-6-0 Class 400 were delivered:

Original Nos	Built	Builder's Nos
403 – 405	1922	188-190
407 – 409	1922	185-187

The ordering of these engines drew criticism in Dail Éireann concerning purchase of locomotives, coaches and wagons from British manufacturers when there was unutilised capacity at Inchicore and personnel had been laid off. These orders were apparently placed on the basis of competitive pricing. Manufacturers and the UK government were seeking contracts from any quarter to relieve post-war unemployment and cost reduction was attractive to

Armstrong Whitworth's 4-6-0 Type XXI [21] Class 400 No 404 as built.

Stothert & Slaughter builder's number unknown: Type II[2]-WKR, originally Waterford & Kilkenny Railway No 5, later No 3 as shown in this photograph at Waterford.

the financially-challenged GSWR. Nevertheless, there were significant delays in final settlement following delivery in October 1922. Civil War damage to permanent way on the Dublin-Cork route held up post-delivery trials which were not completed until June 1923 when the test mileage in the contract was eventually run up. The manufacturers then received the balance due, much to their relief as they could not understand the reason for the delay. Brand new No 405 worked the Presidential train to the re-opening ceremony of the Civil-War damaged Blackwater Viaduct at Mallow.

Avonside Engine Co Ltd, Bristol

Established as Henry Stothert & Company in 1837, this became Stothert, Slaughter & Co from 1841, and Slaughter, Grüning & Co from 1856. It was re-formed as the Avonside Engine Co Ltd in 1864. A fire reportedly destroyed all company records in 1870. Until about 1880, production focussed on main line engines but with increases in size and weight, was re-directed to industrial types. The company went into voluntary liquidation in 1934; Hunslet Engine Co purchased the goodwill and designs.

Supplied by Stothert, Slaughter & Co/ Slaughter, Grüning & Co:

Railway	Nos	GSWR No	Built	W.A.
WLR	1 to 6	-	1846	2-2-2
WKR	4	[251]	1852	2-4-0
	5	-	1852	2-4-0

Supplied by Avonside Engine Co:

Railway	No	GSWR No	Built	Builder's No	W.A.
WCIR	10	257	1873	965	0-4-2
	11	258	1873	966	0-4-2
	12	[259]	1876	1169	0-4-2T
WLR	19	[272]	1876	1126	0-4-2
	26	278	1876	1125	0-4-2
	27	279	1876	1127	0-4-2
	33	[284]	1876	1128	0-4-2

There do not appear to be any surviving manufacturer records for these locomotives, except for a works photograph of WCIR 0-4-2T No 12.

Beyer Peacock & Co, Manchester

Established in 1854 at Gorton Tank, Openshaw, this prominent manufacturer was a prolific supplier to Irish railway companies including the GSWR which purchased 12 members of 0-6-0 Class 101:

GSWR No	Built	Builder's No
147-150	1867	747-750
151-154	1868	780-783
177, 178	1873	1251, 1252
189, 190	1881	2029, 2030

Well-preserved and extensive manufacturers' archives, including official photographs and general arrangement drawings are in the care of the Manchester Museum of Science & Industry,

Bury, Curtis & Kennedy

Formed by Edward Bury in 1826 in Liverpool, this manufacturer's first locomotive was supplied to the Liverpool & Manchester Railway in 1830, soon followed by standard designs of 2-2-0s and 0-4-0s. Known as Bury, Curtis & Kennedy from 1842, the business closed in 1851 following a downturn in trade and default by the Russian government in payment for engineering supplies. GSWR 2-2-2 No 36 is one of only two surviving Bury locomotives.

GSWR No	Built	W.A.
21-40	1846-8	2-2-2
41-50	1845-8	0-4-2
WLR No	**Built**	**2-2-2**
8-10	1848/9	2-2-2

The Bury Archives were supposedly taken to the USA for display at the 1893 World's Fair after which they were passed into the care of the Field Museum, Chicago which then had a substantial transport section. (This body is now a natural history museum only and has no record of these arrangements). "Historian" Clement Stretton (1850-1915) was apparently involved in the matter. By about 1900, Stretton claimed to have recovered the material that had been on loan but as this proved too large for storage by him, it was supposedly donated to the South Kensington Museum, now the Science Museum. However, it seems doubtful whether the records of Bury, Rothwell and EB Wilson were included as they do not appear in the UK National Database of historical documents. The Field Museum ceased to act as repository for World Fair exhibits in 1905. Further inquiries in Chicago and at the Merseyside Maritime Museum, Liverpool Central Library, and Liverpool City archives have produced no information on Bury's archives. The records should be regarded as lost.

Dübs & Co, Glasgow

Set up by Henry Dübs at the Queens Park Works, Glasgow in 1863, this company became a major supplier to railways in the UK plus Australia, New Zealand, and South Africa before combining in 1903 with two other Glasgow manufacturers to form the North British Locomotive Company (NBLC). The Waterford & Limerick Railway was the only constituent company to be supplied by Dûbs:

WLR No	GSWR	Built	Builder's Nos	W.A.
9	262	1886	2194	4-4-0
24	227	1886	2195	0-6-0
10	263	1889	2477	2-4-0
22	275	1890	2662	2-4-0
20/ 23	273/ 276	1892	2880/ 2881	2-4-0
43/ 44	290/ 291	1893	3025/ 3026	2-4-0
45/ 46	233/ 234	1893	3042/ 3043	0-6-0
47/ 48	292/ 293	1894	3109/ 3110	2-4-0
49/ 50	235/ 236	1895	3222/ 3223	0-6-0

The archives for Dübs are held by the National Railway Museum, York together with the files for the North British Locomotive Co.

Bury Curtis & Kennedy 2-2-2, built 1847: Type II [2] No 36 was the last of fourteen engines in the second series of Bury single drivers, withdrawn 1875. It is one of only two surviving Bury locomotives (the other being Furness Railway 0-4-0 No 3 "Old Coppernob"). In this view, No 36 is awaiting resuscitation.

William Fairbairn & Sons

Formed in Manchester by Sir William Fairbairn Bt., this firm's activities included civil, structural and mechanical engineering plus shipbuilding. Between 1839 and 1862, it built around 500 locomotives, of which 62 were supplied to Ireland including:

Railway	Nos	Built	W.A.	
GSWR	70/ 71	1855	2-4-0	
	75	1856	0-4-2	
LER §	1	1859	0-4-2	Later WLR No 1
	2	1854 or 1856	0-4-2	Later WLR No 2
WLR	11/ 12	1853	2-4-0	
	17 to 20	1854	2-4-0	
	21	1855	2-4-0	
WKR	1	1855	2-4-0	Retained by WLR after 1867 (WLR No 26)

§ Limerick & Ennis Railway

This firm's practice was to copy other manufacturers' products which may complicate identification. Fairbairn moved from Manchester to Millwall, Isle of Dogs in 1834-5 as more convenient for shipbuilding. The locomotive business was sold to Sharp Stewart in 1863. William Fairbairn died in 1874 by which time the business faced many difficulties. Liquidation was not completed until 1899 and reportedly company records were then destroyed.

Fossick & Hackworth, Stockton

This firm was founded in 1839 by George Fossick and Thomas Hackworth (brother of Timothy). About 120 locomotives were built before activities moved into marine engineering in 1853. The firm supplied the following:

Railway	Nos	Built	W.A.
WLR	22-4	1862	0-4-2

No records for this company have been located at the Discovery database; the Discovery Museum, Newcastle-upon-Tyne; Tyne and Wear Archives; or Teesside Archives, Middlesbrough.

John Fowler & Co, Hunslet, Leeds

Established in the early 1860s, this firm was a leader in agricultural mechanisation, stemming partly from John Fowler's visit to Ireland in 1849. He recognised the need for new ploughing methods to increase arable acreage and to improve crop yields for famine relief. The firm produced steam ploughs and traction engines plus railway locomotives but moved into

John Fowler & Co 2-4-0T, built 1866: Type V [5]-WKR comprised two of a batch of four locomotives originally destined for railways in the north of Ireland. Having been acquired by the Waterford & Kilkenny Railway (later Waterford & Central Ireland Railway), they were converted to 2-4-0s. The pristine condition of one of the pair as depicted here suggests that it might have recently undergone the conversion.

munitions in World War II. The company merged with Marshall, Sons & Co Ltd in 1947 and finally ceased production in 1968. Four locomotives were ordered by the Belfast, Hollywood & Bangor Railway which could only afford to pay for one; the second went to the Belfast and Co Down Railway and the remaining pair were bought by the WKR (later WCIR):

Railway	Nos	GSWR Nos	Built	W.A.
WKR	6/ 7	[253]/ [254]	1866	2-4-0T

Company's records are with the Museum of English Rural Life, University of Reading. A works photo of one of these engines is in the archives, oddly listed as for the "Irish Midland Railway"; no GA drawings have been traced.

Thomas Grendon & Co, Drogheda, Ireland

Approximately 2200 steam engines operated in Ireland, of which about one-third were built by railway companies for their own use. Some independent enterprises produced components and undertook heavy repairs but there were only ever two Irish commercial manufacturers. Grendon of the Drogheda Ironworks built its first locomotives in February-May 1845 for Dublin & Drogheda Railway (2-2-2 Nos 13-15) and produced at least 38 more. The last was a 2-4-0 for the Belfast & Northern Counties Railway in 1868, but the firm continued to produce castings and to undertake locomotive repairs until the 1890s. Grendon was eventually taken over by Spence's of Cork Street Foundry, Dublin which was Ireland's only other commercial manufacturer, producing 1' 10" gauge engines for Guinness Breweries between 1887 and 1921. Cylinders for the GSWR were supplied by Grendon from 1862 until 1874 when Inchicore opened its foundry and installed steam hammers. Loss of this business had considerable impact on Grendon's fortunes.

GSWR Nos	Built	W.A.
51/ 52	1849	0-4-2

WLR No	Built	W.A.
7	1848 or 1851	2-2-2

Some Grendon records survive in the care of the Irish Railway Record Society, Dublin.

Hawthorns & Co, Leith

R & W Hawthorn Ltd, Newcastle-upon-Tyne acquired the Leith Engine Works, Edinburgh in 1846 for locomotive assembly using components supplied by its main factory. These works were sold in 1850 to another company that traded as Hawthorns & Company and which produced about 400 locomotives before closure in 1872.

WLR No	GSWR No	Built	W.A.
42	[232]	1862	0-6-0WT

No archival source has been traced. An article in The Locomotive *for 15th March 1940 describes the early history of this engine.*

Hunslet Engine Co builder's No 557, built 1892: This company was a specialist in the manufacture of small shunting and industrial tank engines. Originally owned and operated by a contractor, it was later sold to the Tralee & Fenit Pier & Harbour Commissioners, from whom it was purchased by the GSWR in 1901 and numbered 299 (and informally named "Shamrock") – Type LXVI (66). Seen here at Limerick shed.

Hunslet Engine Co, Leeds

Established 1864 in Leeds this company built small tank engines for shunting, quarry, industrial and colliery use:

Previous owner	Name	GSWR No	Built	W.A.
Fenit Harbour Commissioners	*Shamrock*	299	1892	0-6-0ST
Rowlands & Cartland (contractors)	*Cambria*	-	1894	0-4-0ST
Rowlands & Cartland (contractors)	*Erin*	[300]	1894	0-6-0ST

Surviving Hunslet records are held by the Statfold Barn Railway, Tamworth, Staffordshire.

Kitson & Co, Leeds

Established 1835, this company underwent several changes of name before assuming this title in 1863, becoming a major supplier to UK and overseas companies. Trading declined in the 1920s and serious losses resulted from failure of the Kitson-Still 2-6-2T steam-diesel hybrid. The company entered receivership in 1937 and production ceased the following year. The re-organised business produced components until final closure in 1945.

Railway	No	GSWR No	Builder's No	Built	W.A.
WKR	6/ 7	-	320/ 321	1853	2-2-2
WLR	28	[280]	1213	1864	2-2-2
	3/ 7	-	1783/ 4	1872	0-4-2
	51/ 52	294/ 295	3587/ 8	1895	0-4-4T
WLWR	16/ 17	269/ 270	3616/ 7	1896	4-4-2T
	53/ 54	296/ 297	3618/ 9	1896	4-4-0
	55	298	3694	1897	4-4-0
	18/ 21	271/ 274	3689/ 90	1897	4-4-2T
	56 to 58	237 to 239	3691- 3	1897	0-6-0
	2	222	3908	1900	0-6-0

Locomotive works and commercial manufacturers

Robert Stephenson & Hawthorns acquired the records and goodwill in 1938. Most archives for main line engines apparently went to the Merseyside Museum, but they have not been traced, although work continues to catalogue and curate Kitson's order book entries. Line drawings and works photos for some locomotives supplied to the WKR, WLR and WLWR have been obtained via the Stephenson Locomotive Society.

Kitson & Co builder's No 3619 of 1896: WLWR 4-4-0 No 54 *Killemnee* (Type XXXIV [34]-W) at Limerick. This was the second of a group of three built for Waterford-Limerick boat trains.

Kitson & Co builder's No 3908 of 1900: WLWR 0-6-0 No 2 *Shannon* as GSWR No 222 (Type XXXV [35]-W), the last locomotive delivered to Limerick before takeover over by the GSWR. *IRRS*

Manning Wardle & Co

Established in the Hunslet area of Leeds in 1840, this company manufactured approximately 2,000 small shunting, industrial and colliery locomotives. Despite its success, failure to modernise led to closure in 1927. It built two rail motors for the DSER. The locomotive and carriage units were later separated and one locomotive was sold in 1918 to the Dublin & Blessington Steam Tramway where it was found to be too heavy. It was re-sold to the GSWR in 1921 in exchange for the ex-WWR *Cambria*.

Name	GSWR No.	Builder's No.	Built	Wheel arrangement
Imp	-	1693	1906	0-4-0T

Neilson & Co (later Neilson, Reid & Co), Glasgow

This company built marine and stationary engines between 1836 and 1855 but from 1843 moved increasingly into locomotive construction. In 1861, the company moved to a new factory at Springburn, Glasgow to cope with business expansion. Owned by James Reid since 1884, it was renamed Neilson, Reid & Co in 1898. In 1903, it merged with Dübs & Co and Sharp, Stewart & Co to form North British Locomotive Co.

Railway	CYR	GSWR No	Built	Builder's	W.A.
	1 to 3	61 to 63	1859	542 to 544	2-4-0ST
	4/ 5	64/ 65	1860	599/ 600	2-4-0ST
	6 to 8	68 to 70	1861	689 to 691	2-2-2ST
	9/ 10	66/ 67	1862	885/ 886	2-4-0ST
GSWR	-	309 to 314	1903	6313 to 6318	4-4-0

The archives for Neilson, Reid are held by the National Railway Museum, York together with files for the North British Locomotive Co.

North British Locomotive Co, Glasgow

Formed in 1903 through the merger of Dübs & Co, Neilson, Reid & Co and Sharp, Stewart & Co. Following liquidation in 1962 the goodwill, drawings & patterns were acquired by Andrew Barclay. The following were supplied:

GSWR No	Built	Builder's No	W.A.
355 to 361	1903	15943 to 15949	0-6-0
211 to 214	1903	16021 to 16024	0-6-2T

The main archives for North British Locomotive Co are held by the National Railway Museum, York. Some records may held by the University of Glasgow.

Neilson, Reid & Co builder's No 6313 of 1903: Industrial relations difficulties at Inchicore led to what was the first order placed with a commercial manufacturer since 1879. Type XVII [17] Class 309, No 309 was an evolutionary development of two preceding classes of Coey 4-4-0s. This locomotive is standing with a Down train at Ballybrophy.

Top: North British Locomotive Co builder's No 15943 of 1903: By time of delivery, Neilson Reid had become part of North British. No 355 was the prototype of Type XXXVIII [38] Class 355 which comprised seven locomotives and which were found to be front end heavy, necessitating their early rebuilding at Inchicore as 2-6-0s.

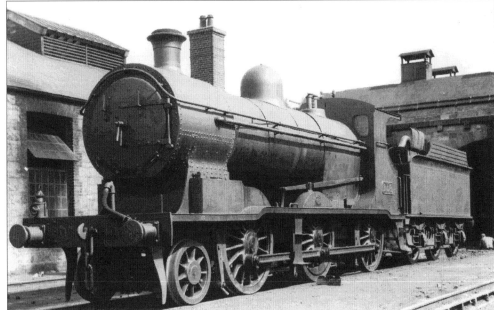

Middle: North British Locomotive Co Builders No 15946 of 1903: Type XXXVIII [38] Class 355 No 358 following its rebuild as a 2-6-0 in 1907, at Inchicore running shed.

Bottom: North British Locomotive Co builders No 16023 of 1903: The four members of 0-6-2T Type LXII [62] Class 211, of which No 213 was the third, were obtained for short-distance freight work in the Dublin area. For reasons that remain unexplained, these locomotives were overweight for their intended duties and two (Nos 211/2) were rebuilt as 0-6-0s, at Inchicore.

Rothwell & Co, Bolton

Established in 1822 as Rothwell, Hick & Rothwell, general engineers, this firm moved into locomotive construction following the Rainhill Trials. The business was re-formed in 1832 as Rothwell & Co. Despite earning a good reputation, a downturn in trade and growing competition led to closure in 1864.

GSWR	Built	Builder's No.	W.A.
53 to 56	1850	131 to 134	0-4-2

As with the Bury archives, those for Rothwell are reported to have passed to the Field Museum, Chicago but their present whereabouts are unknown

Sharp, Stewart & Co, Glasgow (previously Sharp Roberts & Co, then Sharp Bros. of Manchester)

Robert Sharp built 2-2-0 *Experiment* for the Liverpool & Manchester Railway plus three similar locomotives (including *Hibernia*) for the Dublin & Kingstown Railway in 1834. Re-established at Manchester as Sharp Brothers & Co in 1843 at Atlas Works, CP Stewart joined the firm as senior partner in 1852 when the business was renamed Sharp, Stewart & Company. The business moved to Glasgow in 1888, taking over the premises of the Clyde Locomotive Company at Springburn which were renamed Atlas Works.

Railway	No	GSWR No	Builder's No	Built	W.A.
WD #	Later LER§/ WLR No 3		279	1845	0-4-2
GSWR		1 to 10	330-3/ 339/ 40/ 57/ 58, 61/ 62	1846	2-2-2
		11/ 12	393/ 395	1847	2-2-2
		13/ 14	459/ 460	1847	2-2-2
		15/ 16	465/ 466	1847	2-2-2
		17 to 20	490 to 493	1848	2-2-2
		163 to 166	2155-8	1872	0-6-0
		175/ 176	2310/1	1873	0-6-0
		185/ 186	2837/ 2838	1879	0-6-0
WLR	13 to 15	-	736/ 737/ 740	1853	0-4-2
	16	-	764	1854	0-4-2
	4	[223]	1345	1862	0-4-2
	5	-	1346	1862	0-4-2
	6	-	1529	1864	0-4-2
	29	228	1653	1865	0-4-0ST
WDLR	1 to 4	211 to 214	2818 to 2821	1878	0-4-2
	6	216	3665	1891	0-4-2
	7	217	3813	1892	0-4-2
WCIR	1	[250]	3233	1884	0-4-2

WD # William Dargan, contractor
LER § Limerick & Ennis Railway

The archives for Sharp Stewart (including order books and GA drawings for WLR, WDLR and WCIR locomotives are held by the National Railway Museum, York together with files for the North British Locomotive Co.

Robert Stephenson & Co, Newcastle-upon-Tyne

Dating from 1832, this was the first company established specifically for locomotive construction. It merged with Hawthorn Leslie in 1937 and steam construction continued at the original factory until 1959. The works, by then part of the English Electric Group, closed in 1960.

Railway	No	GSWR No	Built	Builder's No	W.A.
WLR	1	221	1879	2379	0-6-0

This engine appears in Stephenson's engine record book and list of engines completed, but no GA drawing or works photos have been located.

Locomotive works and commercial manufacturers

Sharp Stewart builder's No 3233, Type IX [9]-WKR was supplied to the WCIR as their No 1 and is seen here at Waterford. It was withdrawn in 1905 without actually carrying its allocated GSWR number (250).

Vulcan Foundry (formerly Charles Tayleur & Co), Newton-le-Willows

Established in 1832 as Charles Tayleur & Co, general manufacturing engineers, this company moved into locomotive production following the opening of the Liverpool & Manchester Railway. The name was changed to Vulcan Foundry Co in 1847. It was taken over by English Electric in 1957 and locomotive production continued until 1970 although the Vulcan name was dropped in 1962. The Newton-le-Willows works completely closed in 2002.

Supplied by Charles Tayleur:

Railway	Nos	GSWR Nos	Built	Builder's Nos	W.A.
WKR	1 to 3	-	1846	241 to 243	2-2-2-2T

Supplied by Vulcan Foundry:

Railway	Nos	GSWR Nos	Built	Builder's Nos	W.A.
WKR	8	[255]	1867	591	2-4-0
	9	[256]	1868	592	2-4-0
WCIR	4	252	1897	1558	0-4-2
WLR	25/ 30 to 32	[277], 281-3	1874	706 to 709	2-4-0
	8	[261]	1881	910	2-4-0
	35 to 37	285 to 287	1881	911 to 913	2-4-0
	38/ 39	288/ 289	1882	990/ 991	2-4-0
	40/ 41	230/ 231	1883	1010/ 1011	0-6-0
	12	265	1886	1162	4-4-0
	13/ 14	266/ 267	1891	1315/ 1316	2-4-2T

The Merseyside Maritime Museum holds the archives but there are gaps (e.g. the 2-4-0s of 1874-82 for the WLR). The "Abstract Book" for Charles Tayleur for this period is available in the Merseyside Maritime Museum, but does not mention the WKR 2-2-2-2Ts.

Vulcan Foundry Builders No 591, built 1867: Type VI [6]-WKR No 8 was one of a pair of 2-4-0s built with domeless boilers, to which a brass dome was later fitted. The 6-wheel tenders had the relatively uncommon feature of inside bearings.

Type XIX [19]-W 2-4-0 Vulcan Foundry Makers' No 990 as WLR No 38 *Hyacinth* at Limerick. *Locomotive Publishing Co*

EB Wilson and Company, Leeds

This company's origins lay in the Railway Foundry established 1838 in the Hunslet area. The business underwent changes of name and control before assuming this title in 1847. The firm established a reputation for quality, building around 600 locomotives, and was especially famed for the 2-2-2 "Jenny Lind" type. The business closed in 1858 and was re-formed two years later as the Railway Foundry by WS Hudswell and J Clarke.

As with the Bury archives, those for EB Wilson are reported to have passed to the Field Museum, Chicago but their present whereabouts are unknown. Some records may have passed to Manning Wardle, but with periodic culls, few, if any, of these survive.

Railway	No	Built	Builder's No	W.A.
WKR	2	1857	578	0-4-2

Chapter 4
Passenger tender engines
RNC Types I [1] to XX11 [22]

Introduction

Initial expectations were that the GSWR would be predominantly engaged in passenger traffic, as reflected in concentration on the 2-2-2 wheel arrangement. Two leading commercial manufacturers accounted for the passenger fleet during and after the company's opening phase. Twenty locomotives were supplied by Sharp Stewart 1846-8, numbered 1-20 and designated Type I [1] by RN Clements. Between 1845 and 1848, twenty were also provided by Bury, Curtis & Kennedy numbered 21-40; these were Type II [2] although this designation embraced three sub-groups with significant dimensional differences.

Expansion of the 2-2-2 fleet continued in more modest fashion with introduction of No 59 (1864 No 43) in 1853 (RNC Type IV [4]). The first passenger engine built at Inchicore, it was withdrawn in December 1873. Three more (RNC Type 5 [V]) appeared in 1858 as Nos 77-9 (1864 Nos 45-7) and were withdrawn between 1876 and 1878. The final batch of Inchicore-built 2-2-2s comprised nine locomotives delivered in 1859-63. Designated Type VI [6], they were numbered 76, 80, 81, 88-90, 94-96, (1864 Nos 44, 48-55 respectively) and were withdrawn between 1878 and 1882.

The only other passenger locomotives supplied by commercial manufacturers during the 19th Century were a pair of 2-4-0s built by Fairbairn in 1855 as Type III [3] Nos 70 & 71 (1864 No 41 & 42); their working careers exceeded 30 years. No more of this wheel arrangement were added until 1868 when six were built (1864 Nos 56-61) as Type VII [7]. They utilised serviceable components recovered from redundant engines. The recycling policy was also evident in:- Type VIII [8] – fourteen locomotives Nos 1, 3, 4, 9, 11, 12, 14, 16-20, 41, 42 (first introduced 1869 and extinct 1909) and Type IX [9] – two locomotives Nos 62 & 63 (1870 to 1890).

Officially Classed 21, Type X [10] was the first batch of passenger 2-4-0s to be newly built as opposed to re-incarnations of earlier locomotives. Ten appeared between 1873 and 1876, numbered 21-6 and 66-9. Two were withdrawn in 1911/ 2 and the remainder between 1924 and 1928. A pair of 2-4-0s were built in 1875, Nos 64 & 65 (Type XI [11]) which were similar to Type VII [7] and may have been the product of another recycling exercise. They both survived until 1894.

The third wheel arrangement used in passenger locomotives was the 4-4-0, introduced with Class 2 (Type XII [12]) in 1877. By 1880, twelve were in service and withdrawal took place between 1935 and 1953. Enlargements of this form followed with: Class 52 (Type XIII [13]) – twenty locomotives Nos 1, 3, 4, 9, 11, 12, 14, 16, 18, 20, 52-9, 97, 98 built 1883-1890 and withdrawn 1930-1959; and Class 60 (Type XIV [14] – fifteen locomotives Nos 60-65, 85-9, 93-6 built 1885-1891 and withdrawn 1955-60.

Between 1900 and 1913, six classes of 4-4-0s appeared that were recognisably of the modern era in contrast to what had gone before. The first was Class 301 (Type XV [15]) comprising four locomotives Nos 301-4 built 1900 and withdrawn between 1957 and 1960. There followed in 1902 the four-strong Class 305 Type XVI [16] numbered 305-8 which were withdrawn between 1931 and 1959. The following year saw a major break with long-standing tradition when Neilson Reid built Class 309 (Type XVII [17]). Numbered 309-14, these engines were withdrawn in the period 1957-9.

Inchicore built Class 321 (Type XVIII [18]) between 1904 and 1906. The history of these 12 locomotives numbered 321-332 was complex; withdrawal occurred between 1927 and 1960. Class 333 (Type XIX [19]) was built 1907-8 and these eight engines were a variant on the established theme using smaller driving wheels. They lasted until 1955-9. The final GSWR 4-4-0 was the solitary member of Class 341 (Type XX [20]) built in 1913 and withdrawn in 1928.

The company's final passenger locomotives were 4-6-0s. Class 400 (Type XXI [21]) comprised 10 locomotives of which four were built at Inchicore (Nos 400-2, 406) between 1916 and 1921, and six by Armstrong Whitworth (Nos 403-5 and Nos 407-9) in 1922/ 3. Another class with a complex history, withdrawals commenced in 1929 and were completed in 1961. Finally, the company built one member of mixed traffic Class 500 (Type XXII [22]) in 1924, withdrawn 1955. Two more of this class were built by the GSWR's successor.

--- o O o ---

RNC Type: I [1]   **2-2-2/ 2-4-0**   **GSWR Class: n/a**

Nos ±	Built	Maker's Number	Withdrawn	Comments
1	Feb 1846	330	1865	Rebuilt Sep 1866 as 2-4-0; withdrawn 1871; later Type VIII No 1
2	Feb 1846	331	Dec 1873	Last ran Sep 1873; sold to McGowan (scrap dealer) Jan 1874
3	Feb 1846	332	1865	Last ran 1865; scrapped 1868 or 9; parts used in Type VIII No 3
4	Feb 1846	333	1865	Rebuilt 1867 as 2-4-0; withdrawn 1871 or 2; parts used in Type VIII No 4
5	Apr 1846	339	Jun 1875	Last ran Jun 1874; sold less tender to Garvan (flour miller) Jul 1876 for £140
6	Apr 1846	340	Dec 1872	Last ran Sep 1872 sold to McGowan Jan 1874
7	Apr 1846	357	Dec 1874	Last ran Jun 1874; broken up Jun 1875; boiler to steam hammer
8	Jul 1846	358	Jan 1874	Last ran Jan 1874; sold to McGowan Jan 1874
9	Aug 1846	361	1865	Rebuilt Oct 1866 as 2-4-0; withdrawn 1870/ 1; later parts to Type VIII No 9
10	Aug 1846	362	Dec 1874	Last ran Jun 1874; sold Jan 1877 to Bagnall,
11	Feb 1847	393	1865	Rebuilt 1865 as 2-4-0; withdrawn 1871/ 2; later Type VIII No 11
12	Feb 1847	395	1865	No recorded details
13	Nov 1847	459	Dec 1874	Last ran Jun 1874; sold to Stanford (railway contractor) Dec 1876 for £200; used on Waterford, Dungavan & Lismore Railway construction contract
14	Nov 1847	460	1865	Rebuilt Jan 1868 as 2-4-0; withdrawn 1871 or 2; parts to Type VIII No 14
15	Dec 1847	465	Dec 1877	Standing condemned but complete at Tralee Dec 1877; sold Mar 1879 to McGowan for £120
16	Dec 1847	466	1865	Rebuilt Apr 1866 as 2-4-0; withdrawn Mar 1872; parts to Type VIII No 16
17	Jan 1848	490	Dec 1868	Sold to McGowan Aug 1873
18	Jan 1848	491	1865	Rebuilt 1868 as 2-4-0; withdrawn 1871, parts to Type VIII No 18
19	Mar 1848	492	1870	Dates conflict – sold Mar 1877 to Fitzsimons (timber merchant) but reported on duplicate list and still running in 1879 as spare engine at Thurles
20	Mar 1848	493	1868	Donated cylinders to No 1 in 1869; sold to McGowan Aug 1873

Boiler Pressure—80 lb/ sq in   *Heating surfaces*   *Tractive effort - 4,540 lb*
Cylinders – 15" x 20"   *tubes – 798 sq ft*   *Coal capacity – not recorded*
Leading wheels – 3' 3" §   *firebox – 72.8 sq ft*   *Water capacity – 1000 gal*
Driving wheels – 5' 6"   *grate – 12 sq ft*   *Locomotive weight – not recorded*
Trailing wheels – 3' 6" §

± Original identities were retained following the October 1864 re-numbering scheme

Builder: Sharp Bros & Co

§ Sources differ concerning the leading and trailing wheel diameters; suggested alternatives were 3' 3", 3' 6" or 3' 8". Allowing for the different tyre thicknesses, the image indicates the same diameter on both axles. The drawing erroneously states leading diameter at 5' 3" (should read 3' 3").
Board minute dated 12th February 1845 confirmed an order for twenty locomotives (at £1,535 each) and twenty 1000-gal tenders (at £405 each) from Sharp Stewart with the first four to be delivered by February 1846. By March 1846, four were at Inchicore plus two in course of delivery and six more expected by mid-May.

This was a standard manufacturer's design although correspondence dated 21 April 1845 indicated an intention for Nos 11-20 to be built to GSWR specifications, a plan later rescinded. Recorded career mileages were impressive by contemporary standards: No 2 (436,000 miles); No 5 (460,000); No 6 (480,000); No 7 (508,000); No 8 (429,000); No 10 (480,000); No 13 (441,000); No 15 (454,000); No 19 (450,000). As single drivers, they underwent few

Passenger tender engines

Type I [1] No 19
Locomotive Publishing Co

2-2-2 Type I[1] as built.

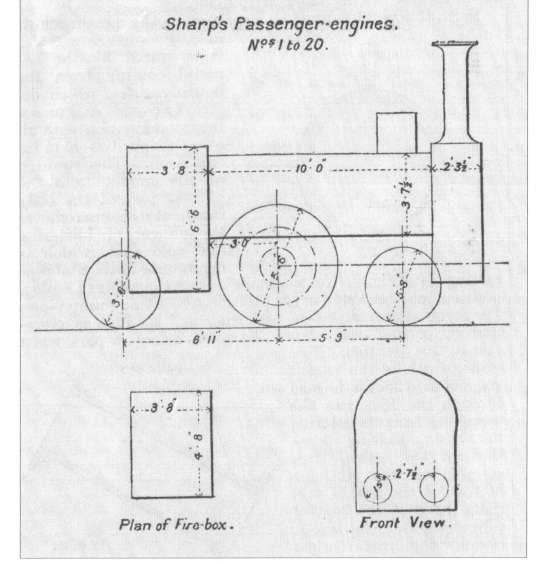

modifications beyond fitting of replacement copper fireboxes to Nos 2 (1864); 5 (1859); 6 (1863); 7 (1858); 8 (1864); 13 (1866); 15 (1863); 19 (1855). No 19 was reported to be fitted with 16" x 20" cylinders while on the duplicate list.

All twenty were still in service at the date of McDonnell's appointment. They played a key role in his early passenger motive power policy, pending introduction of more modern locomotives. Nos 2, 5, 6, 8, 10, 13, 15, 17, 19, 20 were retained in service as 2-2-2s until withdrawal when they sold to third parties for scrap metal. Disposal details are well documented except regarding No 12 and it is speculated that following withdrawal in 1865, it was used to provide spare parts. It is definite that Nos 3 & 7 were broken up at Inchicore to provide components for re-use as detailed in the individual comments above.

On withdrawal, Nos 1, 4, 9, 11, 14, 16, 18 were rebuilt as 2-4-0s with new frames and wheels supplied by Sharp, Stewart. RNC referred to these seven as "hybrids" implying retention of serviceable materials (particularly boilers, cylinders and tenders). Working careers in this condition were relatively short as they were withdrawn and rebuilt a second time in 1871/ 2, still as 2-4-0s. Leading dimensions of the hybrids are unclear but they may have been as for the second rebuilding whereby Type VIII was created. Type I as singles had used 5' 6" diameter driving wheels whereas the coupled wheels for Type VIII were 5' 7½" which suggests no change in design except for thicker tyres. Details covering the second rebuilding as 2-4-0s appear under Type VIII.

The preponderance of 2-2-2s was a distinctive feature of the early GSWR passenger fleet. Inclusion of components in the group of hybrid 2-4-0s seems to have been an interim measure to cope with increased traffic demands and heavier loads.

RNC Type: II [2] 2-2-2/ 2-4-0 GSWR Class: n/a

Built by: Bury, Curtis and Kennedy

Nos ±	Delivered	Withdrawn	Comments
21	Aug 1845	Jun 1873	Shipped new to Drogheda for trials on DDR; rebuilt 1865 with new boiler, tube plates & cylinders; worked at GSWR foundry until 1875
22	Aug 1845	Jun 1873	Shipped new to Drogheda for trials on DDR; rebuilt 1865 with new boiler, tube plates & cylinders; last ran Jun 1872; worked at peat works 1874-5
23	Jul 1846	Jun 1872	Ran until May 1873; boiler sold to Courtney Stephens (engineers) Blackhall Place Jul 1873.
24	Jul 1846	Dec 1872	Sold for £350 to Cork & Bandon Railway as their No 8 Oct 1872; ran 703 miles with C&BR, then broke a valve spindle 13 Nov 1873 & burst a steam pipe 4 days later despite boiler pressure of 70 lb/ sq in; described as "pretty nearly worn out"; withdrawn by C&BR in Nov 1874 and sold by Feb 1875.
25	Aug 1846	Dec 1872	Sold to McGowan Aug 1873.
26	Aug 1846	Dec 1872	Hired to Athenry & Ennis Junction Railway (Feb 1872 until at least Apr 1872); sold to McGowan in Aug 1873.
27	Oct 1846	Apr 1870	Rebuilt Jan 1867 as hybrid with new boiler and coupled wheels to become 2-4-0; last ran in this state Apr 1870; rebuilt again that month and renumbered 62 to become Type IX [9]).
28	Oct 1846	Dec 1873	Reported alternative withdrawal dates of 1870/ 1 were possibly clerical error by Inchicore; last ran Jun 1876; sold to McGowan Aug 1876 for £172; might have run as duplicate No 28A.
29	Oct 1846	Dec 1872	Last ran Jan 1871; sold to Michael Meade & Son (builders & timber merchants) April 1871.
30	Apr 1847	Oct 1870	Rebuilt Mar 1867 with new boiler; last ran Oct 1870; rebuilt again and numbered "Y" in April 1871 to become Type IX [9] No 63.
31	May 1847	Jun 1870	Reported withdrawal date 1867 is an error; in service until Jun 1870; these dates cannot be reconciled as apparently parts from this engine were used in McDonnell's first passenger locomotive which became No 56 built Nov 1868 - see Type VII [7].
32	May 1847	Dec 1876	Last ran Oct 1873; at sawmill 1874/ 5; sold to McGowan Jun 1881; however records also state that parts from No 32 were used in rebuild process that created Type VII [7] No 56; these reports and dates conflict; it is speculated that parts from other Bury 2-2-2s were used for No 58 – see Type VII [7].
33	Jun 1847	1865	Might have worked until Dec 1869 but records conflict as parts from the engine were reportedly used in rebuild that created Type VII [7] No 59.
34	Jun 1847	Dec 1867	Despite reported withdrawal date, apparently in service until May 1870; however, as with Type II No 31 there are discrepancies in official dates; parts from this engine were used in rebuild that result in Type VII [7] No 57.

Passenger tender engines

35	Jun 1847	Dec 1869	Last ran Feb 1868; broken up Aug 1868 despite withdrawal date.
36	Jul 1847	Dec 1875	RNC note suggests withdrawn 1872; preserved; see further details below.
37	Jan 1848	Dec 1873	Rebuilt 1852/ 3 as 2-4-0; last ran Jun 1873; boiler sold to Courtney Stephens July 1873.
38	Jan 1848	Jun 1871	Rebuilt 1852/ 3 as 2-4-0; last ran July 1871; sold to CBR May 1871 as their No 8 for £300; renumbered as CBR No 2 about Jun 1872; replaced Jul 1875 but worked as shunter until Mar 1877; broken up Apr 1877.
39	Jan 1848	Dec 1868	Rebuilt 1852 as 2-4-0; last ran 21 Jul 1868 following a fatal accident near Patrickswell; weld of an inadequately strengthened coupling rod broke, killing driver and fireman; withdrawn & scrapped Dec 1868; a report that engine was later used to drive steam hammer is clearly incorrect as accident resulted in pierced boiler & firebox, and badly damaged motion; steam hammer report might relate to No 35.
40	Feb 1848	1875	Rebuilt 1852/ 3 as 2-4-0; note of withdrawal Dec 1868 possible erroneous duplication of record for No 39; last ran 1875; sold to McGowan Mar 1875.

± Original identities were retained following the October 1864 re-numbering scheme.

In April 1850, No 2 was loaned to the Cork & Bandon Railway and a second locomotive (number unknown) was shortly afterwards. Both were returned in July 1850 after the CBR had acquired its own motive power.

Records suggest that the acquisition process for these locomotives commenced in advance of the Sharp Stewart 2-2-2s (Type I [1]). Orders were placed for one passenger and one goods engine on 18 October 1844, increased to two of each seven days later. In March 1845, a total of 19 engines were on order from Bury, the first two to be ready by the following June for testing on the Dublin & Drogheda Railway (DDR). Between July and September 1845, four locomotives were delivered to the DDR where they were tested for about one month. Bury's invoice for these four was £7,170 which appears to have been nominally cheaper than Type I [1].

Subsequent correspondence dated 1845/ 6 shows the GSWR pressing Bury for delivery of the remainder. There was also discussion about reduction of wheel size (presumably driving wheels) plus increase of heating surfaces and power output. Around this time the GSWR claimed compensation for alleged poor workmanship. Settlement was through deduction by GSWR of £704 3s 11d in amount due to makers for a total of 30 engines. They seemed to have lacked the quality of the Sharp Stewart 2-2-2s, especially as the basic design was apparently modified twice before delivery was completed. Also, there seems to have been no attempt to extend their working careers in later years.

RNC's archives do not distinguish between dates of construction/ delivery to Ireland/ entry into service which begs the question – what happened to the first two between October 1845 and October 1847? They may have been on loan to the civil contractors building the GSWR which would have included the pair of 0-4-2s which were apparently contemporary.

There is a tradition that the first four Bury engines were built as four-wheelers (two passenger as described here would have been 0-2-2 or 2-2-0 and two goods engines of Type XXIII [23] would have been 0-4-0) and this is borne out by the passage of events in England. Edward Bury was a champion of small four-wheeled locomotives as being cheap and easy to construct, albeit deficient in power. As a major locomotive supplier to the London &

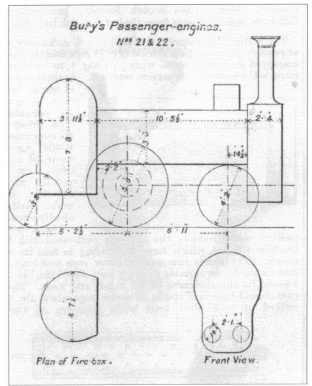

2-2-2 Type II [2] Nos 21 & 22. This drawing shows dome on the leading boiler ring which does not accord with other surviving illustrations.

Birmingham Railway (LBR), by 1844 he was under pressure to change his policy as traffic growth necessitated multiple use of locomotives, and as his designs were increasingly prone to axle breakages.

The following year he commenced construction of six-wheeled locomotives, following the industry trend.

As the LBR was an influential ally of the GSWR, it seems highly probable that the first four locomotives were ordered as four-wheelers in keeping with prevailing Bury policy but that during or following the period of testing on the DDR they were modified. As the goods locomotives are known later to have been 0-4-2s, they would have originally been 0-4-0s. It follows that the passenger locomotives were probably originally 2-2-0s.

This would explain the interval between delivery to Ireland and entry into service of Nos 21 & 22. The need for design modifications might also explain the interval before arrival of more Bury engines. While details of early modifications to Nos 21 & 22 are uncertain, confirmed dimensional variations place the 20 Bury passenger locomotives in three categories:

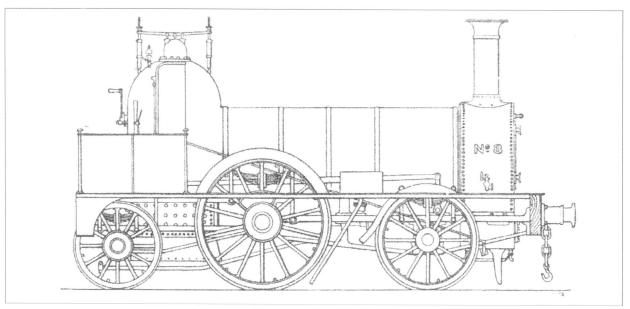

2-2-2 Type II [2] No 24 following sale to Cork & Bandon Railway.

Ex-GSWR Type II [2] No 38 following rebuild as a 2-4-0 in 1852/3 and sale in May 1871 to the Cork & Bandon Railway as their No 8, later No 2. As built, the last four Bury singles differed from the rest in their D-shaped low crown fireboxes.

Sub-type IIA [2A]:

Nos 21 & 22
Boiler pressure – 80 lb/ sq in
Cylinders – 14" x 20"
Leading wheels – 4' 2"
Driving wheels – 5' 8"
Trailing wheels – 3' 8"
Wheelbase – 6' 11" + 6' 2½"

Heating surfaces:
tubes – 709 sq ft
firebox – not recorded
grate – not recorded

Tractive effort – 3,920 lb
Coal capacity – not recorded
Water capacity – 1344 gal
Locomotive weight – c. 19 tons 10 cwt

In November 1845, Bury proposed to increase the power of the 26 locomotives then on order but not yet delivered. The cost was agreed at £170 per locomotive plus £30 for "patent life guards". These comprised eighteen of this Type (plus tender goods locomotives: Type XXIII [23] – two engines and Type XXIV [24] – six engines). This was accepted by the GSWR, resulting in the following dimensional changes to the remaining 2-2-2s to be delivered:

Sub-type IIB [2B]:

Nos 23 to 36
Cylinders – 15" x 20"
Leading wheels – 4' 8"
Driving wheels – 6' 0"
Trailing wheels – 3' 10"
Wheelbase – 7' 9" + 6' 10"

Heating surfaces:
tubes – 1000 sq ft
firebox – 60 sq ft
grate – 12.75 sq ft

Tractive effort – 4,250 lb
Locomotive weight – 22 tons 19 cwt

These dimensions were retained for the final four except that, at maker's suggestion, the leading and driving wheel diameters were reduced. Also it appears that they differed from the earlier engines in being fitted with a D-shaped firebox with low crown.

Sub-type IIC [2C]:

Nos 37 to 40
Leading wheels – 4' 2"
Driving wheels – 5' 8"
These four engines were rebuilt in 1852/ 3 as 2-4-0s. Key dimensions were unchanged except for:
Wheelbase – 7' 2½" + 7' 8"

Tractive effort – 4,500 lb

NB *Railway Magazine* Volume 5 1899 erroneously quotes dimensions for preserved No 36 which are actually those of Nos 21/ 2.

Nos 37 to 40 were delivered as 2-2-2s. However, the board approved their rebuild as 2-4-0s in November 1852 at a cost not exceeding £207 per locomotive. These conversions were undertaken by Miller at Inchicore in 1852/3. As a result of this work, the wheelbase became 7' 2½" + 7' 8"

Around 1864/ 5, an official chart was produced showing diagrams of the locomotive types then in service. However, diagrams for Nos 23 to 36 and 37 to 40 were inexplicably omitted (as was also that Type XXIII [23] – Goods engines Nos 102/ 3). The omission has led to statements that the dimensions for Nos 21/ 2 applied to all 20 Bury 2-2-2s, most prominently in *The Engineer* for January 1896, and in other reference sources. This error also resulted in failures to record the conversion of Nos 37-40 to 2-4-0s.

Subsequent recorded details are sparse but the following is known:

[1] No 22 received a new boiler in 1865; around six years later it was taken out of service.

[2] Three early withdrawals were Nos 27/ 30/ 33 in 1865 (although RNC's records elsewhere state between 1866 and 1870). Two 2-4-0s appeared from Inchicore bearing Nos 27 (January 1867) and 30 (March 1867). They retained cylinders, crank axle and motion from their single driver predecessors while the erstwhile trailing wheels were re-tyred and fitted as leading wheels.

[3] Nos 27 and 30 returned to Inchicore in 1870/ 1. Other than the 6' 1" diameter driving wheels, all the material that had been retained from their single driver days at the first rebuilding was replaced. New cylinders of 16' x 22" dimensions were fitted and the pair were renumbered 62/ 3 respectively. In this state they were categorised by RNC as Type IX [9].

2-2-2 Type II [2] No 36 as withdrawn and prior to restoration.

2-2-2 Type II [2] No 36 as restored for preservation.

Passenger tender engines

Preserved 2-2-2 No 36

Allowing for uncertainties surrounding disposal details of older GSWR locomotives, No 36 was the last Bury 2-2-2 in ordinary service with a recorded mileage of 487, 918 to June 1874. On withdrawal it was stored at Inchicore before display at the Cork Exhibition in 1902 followed by more storage in Cork shed. It later returned north for display at the Dublin Exhibition of 1907. Around this time it was subject to a partial restoration that included provision of splashers and other features that were perhaps not completely historically accurate. It then stood on a pedestal outside the Inchicore offices from about 1908 until 1919. During the Great War, the copper firebox was removed as this metal was then in short supply and needed for the war effort.

There followed unfulfilled plans for public display at Dublin Kingsbridge. No 36 lived in the Inchicore paint shop until its appearance at the Railway Centenary Exhibition at Darlington in 1925, and then at the Royal Dublin Society Bi-Centenary celebrations at Ballsbridge in 1930. It was then dumped at Inchicore throughout World War 2 before undergoing in 1950 what seems to have been its most comprehensive restoration since withdrawal. It was then mounted on a plinth at Cork Station where it has remained ever since.

This locomotive is historically significant as one of the few remaining GSWR mechanical artefacts, and also as one of only two surviving examples of the Bury type, the other being Furness Railway 0-4-0 No 3 of 1846 (nicknamed "Old Copperknob") which is in the care of the National Railway Museum, York.

The recovery of the copper firebox during the Great War might have been significant in that RNC could find no reference to replacements being fitted to the Bury 2-2-2s. Fireboxes on this manufacturer's products elsewhere enjoyed long working lives and RNC speculated that very heavy copper sheeting might have been used. Although the Sharp Stewart 2-2-2s were reputed to be of sounder construction, in the period 1866 to 1875 Bury fireboxes were recorded as incurring repair expenses equivalent to 0.003d per mile. The comparative figure for the Sharp Stewart 2-2-2s was 0.31d per mile.

RNC Type: III [3]		2-4-0			GSWR Class: n/a	
1864 No	Original No	Introduced	Withdrawn for rebuild	Re-entered service	Second rebuild	Withdrawn
41	70	Aug 1855	Aug 1870	1871	1882	Dec 1888
42	71	Aug 1855	Dec 1870	Sep 71	1880	Jun 1887 (last ran)

Built by: Fairbairn

Boiler pressure – 80 lb/ sq in [assumed] Cylinders – 15" x 21" Leading wheels – 3' 8" Driving wheels – 5' 6" Wheelbase – 6' 5½ " + 6' 7½"	Heating surfaces: – not recorded	Tractive effort – 4,870 lb

First rebuild: New boiler, cab and platforms; original frames, cylinders and motion were retained -

Boiler pressure – 80 lb/ sq in [assumed] Cylinders – 15" x 21" Leading wheels – 3' 8" Driving wheels – 5' 6" Wheelbase – 6' 5½ " + 6' 7½"	Heating surfaces: tubes – 910 sq ft firebox – 86.5 sq ft grate – 15 sq ft	Tractive effort – 4,870 lb

Second rebuild: No 41 in 1882; No 42 in 1880 – *Cylinders – 16" x 21"*

These engines were apparently later regarded as part of Type VIII [8] – refer to that section

They had been planned as the first of an order for ten from this manufacturer, an engine to be delivered every month from June 1854. Extended delivery delays ensued and the order was reduced to six in September 1854. Two were delivered in August 1855 and the GSWR declined to accept the remaining four. One was delivered to the Waterford & Limerick Railway in December 1855 as No 21 (Type IV[4]-W). Fairbairn attempted to offer a tank locomotive in lieu of one of the 2-4-0s in June 1854 but the GSWR declined. No information has been traced about the careers of Nos 41/ 2 except that their recorded career mileages were 663,343 and 535,210 respectively. See Diagram Page 82.

RNC Type: IV [4] 2-2-2 GSWR Class: n/a

1864 No	Original No	Introduced	Withdrawn	Comments
43	59	Jul 1853	Dec 1873	First passenger engine built at Inchicore

Designer: Miller/ Wakefield

Boiler pressure – 80 lb/ sq in Cylinders – 15" x 22" § Leading wheels – 4' 6" Driving wheels – 6' 0" Trailing wheels – 3' 6" Wheelbase – 7' 9½" + 7' 10½"	Heating surfaces: tubes – 179 tubes firebox – not recorded grate – not recorded	Tractive effort – 4,670 lb
§ Some sources quote 15" x 20". *(The firebox was raised and the dome on middle of boiler).*		

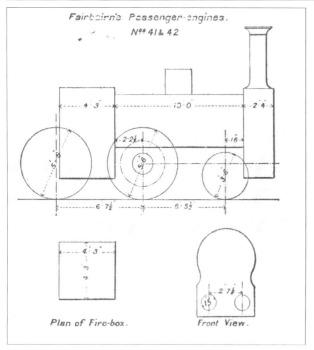

2-4-0 Type III [3] Nos 41 & 42 (previously Nos 70 & 71). See type history on Page 81.

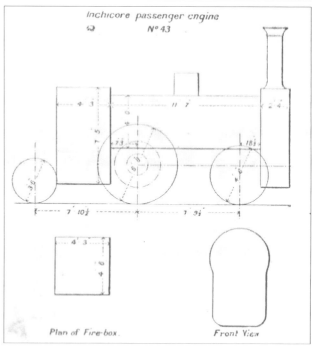

2-2-2 Type IV [4] No 43 (previously No 59).

Apparently, Miller was instructed to build a locomotive at a cost not exceeding £1900 which would have been a significant reduction on the unit prices charged for Types I [1] and II [2]. The actual cost was recorded as £1756 including £1147 for materials. The repair history suggests that this locomotive was not a success. It required a replacement crank axle in March 1859 after 116,786 miles, a further crank axle in January 1864 (131,010

miles), and a third in October 1864 (193,275 miles). It received a new set of motion in 1866.

This locomotive might have been rebuilt as an 0-4-2 with 15" x 20" cylinders at an unknown date. It is believed to have stopped normal service in 1873 but to have then been employed in driving a steam hammer from Oct 1874 before final withdrawal for scrapping sometime between 1878 and 1880.

RNC Type: V [5] 2-2-2 GSWR Class: n/a

1864 No	Original No	Introduced	Withdrawn	Comments
45	77	Mar 1858	Dec 1878	Sold to McGowan Dec 1878.
46	78	Apr 1858	Jun 1878	Leading wheels to No 80 in Dec 1878; remainder sold to McGowan.
47	79	Apr 1858	Jun 1876	Tubes to No 125 and leading wheels to No 78 in Sep 1876.

Designer: Miller/ Wakefield **Built at inchicore**

Boiler pressure – 80 lb/ sq in (assumed) *Heating surfaces:* *Tractive effort – 3,920 lb*
Cylinders – 15" x 20" *not recorded*
Leading wheels – 4' 6"
Driving wheels – 6' 6"
Trailing wheels – 3' 8"
Wheelbase – 6' 8" + 7' 0"

Ahrons records the cylinder dimensions as 15" x 22". Little information is available on this Type's history but recorded mileages to 30/6/1876 were:

No	Total	Average pa
45 (77)	427,060	23,726
46 (78)	438,614	24,367
47 (79)	407,861	22,639

If these figures are accurate, these locomotives achieved impressive usage and availability by contemporary standards. They were provided with cabs and were among the earliest to be so fitted anywhere. Their external styling was similar to that of McConnell's "Bloomers" on the London & North Western Railway.

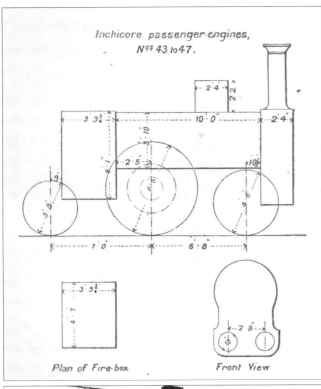

Left: 2-2-2 Type V [5] Nos 45 to 47. Note that reference to locomotives 43 & 44 on Diagram is an error.

Bottom: 2-2-2 Type V [4] Nos 45 to 47. No photograph has been traced but this Type is believed to have resembled the 2-2-2 small-boilered Bloomers with 6' 6" driving wheels built by the LNWR in 1861 as shown here.

Locomotives of the Great Southern & Western Railway

RNC Type: VI [6] 2-2-2 **GSWR Class: n/a**

1864 No	Original No	Introduced	Withdrawn	Comments
44	76	Dec 1859	Jun 1878	Sold to McGowan Dec 1878
48	80	Dec 1859	Jul 1881	Sold to McGowan Jun 1881
49	81	Dec 1859	May 1882	New motion set fitted in 1865 after 227,940 miles in replacement of the original Wakefield motion
50	88	Aug 1861	Dec 1878	Broken up Inchicore Dec 1881
51	89	Aug 1861	Jan 1882	Last ran Dec 1881; sold to McGowan Jun 1862
52	90	Oct 1861	Dec 1882	Last ran Jun 1880; boiler sold to T&C Martin in Aug 1882 for £150; assorted parts to McGowan Oct 1882
53	94	Oct 1862	Jun 1882	Last ran Dec 1881; sold to McGowan Jun 1882
54	95	Dec 1862	Dec 1878	Last ran and sold to McGowan Dec 1878
55	96	Jan 1863	Jan 1882	Last ran Dec 1881; sold to McGowan Jun 1882

Designer: Miller/ Wakefield **Built at Inchicore**

Boiler pressure – 80 lb/ sq in (assumed)
Cylinders – 15" x 22"
Leading wheels – 4' 6"
Driving wheels – 6' 6"
Trailing wheels – 3' 8"
Wheelbase – 7' 6" + 7' 4"

Heating surfaces:
tubes – 966 sq ft
firebox – 81 sq ft
grate – not recorded

Tractive effort – 4,310 lb
Locomotive weight – 25 tons 14 cwt
Max axle loading – 11 tons 8 cwt

No rebuilding details have been traced but it might be possible that these locomotives were converted to 0-4-2s. They were the last single driver locomotives built for the GSWR. Reported mileages to 30th June 1876:

No	Total	Average pa	No	Total	Average pa
44	455,744	27,621	52	438,228	30,016
48	444,735	26,954	53	425,104	31,258
49	454,583	27,550	54	447,611	33,156
50	440,812	29,785	55	442,023	34,265
51	428,002	28,919			

Above and opposite: 2-2-2 Type VI [6] Nos 44, 48 to 55. This locomotive is No 48. *Locomotive Publishing Co*

Passenger tender engines

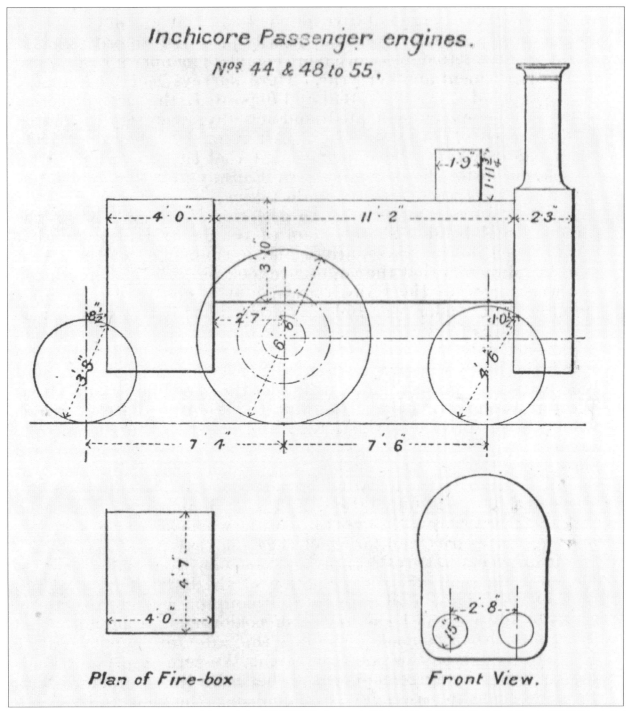

RNC Type: VII [7]		2-4-0		GSWR Class: n/a
1864 No	No of Type II [2] Parts donor	Interim No during conversion	Introduced	Withdrawn
56	31	-	Nov 1868	1887
57	34	-	Dec 1868	1887
58	32	-	Feb 1869	Jun 1887
59	33	-	Mar 1869	Jun 1887
60	-	"T"	Oct 1870	Feb 1891
61	-	"U"	Nov 1870	May 1891

Locomotives of the Great Southern & Western Railway

Designer: McDonnell **Built at Inchicore**

Boiler pressure – 120 lb/ sq in (assumed)
Cylinders – 16" x 22"
Leading wheels – 4' 0"
Driving wheels – 6' 6"
Wheelbase – 7' 0" + 7' 9"
Length over buffers – 24' 9"

Heating surfaces:
tubes – 898 sq ft
firebox – 95 sq ft
grate – 17.6 sq ft

Tractive effort – 7,360 lb
Coal capacity – 2 tons 5 cwt
Water capacity – not recorded
Locomotive weight – 32 tons 7 cwt
Adhesive weight – 22 tons 2 cwt
Max axle loading – 11 tons 1 cwt

All are believed to have been fitted with 17" x 22" cylinders between July 1877 and March 1883.

This was McDonnell's first passenger design. Nos 56-59 used parts recovered from withdrawn 2-2-2 Type II [2] Nos 31-34 as detailed above, and were considered to be rebuilds. The conversion process incorporated new components supplied by:- Beyer Peacock (wheels); Vickers (axles); Beyer Peacock and Sharp Stewart (frames); Beyer Peacock and Grendon (cylinders). Nos 31 and 34 were donors for parts used in the rebuilding of Nos 56 and 57. Nos 60 & 61 were completely new locomotives using parts obtained from these suppliers. Following withdrawal as 2-4-0s between 1887 and 1891, components from Nos 56 to 59 were used in construction of 4-4-0 Class 52 Type XIII [13] which carried the same running numbers.

Career mileages to 30/6/1876.

No	Total	Average pa	No	Total	Average pa
56	192,215	25,291	59	167,320	23,239
57	186,617	24,882	60	190,164	32,787
58	205,694	28,177	61	203,376	35,680

2-4-0 Type VII [7] Nos 56 to 61. *LGRP*

RNC Type: VIII [8] **2-4-0** **GSWR Class: n/a**

No	Introduced	Withdrawn	Comments
1	Feb 1871	Jun 1887	Ran Sep 1866 to 1871 as a "hybrid" (see Type I [1]), renewed as 2-4-0 retaining same number; last ran Dec 1886; broken up Jan 1887
3	May 1869	Oct 1887	Last ran Jun 1890, despite official withdrawal date. Regarded as new engine built at Inchicore; withdrawal date recorded as Oct 1887 but reprieved following fitting of cylinders recovered from withdrawn No 9 of same class; might have run as duplicate No 3A from 1888; finally withdrawn 1889; hired Sep 1890 to Murphy, contractor for construction of Fermoy-Mitchelstown branch

Passenger tender engines

No	Built	Withdrawn	Notes
4	Mar 1872	Apr 1888	Ran Oct 1867 to 1872 as a "hybrid" (see Type I [1]), renewed as 2-4-0 retaining same number; last ran Jun 1888
9	Oct 1874	May 1884	Ran Oct 1866-71 as a "hybrid" (see Type I [1]), renewed as 2-4-0 retaining same number; last ran Dec 1883; broken up 1886; cylinders transferred to No 3
11	Mar 1872	Jun 1888	Ran 1865-72 as a "hybrid" (see Type I [1]), renewed as 2-4-0 retaining same number; last ran Jun 1888
12	Jun 1869	Jan 1889	Regarded as new engine built at Inchicore; despite withdrawal date appears to have run until Jun 1889; broken up 1890
14	Nov 1872	Mar 1887	Ran Jan 1868 to Nov 1872 as a "hybrid" (see Type I [1]), renewed as 2-4-0 retaining same number; last ran Dec 1886; broken up Mar 1887
16	Jan 1873	Nov 1885	Ran Apr 1866 to Mar 1872 as a "hybrid" (see Type I [1]), renewed as 2-4-0 retaining same number; last ran Jun 1884
17	Jun 1872	1909	Regarded as new engine; rebuilt at Inchicore Dec 1892 which resulted in dimensions similar to Type X [10]; the similarity was such that it was effectively assimilated into that type
18	Dec 1871	Apr 1888	Ran Feb 1868 to 1871 as a "hybrid" (see Type I [1]), renewed as 2-4-0 retaining same number; last ran Jun 1888
19	Jul 1872	Jan 1891	Regarded as new engine built at Inchicore; accumulated mileage 467,513
20	Feb 1870	Oct 1888	Regarded as new engine built at Inchicore; carried No "L" during construction; running number applied later; last ran Dec 1888 despite officially broken up Oct 1888
41	Aug 1871	Dec 1888	Either a new build or a rebuild of Type III No 41 which had been withdrawn Aug 1870 – records are unclear; rebuilt again in 1882; last ran Dec 1888; broken up Apr 1889
42	Sep 1871	Jun 1887	Either a new build or a rebuild of Type III No 42 which had been withdrawn Dec 1870 – records are unclear; rebuilt again in 1880; last ran Jun 1887; broken up Dec 1888

Designer: McDonnell **Built at Inchicore**

Boiler pressure – 140 lb/ sq in
Cylinders – 15" x 20"
– [16" x 20" later]
Leading wheels – 3' 8"
Driving wheels – 5' 7½"
Wheelbase – 6' 0" + 7' 11"

Heating surfaces:
not recorded

Tractive effort – 7,930 lb [9,030 lb]
Locomotive weight – 29 tons 8 cwt
Adhesive weight – 19 tons 12 cwt
Max axle loading – 9 tons 16 cwt

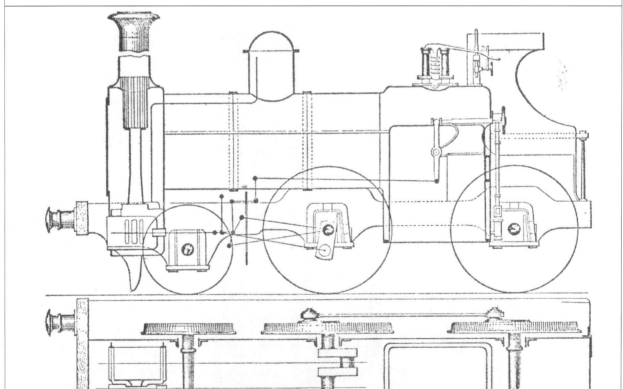

2-4-0 Type VIII [8] Nos 1, 3, 4, 9, 11, 12, 14, 16-20, 41, 42.

2-4-0 Type VIII [8] Nos 1, 3, 4, 9, 11, 12, 14, 16-20, 41, 42. This locomotive is No 20 c. 1886. *Locomotive Publishing Co*

The origins of this class are varied:
Nos 1, 9, 16 used existing frames from withdrawn 2-2-2's of Type I.
Nos 4, 11, 14, 18 used new frames supplied by Sharp Stewart at a price of £48 15s per pair.
Nos 3, 12, 17, 19, 20 were regarded as new engines.
Nos 41, 42 were replacements of Type III but as noted above their precise origins are uncertain.

Career mileages to 30th June 1876:

No	Total	Average pa	No	Total	Average pa
1	273,972	28,245	16	228,668	22,418
3	243,638	34,805	17	153,065	38,266
4	244,772	26,606	18	278,943	34,017
9	226,032	23,302	19	111,317	22,718
11	232,769	26,451	20	221,458	35,152
12	212,057	30,294	41	116,340	24,238
14	230,506	28,110	42	94,723	20,154

Late survivor No 17 was almost dimensionally identical with Type X [10]. Apparently, it was later regarded as part of the latter.

RNC Type: IX [9]		2-4-0		GSWR Class: n/a
1864 No	Original No	Introduced		Withdrawn
62	27	Apr 1870		Dec 1888
63	30	Apr 1871		Jun 1890
Designer: McDonnell				**Built at Inchicore**

Boiler pressure – 80 lb/ sq in (assumed)
Cylinders – 16" x 22"
Leading wheels – 4' 0"
Driving wheels – 6' 1"
Wheelbase – 8' 0" + 7' 11"

Heating surfaces:
tubes – 835 sq ft
firebox – 96 sq ft
grate – not recorded

Tractive effort – 9,180 lb

These engines were dimensionally similar to Type VII [7] except for the heating surfaces and the driving wheel diameter. By the time of their construction, McDonnell had adopted 5' 8" and 6' 7" as standardised diameters for passenger locomotives; the reason for the unique dimension of 6' 1" is not recorded.

There appears to be conflicting information concerning the early lives of this pair. One report states them to be very similar to Type VII [7] Nos 56-61 built 1868-1870. Another indicates that while No 62 was built as a 2-4-0, No 63 was actually a 2-2-2 until provision of new wheels and conversion to 2-4-0 in 1871. See Type II [2] for earlier history.

RNC Type: X [10]		2-4-0	GSWR Class 21
No	Introduced	Withdrawn	Comments
21	Jun 1873	1928	Rebuilt Dec 1890 & Feb 1906
22	Jul 1873	1928	Rebuilt Aug 1893 & Aug 1920
23	Oct 1873	1912	Rebuilt Feb 1894
24	Sep 1873	1924	Rebuilt Apr 1892; civil war loss
25	Oct 1873	1924	Rebuilt Feb 1892 & Oct 1917; civil war loss
26	Nov 1873	1928	Rebuilt Dec 1893
66	Mar 1876	1928	Rebuilt Jul 1895 & Mar 1921
67	Mar 1876	1928	Rebuilt Jun 1894 & Jan 1903
68	May 1876	1928	Rebuilt 1893 & May 1922
69	Jun 1876	1911	Rebuilt Nov 1896

(Refer also to No 17 of Type VIII [8] which following rebuilding in Dec 1892 was dimensionally similar; withdrawn 1909).

Designer: McDonnell **Built at Inchicore**

Boiler pressure – 140 lb/ sq in	Heating surfaces:	Tractive effort – 8,900 lb
Cylinders – 16" x 20"	tubes – 774 sq ft	Coal/ water capacities – refer Chapter 9
Leading wheels – 3' 8"	firebox – 83.8 sq ft	Locomotive weight – 30 tons
Driving wheels – 5' 8½"	grate – 16 sq ft	Adhesive weight – 20 tons
Wheelbase – 6' 0" + 7' 11"		Max axle loading – 10 tons
Locomotive length – 22' 11" (estimated)		

All class members were rebuilt with boilers dimensionally identical with the originals. Where a second rebuilding took place this involved installation of a two-ring boiler with similar heating surfaces. It appears that concurrent with the second rebuilding, boiler pressure was increased to 150 lb/ sq in which would have raised the tractive effort to 9,530 lb.

No 22 was the last locomotive to be converted from Smith Automatic brake to the GSWR two-pipe Automatic Vacuum system in 1893.

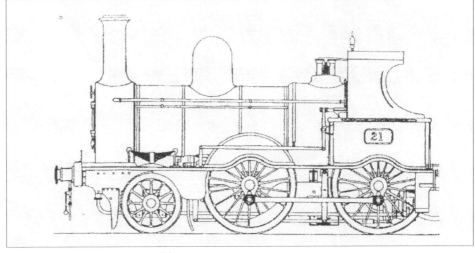

2-4-0 Type X [10] Class 21.

2-4-0 Type X [10] Class 21. *Photo courtesy Ken Nunn.*

RNC Type: XI [11] 2-4-0 **GSWR Class: n/a**

No	Introduced	Withdrawn	Comments
64	Jul 1875	1894	Broken up 1897
65	Aug 1875	1894	Broken up 1898

At official withdrawal, both were replaced in the capital list by 4-4-0 Class 60 Nos 64 & 65 of Type XIV [14]. However, according to Ahrons both 2-4-0s were retained as pilots at Limerick Junction, still carrying their running numbers, and were known as "old No 64" and "old No 65" until they were broken up.

Designer: McDonnell **Built at Inchicore**

Boiler pressure – 130 lb/ sq in
Cylinders – 17" x 22"
Leading wheels – 4' 0"
Driving wheels – 6' 6"
Wheelbase – 7' 0" + 7' 9"
Locomotive & tender length – 45' 10" (estimated)

Heating surfaces:
tubes – 96 sq ft
firebox – 835 sq ft
grate – 17.5 sq ft

Tractive effort – 10,330 lb
Coal/ water capacities – refer Chapter 9
Locomotive weight – 30 tons 6 cwt
Adhesive weight – 20 tons 6 cwt
Max axle loading – 10 tons 16 cwt

(Recorded dimensions: boiler 4' 0" x 9' 7"; firebox casing 5' 1" x 4' 6"; 185 brass tubes 1¾" diameter)

These locomotives were very similar to Type VII [7], also retaining the non-standard driving wheel diameter. One of this type is recorded as taking 14 coaches unassisted out of Kingsbridge in 1879.

Passenger tender engines

2-4-0 Type XI [11] Nos 64, 65. *Locomotive Publishing Co*

RNC Type: XII [12]   **4-4-0**   **GSWR Class 2**
"Kerry Bogie"

No	Introduced	Rebuilt §	Rebuilt §§	Withdrawn	No	Introduced	Rebuilt §	Rebuilt §§	Withdrawn
2	May 1877	Dec 1897		Mar-53	13	Oct 1880	1900		Jun 1953
5	Jun 1877	Aug 1894		1949	15	Oct 1880	Jul 1896		Sep 1951
6	Aug 1877	Aug 1897	May 1923	Jul-52	43	Jun 1878	Apr 1898	Jul 1922	1945
7	Sep 1877	1894		May-53	44	Jul 1878	Dec 1901	Jun 1917	Jul 1950
8	Jul 1880	May 1901		1945	45	Oct 1878	Jan 1901	Jun 1919	1945
10	Jul 1880	Sep 1900	Jul 1922	Feb-52	46	Nov 1878	Nov 1898	Apr 1905	1935

Designer: McDonnell   **Built at Inchicore**

Boiler pressure – 150 lb/ sq in
Cylinders – 16" x 20"
Bogie wheels – 3' 0"
Driving wheels – 5' 8½ "
Wheelbase – 5' 3" + 5' 6¾" + 7' 11"
Locomotive length – 25' 3"

Heating surfaces:
tubes – 770 sq ft
firebox – 83.8 sq ft
grate – 16 sq ft

Tractive effort – 9,530 lb
Coal/ water capacities – refer Chapter 9
Locomotive weight – 31 tons 8 cwt
Adhesive weight – 20 tons 12 cwt
Max axle loading – 10 tons 6 cwt

As rebuilt §: Rebuilt with replacement three-ring boiler, dimensions unchanged
        §§: Rebuilt with two-ring boiler in place of original three-ring type

	Heating surfaces: *tubes – 757 sq ft* *firebox – 83.8 sq ft*	*Locomotive weight – 31 tons 4 cwt* *Adhesive weight – 21 tons 7 cwt* *Max axle loading – 10 tons 15 cwt*

Class 21 (Type X [10]) had been built for the Kerry branches but its 2-4-0 wheel arrangement was found to be too rigid for those curvaceous lines. To circumvent these problems, Class 2 was introduced with swing-link bogies of American design. Apart from the wheel arrangement and a minor variance in heating surfaces, the two types were dimensionally identical. No 2 was the first 4-4-0 in Ireland and among the first of this wheel arrangement to run in these islands. The working career of this locomotive at 76 years underlines the success of the class.

Locomotives of the Great Southern & Western Railway

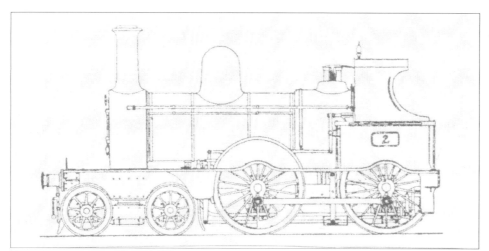

Left and below:
4-4-0 Type XII [12] Class 2
Photo courtesy Ken Nunn.

RNC Type: XIII [13]   **4-4-0**   **GSWR Class 52**

Running No [Interim No]		Introduced	Rebuilt	Withdrawn	Running No [Interim No]		Introduced	Rebuilt	Withdrawn
1	[O]	Mar 1890	Mar 1900	Jun 1955	52	[A]	Nov 1883	1923	1949
3	[P]	Mar 1890	Dec 1910	Nov 1957	53	[B]	Dec 1883	Sep 1900	1925
4	[K]	Apr 1888	Dec 1922	Mar 1957	54	[C]	Dec 1883	May 1903	Oct 1959
9	[E]	Dec 1886	Nov 1904	Oct 1955	55	[D]	Feb 1884	Feb 1899	Jun 1955
11	[L]	Apr 1888	Aug 1921	1949	56		Sep 1888	-	1951
12	[Q]	May 1890	Jun 1924	1949	57		Oct 1888	-	1957
14	[M]	May 1888	Jul 1913	Mar 1951	58		Oct 1888	Jul 1903	Sep 1953
16	[F]	Dec 1886	Jul 1905	Oct 1959	59		Oct 1888	Dec 1911	Apr 1955
18	[N]	Jun 1888	Jul 1918	Oct 1959	97	[G]	Feb 1887	Aug 1902	1930
20	[R]	Jun 1890	-	Aug 1959	98.	[H]	Feb 1887	Jun 1904	Dec 1954

Passenger tender engines

Designer: Aspinall   **Built at Inchicore**

Boiler pressure – 160 lb/ sq in
Cylinders – 17" x 22"
Chapter Bogie wheels – 3' 0"
Driving wheels – 6' 7"
Wheelbase – 5' 3" + 6' 5¼" + 7' 9"
Locomotive length – 27' 6½"

Heating surfaces:
tubes – 835 sq ft
firebox – 96 sq ft
grate – 17.5 sq ft

Tractive effort – 10,940 lbs
Coal/ water capacities – refer Chapter 9
Locomotive weight – 36 tons 8 cwt
Adhesive weight – 24 tons 10 cwt
Max axle loading – 12 tons 8 cwt

As rebuilt: Replacement of the original three-ring boiler with a two-ring version, retaining raised firebox.

Heating surfaces:
tubes – 754 sq ft
firebox – 97.1 sq ft

Locomotive weight – 36 tons 15 cwt
Adhesive weight – 24 tons 7 cwt
Max axle loading – 12 tons 7 cwt

This was the first passenger class to be built with 6' 7" diameter driving wheels, a dimension used with all subsequent express passenger locomotives built at Inchicore. Earlier express designs had been built with 6' 6" driving wheels (2-2-2 Type V [5] and 2-4-0 Type VII [7]). It was quite usual in the 19th Century for wheel diameters to increase through the fitting of thicker tyres. Nos 56-59 were regarded as renewal of Class 56 locomotives carrying the same numbers (Type VII [7]).

4-4-0 Type XIII [13]
Class 52 No 52.

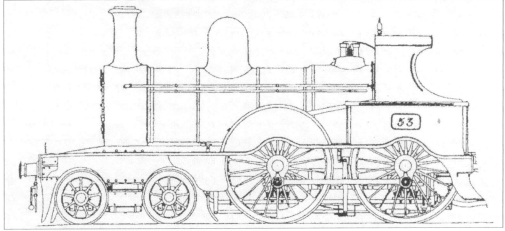

RNC Type: XIV [14]   **4-4-0**   **GSWR Class 60**

No	Built	Rebuilt	Withdrawn	No	Built	Rebuilt	Withdrawn
60	Oct 1891	Mar 1908	1957	87	1886	Dec 1898	Mar 1957
61	Nov 1891	-	Jun 1955	88	1886	Nov 1904	Mar 1957
62	Dec 1891	Jan 1903	Dec 1959	89	1886	-	Feb 1960
63	Dec 1891	Oct 1910	Jun 1955	93	Jun 1885	Aug 1894 §	Oct 1959
64	Oct 1895	Apr 1907	Aug 1959	94	Aug 1885	Feb 1903	Aug 1959
65	Oct 1895	1903	Aug 1959	95	Oct 1885	1898	Jun 1955
85	1886	Jan 1903	Aug 1959	96	Nov 1885	Jul 1905	Oct 1959
86	1886	May 1904	Aug 1957				

Designer: Aspinall   **Built at Inchicore**

Boiler pressure: Nos 85-96 140 lb/ sq in, later increased to 150 lb/ sq in; Nos 60 to 65 were built at higher pressure

Boiler pressure – 140 lb/ sq in
              – 150 lb/ sq in
Cylinders – 18" x 24"
Leading wheels – 3' 0"
Driving wheels – 6' 7"
Wheelbase – 5' 3" + 6' 11" + 8' 3"
Locomotive length – 28' 6"
	Heating surfaces:
	tubes – 938 sq ft
	firebox – 112.5 sq ft
	grate – 18.8 sq ft
		Tractive effort – 11,710 lb
		              – 12,550 lb
		Coal/ water capacities – refer Chapter 9
		Locomotive weight – 39 tons 10 cwt
		Adhesive weight – 25 tons 18 cwt
		Max axle loading – 12 tons 19 cwt

As rebuilt: *Fitted with two ring boiler and new driving wheels*

Boiler pressure – 160 lbs/ sq in	Heating surfaces tubes – 878.6 sq ft firebox – 112.5 sq ft grate area – 18.8 sq ft	Tractive effort – 13,390 lbs Locomotive weight – 39 tons 10 cwt Adhesive weight – 26 tons 11 cwt Max axle loading – 13 tons 9 cwt
The boiler pressure was later reduced to 150 lbs/ sq in		

§ As rebuilt: *Experimentally converted to 2-cylinder compound retaining three-ring boiler; reverted to simple expansion in 1901.*

Boiler pressure – 150 lbs/ sq in Cylinders – (1) 18" x 24" & (1) 26" x 24" Wheelbase – 5' 8" + 9' 6½" + 8' 3"	Heating surfaces: tubes – 824 sq ft firebox – 112.5 sq ft grate – 18.8 sq ft	Locomotive weight – 39 tons 9 cwt Adhesive weight – 25 tons 11 cwt Max axle loading – 13 tons 0 cwt

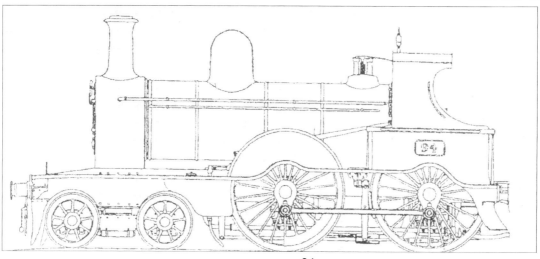

4-4-0 Type XIV [14] Class 60.

4-4-0 Type XIV [14] Class 60.

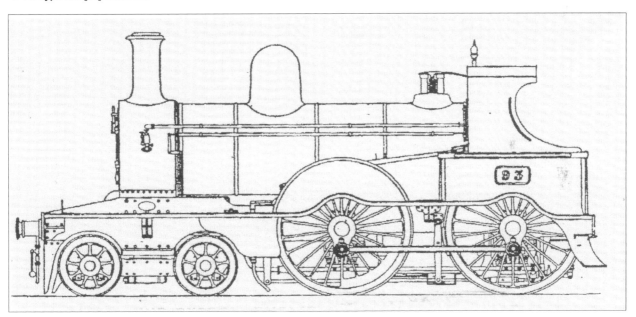

4-4-0 Type XIV [14] Class 60 as experimentally modified to work as a compound locomotive.

These locomotives were a further evolution and enlargement of the concept initiated with the Kerry Bogies. They were subject to additional experiments: No 89 was fitted (date unknown) with a side-window cab until 1925. No 62 was fitted with a steam drier from 1896 for about six months; this was removed because lubrication difficulties led to excessive valve wear. The unusual wheelbase with No 93 as rebuilt in 1895 was necessary to accommodate the differing cylinder dimensions. This locomotive reverted to simple form in 1901, retaining the modified wheelbase. The GSWR's experiments involving this locomotive and 0-6-0 Class 101 No 165 are described in Chapter 2 Design and construction, Period II (1864 to 1895).

No 87 was displayed at the Manchester Exhibition in 1897.

RNC Type: XV [15]   4-4-0   **GSWR Class 301**

No	Name	Introduced	Withdrawn	No	Name	Introduced	Withdrawn
301	*Victoria*	Apr 1900	1960 & 1962	303	*St. Patrick*	Jun 1900	Oct 1959
302	*Lord Roberts*	Apr 1900	Aug 1957	304	*Princess Ena*	Jun 1900	Nov 1959

Designer: Coey   **Built at Inchicore**

Boiler pressure – 160 lbs/ sq in	Heating surfaces: §	Tractive effort – 14,500 lbs
Cylinders – 18" x 26"	tubes – 1100 sq ft	Coal/ water capacities – refer Chapter 9
Bogie wheels – 3' 6"	firebox – 120 sq ft	Locomotive weight – 47 tons 0 cwt
Driving wheels – 6' 7"	grate – 20.4 sq ft	Adhesive weight – 30 tons 11 cwt
Wheelbase – 6' 4" + 6' 10" + 8' 6"		Max axle loading – 15 tons 19 cwt
Locomotive length – 29' 11"		
§ As built, subsequently modified to: tubes – 1011.75 sq ft, firebox – 116 sq ft at dates unknown		

This was the first GSWR express passenger class to reflect 20th Century practice. Designed to work Dublin-Cork express services, they were found to have poor steaming capacity and the modifications to heating surfaces detailed above might have been carried out early in an attempt at improvement. Apparently fitted from new with Drummond spark arresters, this equipment was removed about the same time. On opening of the new Cork-Rosslare route in 1906 they were transferred to that section where they also proved unsuccessful, particularly as their large driving wheels made them unsuitable for the hilly route. They remained in that area for around a year before transfer to secondary passenger duties on the Dublin-Cork line.

It seems that they were subject to several modifications, details and dates for which have not been recorded. There are unverified references to the fitting of Belpaire fireboxes and piston valves to Nos 301/ 2. The rationale for the former was an attempt to improve steaming; the purpose of the latter is unclear. It seems certain that they had reverted to original condition at least by 1924 and probably much earlier. Their names were removed at the time of their relegation from Dublin-Cork work in 1906, possibly in acknowledgment of their reduced status.

No 301 earned the sad distinction of being the last ex-GSWR 4-4-0 in service when after an extended period withdrawn and semi-derelict at Limerick, it was revived in late 1960 to work services affected by flooding in the Ballycar area. It then worked from Ennis and later in the Dublin area before serving as a stationary boiler at Inchicore until mid-1962.

4-4-0 Type XV [15] Class 301.

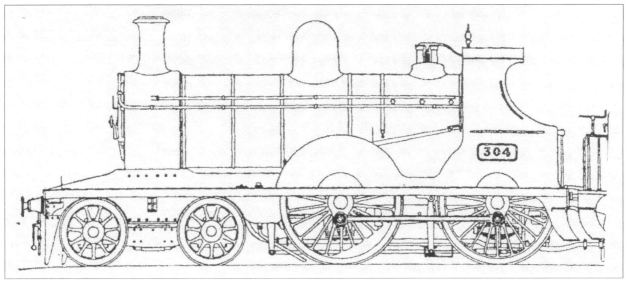

4-4-0 Type XV [15] Class 301.

RNC Type: XVI [16]				4-4-0			GSWR Class 305
No	Introduced	Rebuilt	Withdrawn	No	Introduced	Rebuilt	Withdrawn
305	Mar 1902	1906	Apr 1957	307	Jun 1902	1906	Oct 1959
306	Jun 1902	1906	Oct 1959	308	Jun 1902	1904	Aug 1931

Designer: Coey   **Built at Inchicore**

Boiler pressure – 160 lbs/ sq in Cylinders – 18" x 26" Bogie wheels – 3' 6" Driving wheels – 6' 7" Wheelbase – 6' 4" + 6' 10" +8' 6" Locomotive length – 29' 11"	Heating surfaces: tubes – 1148 sq ft firebox – 127 sq ft grate – 21 sq ft	Tractive effort – 14,500 lbs Coal/ water capacities – refer Chapter 9 Locomotive weight – 46 tons 18 cwt Adhesive weight – 30 tons 11 cwt Max axle loading – 14 tons 16 cwt

As rebuilt with tapered boiler (1904-6):

	Heating surfaces: tubes – 1284 sq ft firebox – 128 sq ft grate – 21 sq ft	Locomotive weight – 49 tons 15 cwt Adhesive weight – 31 tons 9 cwt Max axle loading – 15 tons 15 cwt
(The firebox outer casing was 6' 0" x 4' 6", internally 5' 5" by 10' 3". The boiler was 10' 3" long with a diameter of 5' ½" at the front, increasing to 5' 6½" at the firebox end).		

Originally dimensionally similar to Class 301, rebuilding which commenced when these engines were barely two years old marked a significant divergence from established Irish locomotive practice. The background lay in the 1902 announcement by GJ Churchward, Locomotive Superintendent of the GWR, of his intention to build express locomotives capable of exerting two tons drawbar pull at 70 mph. Although believed impossible by the engineering establishment, early GWR 2-cylinder 4-6-0s quickly proved the realism of these claims. Churchward had exposed the fallacy that efficient steam-raising was determined solely by size and heating area, and that boiler shape was also important. The hottest part of the boiler is at the throatplate, immediately adjacent to the firebox front and it thus made sense to maximise the volume of water at that point. Coey was clearly sufficiently influenced by the GWR's progress to try out the concept.

Performance records have not been traced for the GSWR's tapered boiler 4-4-0s but it may have been that operating conditions were not sufficiently demanding to justify retention of this feature when new boilers were fitted in the 1930s. A tapered boiler is more expensive to manufacture and the cost increases substantially when combined with a

Belpaire firebox which is similarly advantageous in maximising water volume where heat is more intense. Subsequent policy with the GSWR, and later GSR, favoured Belpaire fireboxes over tapered boilers.

This class served as guinea pig for other attempts at improved performance. No 306 was modified to run as an oil burner in July 1903 and apparently proved satisfactory in this condition. No information has been found about the type of system used, nor how long the equipment was in place. In 1904, Marshall valve gear was fitted to No 307. More of a cosmetic nature, at unknown dates Nos 305/ 6 were refashioned with running plates rising above the coupling rods, the former concurrently also receiving a canopy cab. No 308's early demise was due to cracked frames.

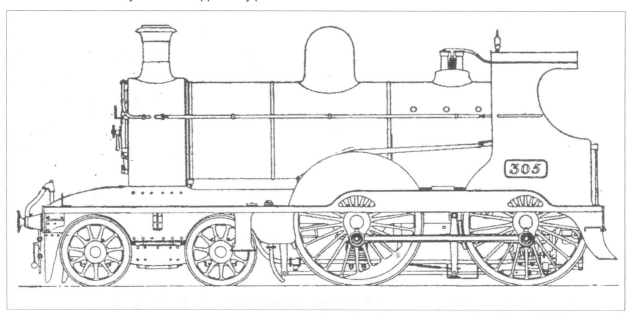

4-4-0 Type XVI [16] Class 305 with parallel boiler.

4-4-0 Type XVI [16] Class 305 with tapered boiler.

Passenger tender engines

4-4-0 Type XVI [16] Class 305 with tapered boiler.

RNC Type: XVII [17]   **4-4-0**   **GSWR Class 309/ 310**

No	Introduced	Makers No	Rebuilt §	Withdrawn	No	Introduced	Makers No	Rebuilt §	Withdrawn
309	Jun 1903	6313	Apr 1913	Oct 1959	312	Jun 1903	6316	Jun 1920	Oct 1959
310	Jun 1903	6314	-	Nov 1957	313	Jun 1903	6317	-	Dec 1957
311	Jun 1903	6315	-	Oct 1959	314	Jun 1903	6318	-	Dec 1957

Designer: Coey   **Built by Neilson, Reid & Co**

Boiler pressure – 160 lb/ sq in
Cylinders – 18½" x 26"
Bogie wheels – 3' 6"
Driving wheels – 6' 7"
Wheelbase – 6' 4" + 6' 10" + 9' 0"
Locomotive length – 30' 0"

Heating surfaces:
tubes –1110 sq ft
firebox – 135 sq ft
grate – 23 sq ft

Tractive effort – 15,320 lb
Coal/ water capacities – refer Chapter 9
Locomotive weight – 49 tons 10 cwt
Adhesive weight – 30 tons 18 cwt
Max axle loading –16 tons 0 cwt

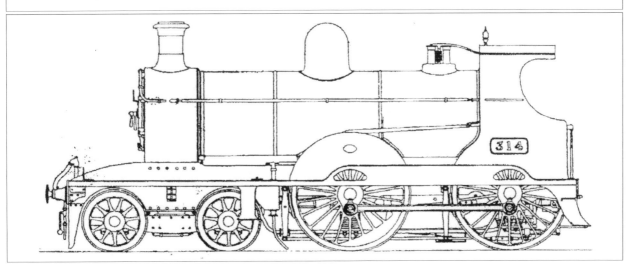

Type XVII [17] Class 309 as built with parallel boiler.

These locomotives were the first to be supplied by a commercial manufacturer in many years, necessitated by a protracted strike at Inchicore works, May-October 1902. Neilson Reid GA drawing states 124.5 firebox. Another source states that deliveries commenced from 28th March 1903.

§ As rebuilt with tapered saturated Class 321 type boiler

	Heating surfaces: tubes – 1283.9 sq ft firebox – 145 sq ft grate – 23 sq ft	Tractive effort – 15,320 lb Locomotive weight – 52 tons 1 cwt Adhesive weight – 33 tons 10 cwt Max axle loading – 16 tons 16 cwt

Consequent upon its rebuilding, No 309 was re-designated a member of Class 321, and the Class 309 identity was changed to 310. With the similar rebuilding of No 312 in 1920, this locomotive also became part of Class 321. A large canopy cab was also installed

RNC Type: XVIII [18]			4-4-0				GSWR Class 321
No	**Introduced**	**Rebuilt**	**Withdrawn**	**No**	**Introduced**	**Rebuilt**	**Withdrawn**
321	Dec 1904	Apr 1924 ±	1957	327	Jun 1905	Sep 1922 §	Oct 1959
322	Jan 1905	May 1924 ±	Feb-60	328	Jun 1905	May 1922 §	Aug 1959
323	Jan 1905	Jun 1924 ±	Jun-55	329	Nov 1906	Nov 1921 §	Feb 1960
324	Feb 1905	-	1928	330	Dec 1906	Sep 1919 §	Mar 1957
325	May 1905	-	1928	331	Oct 1906	Sep 1918 §	Aug 1959
326	Jun 1905	1912 / Dec 1915 §§	1927	332	Oct 1906	Jan 1919 §	Oct 1959

Designer: Coey   **Built at Inchicore**

As built with round-topped tapered boiler:

Boiler pressure – 160 lbs/ sq in Cylinders – 18½" x 26" Leading wheels – 3' 6" Driving wheels – 6' 7" Wheelbase – 6' 4" + 6' 10" + 9' 0" Locomotive length – 30' 4" (Nos 321 to 328 when built had heating surface: tubes 1366 sq ft)	Heating surfaces: tubes – 1283.9 sq ft firebox – 145 sq ft grate – 23 sq ft	Tractive effort – 15,320 lbs Coal/ water capacities – refer Chapter 9 Locomotive weight – 52 tons 1 cwt Adhesive weight – 33 tons 10 cwt Max axle loading – 16 tons 16 cwt

§§ Rebuilt with Schmidt superheater and extended smokebox:

Boiler pressure – 160 lbs/ sq in Cylinders – 20" x 26"	Heating surfaces: tubes – 1153 sq ft superheater - 345 sq ft firebox – 145 sq ft grate – 23 sq ft	Tractive effort – 17,900 lbs Locomotive weight – 53 tons 2 cwt Adhesive weight – 33 tons 14 cwt

Apart from Class 60 No 62 fitted with steam dryer, this was the GSWR's first superheater locomotive.
It reverted original condition in December 1915 but retained extended smokebox.

§ Rebuilt with deeper & thicker frames, extended smokebox, and Belpaire saturated boiler:

Boiler pressure – 170 lbs/ sq in	Heating surfaces: tubes – 1355 sq ft firebox – 148 sq ft grate – 23 sq ft	Tractive effort – 16,280 lbs Locomotive weight – 54 tons 10 cwt Adhesive weight – 35 tons 10 cwt Max axle loading – 16 tons 17 cwt

A saddle was installed to support the smokebox and the running pate was raised over the coupling rods

± Rebuilt with new frames and Belpaire saturated boiler:

Boiler pressure – 180 lbs/ sq in	Heating surfaces: tubes – 1355 sq ft firebox – 148 sq ft grate – 23 sq ft	Tractive effort – 17,230 lbs Locomotive weight – 54 tons 10 cwt Adhesive weight – 35 tons 10 cwt Max axle loading – 18 tons 0 cwt

A large canopy cab was also installed.

The GSWR rebuilding history of this class was dictated by the search for improved thermal efficiency, greater power output, redress of frame weaknesses, yet constrained by weight and axle loading limits imposed by the Civil Engineer. The maximum permitted axle loading was apparently 16 tons on the Dublin-Cork route at time of introduction and this was not eased until 1907. How the evident conflict over axle loading during that period was resolved Is not clear. The effort to keep weight down appears to have resulted in sub-standard frames as apparent with further rebuilding post-1925. No 332 was equipped with Marshall valve gear for a period but specific dates are unknown. No 322 undertook exchange trials with Great Northern Railway 4-4-0 QL Class No 113 in 1911 but no substantive conclusions appear to have resulted.

Above: 4-4-0 Type XVIII [18] Class 321 No 323.

Centre: 4-4-0 Type XVIII [18] Class 321 with tapered boiler.

Bottom: 4-4-0 Type XVIII [18] Class 321 No 326 as modified with Schmidt superheater.
The Locomotive

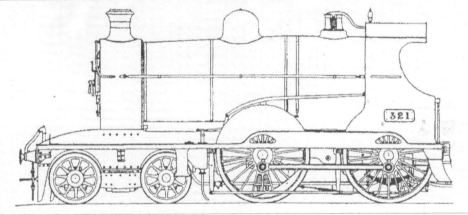

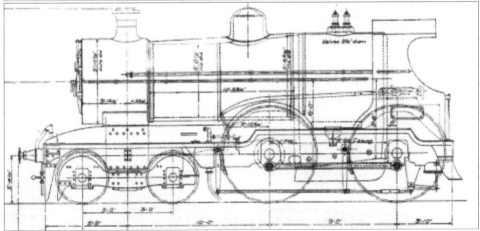

4-4-0 Type XVIII [18] Class 321 with parallel boiler and Belpaire firebox.

RNC Type: XIX [19]			4-4-0		GSWR Class 333
No	Introduced	Withdrawn	No	Introduced	Withdrawn
333	Jun 1907	Aug 1955	337	Jun 1908	Jun 1955
334	Jun 1907	Jun 1955	338	Jun 1908	Oct 1959
335	Jun 1907	Jun 1955	339	Jun 1908	Dec 1959
336	Jun 1907	Apr 1957	340	Jun 1908	Dec 1955

Designer: Coey **Built at Inchicore**

4-4-0 Type XIX [19] Class 33 No 334 fitted with the Aspinall twin-pipe continuous brake on the front buffer beam which appears to have been unusual for tender locomotives. *Kelland Collection*

Boiler pressure – 160 lb/ sq in	Heating surfaces:	Tractive effort – 16,730 lb
Cylinders – 18" x 26"	tubes – 1283.9 sq ft	Coal/ water capacities – refer Chapter 9
Bogie wheels – 3' 0"	firebox – 128.1 sq ft	Max axle loading – 16 tons 5 cwt
Driving wheels – 5' 8½"	grate – 21 sq ft	Loco weight Adhesive weight
Wheelbase – 6' 4" + 6' 10" + 8' 6"	Nos 333-336:	50 tons 2 cwt 31 tons 18 cwt
Locomotive length – 29' 8"	Nos 337-340:	50 tons 6 cwt 32 ton 0 cwt

These locomotives were a mixed traffic variant of (taper boiler) Class 321 with smaller driving wheels, and were intended for Cork-Rosslare services where they were concentrated until displacement by Woolwich moguls in GSR days. The first four had a tendency for the bogie journals to run hot so Nos 337-340 were built with outside-framed bogies, resulting in an increase in weight. About 1909, a new type of lubricant and minor axle box modifications resolved the overheating issue.

4-4-0 Type XIX [19] Class 333 No 339 with outside-frame bogie.

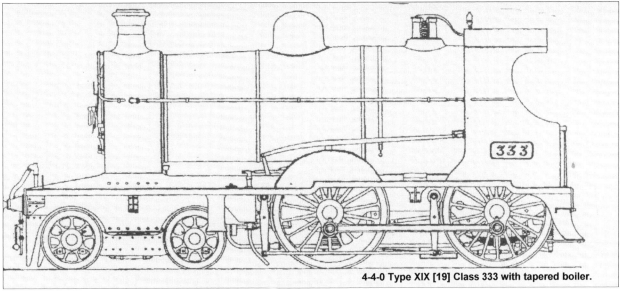

4-4-0 Type XIX [19] Class 333 with tapered boiler.

4-4-0 Type XIX [19] Class 333 outside-framed bogie version with tapered boiler.

RNC Type: XX [20]	4-4-0	GSWR Class 341
No **Name**	**Introduced**	**Withdrawn**
341 *Sir William Goulding*	May 1913	1928
Designer: Coey/ Maunsell		**Built at Inchicore**

Boiler pressure – 160 lb/ sq in (later 175 lb/ sq in) Cylinders – 20" x 26" (later 19" x 26") Piston valves – 9" Driving wheels – 6' 7" Bogie wheels – 3' 0" Wheelbase – 6' 4" + 7' 11" + 9' 11" Locomotive length – 32' 2"	Heating surfaces: tubes – 1364.9 sq ft firebox – 155.9 sq ft superheater – 335.1 sq ft grate – 24.8 sq ft	Tractive effort – 17,910 lb (later 17,680 lb) Coal/ water capacities – refer Chapter 9 Locomotive weight – 60 tons 3 cwt Adhesive weight – not known Max axle loading – 19 tons 2 cwt

As Coey retired through ill health during construction of this locomotive, its completion and modern features were attributed to Maunsell. The parallel boiler was significantly larger than those carried by preceding 4-4-0s, and it was unique in being fitted with Walschaerts valve gear. Performance was impressive leading to comparisons with the succeeding 4-6-0 Class 400, to the detriment of the latter. The contemporary technical press noted that it was to be the first of a series and further frames may have been cut but Watson was more interested in pursuing Class 400 development so No 341 remained a singleton. Another reason why no more were built was the civil engineer's concern about possible weight and axle loading constraints, and he insisted that the locomotive be re-weighed every six months. Its early withdrawal was widely regretted by locomotive crew and observers.

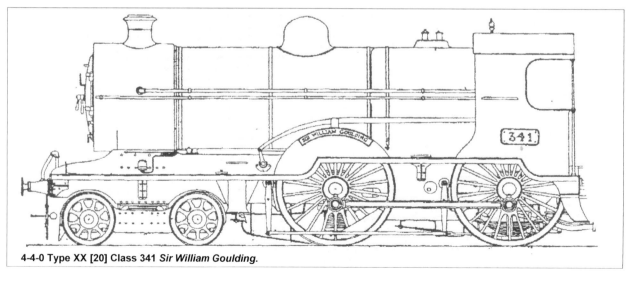

4-4-0 Type XX [20] Class 341 *Sir William Goulding*.

Passenger tender engines

4-4-0 Type XX [20] Class 341 *Sir William Goulding*.

RNC Type: XXI [21]   **4-6-0**   **GSWR Class 400**

No	Introduced	Built by	Builders No	Withdrawn	No	Introduced	Built by	Builders No	Withdrawn
400	Aug 1916	Inchicore		1929	405	Jun 1923 ±	AW	190	Sep 1955
401	Apr 1921	Inchicore		Mar 1961	406	Nov 1921	Inchicore		Mar 1957
402	Aug 1921	Inchicore		Mar 1961	407 *	Jun 1923 ±	AW	185	Mar 1955
403	Jun 1923 ±	AW	188	1959	408 *	Jun 1923 ±	AW	186	1930
404 §	Jun 1923 ±	AW	189	1930	409 *§	Jun 1923 ±	AW	187	Mar 1958

(AW = Armstrong Whitworth)
± Completed and delivered in October 1922 but did not enter service until June 1923, due to Civil War situation.
* Built with saturated boilers; rebuilt with superheaters – No 407 in 1925 and Nos 408/ 409 in 1924
§ Nos 404 and 409 swapped identities in 1930, i.e. No 409 was withdrawn in 1930 carrying identity of No 404.

Designer: Watson

No 400 as built:

Boiler pressure – 175 lbs/ sq in Cylinders – (4) 14" x 26" Piston valves – 8" Bogie wheels – 3' 0" Driving wheels – 6' 7" Wheelbase – 6' 4" + 5' 6" + 7' 0" + 8' 3" Locomotive length over buffers – 36' 9"	Heating surfaces: tubes – 1614 sq ft firebox – 158 sq ft superheater – 440 sq ft grate – 28 sq ft	Tractive effort – 19,190 lbs Coal/ water capacities – refer Chapter 9 Locomotive weight – 70 tons 14 cwt Adhesive weight – 50 tons 14 cwt Max axle loading –17 tons 6 cwt

No 401, 402 and 406 as built:

	Heating surfaces: tubes – 1590 sq ft firebox – 158 sq ft superheater – 350 sq ft grate – 28 sq ft	Coal/ water capacities – refer Chapter 9 Locomotive weight – 76 tons 7 cwt Adhesive weight – 55 tons 4 cwt Max axle loading –18 tons 11 cwt

No 403 to 405 as built:

	Heating surfaces: tubes – 1614 sq ft firebox – 158 sq ft superheater – 366 sq ft grate – 28 sq ft	

No 407 to 409, as built saturated:

Boiler pressure 225 lb/ sq in	Heating surfaces: tubes – 1870 sq ft firebox – 158 sq ft grate – 28 sq ft	Tractive effort – 24,680 lbs Weights not recorded
(On conversion to superheated condition, Nos 407 to 409 became identical with Nos 403 to 405)		

Prior to appointment as Works Manager at Inchicore, EA Watson had been an Assistant Works Manager at Swindon with responsibility for carriage and wagon matters. He returned to Ireland convinced of the superiority of the GWR's motive power practices and his repeated preaching on the subject increasingly annoyed Maunsell. Ironically, the latter became an early disciple of Swindon's standards following his move to the South Eastern & Chatham Railway at Ashford, to the ultimate benefit of the GSR in the form of the Woolwich Moguls.

While the Coey/ Maunsell 4-4-0 Type XX Class 341 had broken new ground in applying modern concepts, Watson chose to go further with a 4-6-0 type and revoked plans for more 4-4-0s and is believed to have scrapped frames that had already been cut for those locomotives. Also, he ignored the possibility of a 4-4-2 that could have circumvented the weight constraints that afflicted the 4-4-0 while providing a larger firebox more suited to variable quality fuel. Watson has been criticised for his iconoclasm but the GSWR's experience with 20th Century 4-4-0s had been varied. No 341 was the best but given weight and axle loading constraints, Watson was justified in turning to a ten wheeled design, even if the outcome of the exercise was disappointing.

From the drawings sequence described below, a 2-cylinder 4-6-0 was initially considered before moving to the 4-cylinder concept. Arguments in favour rested on emerging recognition of the damaging impact of hammer blow with a 2-cylinder high speed locomotive. This factor increases exponentially with faster speeds but can be significantly ameliorated with three or four cylinders as exemplified with the Bulleid 3-cylinder Pacifics that were so well balanced as not to require any driving wheel balance weights.

Influenced by the impressive performance of the GWR Star Class, Watson opted for 4-cylinder divided drive and in so doing added to the list of 4-cylinder 4-6-0 types that proved below par in these islands. Only the GWR mastered the concept with unqualified success, and Class 400 proved one of the more unsatisfactory examples of the genre. Several faults were attributed to the class but RN Clements maintained that the root cause lay in poor chassis design and weak frames. Adoption of outside valve motion was ostensibly an advance on the GWR practice of placing this equipment between the frames. However, the greater distance between the sets of valve motion accentuated fore-aft lateral stresses on the frames at their weakest point where sections were cut away to accommodate bogie and wheels. This factor was recognised with the Stars which had thicker plate frames and substantially stronger cross-bracing in the cylinder area.

Any successful, ground-breaking design usually relied on an iterative process to determine the optimal configuration. Much of the Star's success

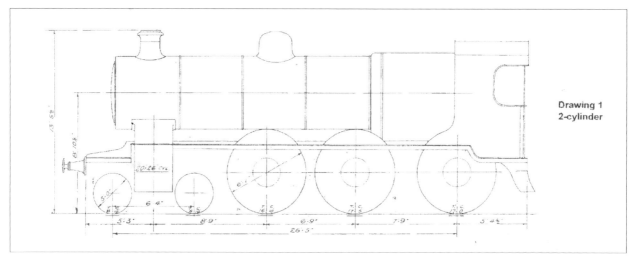

4-6-0 Type XXI [21] Class 400 Proposed designs No 1.

rested on Churchward's leadership of the Swindon Drawing Office, and his adherence to MBWA (management by wandering around). If a draughtman was stuck with a difficult problem, Churchward would assemble an impromptu meeting of those nearby at which all were encouraged to express opinions, regardless of relative seniority. Watson appears to have cast his net wide in considering design alternatives but his arrogant, opinionated approach probably extinguished worthwhile collaborative discussion with his subordinates to the detriment of the final outcome.

Drawing Reference 1: This was the earliest (dated January 1914) and depicts a 2-cylinder engine reminiscent of the first, large wheeled 2-cylinder 4-6-0s of the Great Central Railway. There is no record of JG Robinson having had any direct association with Inchicore but his work would have been familiar through acquisition of thirty-three of his locomotives following the amalgamation with the Waterford Limerick & Western Railway in January 1901.

Drawing Reference 2: Dated February 1914, this was apparently a re-working of the initial proposal to accommodate four cylinders in line, all connecting with the leading driving axle as in the London & North Western Railway 4-6-0 Claughton Class of 1913. This version does not seem to have been fully worked out. The frame was 1' 4¼" longer, and the chassis would have been structurally more complex with four cylinders and associated valve motion, yet the weight increase would supposedly have been only 1 ton 5 cwt.

Drawing Reference 3: Also dated February 1914, this depicts 4-cylinder divided drive. A more realistic weight increase over the original 2-cylinder proposal is indicated but the layout seems impracticable. The outside cylinders would have been set further back than was the case with Class 400 as eventually built (and also with the Stars). This would have allowed insufficient space for the outside valve motion and for the connecting rod to drive the centre coupled axle. The 10' distance (9' with the Star) between the bogie centre and the leading coupled axle suggests that this variant contemplated inside valve motion to activate the outside valves through rocking levers (ie the GWR 4-cylinder format). Estimated as the heaviest of the proposed design variants, it seems that efforts were made to reduce weight at the rear end. The resultant 13' 6" coupled wheelbase would have cramped the space around the firebox area with limited clearance for the trailing coupled axle. Recognition of potential weight problems is also reflected in the alternative round-topped firebox.

Drawing Reference 4: The dimensions closely accord with No 400 as built in 1916 but differ in two key respects. The smokebox on the actual locomotive was deeper than that proposed in the earlier drawings, presumably due to changes in the superheater. Also, the location of the front fall in the running plate would have precluded the use of rocking levers to activate the outside valves, presumably an oversight in preparation of the drawing.

The table overleaf summarises the lengths and estimated weight variances between the four proposals, and the actual No 400:

Apart from the outside valve motion, No 400 differed from the Swindon format in the use of a parallel boiler, probably to reduce weight and to contain construction cost. The boiler seems to have performed well with high degree superheat and 175 lb/ sq in pressure, which followed the LNWR Claughton standard. Major contention concerned

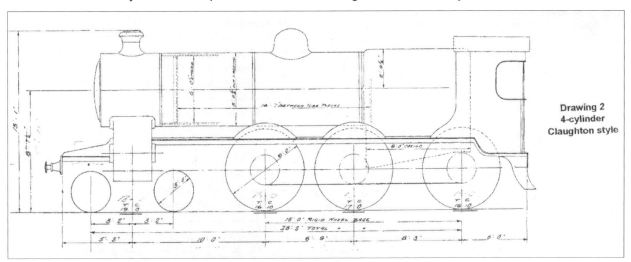

Drawing 2
4-cylinder
Claughton style

4-6-0 Type XXI [21] Class 400 Proposed designs No 2.

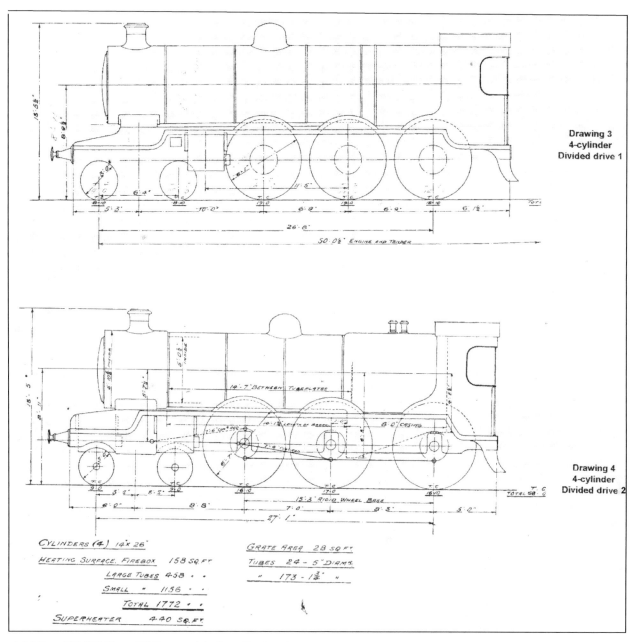

4-6-0 Type XXI [21] Class 400 Proposed designs Nos 3 and 4.

	Drawing 1 2-cylinder	Drawing 2 4-cylinder Claughton style	Drawing 3 4-cylinder Divided drive 1	Drawing 4 4-cylinder Divided drive 2	No 400 As built
Cylinders	20" x 26"	Not stated	Not stated	14" x 26"	14" x 26"
Driving wheel diameter	6' 1"	6' 0"	6' 1"	6' 7"	6' 7'
Locomotive length					
- buffer beam to bogie centre	5' 3"	5' 3"	5' 3"	6' 0"	6' 0"
- bogie centre to leading driving axle	8' 9"	10' 0"	10' 0"	8' 8"	8' 8"
- leading to centre driving axle	6' 9"	6' 9"	6' 9"	7' 0"	7' 0"
- centre to trailing driving axle	7' 9"	8' 3"	6' 9"	8' 3"	8' 3"
- trailing driving axle to frame end	5' 4½ "	5' 0"	6' 1½"	5' 0"	5' 0"
Total	**33' 10½"**	**35' 3"**	**34' 10½"**	**34' 11"**	**34' 11"**
Axle loadings:					
- bogie	17 0 c	19t 0c	17t 0c	18t 0c	20t 0c
- leading driving axle	16t 10c	16t 10c	19t 0c	16t 10c	17t 6c
- centre driving axle	17t 5c	17t 0c	19t 0c	17t 0c	17t 1c
- trailing driving axle	17t 0c	16t 10c	18t 10c	16t 10c	16t 7c
Total	**67t 15c**	**69t 0c**	**73t 10c**	**68t 0c**	**70t 14c**

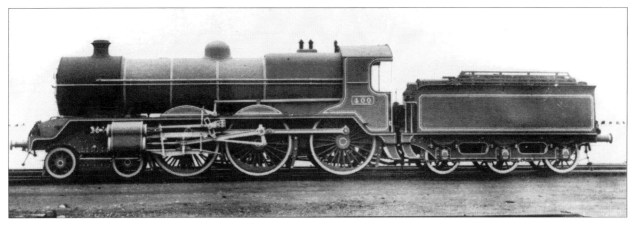

4-6-0 Type XXI [21] Class 400 No 400 as built.

Armstrong Whitworth builder's No 189, built 1923: 4-6-0 Type XXI [21] Class 400 No 404. Continuing problems with this design led to early instructions for withdrawal of Nos 400 (1929) and 404/ 8 (1930). The fate of No 404, seen here in original condition between 1923 and 1930 at Inchicore, was unusual. This engine was regarded by its operators as the best of the surviving 4-cylinder engines so at local level and without formal authority, its identity was swapped with that of No 409 (one of the originally saturated trio). Masquerading as No 409, No 404 was converted to a 2-cylinder engine in 1935 and withdrawn in 1958.

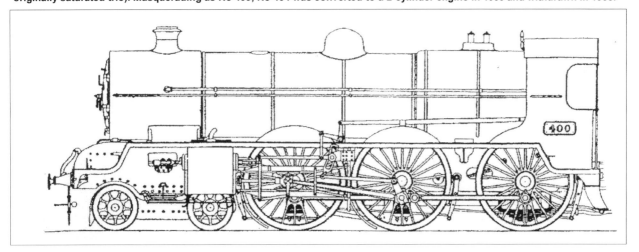

Type XXI [21] Class 400 as built.

valve lap where Chief Draughtsman EE Joynt advocated 7/8" in full gear while Watson wished for a significantly greater length. Despite his enthusiasm for the Swindon format, the latter seems to have been unable adequately to argue the point and a compromise was reached at 1¼". Blame for sluggish performance and high fuel consumption is typically laid at Watson's feet and ultimately, he was responsible as Locomotive Superintendent. Nevertheless, Joynt's chronically out-dated ideas were the primary source of the design's poor performance on the road; the GWR's standard valve lap was 1.63".

Orders for nine more were instigated in 1918 but supplies were impeded by difficulties arising from the Great War and delivery was significantly delayed. The dimensional differences enumerated above provided cogent evidence of dissatisfaction with No 400. Other changes included superheater modifications; introduction of Detroit three-feed lubrication; simplification and enlargement of internal steam passages; and strengthening of frames and valve motion. The construction of Nos 407-9 in saturated condition, personally approved by Watson, suggests a desperate attempt to remedy a deficient design despite contemporary evidence that superheating was obligatory.

In essence, the GSWR passed to its successor ten modern 4-6-0s plagued with problems, of which No 400 was undoubtedly the worst. Resolution of these difficulties proved to be a drawn-out affair under GSR auspices. Full details of the complex programme of rebuilding and modifications appear in *Locomotives of the GSR*.

RNC Type: XXII [22]	**4-6-0**	**GSWR Class 500**
No	**Built**	**Withdrawn**
500	Apr 1924	Jun 1955
Also, under GSR auspices:		
501	Feb 1926	Jun 1955
502	Mar 1926	Aug 1957
Designer: Bazin		**Built at Inchicore**

Boiler pressure – 180 lbs/ sq in	Heating surfaces:	Tractive effort – 23,780 lbs
Cylinders – 19½" x 28"	tubes – 1614 sq ft	Coal/ water capacities – refer Chapter 9
Piston valves – 10"	firebox – 158 sq ft	Locomotive weight – 74 tons 10 cwt
Bogie wheels – 3' 0"	superheater – 440 sq ft	Adhesive weight – 53 tons 17 cwt
Driving wheels – 5' 8½"	grate – 28 sq ft	Max axle loading – 18 tons 10 cwt
Wheelbase – 6' 8" + 5' 10½" + 7' 0" + 7' 4"		
Locomotive length – 37' 1"		

4-6-0 Type XXII [22] Class 500. *Locomotive Publishing Co*

It is probable that this class would have been multiplied further, but for the success of the bargain-priced Woolwich Moguls. No 500 was the last locomotive built by the GSWR, and No 502 the last built to the company's specific design.

The superheated/ saturated debate had been resolved by the time No 500 was delivered; that fitted to the prototype had been supplied by Marine & Locomotive Superheater Ltd with 24 elements. This was a successful and well-regarded class. Maunsell was the first Locomotive Superintendent in these islands to recognise the potential embedded in the design principles of Churchward's 2-cylinder "Saint" Class, as expressed in his 2-6-0 Class N for the South Eastern & Chatham Railway and in his improvements to the London & South Western's 4-6-0 family after the 1923 Grouping. He and Bazin enjoyed a co-operative working relationship, and No 500 appears to have been a happy product of this association.

No 500 was therefore a locomotive of historic significance that has been rarely fully recognised. As an effective mixed traffic 4-6-0, it was an early example of a type that would be built in substantial numbers in the form of Stanier's "Black 5" for the London Midland & Scottish Railway, and of Thompson's Class B1 for the London & North Eastern Railway.

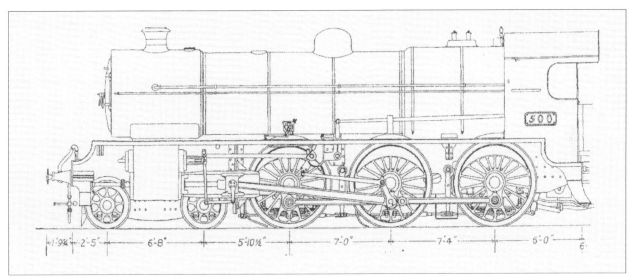

4-6-0 Type XXII [22] Class 500.

Type XXII No 500 at Mallow on the 11.50 am Cork to Dublin 15th June 1954. *B K B Green*

Chapter 5
Goods tender engines
RNC Types XXXIII [23] to XL111 [43]

Introduction

Four-coupled locomotives for goods duties were favoured from the outset, the GSWR's first locomotives being a pair delivered by Bury, Curtis & Kennedy in 1845. As discussed in Chapter 4 they may have been built as 0-4-0s but if so, they were probably converted to 0-4-2s before entering normal service. Two more were delivered in 1847 with all four numbered 41-4 (Nos 100-3 under the 1864 renumbering scheme) and categorised as Type XXIII [23|; they were withdrawn between 1865 and 1880.

Six more 0-4-2s were supplied by Bury in 1847-8. RNC's Type XXIV [24], numbered 104-9 (1864 Nos 45-50) and withdrawn 1868-76. A pair of locomotives, Nos 51/ 2 (1864 Nos 110/ 1) built by Grendon followed in 1849 as Type XXV [25]; they worked until 1867. The next supplier was Rothwell which built four in 1850 (Nos 53-6, 1864 Nos 112-5 as Type XXVI [26]). They were withdrawn between 1865 and 1869. A further 0-4-2 was provided by Fairbairn as No 75 (1864 No 116) in 1856, Type XXVII [27]. This engine was later converted to 0-4-2T when the name *Sambo* was later substituted for the number.

Construction of goods locomotives commenced at Inchicore in 1852 with Type XXVIII [28] Nos 57/ 8 (1864 Nos 117/ 8) and they worked until 1865/ 73. These engines appeared in parallel with the first 2-2-2 built by the GSWR. By 1853, passenger locomotives still predominated with forty-one 2-2-2s all but one supplied by outside builders, plus nineteen 0-4-2s of which only two were Inchicore products.

Two Type XXX [30] 0-4-2s numbered 62/ 3 (1864 Nos 122/ 3) appeared from Inchicore in 1854 and lasted until 1879/ 82. Between 1860 and 1862, nine of Type XXXI [31] entered traffic; withdrawals took place between 1879 and 1884. The final group of 0-4-2s to be added to the fleet were built at Inchicore as Type XXXII [32]. Three appeared as Nos 97-99 (1864 Nos 133-5) in 1863, and three more in 1865 (nominally Nos 100-2 but actually Nos 136-8 under the 1864 system). Unlike certain other railways, the 0-4-2 wheel arrangement was by then regarded as an obsolete concept and all of this type had been withdrawn by 1886.

The only 2-4-0s built specifically for goods duties were Type XXIX [29] Nos 64-6 (1864 Nos 119-121) introduced in 1855, all of which worked until 1873. In 1854, the first engines built as 0-6-0s, as opposed to rebuilds, were Type XXXIII [33] Nos 60/ 61 (Nos 139/ 40) which last ran in 1874/ 6 respectively. Another batch of 0-6-0s totalling six were built in 1856, Type XXXIV [34] Nos 67-69, 72-74 (1864 Nos 141-146). Two (Nos 144/ 5) were rebuilt as 0-6-0Ts in 1868 and all six were withdrawn 1873-9.

The pre-McDonnell policy of small batches of contractor- and Inchicore-built locomotives to meet expanding goods traffic denied the benefits of standardisation. The foundation stone of McDonnell's construction programme was nine 0-6-0s fashioned out of components donated by a heterogenous collection of earlier machines. This group of nine "hybrids" (Nos 103, 105, 110-115, 118) contained components of divergent dimensions, differing quality, and with varying degrees of wear for which reason a Type XXXV [35] Hybrid has been added to the RNC Type list. The analysis in Chapter 2 (Page 38) of the evolution of 2-4-0 No 16 underlines the reality that such measures could only be a short term expedient. The prevailing pressure on the works demanded mass production of a versatile, reliable 0-6-0 that was then beyond Inchicore's capacity. Analysis of contemporary data confirms that the prototype of what became Class 101 was actually Beyer Peacock works No 747 (locomotive No 147) of May 1867 and that the preceding motley group of hybrids were rebuilt/ renewed later in their progressive assimilation into a class whose longevity was slightly shorter than earlier accounts would claim.

Following its introduction, Class 101 had a profound impact upon the motive power fleet. Construction was continued by McDonnell's successors without significant modification so that by the end of 1899, a total of 99 were in service as Type XXXV [35]. Twelve of an improved version were built by Coey in 1902-5 as Type XXXVI [36] Class 200. These engines set the pattern for up-grading Type XXXV [35] and in due course they were absorbed into Class 101. Expansion of the class encouraged fleet rationalisation through renewal or replacement of older locomotives after careers lasting around 20 years, and heralded a substantial lengthening of working lives. Originally intended as a goods locomotive, Class 101 later assumed a genuine mixed traffic role.

For all the effectiveness of Classes 101/ 200, heavier loads and faster schedule presented a case for something larger. In 1903, four 0-6-0s were introduced that were modern in appearance but failed to deliver the anticipated advance in performance.

Numbered 351-4 and allocated Type XXXVII [37] by RNC, they were followed by four more in 1912 as Nos 249-252 with sufficient detail differences for them to be designated Type XLII [42] although the GSWR treated all eight as Class 351. One was withdrawn in 1931 following a collision and the remainder worked until 1961-4. Concurrent with the introduction of Class 351, seven larger locomotives numbered 355-61 were delivered by North British Locomotive Co to Coey's specification. The weight increase of *circa* 4 tons made them front end heavy necessitating rebuild by Inchicore as ungainly 2-6-0s in 1906/ 8. Classified 355 (Type XXXVIII [38]), the prototype was withdrawn in 1928 but the remainder stayed in service until 1957-60.

A pair of 0-6-0s, the products of North British, were added in 1907. They had been purchased in 1903 as part of a batch of four 0-6-2Ts (RNC Type LXII [62]) to Coey's design specification. They were also found to be overweight; two remained as tank locomotives with reduced water capacity while Nos 211/ 2 were converted to 0-6-0s of Class 211 (Type XL [40]); they worked until 1949/ 51.

Modern design trends were reflected in the GSWR's last 0-6-0, Maunsell's Class 257 (Type XLIII [43]) of which eight (Nos 257-264) were built 1913/ 4. They were the best goods engines introduced since Class 101 and should have been the basis for further construction by the GSWR's successor in preference to the two mediocre 0-6-0 classes that were actually introduced. Class 257 was withdrawn 1959-1965; Nos 261/ 2 were the last steam locomotives in service with Corás Iompair Eireann.

Coey introduced two purpose-designed larger goods classes with alternative wheel arrangements. Six of 4-6-0 Class 362 (Type XXXIX [39]) were built in 1905 -7 to some fanfare as they were then Ireland's largest locomotives. They followed the popular concept elsewhere of inside-cylindered 4-6-0s for goods and mixed traffic work but suffered from very poor riding, leading to their withdrawal 1928-31. The final large goods design was 2-6-0 Class 368 (Type No XLI [41]) of which four were built in 1909 as Nos 368-71. These engines were a development of Class 355 with a lengthened wheelbase. Nos 368 and 371 were withdrawn in 1928 but the other two lasted until 1957.

--- o O o ---

RNC Type: XXIII [23]	0-4-2	GSWR Class: n/a

1864 No [Original No]	Introduced	Withdrawn	Comments
100 [41] §	Aug 1845	Dec 1873	Shipped new to Drogheda for trials on Dublin & Drogheda Railway; sold for scrap, probably to Delany, Jun 1874
101 [42] §	Sep 1845	Dec 1880	Shipped new to Drogheda for trials on DDR; condemned Jan 1880 but not withdrawn until following Dec when broken up; remains sold to McGowan Jun 1881
102 [43]	Sep 1847	Jun 1871	Sold to Athenry & Tuam Railway for £450; became ATR No 3 (see Chapter 8)
103 [44]	Sep 1847	Dec 1865	Sold to Cork & Bandon Railway for £450 Dec1865; became CBR No 8, renumbered 1 in 1868; withdrawn by CBR Sept 1874; NB Sources conflict on identify of this locomotive

§ These locomotives may have been at first named *Buffalo* and *Urus* respectively.

Built by Bury Curtis & Kennedy

Boiler pressure – 80 lb/ sq in	Heating surfaces:	Tractive effort – 5,330 lb
Cylinders – 14" x 24"	tubes – 1000 sq ft	Coal capacity – not recorded
Driving wheels – 5' 0"	firebox – 60 sq ft	Water capacity – not recorded
Trailing wheels – 3' 0"	grate – 12.75 sq ft	Locomotive weight – 24 tons 1 cwt
Wheelbase – 8' 0"+ 6' 8"		

This was a typical Bury goods design with that manufacturer's characteristic feature of cylinders inclined downward towards the front with the motion working below the leading axle. Sources vary on some dimensions. A scale drawing of 103 (as possibly sold to the CBR) indicates a wheel base of 8' + 6' 1". All were probably built with 14" x 24" cylinders but Nos 102/ 3, apparently later acquired 15" or 16" diameter cylinders. There was also a report of 14" x 20" cylinders but this seems doubtful; locomotive's identity is unknown.

No 100 was on hire to the Athenry & Tuam Railway from April 1872 to January 1873; estimated daily mileage was 100 which roughly equates to three return trips Athenry-Tuam.

0-4-2 Type XXIII [23] No 103 running as Cork & Bandon Railway No 1. The few other illustrations of this type indicate that they had domed boilers. The absence in this drawing might be an error. *The Locomotive*

0-4-2 Type XXIII [23] No 101 in original condition except for the addition of a rudimentary extension to the cab sides to improve crew protection. *Locomotive Publishing Co*

RNC Type: XXIV [24]			0-4-2	GSWR Class: n/a
1864 No [Original No]	**Introduced**	**Rebuilt §**	**Withdrawn**	**Comments**
104 [45]	Dec 1847	1863/ 4	Dec 1870	Sold to McGowan Aug 1873
105 [46]	Dec 1847	1863/ 4	1868	Refer to Type XXXV [35] Hybrid; cylinders to No 107 in 1869
106 [47]	Dec 1847	1863/ 4	Jun 1871	Sold to Meade Dec 1871 for £250
107 [48]	Jan 1848	-	Dec 1875	Sold to McGowan March 1879 for £120
108 [49]	Jan 1848	-	Dec 1874	Sold to Whitehaven Colliery for £240 Dec 1876; there are doubts about the disposal – see Type XXXV [35] Hybrid
109 [50]	Jan 1848	-	Dec 1876	To Inchicore rolling mill 1877

§ Rebuilt as either side or saddle tanks; No 105's cylinders were fitted to No 107 in 1869, which implies that it worked until about 1868.

Goods tender engines

Built by Bury Curtis & Kennedy

Boiler pressure – 80 lb/ sq in	Heating surfaces:	Tractive effort – 6,960 lb
Cylinders – 16" x 24"	tubes – 1001 sq ft	Coal capacity – not recorded
Driving wheels – 5' 0"	firebox – not recorded	Water capacity – 1344 gal
Trailing wheels – 3' 0"	grate – not recorded	Locomotive weight – 24 tons 1 cwt
Wheelbase – 8' 0" + 6' 8"		

A board minute dated Sept 1863 authorised Miller to convert three old goods engines into tank locomotives to work traffic from Cork to Kilbarry and Rathpeacon, cost not to exceed £75 each. These locomotives had a D-shaped firebox with low crown.

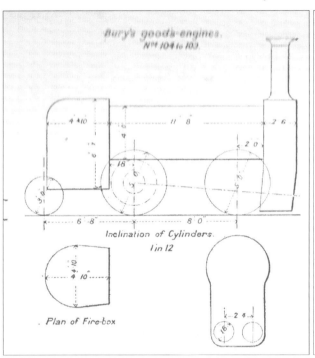

0-4-2 Type XXIV [24].

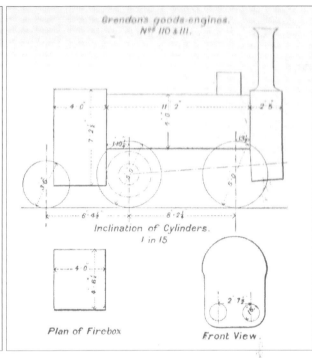

0-4-2 Type XXV [25].

RNC Type: XXV [25]   **0-4-2**   **GSWR Class: n/a**

1864 No [Original No]	Introduced	Withdrawn	Comments
110 [51]	1849	1867	Broken up 1867-9
111 [52]	1849	1867	Broken up 1868; see Type XXXV [35] Hybrid

Built by Grendon.

Boiler pressure – 80 lb/ sq in	Heating surfaces:	Tractive effort – 6,120 lb
Cylinders – 15" x 24"	not recorded	
Driving wheels – 5' 0"		
Trailing wheels – 3' 6"		
Wheelbase – 8' 2¼" + 6' 4½"		

In September 1848, the company invited tenders from Grendon, the Haigh Foundry, Benjamin Hick, Jones & Potts, Nasmyth, Rothwell and Stephenson. To approach so many manufacturers for such a modest order suggests a conscious effort to move away from the company's original two suppliers.

These locomotives had a dome on the front boiler rings and a raised firebox. The diagram shows 15" diameter cylinders although some sources suggest 16". It has been suggested that they were built specifically for the Mallow-Killarney line. These locomotives were ordered concurrently with Type XXVI [26].

RNC Type: XXVI [26]			0-4-2		GSWR Class: n/a
1864 No [Original No]	**Builder's No**	**Introduced**	**Withdrawn**	**Comments**	
112 [53]	131	1850	Jun 1865		
113 [54]	132	1850	1865		
114 [55]	133	1850	Jul 1869	Wheels used for No 123 in Jul 1869	
115 [56]	134	1850	1868	Wheels used for No 109 in Mar 1868	

All four locomotives donated parts for conversion from 0-4-2 to 0-6-0 – refer to Type XXXV [35] Hybrid.

Built by Rothwell

Boiler pressure – 80 lb/ sq in (assumed) Heating surfaces: Tractive effort – 6,960 lb Cylinders – 16" x 24" not recorded Driving wheels – 5' 0" Trailing wheels – 3' 0" Wheelbase – 7' 2¾ " + 6' 9½

These were the only Rothwell machines supplied to Ireland. They had a dome on the front of the boiler and a raised firebox. The order for these locomotives was placed concurrently with Grendon 0-4-2 Nos 110, 111 (Type XXV [25]). In both cases, solid wrought iron wheels were specified at an increased cost of £100 per locomotive.

A cleaner accidentally opened the regulator of No 54 on 30th December 1853 and the locomotive set off on its own, destroying Inchicore's shed doors.

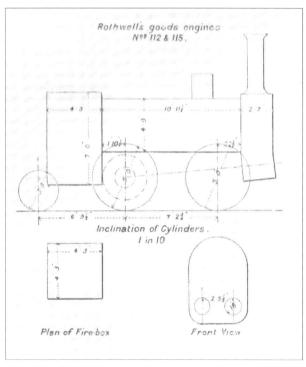

0-4-2 Type XXVI [26].

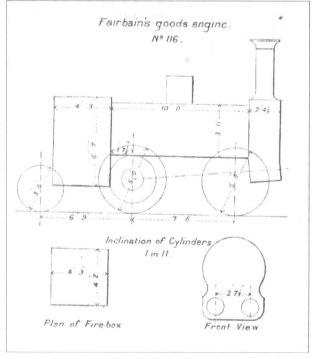

0-4-2 Type XXVII [27].

RNC Type: XXVII [27]			0-4-2/0-4-2T		GSWR Class: n/a
No [Original No]	**Built**	**Name**	**Rebuilt**		**Withdrawn**
116 [75]	1856	(Sambo)	1870/ 1885/ 1892		c. 1913

Goods tender engines

Built by Fairbairn

Boiler pressure – 80 lb/ sq in (assumed) Cylinders – 16" x 22" Driving wheels – 5' 0" Trailing wheels – 3' 6" Wheelbase – 7' 6" + 6' 9"	Heating surfaces: not recorded	Tractive effort – 6,380 lb Coal capacity – not recorded Water capacity – not recorded Locomotive weight –26 tons 4 cwt Adhesive weight – 20 tons 8 cwt Max axle loading –10 tons 4 cwt

As built, this locomotive had a raised firebox and dome in the centre of the boiler. Taken into Inchicore works in October 1868, it underwent a leisurely rebuilding during which it was identified as "M" and re-entered traffic in January 1870, retaining the number 116:

Boiler pressure – 140 lb/ sq in	Heating surfaces: Tubes – 838 sq ft firebox – 86 sq ft grate – 17.5 sq ft	Tractive effort –11,170 lb

In 1885, it was rebuilt as a saddle tank, apparently with no change to leading dimensions. It is believed that it was transferred to departmental stock following this conversion to serve as the Inchicore works shunter; the number was removed and name *Sambo* substituted in May 1890. It was reboilered in May 1892:

Boiler pressure – 140 lb/ sq in	Heating surfaces: Tubes – 856 sq ft firebox – 101 sq ft grate – 17.5 sq ft (unconfirmed)	Tractive effort – 11,170 lb

On withdrawal, it was replaced by a "new" Inchicore shunter 0-4-2ST named *Sambo* (Type LXIV [64]) which was cobbled together out of sundry surplus material, and which might have contained components from this locomotive.

RNC Type: XXVIII [28]			0-4-2	GSWR Class: n/a
1864 No **[Original No]**	**Introduced**	**Withdrawn**	**Comments**	
117 [57]	Sep 1852	Jun 1873	First goods engine built at Inchicore; last ran Apr 1873; sold to McGowan Jan 1874	
118 [58]	1852	1865	Last ran July 1866; following withdrawal, parts used in construction of 0-6-0 with the same number - Type XXXV [35] hybrid	

Designer: Miller/ Wakefield   **Built at Inchicore**

Boiler pressure – 80 lb/ sq in (assumed) Cylinders – 15" x 24" Driving wheels – 5' 0" § Trailing wheels – 3' 6" Wheelbase – 8' 3½" + 6' 10½"	Heating surfaces: not recorded	Tractive effort – 6,120 lb Coal capacity – not recorded Water capacity – not recorded Locomotive weight – not recorded

§ Ahrons gives 5' 2"; other sources say 5' 10". The GSWR diagram shows 5' 0", the standard size for goods locomotives supplied up to this date. The dome was on the boiler centre ring and a raised firebox was fitted. Either No 117 or 2-2-2 Type IV [4] No 43 was the first locomotive built at Inchicore.

In 1851, the board authorised building two goods engines at Inchicore, using wheels, axles and cylinders from an external supplier. The first was completed in September 1852 and a board minute dated 15th November noted Miller's report that both engines had proved satisfactory in trials. The cost of £1,882 each was estimated at about 15% less than a locomotive supplied by a manufacturer. These engines were the first of nineteen 0-4-2 goods engines (the others were original Nos 62-63/ 82-87/ 91-93/ 97-102) built at Inchicore before the 0-6-0 wheel arrangement was adopted for goods traffic.

Locomotives of the Great Southern & Western Railway

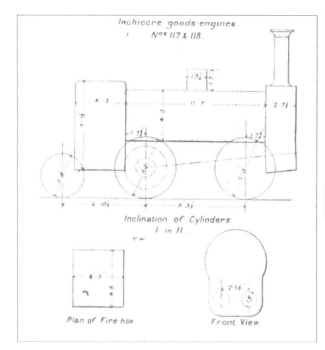
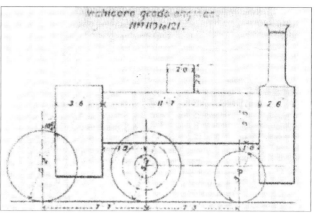

Left: 0-4-2 Type XXVIII [28].

Above: 2-4-0 Type XXIX [29].

RNC Type: XXIX [29]		2-4-0		GSWR Class: n/a
1864 No [Original No]	**Built**	**Last ran**	**Withdrawn**	
119 [64]	Jul 1855	Dec 1873	Dec 1873	
120 [65]	Jul 1855	Dec 1873	Dec 1873	
121 [66]	Jul 1855	Nov 1873	Dec 1873	
Designer: Miller/ Wakefield				**Built at Inchicore**

Boiler pressure – 80 lb/ sq in (assumed)	Heating surfaces:	Tractive effort – 5,070 lb
Cylinders – 14½" x 22"	tubes – 874 sq ft	Coal capacity – not recorded
Leading wheels – 3' 8"	firebox – 67.8 sq	Water capacity – not recorded
Driving wheels – 5' 2"	grate – 11 sq ft est.	Locomotive weight – 22 tons 2 cwt
Wheelbase – 7' 3" + 7' 7"		Adhesive weight – 13 tons 16 cwt
		Max axle loading – 9 tons 10 cwt

These locomotives had the dome in the middle of the boiler and a raised firebox. All three sold as scrap to McGowan for £625 in a single transaction Jan 1874.

RNC Type: XXX [30]		0-4-2		GSWR Class: n/a
1864 No [Original No]	**Introduced**	**Withdrawn**	**Comments**	
122 [62]	Oct 1854	Jan 1882	Sold to McGowan Jun 1882	
123 [63]	Nov 1854	Jun 1879		
Designer: Miller/ Wakefield				**Built at Inchicore**

Boiler pressure – 80 lb/ sq in	Heating surfaces:	Tractive effort – 6,740 lb
Cylinders – 16" x 24"	tubes – 1128 sq ft	
Driving wheels – 5' 2"	firebox – 89.5 sq ft	
Trailing wheels – 3' 8"	grate – 15.4 sq ft	
Wheelbase – 8' 3½ " + 6' 10½"		

Goods tender engines

It was reported that No 123 received leading and driving wheels from No 114 in 1869 but this conflicts with information that this engine was converted into a short wheelbase Type XXXV [35] Hybrid.

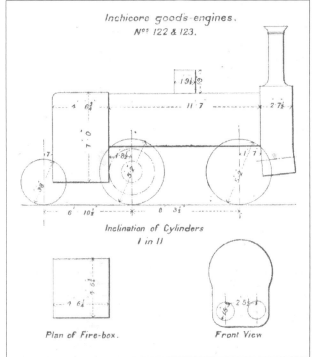

0-4-2 Type XXX [30].

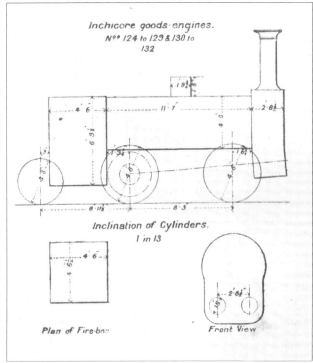

0-4-2 Type XXXI [31].

RNC Type: XXXI [31]   **0-4-2**   **GSWR Class: n/a**

1864 No Original No	Introduced	Withdrawn	Comments
124 [82]	Aug 1860	Dec 1880	Last ran Jun 1882; sold to Cunningham for £200 Oct 1882 with axles, wheels and tyres
125 [83]	Aug 1860	Dec 1880	Last ran Jun 1880; when broken up, boiler went to new fitting shop at Cork
126 [84]	Oct 1860	Jun 1883	Last ran & broken up Jun 1883
127 [85]	Feb 1861	Mar 1879	Last ran Mar 1879; sold to McGowan Mar 1879 for £170; leading & driving wheels to No 131 Jun 1879; trailing wheels to No 126 Aug 1880
128 [86]	Mar 1861	Jul 1882	Last ran Dec 1881; sold to McGowan Dec 1882
129 [87]	Mar 1861	Oct 1881	Last ran Dec 1881; broken up Inchicore Jun 1882; tubes to No 77 Jan 1883
130 [91]	Mar 1862	Dec 1880	Last ran Dec 1880; broken up at Inchicore and cylinders to No 132
131 [92]	Apr 1862	Aug 1881	Last ran Dec 1881; broken up at Inchicore Jun 1882
132 [93]	Apr 1862	Jan 1884	Last ran Dec 1883; broken up 24 Apr 1884

Designer: Miller/ Wakefield   **Built at Inchicore**

Boiler pressure – 80 lb/ sq in
Cylinders – 15" x 24" later 16" x 24"
Driving wheels – 4' 6"
Trailing wheels – 3' 6"
Wheelbase – 8' 3" + 6' 11½"

Heating surfaces:
tubes - 11334 sq ft
firebox - 85.9 sq ft
grate - not recorded

Tractive effort – 6,800 lb (later 7,740 lb)

These locomotives were built in three batches of three. Nos 124-6 used frames by Fairbairn, wheels and cylinders by Beyer Peacock, crank axle by Mersey, other axles by Cooper [price £1874 for each locomotive]. Nos 127-9 used frames and wheels by Neilson, cylinders by Beyer Peacock, crank axle by Mersey, other axles by Cooper [price £2007 each]. Nos 130-2 used frames and wheels by Slaughter, cylinders by Beyer Peacock, crank and other axles by Taylor [price £2070 each].

McDonnell wished to repair No 127 but was overruled and the sale proceeded. However, he appears to have recovered reusable components before delivery to the scrap merchant.

RNC Type: XXXII [32] 0-4-2 **GSWR Class: n/a**

1864 No [Original No]	Built	Withdrawn	Comments
133 [97]	May 1863	June 1883	Last ran Dec 1882; sold complete to McGowan May 1883
134 [98]	Jul 1863	Dec 1884	Last ran Dec 1881; crank to No 138 Jul 1883
135 [99]	Aug 1863	Jul 1881	Last ran Jun 1881; broken up Inchicore Dec 1881
136 [100]	Apr 1865	Jun 1884	Last ran Jun 1884; broken up Mar 1885
137 [101]	May 1865	Dec 1884	Last ran Dec 1883; broken up Feb 1885
138 [102]	May 1865	Jun 1886	Last ran Jun 1886; broken up Nov 1886.

Nos 100-102 were allocated but not carried.

Designer: Miller/ Wakefield **Built at Inchicore**

Boiler pressure – 120 lb/ sq in	Heating surfaces:	Tractive effort –10,440 lb
Cylinders – 16" x 24"	tubes – 1112 sq ft	Coal capacity – not recorded
Driving wheels – 5' 0"	firebox – 85 sq ft	Water capacity – not recorded
Trailing wheels – 3' 6"	grate – 14.7 sq ft	Locomotive weight – 27 tons 19 cwt
Wheelbase – 8' 3" + 6' 11½"		Adhesive weight – 22 tons 8 cwt
Locomotive length – 24' 2½"		Max axle loading – 11 tons 6 cwt

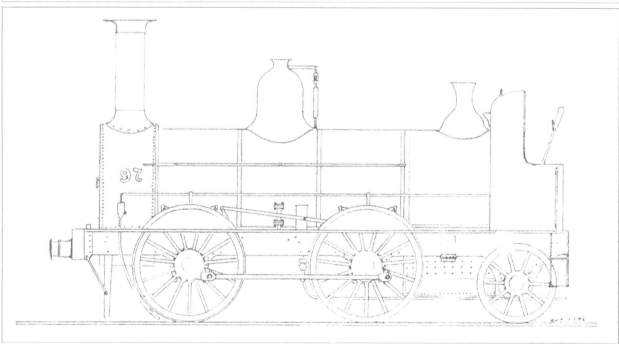

0-4-2 Type XXXII [32].

Nos 133-5 used frames by Sharp, wheels by Beyer Peacock, cylinders by Grendon, crank axles by Taylor, ordinary axles by Cooper at aggregate cost £2107. Nos 136-8 used frames by Sharp, wheels by Neilson, cylinders by Grendon, crank axles by Taylor, ordinary axles by Cooper at aggregate cost £2044.

They had the dome in the middle of the boiler and a flush firebox. They suffered the usual mishaps for engines of this period. No 134 had a particularly unlucky year in 1878, bursting a tube on the Athlone branch in April and breaking an axle at Roscrea in May. No 99 (later No 135) was supposedly intended for the new Nenagh branch.

There is a reference to four of these engines having been rebuilt as 0-6-0s but it has not been possible to confirm this information. No dimensional details have been traced. The suggested engines and rebuilt dates are Nos 133 (Sep 1868), 134 (Jan 1871), 135 (Sept 1871), 137 (May 1871).

This design was compared by Zerah Colburn with contemporary Beyer Peacock 0-4-2s supplied to the Smyrna & Cassaba Railway, Turkey. It was found to be wanting in steaming ability, valve design and frame construction. It is believed that this criticism was partly instrumental in the replacement of Wakefield and in the re-establishment of the role of Locomotive Superintendent.

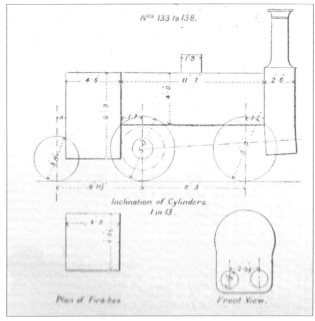

0-4-2 Type XXXII [32]

Note regarding numbering of 0-6-0s

Between 1852 and 1863, locomotive numbers were allocated in chronological order of construction and this sequence was maintained for the most part in allocating 1864 numbers to the goods fleet. However, from the table below, it is apparent that this discipline was ignored in respect of 0-6-0s which were renumbered 139 to 146 within the 1864 exercise, evidently to segment this wheel arrangement from the four-coupled goods types. This change would appear to have been initiated soon after McDonnell's arrival, possibly in advance of the main renumbering scheme. It suggests an early executive decision that future goods locomotive construction would be of the 0-6-0 wheel arrangement only, as was to prove the case until early in the 20th Century.

Type	Built	Wheel arrangement	Original Nos	1864 Nos
XXVIII [28]	Sep 1852	0-4-2	57/ 8	117/ 8
IV [4]	Jul 1853	2-2-2	59	43
XXXIII [33]	Apr/ May 1854	0-6-0	60/ 1	139/ 140
XXX [30]	Oct/ Nov 1854	0-4-2	62/ 3	122/ 3
XXIX [29]	Jul 1855	2-4-0	64-6	119-21
XXXIV [34]	Feb to Apr 1856	0-6-0	67-69	141-143
III [3]	Aug 1855	2-4-0	70/ 71	41/ 2
XXXIV [34]	Oct to Dec 1856	0-6-0	72-74	144-146
XXVII [27]	1856	0-4-2	75	116
VI [6]	Dec 1859	2-2-2	76	44
V [5]	Mar 1858 to Apr 1858	2-2-2	77-79	45-47
VI [6]	Dec 1859	2-2-2	80/ 81	48/ 49
XXXI [31]	Aug 1860 to Mar 1861	0-4-2	82-87	124-129
VI [6]	Aug to Oct 1861	2-2-2	88-90	50-52
XXXI [31]	Mar/ Apr 1862	0-4-2	91-93	130-132
VI [6]	Oct 1862 to Jan 1863	2-2-2	94-96	53-55
XXXII [32]	May 1863 to May 1865	0-4-2	97-102	133-138 §

§ Type XXXII [32]:- Nos 100-102 allocated but not carried; Nos 136-138 applied when built.

| RNC Type: XXXIII [33] | | 0-6-0 | | GSWR Class: n/a |

1864 No Original No	Built	Withdrawn	Comments
139 [60]	Apr 1854	Jun 1874	Last ran Jun 1874; sold to McGowan Mar 1875
140 [61]	May 1854	Jun 1876	Last ran Jun 1876; sold to McGowan Aug 1876 for £240

Designer: Miller/ Wakefield **Built at Inchicore**

Boiler pressure – 120 lb/ sq in Cylinders – 17" x 24" Driving wheels – 5' 0" Wheelbase – 6' 10" + 7' 4 ½"	Heating surfaces: tubes – 1112 sq ft firebox – 85 sq ft grate – not recorded	Tractive effort –11,790 lb Coal capacity – not recorded Water capacity – not recorded Locomotive weight – 28 tons 15 cwt Adhesive weight – 23 tons 4 cwt Max axle loading – 11 tons 14 cwt

These were the GSWR's first six-coupled engines and had the dome in the middle of the boiler and a raised firebox. It seems they were designed as tank engines, but altered to a tender design either during construction or shortly after completion. They were originally intended for banking trains from Cork Glanmire Road station.

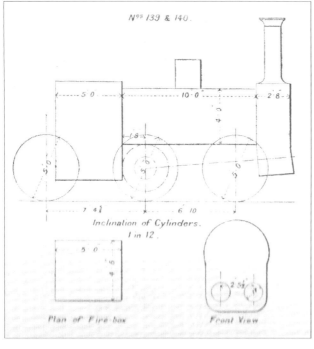

0-6-0 Type XXXIII [33].

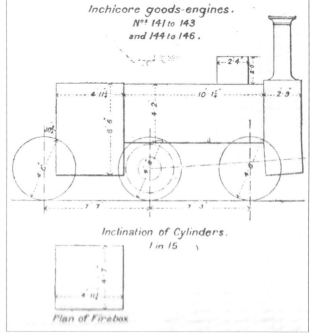

0-6-0 Type XXXIV [34].

| RNC Type: XXXIV [34] | | | 0-6-0/ 0-6-0T | | GSWR Class: n/a |

1864 No [Original No]	Built	Rebuilt	Withdrawn	Comments
141 [67]	Feb 1856	-	Dec 1878	Last ran and withdrawn Dec 1878; sold to McGowan
142 [68]	Mar 1856	-	Jun 1873	Last ran Feb 1873; broken up Nov 1873
143 [69]	Apr 1856	-	Dec 1874	Last ran Dec 1874; Sold to McGowan Mar 1875
144 [72]	Oct 1856	Jun 1868	Mar 1879	Sold to McGowan for £130
145 [73]	Oct 1856	Mar 1868	Dec 1874	Sold to McGowan March 1875 for £130: cylinders to No 131 in 1875
146 [74]	Dec 1856	-	Dec 1877	Last ran Jun 1877; wheels and axles to No 129 Jan 1878

Goods tender engines

Designer: Miller/ Wakefield **Built at Inchicore**

Boiler pressure – 80 lb/ sq in (assumed)	Heating surfaces:	Tractive effort – 7,740 lb
Cylinders – 16" x 24"	tubes – 1112 sq ft	Coal capacity – not recorded
Driving wheels – 4' 6"	firebox – 85 sq ft	Water capacity – not recorded
Wheelbase – 7' 3" + 7' 7"	grate – not recorded	Locomotive weight – 28 tons 15 cwt
		Max axle loading – 11 tons 14 cwt

Rebuilt as 0-6-0T

	Coal capacity – 1 ton 10 cwt
	Water capacity – 820 gal
	Locomotive weight – 36 tons 10 cwt
Locomotive length over buffers - 29' 2"	Max axle loading – 14 tons 14 cwt

As a consequence of the protracted delivery of the Fairbairn engines (Type III [3]) in 1855-6, Inchicore returned to building for its own needs with this class. After this batch, Wakefield reverted to provision of 0-4-2s, possibly as they were considered more flexible for mixed traffic duties. No more six-coupled engines were built until after McDonnell's appointment. These engines had the dome on the front of the boiler and a flush firebox.

RNC Type: XXXV [35] HYBRID and Class 101 origins

McDonnell arrived at Inchicore in 1864 with a reputation as a railway engineer and builder rather than as a locomotive engineer experienced in design and construction. Nevertheless he recognised the magnitude of the challenge to modernise and expand the motive power fleet. Described in Chapter 2 is his interim solution to produce 2-4-0 passenger locomotives using significant components recovered from Sharp 2-2-2s, as analysed in the story of 2-2-2 later 2-4-0 No 16. Goods locomotive development followed a parallel course although here the potential donors for parts had been built in small batches by three commercial manufacturers (Bury, Fairbairn, Grendon and Rothwell) plus Inchicore. The candidates for conversion were all four-coupled, mostly with 5' diameter driving wheels and 15/ 16" x 24" cylinders but dimensional variation among other reusable components probably made the exercise more complex than had been the case when relying solely on Sharp Stewart-built 2-2-2s to create the new 2-4-0s.

The design origin for what eventually became 0-6-0 Class 101 is generally thought to have stemmed from Beyer Peacock (BP) and there is persuasive evidence to support this contention. BP established its business at Gorton Foundry, Manchester in 1855 and soon gained a reputation for reliable, well-built machines. The company actively supplied foreign markets with its first 0-6-0s sold to the Egyptian Government in 1857. Between then and 1860, more 0-6-0s were sold in the UK to the Great Western, Shrewsbury & Hereford and Midland railways plus overseas to the Madras and Victorian railways, and another pair to Egypt.

In 1859, the Danube & Black Sea Railway (DBSR) ordered six 0-6-0s (builder's Nos 120-5) but only took delivery of the first two for service over the newly-built line between Constanza and Cernavoda in what is modern day Romania. Builder's Nos 122-5 were not immediately required by the DBSR; they were spotted by Ramsbottom as for sale on a visit to Gorton Foundry on 28th December 1859. He gained approval for their purchase on 2nd January 1860 on the grounds that they were "very similar in size and type to those we are now making" i.e. class DX which eventually totalled 943 engines. The LNWR then ordered four more (builder's Nos 191-4) which were delivered direct to the DBSR to compensate for the earlier truncated delivery. BP sold a further two almost identical 0-6-0s to the DBSR in 1862.

McDonnell joined the DBSR that same year and these transactions would have alerted him to the generic virtues of the BP product. Coupled with his prior association with the LNWR by way of the Newport, Abergavenny & Hereford Railway, McDonnell would have been well placed to obtain technical support in the creation of the new 0-6-0 class. Despite the external similarity between LNWR Class DX and GSWR Class 101, the former was slightly larger and there were sufficient dimensional differences to discount the supposition that it was the template for the Irish locomotives.

McDonnell started to produce "new" 0-6-0s at Inchicore in 1866 and these took the numbers of 0-4-2s that had been taken out of service. In keeping with practice in the early years of his tenure these locomotives were in the form of hybrids and are known to have used components recovered from the earlier engines. The process would have been helped by all the donor machines having 5' diameter driving wheels and cylinder dimensions of either 15" or 16" x 24".

It is uncertain how many locomotives were hybrids. Judging by the numbering sequences and the nature of the recorded dimensional variations, it seems probable that in chronological order of introduction Nos 112/ 113/ 118/ 103/ 111/ 105/ 110 / 114/ 115 passed through the hybrid phase. RNC specifically nominated only Nos 112/ 113/ 118 as having been hybrids but the authors opine that the next six locomotives that emerged from Inchicore were also in this category. The rationale for this assertion is detailed below.

Acknowledging McDonnell's relative inexperience in locomotive design and construction at that point, it seems probable that he relied on the drawings that Beyer Peacock prepared for their series production (which started with No 147 in May 1867) to use as a template on which to base his conversion work. If this was the case, then the hybrids might have differed externally from the newly-built Beyer Peacock machines.

Construction in the period 1866-1869 of Hybrids that eventually became part of Class 101 is summarised as follows:

"New" 0-6-0 introduced	No	Original Builder	Original Type	Cyl	Year 0-4-2 Withdrawn
Jun 1866	112	Rothwell	XXVI [26]	16" x 24"	1865
Dec 1866	113	Rothwell	XXVI [26]	16" x 24"	1865
May 1867	118	Inchicore	XXVIII [28]	15" x 24"	1866
Aug 1867	103	Bury	XXIII [23]	15" or 16" x 24"	1865
Sep 1867	111	Grendon	XXV [25]	15" x 24"	1867
May 1868	105	Bury	XXIV [24]	16" x 24"	1868
Jul 1868	110	Grendon	XXV [25]	15" x 24"	1867
Aug 1869	114	Rothwell	XXVI [26]	16" x 24"	1869
Oct 1869	115	Rothwell	XXVI [26]	16" x 24"	1868

Regarding the earlier histories of locomotives carrying these numbers :

No 112: RNC states that this was a hybrid 0-6-0 introduced in June 1866. However, this date conflicts with his own notes which state that this locomotive's frames, cylinders, crank axles, driving wheels, motion were installed in an 0-6-0 in November 1872.

No 113: Introduced December 1866, otherwise as for No 112 except that the notes indicate that the components were installed in an 0-6-0 in December 1872

No 118: Modified frames, crank axle and one straight axle, and four wheels were apparently used in the "new 0-6-0" until April 1870, implying that its recycled parts were then replaced with new components.

No 103: Despite RNC's statement that this was a hybrid, records conflict. Some reports state that Type XXIII [23] Bury 0-4-2 No 103 was sold to the Cork & Bandon Railway as their No 8 (later No 1) in Dec 1865 for £450 (which appears to accord with the prevailing market value for a large working engine). As sale of a complete working locomotive, no surplus parts would have been recovered for the hybrid exercise. However, it is also claimed that the CBR actually purchased Bury 0-4-2 No 108 whereas elsewhere this locomotive is reported as sold to the Whitehaven Colliery in England, apparently for use as a stationary boiler in 1876. It is thus not possible to determine the likely source of components used in the creation of Hybrid 0-6-0 No 103.

No 111: Allowing for uncertainties over the withdrawal date, Grendon Type XXV [25] was definitely out of service in the period before the 0-6-0 version was delivered.

No 105: No details recorded.

No 110: No details recorded.

No 114 (short wheelbase): The wheels (with 1866-vintage tyres) were reportedly transferred to No 123 in July 1869 but unfortunately this locomotive was not built until July 1881

No 115 (short wheelbase): New tyres were fitted to this locomotive in March 1868, shortly before its earliest possible withdrawal date. These wheels were apparently fitted No 109 when built in January 1877. There is no record of what parts from the 0-4-2 were used in creation of 0-6-0 No 115.

The remaining short wheelbase locomotives, Nos 155 & 156, were introduced as new engines. It appears that production of new standard Class 101 locomotives at Inchicore (as opposed to hybrid conversions) commenced with No 159 in September 1871.

Goods tender engines

RNC Type: XXXV [35]   **0-6-0**   **GSWR Class 101**
Designer: Beyer Peacock/ McDonnell

A total of 107 locomotives were built that became Class 101, Ireland's numerically largest. This table summarises construction and withdrawal dates by order of running numbers:

No	Built	W'drawn	No	Built	W'drawn	No	Built	W'drawn
101	Sep 1882	1962	131	Dec 1882	1963	165	Aug 1872	1945
102	Jan 1873	1962	132	Dec 1888	1965	166	Aug 1872	1963
103 1st	Aug 1867	1886	133	Jun 1885	1963	167	Mar 1873	1960
103 2nd	Aug 1889	1957	134	Jun 1885	1961	168	Apr 1873	1962
104	Jan 1873	1965	135	Sep 1885	1957	169	Mar 1874	1928
105 1st	May 1868	1895	136	Dec 1888	1962	170	Apr 1874	1963
105 2nd	Jun 1896	1963	137	Dec 1888	1960	171	Jul 1874	1961
106	Jan 1874	1964	138	Dec 1888	1962	172	Aug 1874	1964
107	Feb 1881	1957	139	Apr 1881	1961	173	Sep 1874	1933
108	Feb 1875	1959	140	May 1881	1961	174	Nov 1874	1953
109	Jan 1877	1964	141	May 1881	1959	175	Aug 1873	1956
110 1st	Jul 1868	1890	142	Mar 1875	1928	176	Aug 1873	1959
110 2nd	Dec 1890	1963	143	Dec 1877	1960	177	Dec 1873	1927
111 1st	Sep 1867	1888	144	Feb 1878	1954	178	Dec 1873	1926
111 2nd	Mar 1891	1963	145	Feb 1878	1926	179	Apr 1875	1963
112	Jun 1866	1929	146	Feb 1878	1955	180	May 1875	1928
113	Dec 1866	1930	147 1st	May 1867	1888	181	Aug 1879	1959
114 1st	Aug 1869	1885	147 2nd	May 1891	1956	182	Sep 1879	1962
114 2nd	Aug 1889	1961	148	Jun 1867	1953	183	Jan 1880	1965
115	Oct 1869	1929	149 1st	Jun 1867	1887	184	Feb 1880	1963 §
116	Aug 1896	1964	149 2nd	Oct 1889	1962	185	Aug 1879	1959
117	Mar 1874	1930	150	Jul 1867	1957	186	Nov 1879	1964 §
118 1st	May 1867	1890	151	Mar 1868	1965	187	Mar 1882	1957
118 2nd	May 1891	1966	152	Mar 1868	1959	188	Jul 1882	1959
119	Jan 1877	1962	153	Mar 1868	1954	189	May 1881	1923
120	Feb 1877	1955	154	Mar 1868	1962	190	May 1881	1963
121	Feb 1877	1963	155	Feb 1871	1930	191	Oct 1885	1962
122	Sep 1882	1963	156	Apr 1871	1961	192	Sep 1898	1956
123	Jul 1881	1963	157	Mar 1872	1963	193	Sep 1898	1963
124	Sep 1881	1965	158	Apr 1872	1957	194	Nov 1898	1959
125	Oct 1881	1965	159	Sep 1871	1949	195	Dec 1898	1965
126	Nov 1881	1959	160	Oct 1871	1955	196	May 1899	1961
127	Feb 1882	1963	161	Oct 1871	1963	197	Jun 1899	1961
128	Mar 1882	1963	162	Dec 1871	1963	198	Jun 1899	1965
129	Sep 1889	1940	163	Jul 1872	1955	199	Nov 1899	1954
130	Dec 1882	1965	164	Aug 1872	1963		§ Preserved	

Locomotives of the Great Southern & Western Railway

Eight locomotives were withdrawn early and replaced by new locomotives carrying the same numbers. In contrast to the normal practice of rebuilding and renewal, it has been confirmed that in each of these cases the first machine was genuinely withdrawn and dismantled. The replacement was therefore a new locomotive. The numbers concerned (distinguished by 1st and 2nd) were 103/ 105/ 110/ 111/ 114/ 115/ 147/ 149.

Chronological order of construction

No	Built	New boiler	4' 4" boiler	Wdn	No	Built	New boiler	4' 4" boiler	Wdn	No	Built	New boiler	4' 4" boiler	Wdn
112	1866	1889	1911	1929	178	1873	1894	1912	1926	126	1881		1904	1959
113	1866	1889	1903	1930	106	1874	1894	1921	1964	127	1882	1900	1914	1963
118	1867			1890	117	1874	1893	1904	1930	128	1882		1914	1963
147	1867			1888	169	1874	1890	1921	1928	187	1882		1928	1957
148	1867	1892	1907	1953	170	1874	1890	1917	1963	188	1882	1899	1923	1959
149	1867			1887	171	1874	1896	1929	1961	101	1882		1924	1962
150	1867		1925	1957	172	1874	1897	1906	1964	122	1882		1901	1963
103	1867			1886	173	1874	1893	1902	1933	130	1882		1902	1965
111	1867			1888	174	1874	1889	1929	1953	131	1882		1909	1963
151	1868	1883	1904	1965	108	1875	1897	1922	1959	133	1885		1904	1963
152	1868	1882	1901	1959	142	1875	1893	1907	1928	134	1885		1922	1961
153	1868	1890	1904	1954	179	1875	1894	1920	1963	135	1885		1903	1957
154	1868	1890	1915	1962	180	1875	1893	1912	1928	191	1885		1914	1962
105	1868	1885		1895	109	1877	1896	1912	1964	132	1888		1905	1965
110	1868			1890	119	1877	1897	1928	1962	136	1888		1905	1962
114	1869			1885	120	1877	1896	1920	1955	137	1888		1902	1960
115	1869	1889		1929	121	1877	1896	1916	1963	138	1888		1903	1962
155	1871	1882		1929	143	1877	1889	1906	1960	103	1889		1921	1957
156	1871	1889		1961	144	1878	1897	1910	1954	114	1889		1907	1961
159	1871	1889	1912	1949	145	1878		1922	1926	129	1889		1907	1940
160	1871	1891	1907	1955	146	1878	1895	1912	1955	149	1889		1903	1962
161	1871	1886	1925-7	1963	181	1879	1897	1920	1959	110	1890		1922	1963
162	1871	1891	1909	1963	185	1879	1898	1929	1959	111	1891		1913	1963
157	1872	1889	1911-2	1963	182	1879	1897	1925	1962	118	1891		1927	1966
158	1872	1889	1905	1957	186	1879	1898	1910	1964	147	1891		1909	1956
163	1872		1923	1955	183	1880		1929	1965	105	1896		1910	1963
164	1872	1890	1924	1963	184	1880	1899	1921	1963	116	1896		1908	1964
165	1872	1891	1921	1945	107	1881		1919	1957	192	1898		1908	1956
166	1872	1892	1923	1963	139	1881	1898	1909	1961	193	1898		1910	1963
102	1873	1892	1904	1962	140	1881	1894	1909	1961	194	1898		1908	1959
104	1873	1892	1908	1965	141	1881	1894	1923	1959	195	1898		1909	1965
167	1873	1895	1918	1960	189	1881		1904	1923	196	1899		1911	1961
168	1873	1892	1920	1962	190	1881		1916	1963	197	1899		1912	1961
175	1873	1892	1924	1956	123	1881	1899	1909	1963	198	1899		1911	1965
176	1873	1891	1922	1959	124	1881		1901	1965	199	1899		1913	1954
177	1873	1892	1921	1927	125	1881		1915	1965					

Some of the numbers were used twice i.e. following early withdrawals. See previous table for locomotive identities. All were built at Inchicore excepting for the following:

Goods tender engines

Beyer Peacock:

Builder's No	Running No
747, 748	147 (1st), 148
749, 750	149, 150
780-783	151-154
1251, 1252	177, 178
2029, 2030	189, 190

Sharp, Stewart:

Builder's No	Running No
2155-2158	163-166
2310, 2311	175, 176
2837, 2838	185, 186

It was inevitable that with a class of 107 locomotives built over a period of 33 years and which survived largely intact until 1925, there should be detail variations among individual engines. Most important was the re-boilering programme. The GSWR fitted the majority with replacements to the same leading dimensions as the originals, and then followed up with a programme of enlargement in the form of the 4' 4" diameter boiler. Replacement years are believed to be accurate except where noted below. The years quoted in the chronological table above for boiler changes are drawn from the RNC Archives, in some instances other sources quote different dates as listed below:

Boiler renewals to original dimensions:

No	Alternative date	No	Date
163	1889	128	1901
150	1895	187	1901
190	1898	191	1903
101	1898	183	1904
131	1898	107	1904
125	1901		

4' 4" diameter boiler renewals:

No	Alternative date	No	Alternative date	No	Alternative date
126	1901	121	1913	168	1921
147	1907	167	1916	171	1924
178	1909	127	1917	119	1926
198	1910	157	1918	174	1927
123	1911	185	1918	183	1927
191	1911	190	1918	187	1927
199	1912	120	1921		
104	1913	150	1921		

Sixty-seven were fitted by the Great Southern Railways with the Type Z superheated Belpaire boiler which extended working careers and improved performances. This programme lies beyond the remit of this work; reference should be made to *Locomotives of the GSR* for details.

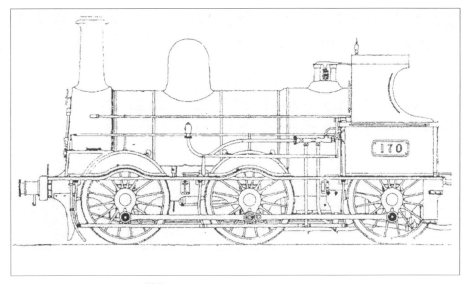

0-6-0 Type XXXV [35] No 170, as built in 1874.

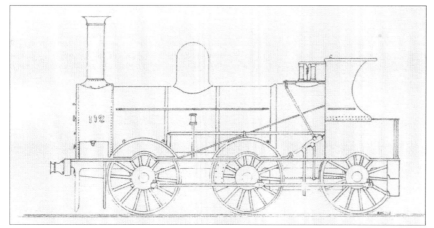

Drawing of Hybrid Type XXXV [35] No 112 (later part of Class 101).

No 112's origins lay at least in part with Type XXVI [26] 0-4-2 built by Rothwell in 1850. It was rebuilt in Jun 1866 as the first of Hybrid Type XXXV [35] (as seen here) although some components might have been used in another rebuilding exercise in 1872. Its original 16" x 24" cylinders were later enlarged to 17" and then 18" diameter. It was reboilered in 1889 and again in 1911 when it received a 4' 4" boiler.
It was finally withdrawn in 1929, although it seems likely that by then little of the original engine remained.
LGRP

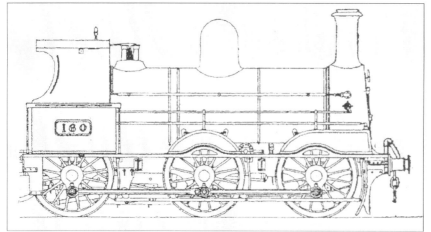

0-6-0 Type XXXV [35] No 160, as rebuilt 4' 4" boiler in 1907.

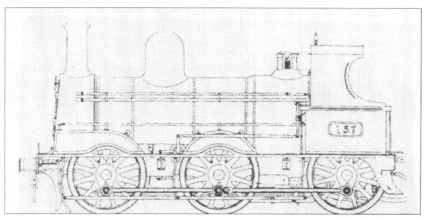

0-6-0 Type XXXV [35] No 137, as built in 1888.

Goods tender engines

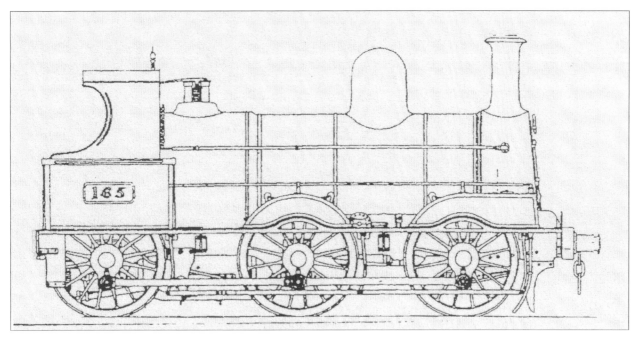

0-6-0 Type XXXV [35] No 165 rebuilt as a compound locomotive in 1891.

As built by Inchicore:

Boiler pressure – 140 lb/ sq in
    [later – 150 lb/ sq in]
Cylinders – 17" x 24"
Driving wheels – 5' 0" [see comments below]
Wheelbase – 7' 3" + 8' 3"
Locomotive length – 24' 10"
	Heating surfaces:
	tubes – 856 sq ft
	firebox – 96 sq ft
	grate – 17.5 sq ft
		Tractive effort – 13,760 lb
		    [later – 14,740 lb]
		Locomotive weight – 32 tons 4 cwt
		Max axle loading – 11 tons 14 cwt

The Riley record and other sources confirm that the driving wheel diameter initially was 5' 0" as with the four-coupled locomotives that on withdrawal donated wheels, cylinders and other parts for the early Inchicore-built class members. However as discussed in Chapter 2, at the time of McDonnell's arrival and for some years thereafter, the GSWR trackwork was in poor condition, accounting for an unacceptable number of breakages in springs, wheels and axles. Creation of stronger driving wheels through fitting of thicker rims and tyres was an obvious measure against equipment failures and from the 1870s, 5' 1¼" diameter wheels were introduced although the official size is more often quoted as 5' 2".

Beyer Peacock-built locomotives (Nos 147/ 148/ 149 1st/ 150-154):

	Heating surfaces: tubes – 922 sq ft firebox – 95 sq ft grate – 19.6 sq ft	Weight – 29 tons 15 cwt (empty) Max axle loading – 11 tons 6 cwt

Beyer Peacock-built locomotives (Nos 177/ 178/ 189/ 190):

	Heating surfaces: tubes – 856 sq ft firebox – 93 sq ft grate – 17.6 sq ft	

NB It is unclear why these dimensions are less than for the earlier BP-built locomotives.

Inchicore-built short wheelbase Nos 114 1st/ 115/ 155/ 156:

Boiler pressure –140 lb/ sq in	*Heating surfaces*	*Tractive effort – 12,190 lb [16" x 24" cylinders]*
Cylinders [114, 115] – 16" x 24"	*tubes – 846 sq ft*	*– 13,760 lb [17" x 24"]*
[later – 17" x 24"]	*firebox – 86 sq ft*	*– 15,420 lb [18" x 24"]*
[155, 156] – 17" x 24"	*grate – 17.5 sq ft*	*Locomotive weight – 30 tons 4 cwt*
[later – 18" x 24"]		*Max axle loading – 11 tons 6 cwt*
Wheelbase – 7' 3" + 7' 9"		
Locomotive length – unknown		

NB Heating surfaces, weight and axle loading are estimates as records are unclear.

These engines had a shorter firebox, hence reduced rear coupled wheelbase. In view of McDonnell's commitment to standardisation, production of four short wheelbase class members is a curiosity. They appear to have resulted from a conscious deign decision, having been built consecutively within the Class 101 construction programme. It is believed that they were required for a route that had sharp curves (e.g. Mallow-Tralee but this is speculative).

The fixed wheelbases of preceding four-coupled goods locomotives were in the 7' 3" to 8' 3" range (assuming an element of side play in the carrying axles). By comparison, a Class 101 with a coupled wheelbase of 15' 6" was substantially more rigid. Pending track modifications, a 6" reduction might have been a short-term solution. No 114 2nd was built with the standard wheel base.

0-6-0 Type XXXV [35] Class 101 No 119. *Hamish Stephenson Collection*

New construction from July 1874:

Boiler pressure –150 lb/ sq in	*Heating surfaces:*	*Tractive effort – 15,990 lb*
Cylinders – 18" x 24"	*tubes – 856 sq ft*	*Locomotive weight – 30 tons 4 cwt*
Driving wheels – 5' 2"	*firebox – 96 sq ft*	*Max axle loading – 11 tons 6 cwt*
	grate – 17.5 sq ft	

This change was accompanied by a programme to up-rate earlier locomotives. It was reported that by 1903 only Nos 104/ 152/ 153/ 159/ 167/ 176/ 177 were still working with 17" diameter cylinders.

Goods tender engines

Revised dimensions following fitting of new boilers from 1882 onwards:

Boiler pressure –160 lb/ sq in	Heating surfaces:	Tractive effort – 17,060 lb
Cylinders – 18" x 24"	tubes – 764 sq ft	Locomotive weight – 33 tons 8 cwt
Driving wheels – 5' 2"	firebox – 96 sq ft	Max axle loading – 12 tons 2 cwt
Wheelbase – 7' 3" + 8' 3"	grate – 17.5 sq ft	

Revised dimensions following fitting of 4' 4" diameter boiler from 1901 onwards:

Boiler pressure –160 lb/ sq in	Heating surfaces:	Tractive effort – 17,060 lb
Cylinders – 18" x 24"	tubes – 925 sq ft	Locomotive weight – 35 tons 16 cwt
Driving wheels – 5' 2"	firebox – 116 sq ft	Max axle loading – 13 tons 0 cwt
Wheelbase – 7' 3" + 8' 3"	grate – 19.3 sq ft	

No 165 as a 2-cylinder compound:

Boiler pressure –150 lb/ sq in	Heating surfaces:	Locomotive weight – 34 tons 10 cwt
Cylinders – 18"/ 26" x 24"	tubes – 925 sq ft	Max axle loading – 13 tons 2 cwt
Driving wheels – 5' 2"	firebox – 116 sq ft	
Wheelbase – 7' 3" + 8' 3"	grate – 19.3 sq ft	

This modification proved unsuccessful; the locomotive worked as a compound between 1891 and 1896; see Chapter 2 for details.

0-6-0 Type XXXV [35] Class 101 No 158. *Ken Nunn*

0-6-0 Type XXXV [35] Class 101 No 187. *Locomotive Publishing Co*

There were numerous dimensional variations among this class during GSWR days. The principal differences when constructed, as categorised by RNC, were:

A. Hybrid locomotives: Because of their origins, these locomotives had varied detailed dimensions, details of which are not available. Nos 112, 113, 118 (1st) were definitely hybrids and as discussed above, possibly Nos 103, 105(1st), 110(1st), 111(1st), 114 (1st), 115.

B. The Beyer Peacock engines were built with 1 1/8" thick frames as opposed to the 1" standard. They were also fitted with 5' 7" long fireboxes with accounted for the larger grate surface area. BP engines were: Nos 147(1st)/ 148/ 149(1st)/ 150-154 [8 locomotives].

C. These engines had similar dimensions to B. but with 1" frames and 15" diameter cylinders. Cylinders were increased to 17" diameter in 1870/ 1. Locomotives Nos 103(1st)/ 111.

D. Nos 105/ 110 were built as for C. except for 17" diameter cylinders; those on No 110 were increased to 18" in 1877.

E. Nos 114/ 114/ 155/ 156 were short wheelbase locomotives built with 5' 1" fireboxes and 16" cylinders. Larger cylinders were fitted as follows: 17" to No 114 [1874] and to No 115 [1876].

F. Nos 155/156 which had been built with 17" cylinders; they were fitted with 18" cylinders as follows: No 155 [1878] and No 156 [1889].

G. These were built as a development of category F but with standard wheelbase, lighter frames and a flat grate. In order of construction, they were Nos 159-162/ 157/ 158/ 163-166/ 102/ 104/ 167/ 168/ 175-178/ 106/ 117/ 169/ 170 [22 locomotives].

H. Similar to category G. but built with 18" cylinders. In order of construction: Nos 171-174/ 108/ 142/ 179/ 180/ 109/ 119-121/ 143-146/ 181/ 185/ 182/ 186/ 183/ 184/ 107 [23 locomotives].

I. Similar to category H. but built with steel boiler. In order of construction: Nos 139-141/ 189/ 190/ 127 [6 locomotives].

J. Similar to category I. but built with steel frames. Nos 123-126 [4 locomotives]

K. As category H. but with deeper iron frames. In order of construction: Nos 128/ 187/ 188/ 101/ 122/ 130/ 131/ 133 [8 locomotives].

L. As category K. but with steel frames. In order of construction: Nos 134/ 135/ 191/ 132/ 136-138/ 103

(2nd)/ 114(2nd)/ 129/ 149(2nd)/ 110(2nd)/ 111(2nd)/ 118 (2nd)/ 147(2nd)/ 105(2nd)/ 116 [17 locomotives].

M. Exactly as category L. but with single slide bars. Nos 192-199 [8 locomotives].

In addition, three tube sizes and differing numbers of tubes were fitted. From 1866 until January 1873, 2" diameter tubes were used (and also on Beyer Peacock engines Nos 177 & 178 built December 1873). From April 1873, 1¾" tubes were fitted (Nos 168 to 199). No 167 was unique in being built in March 1873 with 234 x 1½ " tubes. All these were as new; changes were probable later in their careers. Numbers of tubes fitted varied as follows: 2" x 157/ 158/ 159/ 160/ 172/ 174/ 175; 1¾ x 173/ 175/ 185/ 200.

--- o O o ---

This class's accreditation as a standard type and its active career almost to the end of steam on Corás Iompair Eireann bears testimony to its competence and versatility. The GSWR had introduced two groups of 0-6-0s for goods work before reverting to 0-4-2s but the arrival of what eventually became Class 101 effectively declared four-coupled goods locomotives an obsolete concept. Anticipating possible problems with the longer coupled wheelbase, the new 0-6-0s were fitted with thinner flanges on the centre driving wheels but they quickly proved their operational flexibility. They enjoyed a very wide sphere of availability which allowed them access to virtually all routes and most sidings. Although intended primarily to use Welsh coal, they proved excellent steamers on less suitable fuel and capable of handling loaded 45-wagon goods train (aggregate weight *circa* 500 tons). They excelled both on main line goods services and in working over difficult lines such as that to Valentia Harbour.

With growing class numbers, the range of duties expanded and they matured into genuine mixed traffic machines. They were called upon as assisting locomotives for heavier main line passenger trains while becoming favourites for secondary and branch passenger services. Apart from the eight members withdrawn in the 19th Century, the Class remained intact for the remainder of the GSWR's existence except for a Civil War Casuality No 189 at Ballyvoyle on 31st January 1923.

0-6-0 Type XXXV [35] Class 101 No 128 (4-4-0 Type 14 No 63 to the left). *Locomotive Publishing Co*

Locomotives of the Great Southern & Western Railway

RNC Type: XXXVI [36] later XXXV [35]   0-6-0   **GSWR Class 200 later 101**

No	Introduced	Withdrawn	No	Introduced	Withdrawn
200	Feb 1903	Nov 1960	242	Dec 1902	May 1957
223	Feb 1903	Nov 1960	243	Jan 1903	Nov 1955
229	Mar 1903	1960	253	1903	1963
232	Mar 1903	1963	254	1903	May 1961
240	Oct 1902	Dec 1957	255	1903	1964
241	Dec 1902	Aug 1957	256	1903	Oct 1959

Designer: Coey   **Built at Inchicore**

Boiler pressure – 160 lb/ sq in *Heating surfaces:* *Tractive effort – 17,120 lb*
Cylinders – 18" x 24" *tubes – 925 sq ft* *Coal/ water capacities – refer Chapter 9*
Driving wheels – 5' 1¾" *firebox – 116 sq ft* *Locomotive weight – 35 tons 16 cwt*
Wheelbase – 7' 3" + 8' 3" *grate – 19.3 sq ft* *Max axle loading – 13 tons 0 cwt*

When introduced, this type was identified as Class 200 being essentially a standard Class 101 fitted with larger 4' 4" diameter boiler and a modified cab.

This boiler was later fitted to many of the older locomotives, and Class 200 was in due course assimilated into Class 101. There is a report that No 223 was rebuilt in 1923 but details are unknown.

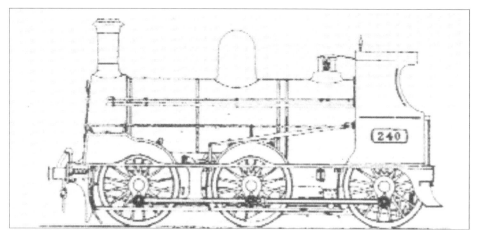

0-6-0 Type XXXVI [36] Class 200 as built.

0-6-0 Type XXXVI [36] Class 200 No 232.

RNC Type: XXXVII & XLII [37 & 42] 0-6-0 GSWR Class 351

No	Introduced	Withdrawn	Comments
249	Apr 1912	1963	
250	May 1912	1963	
251	May 1912	1964	
252	Jun 1912	Mar 1961	
351	Nov 1903	1964	
352	Dec 1903	Jun 1955	
353	Dec 1903	1931	Withdrawn following collision at Monasterevan
354	Dec 1903	1962	

Designer: Coey **Built at Inchicore**

Nos 249-52 (Type XLII [42]) as built:

Boiler pressure – 160 lb/ sq in *Cylinders – 18" x 26"* *Driving wheels – 5' 1¾"* *Wheelbase – 7' 7" + 8' 6"* *Locomotive length – 27' 11¾"*	*Heating surfaces:* *tubes – 1040 sq ft* *firebox – 118 sq ft* *grate – 20.4 sq ft*	*Tractive effort – 18,560 lb* *Coal/ water capacities – refer Chapter 9* *Locomotive weight – 45 tons 1 cwt* *Max axle loading –16 tons 3 cwt*

Nos 351-4 (Type XXXVII [37]) as built:

Locomotive length – 26' 9	*Heating surfaces:* *tubes – 1129 sq ft* *firebox – 118 sq ft* *grate – 20.4 sq ft*	*Locomotive weight – 43 tons 16 cwt* *Max axle loading –15 tons 12 cwt*

Construction of the 1903 batch followed closely upon completion of Class 200 (Type XXXVI [36]). They incorporated cylinders and boiler similar to those used in 4-4-0 Class 310, and with a splasher style resembling that used in Class 200. They represented a significant increase in size and weight, at the expense of route availability and seemed to have been confined to mainline goods duties on the Dublin-Cork main line, and also on seasonal beet trains over the Rosslare route. They replaced older members of Class 101 which were then transferred to the recently acquired ex-WCIR and ex-WLWR sections. They had a surprising turn of speed for a goods design and could handle lighter passenger trains at speeds up to 50 mph. They were nevertheless officially regarded as fitted with poor valve gear, making them generally sluggish and heavy on coal. The four added by Maunsell in 1912 were mechanically similar except for raised running plates over the coupling rods, larger cabs and extended smokeboxes.

Post-GSWR, these locomotives were rebuilt, some more than once; refer to *Locomotives of the GSR*.

0-6-0 Type XXXVII [37] Class 351 as rebuilt in GSR days with Belpaire boiler. This photograph shows the earlier pattern of valences and splashers used on the first four members of Class 351.
P McKeown via Charles Friel

0-6-0 Type XLII [42] Class 249. The four locomotives built by Maunsell differed in the raised running plate over the driving wheels, a style that would be repeated on his own 0-6-0 design (Type XLIII of 1913).

RNC Type: XXXVIII [38]   **0-6-0 later 2-6-0**   **GSWR Class 355**

No	Introduced	Makers' No	Withdrawn	Comments
355	Nov 1903	15943	1928	To 2-6-0 1907; rebuilt 1914 ±
356	Nov 1903	15944	Mar 1957	To 2-6-0 1908; rebuilt 1925
357	Dec 1903	15945	Feb 1960	To 2-6-0 by 1907
358	Dec 1903	15946	Mar 1957	To 2-6-0 1907
359	Dec 1903	15947	Dec 1959	To 2-6-0 1908
360	Dec 1903	15948	Jun 1955	To 2-6-0 1906; rebuilt 1921 ±
361	Dec 1903	15949	Oct 1959	To 2-6-0 1907; rebuilt 1923 §

Designer: Coey   **Built by North British Locomotive Co**

As built:

Boiler pressure – 160 lb/ sq in
Cylinders – 19" x 26"
Driving wheels – 5' 1¾"
Wheelbase – 8' 0" + 9' 0"
Locomotive length over buffers - 31' 3¾"

Heating surfaces:
tubes – 1403 sq ft
firebox – 132 sq ft
grate – 24.8 sq ft

Tractive effort – 20,670 lb
Coal/ water capacities – refer Chapter 9
Locomotive weight – 49 tons 3 cwt (full)
Axle loadings –
Leading – 17 tons 11 cwt
Driving – 17 tons 3 cwt
Trailing – 14 tons 9 cwt

As converted to 2-6-0:

Nos 356-361 [No 355 had smokebox extended by 15 inches at this rebuild]
Pony wheels – 3' 0"
Wheelbase – 5' 0" + 8' 0" + 9' 0"

Heating surfaces:
tubes – 1318 sq ft
firebox – 132 sq ft
grate – 24.8 sq ft

Locomotive weight – 52 tons 15 cwt
[53 tons 7 cwt]
Axle loadings –
Pony – 6 tons 11 cwt [6 tons 13 cwt]
Leading – 14 tons 4 cwt [14 tons 8 cwt]
Driving – 16 tons 0 cwt [15 tons 8 cwt]
Trailing – 16 tons 0 cwt [16 tons 18 cwt]

Goods tender engines

± As rebuilt with Class 368 saturated boiler:

Boiler pressure – 180 lb/ sq in	Heating surfaces tubes – 1416 sq ft firebox – 138.5 sq ft	Tractive effort – 23,255 lb

§ As rebuilt with Belpaire saturated boiler:

Boiler pressure – 180 lb/ sq in	Heating surfaces: - tubes – 1498 sq ft - firebox – 139 sq ft	Locomotive weight – 57 tons 2 cwt Axle loadings Pony – 8 tons 10 cwt Leading – 15 tons 12 cwt Driving – 16 tons 10 cwt Leading – 16 tons 10 cwt

Due to the prolonged strike at Inchicore, these locomotives were ordered from North British but the leading axle loading exceeded the 16 tons maximum stipulated by the Civil Engineer; there was also a propensity to derailment. These problems were solved by rebuilding No 360 as a 2-6-0 and the remainder followed suit. It is unclear why the tube surfaces should have been reduced with the rebuilding; perhaps weight constraint was a factor.

No 356 was fitted with a Bissell truck in December 1925 resulting in a modified wheelbase of 6' 6" + 8' 0" + 9' 0". No 355 acquired an extended smokebox, possibly at the 1914 rebuilding.

0-6-0 Type XXXVII [38] Class 355 showing the original front-end heavy form in which these locomotives were supplied.

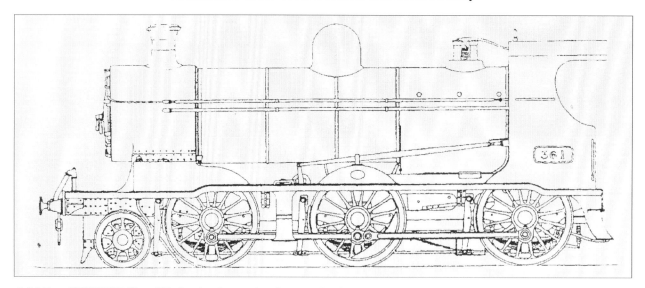

2-6-0 Type XXXVII [38] Class 355 showing the results of conversion from the original 0-6-0 design, undertaken in 1906-8.

2-6-0 Type XXXIX [39] No 359 at Cork.

RNC Type: XXXIX [39]				4-6-0			GSWR Class 362
No	**Introduced**	**Modified §**	**Withdrawn**	**No**	**Introduced**	**Modified §**	**Withdrawn**
362	Dec 1905	Apr-18	1928	365	Dec 1905	May-17	1928
363	Dec 1905	Jul-16	1928	366	Jun 1907	Oct-16	1931
364	Dec 1905	Sep-18	1928	367	Jun 1907	Oct-17	1928

§ Date provided with extended smokebox

Designer: Coey   **Built at Inchicore**

Weights as built; post modification weights in brackets [ ]:
Boiler pressure – 160 lb/ sq in   *Heating surfaces:*   *Tractive effort – 21,220 lb*
Cylinders – 19¼" x 26"   *tubes – 1466.7 sq ft*   *Locomotive weight – 57 tons 0 cwt [57 tons 10 cwt]*
Bogie wheels – 3' 0"   *firebox – 133 sq ft*   *Axle loadings:*
Driving wheels – 5' 1¾"   *grate – 24.8 sq ft*   *Bogie –   12 tons 18 cwt [12 tons 18 cwt]*
                                                                         Leading coupled – 14 tons 9 cwt   [14 tons 17 cwt]
Wheelbase – 5' 3" + 5' 1½" + 6' 9" + 7' 9"   *Centre coupled –   15 tons 11 cwt [14 tons 18 cwt]*
Locomotive length over buffers - 26' 9¾"   *Trailing coupled – 14 tons 2 cwt   [14 tons 17 cwt]*
.   *Coal/ water capacities – refer Chapter 9*

This was Ireland's first 4-6-0 design and when built they were the largest locomotives at work on the island. They were a source of pride to the GSWR and No 366 was displayed at the 1907 Dublin Exhibition. Inclusion of the leading bogie was intended to provide a powerful engine without exceeding the 16 ton axle load limit that had proved so problematic with Class 355 (Type XXXVIII [38]). Cylinders and coupled axles were similar to Class 355, with drive onto the middle coupled axle. Unfortunately, the class proved too light on the bogie and also prone to derailment. They were notorious for rough riding; footplate crews with false teeth were said to remove their dentures before taking them out on the road. They were supposedly nick-named "Long Toms."

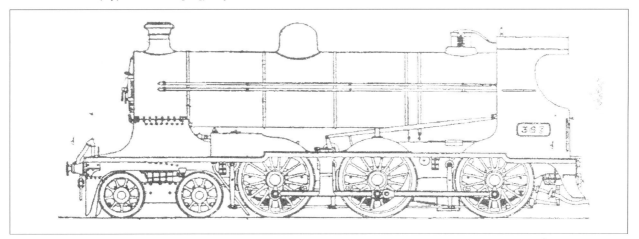

4-6-0 Type XXXIX [39] Class 362 as built.

Locomotives of the Great Southern & Western Railway

RNC Type: XL [40] 0-6-0 **GSWR Class 211**

No	Introduced as 0-6-2T	Makers No	Rebuilt as 0-6-0	Withdrawn
211	Dec 1903	16021	1907	1949
212	Dec 1903	16022	1907	1951

Designer: Coey **Built by North British Locomotive Co**

Boiler pressure – 160 lb/ sq in	*Heating surfaces:*	*Tractive effort – 22,020 lbs*
Cylinders – 18" x 26"	*tubes – 1129 sq ft*	*Coal/ water capacities – refer Chapter 9*
Driving wheels – 4' 6½"	*firebox – 118 sq ft*	*Locomotive weight – 44 tons 0 cwt*
Wheelbase – 7' 7" + 8' 6"	*grate – 20.4 sq ft*	*Max axle loading – 15 tons 3 cwt*

These locomotives formed part of an order of four 0-6-2Ts (Type LXII [62]) for the Drumcondra link line. Proving too heavy, two were rebuilt at Inchicore as tender engines. Although powerful, they were heavy on coal and water, and their small driving wheels limited their use to goods duties on hilly routes such as Waterford-Mallow-Tralee. They also worked the Limerick-Waterford night goods for many years.

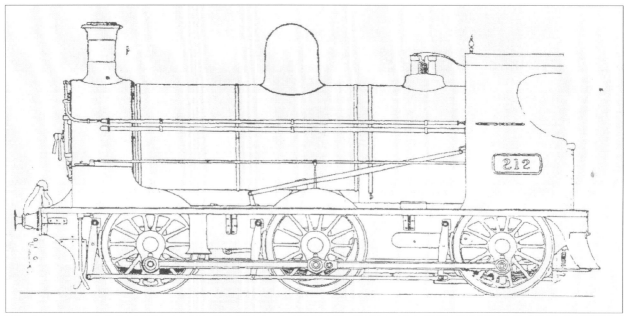

0-6-0 Type XL [40] Class 211 as rebuilt from 0-6-2T Type LXII [62], with extra plating to reduce cab-side cut-out. *LGRP*

Goods tender engines

RNC Type: XLI [41]		2-6-0	GSWR Class 368
No	**Introduced**	**Rebuilt**	**Withdrawn**
368	Sep 1909	-	1928
369	Sep 1909	-	Mar 1957
370	Sep 1909	-	Mar 1957
371	Sep 1909	1923 §	1928

Designer: Coey   **Built at Inchicore**

Boiler pressure – 160 lb/ sq in Cylinders – 19" x 26" Pony wheels – 3' 0" wheels – 5' 1¾" Wheelbase – 5' 9" + 7' 3" + 8' 9" Locomotive length – 31' 3¾"	Heating surfaces: tubes – 1446.5 sq ft firebox – 138.5 sq ft grate – 24.8 sq ft	Tractive effort – 20,670 lb Coal/ water capacities – refer Chapter 9 Locomotive weight – 53 tons 1 cwt Driving Adhesive weight – 44 tons 18 cwt Max axle loading – 15 tons 11 cwt

§ Rebuilt with alternative saturated Belpaire boiler and extended cab

Boiler pressure – 180 lb/ sq in	Heating surfaces: tubes – 1498 sq ft firebox – 139 sq ft grate – 24.8 sq ft	Tractive effort – 23,255 lb Locomotive weight – 57 tons 2 cwt Adhesive weight – 47 tons 10 cwt Max axle loading – 16 tons 10 cwt

The problems with 4-6-0 Class 362 and the improved performance of Class 355 following rebuilding persuaded Coey to produce more 2-6-0s in Class 368. They were similar to Class 355 but with a slightly different wheelbase and they were the first Inchicore-built locomotives to carry Belpaire boilers from new. In service, Classes 355 and 368 were treated as inter-changeable, being regarded as powerful and useful goods engines. They were also used on passenger duties, such as the Cork-Rosslare boat trains and Tralee-Mallow services.

2-6-0 Type XLI [41]
Class 368.

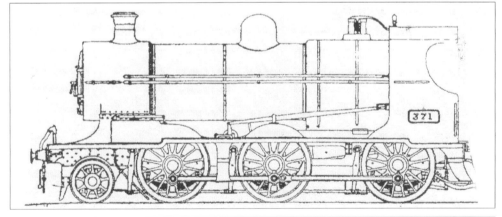

RNC Type: XLIII [43]   0-6-0   GSWR Class 257

No	Introduced	Withdrawn	No	Introduced	Withdrawn
257	Oct 1913	Nov 1960	261	Nov 1914	1965
258	Oct 1913	1963	262	Nov 1914	1965
259	Nov 1913	Oct 1959	263	Dec 1914	1962
260	Nov 1913	1962	264	Dec 1914	May 1960

Designer: Maunsell   **Built at Inchicore**

Boiler pressure – 160 lb/ sq in
Cylinders – 19" x 26"
Driving wheels – 5' 1¾"
Wheelbase – 7' 7" + 8' 6"
Piston valves – 8"
Locomotive length – 28' 2¼ "

Heating surfaces:
tubes – 844 sq ft
superheater – 224 sq ft
firebox – 118 sq ft
grate – 20.4 sq ft

Tractive effort – 20,670 lb
Coal/ water capacities – refer Chapter 9
Locomotive weight – 47 tons 5 cwt
Max axle loading – 17 tons 8 cwt

These locomotives were outwardly similar to 0-6-0 Nos 249-252 (Type XLII [42]) but significantly more modern being built with piston valves and superheaters: Nos 257-61 had Schmidt while Nos 262-4 had the Inchicore modified version. Although accorded the same power rating as Class 351, they were superior in performance and regarded as the best 0-6-0s since Class 101. They were popular on goods duties, secondary passenger trains and beet trains on the Rosslare route. They were excellent steamers except for No 263 (the "Whistling Gypsy" because it emitted a peculiar high-pitched note on its fourth exhaust beat). Nos 261/ 2 were the last GSWR locomotives in service and CIE's last steam power.

0-6-0 Type XLIII [43] Class 257.

Chapter 6
Tank Locomotives
RNC Types XLIV [44] to LXV [65]

Passenger tanks

The first passenger tank locomotives entered service with the GSWR in 1869/ 70, in the form of a pair of 0-4-4 Single Fairlies of Type XLV [45], Nos 33 and 34. A revolutionary concept in the early development of locomotive bogies, they enjoyed working lives of around 20 years. More might have been built but for unreasonable royalty demands by Robert Fairlie. The GSWR therefore built eight more 0-4-4BTs of Type XLVI [46] where the superstructure was virtually identical but with the driving wheels mounted in a rigid frame. (BT refers to 'Back tank' where the tank was located behind the cab, usually on the floor of the bunker; in some cases a BT might also incorporate an additional well tank set between the frames.)

Four more 0-4-4BTs were built in 1879 and designated by RN Clements as Type L [50] although dimensionally very close to the preceding eight. On construction, No 40 was recognised as the 100th locomotive built at Inchicore and in conjunction with the relative celebrations, it was temporarily numbered 100. However, this process ignored the 43 locomotives built prior to McDonnell's arrival and also must have required some liberal interpretation given the preceding complexity of renewals and rebuildings.

The numerically largest tank class comprised twenty 0-4-4BTs built between 1883 and 1887 and numbered 47-51, 70-84. They were identified under RNC as Type LII [52] but by then the company's formal classification system was in place whereby they were known as Class 47. They were dimensionally similar to Type L [50], with a few minor differences. The long-surviving Type LII [52], No 40, was absorbed into this class apparently for administrative convenience.

While the 0-4-4BTs had been built for medium distance Dublin-Kildare/ Kilkenny passenger services, the next passenger tanks were 2-4-2Ts introduced in 1892 by Ivatt for branch line work in Kerry. They totalled six of which four (Nos 33, 34, 41, 42) built in 1892/ 3 were allocated Type LV [55]. Two (Nos 35 & 36) built in 1894 with slightly altered dimensions were separately recognised by RNC as Type LVI [56]. However, all six were treated by the GSWR (and by this work) as Class 33. These were successful engines and withdrawals took place between 1957 and 1963.

In 1894 Ivatt adopted the 4-4-2T wheel arrangement for a pair of passenger engines (RNC Type LVII [57]), numbered 37 and 38. Coey built four more in 1901 with slightly increased weight but otherwise dimensionally identical. Numbered 317-320, they were treated separately by RNC as Type LXI [61]. The GSWR included them all in Class 37. Withdrawals commenced in 1950 and they were extinct by 1955. Class 27 (RNC reference Type LIX [59]) was the company's final passenger tank design and an enlargement of Class 37. There were four (Nos 27, 30-32) built 1900/ 1 and they were withdrawn 1950 to 1953.

Goods tanks

The first purpose-built six-coupled tank locomotives appeared in 1876 as a pair of 0-6-4BTs (Type XLIX [49]) numbered 201/ 2. Both underwent modifications as detailed in the Type history and were officially transferred to the departmental list in 1897, one of the few cases where such engines can be clearly identified. Four 0-6-4Ts were built in 1879/ 80 numbered 203-206. Despite the rebuild of No 204 as an 0-6-0T in 1914, all four remained in Type LI (51) under RNC's system. However, the GSWR placed Nos 203/ 5/ 6 in Class 203 and the 0-6-0T in Class 204. Nos 205/ 6 were withdrawn in 1928 and No 203 in 1940. 0-6-0T No 204 lasted until 1952.

Four 0-6-0Ts appeared in 1887 numbered 207-210 and recognised by RNC as Type LIII [53]. Two more almost identical 0-6-0Ts were added in 1895 which RNC chose to identify as Type LVIII [58]. They were numbered 201/ 2 on construction which identities evidently duplicated Type XLIX [49] before the latter received names in substitution. Obviously, a useful design, four more with minor modifications were added in 1901, and once again accorded a separate identity by RNC becoming Type LX [60]. All ten locomotives (i.e. Nos 201/ 2/ 7-10/ 17-20) were classified 201 by the GSWR.

The final batch of six-coupled tank engines were four 0-6-2Ts numbered 211-4 supplied by North British Locomotive Co in 1903 (RNC Type LXII [62]). Quite unlike the archaic-looking Inchicore products, they were acquired to work the newly opened Drumcondra link line, but were found to be too heavy for these duties. The water capacity of Nos 213/ 4 was therefore reduced to lower the overall weight while Nos 211/ 2 were rebuilt as 0-6-0s (Type XL [40]).

Ireland's only 5' 3" gauge eight-coupled design was 4-8-0T No 900 built in 1915 (Type LXV [65]) with a second example delivered shortly after the GSWR ceased to exist. No 900 was intended as a heavy shunter/ banking locomotive but considered unsuccessful, it was withdrawn in 1928.

Miscellaneous tanks

The remaining formed a motley crew. Type XLIV [44] *Sprite* was the 0-2-2 section of an early combined 6-wheeled locomotive and coach vehicle. Two 0-4-2Ts both named *Sambo*, were Inchicore works shunters; Type LVIV [64] (1914-1962) is detailed here whereas its predecessor appears as Type XXVII [27] in Chapter 5. There were also two small 0-4-2Ts of Type XLVII [47] (*Fairy* and a second *Sprite*). Type XLVIII [48] comprised three 0-6-4T combined engine and coach units (two later converted to conventional 0-6-Ts). There were two small 0-6-0Ts of type LIV [54] and a solitary steam rail motor of Type LXIV [64]. Finally there was *Pat*, an unclassified self-propelled tractor unit regarded as plant.

RNC Type: XLIV [44]	0-2-4T steam carriage	GSWR Class n/a

Name	**Built**	**Withdrawn**
Sprite §	1857	1871-2

§ This unit may have been numbered 76 until *circa* 1859

Designer: Miller   **Built at Inchicore**

Boiler pressure – not recorded *Cylinders – 6 ½" x 12"* *Driving wheels – 4' 6"* *Trailing wheels – 3' 0" (below footplate)* *– 3' 6" (below carriage section)* *Wheelbase – 8' 2" + 7' 2"*	*Heating surfaces:* *tubes – 290.9 sq ft* *firebox – 30.5 sq ft* *grate – 6.18 sq ft*	*Tractive effort – not recorded*

In July 1856, Miller sought Board authority to build a small locomotive and carriage unit for "inspection down the line and special services" at a cost of £950, and it was completed at Inchicore the following year. In comprised a rigid frame structure that supported both locomotive and carriage section, and thereby allowed the unusual wheel arrangement. The carriage body was 9' 7" long and 8' 0" wide, with large rear windows for inspection, but there was no means of communication between this section and the footplate. The cab extended only five inches behind the firebox but a covered space 22" wide either side of the firebox directly above the cylinders provided crew protection. There may have been some form of canopy over the remainder of the footplate but this is uncertain. The cab comprised a front weather board with four spectacles plus two of the same size in each side sheet.

The drawing appearing below was based on an original, incomplete document found in Inchicore works but which does not record details of outside running plate, splashers or chimney. These features are speculative. Also there is an error in the oak front buffer beam on which the coupling hook is mounted at the same height as the centre line of the buffers. The end elevation, now lost, showed that the buffer beam was curved downward toward the centre and the hook was actually 9 inches lower than the position depicted. The design appears to have been influenced by Adams's light engines and steam carriages supplied between 1849 and 1853 to the Cork & Bandon, Londonderry & Enniskillen and Londonderry & Coleraine railways. No specific record survives of what work was undertaken by *Sprite* but it seems to have been employed at least on pay train duties. It was reported as "nearly worn out" in July 1871. McDonnell was authorised to rebuild the machine, but it seems unlikely that anything much beyond the 3' 6" rear wheels on a new axle were incorporated into the second GSWR *Sprite:* (see type XLVII [47]).

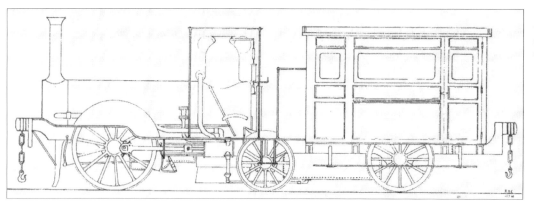

Type XLIV [44] 0-2-4T Steam carriage *Sprite*

Tank Locomotives

RNC Type: XLV [45]   **0-4-4T**   **GSWR: n/a**
(Single Fairlie)

No	Introduced	Rebuilt	Withdrawn
"P" later 33	Dec 1869	Jun 1885 §	1890
"Q" later 34	May 1870		1892

§ With larger cylinders.

No 33 last ran Jun 1889; cranks and wheels were recovered and fitted to 4-4-0 Type XII [12] Class 2 No 6; remainder of locomotive was broken up Sep 1890. No 34 last ran Dec 1889; cranks and wheels were recovered and fitted to 2-4-0 Type X [10] Class 21 No 66.

Designer: McDonnell   **Built at Inchicore**

Boiler pressure – 150 lb/ sq in	*Heating surfaces:*	*Tractive effort – 8,500 lb*
Cylinders – 15" x 20"	*tubes – 843 sq ft*	*later – 9,670 lb*
later – 16" x 20"	*firebox – 81 sq ft*	*Coal capacity – 1 ton 10 cwt*
Driving wheels – 5' 7½"	*grate – 14.6 sq ft*	*Water capacity – 800 gal*
Trailing bogie wheels – 2' 11"		*Locomotive weight – 35 tons 17 cwt*
Wheelbase – 6' 0" + 9' 6" + 5' 0"		*Adhesive weight – 22 tons 0 cwt*
Distance between bogie centres – 14' 7"		*Max axle loading – 11 tons 0 cwt*
Distance between power bogie pivot & crank axle – 2' 7"		*(compensated)*
Fayle records different heating surfaces but these are unsubstantiated		

Born in 1831, Robert Fairlie trained at Swindon and Crewe before becoming Engineer & General Manager of the Londonderry & Coleraine Railway in 1853, and later working with the Bombay & Baroda Railway. By the early 1860s he was a consultant in London who advised on railway projects in South America and India. In 1864, he produced a paper analysing shortcomings in conventional design, and extolling the potential advantages of double ended articulated locomotives. These included superior steaming capacity through use of two boilers, greater haulage potential through maximum adhesion power bogies, ability to traverse sharp curves, and elimination of the need for turntables. He firmly advocated that the conventional locomotive was inherently inefficient through reduced adhesive weight where carrying wheels or a tender were needed to bear coal and water. His system (patented in 1864) which became known as the Double Fairlie type had at its core the maximum adhesion principle. The first manifestation was 0-4-4-0T *Progress* built the following year for the Neath & Brecon Railway. Fairlie gained widespread recognition through successful trials with 0-4-4-0T *Little Wonder* on the 1'11½" gauge Festiniog Railway in 1870. It is not widely recognised that McDonnell at Inchicore had already successfully applied some of the Fairlie principles in his No 33 of the previous year.

As an early exponent of bogie technology, McDonnell recognised possibilities with a Fairlie power bogie but also acknowledged the limitations of finding adequate room for coal and water. Accordingly he ignored the core objective of maximum adhesion in a compromise which involved a single boiler and conventional coal and water storage. The result was the world's first example of what later became known as the Single Fairlie type. Forms of "hybrid-Fairlies" had been designed previously but this was the first variant to take physical form.

Being an 0-4-4BT and lacking maximum adhesion there is doubt whether Nos 33 and 34 fell within the jurisdiction of the patent. No record has been traced to show that Robert Fairlie played any direct role in design and construction, and it could well have been that these engines were a pure McDonnell-Inchicore creation. Determination of any breach of patent would seem to be a purely legal matter.

In service, the pair proved sufficiently satisfactory for McDonnell to seek authority to build 25 more. However, Robert Fairlie who had a reputation for avarice, apparently demanded compensation consisting of a down payment of £500 plus an annual royalty of £50 for each locomotive. The GSWR Board flatly rejected these terms and the matter was ultimately settled on 20th October 1869 by means of a single payment of £50 per locomotive then in service; no further examples were built for Ireland.

The pair, which predated the Kerry Bogies by eight years, typified McDonnell's innovative spirit in seeking a creative solution to the problem of accommodating larger eight-wheeled locomotives on curvaceous routes, and in overcoming problems that might arise from an overall wheelbase that would exceed 20 feet. Up until then Fairlies had been regarded solely as slow speed freight haulers while the GSWR pair were specifically intended for passenger duties. They were unique in being the only Fairlies of any genre (Double/ Single/ Mason) to have only inside cylinders. They were also markedly more effective than the only other standard gauge Fairlie to work in these islands, the unsuccessful 4-cylinder single variant tried on the Swindon, Marlborough & Andover Railway.

--- o O o ---

Nos 33 and 34 were a synthesis of parts purchased from leading manufacturers: boilers and wheels were supplied by Beyer Peacock; frames from Sharp Stewart; trailing bogie from Avonside; cylinders from Grendon. The main interest however lay in the power bogie and suspension system, design of which has been attributed to McDonnell, despite Robert Fairlie's proprietorial claims.

The power and trailing bogies were both connected to a single mainframe structure that supported boiler, bunker and cab. The pivot of the power bogie had a flat face that rested in a recessed socket set between the frames. Most of the weight was carried on the pivot but there were also load checking springs made of India-rubber on each side in cup brackets attached to each mainframe. This layout allowed the steam bogie and the carrying frame to tilt in unison while the trailing Adams bogie below the bunker could tilt independently of the main frames. Any tendency to pitch by the power bogies was checked by India-rubber springs fixed to a bracket carried in the centre of a transverse frame stay set in front of the firebox. Compensating levers connected the springs of the coupled wheels while the trailing bogie relied on a single inverted spring on each side.

Steam was taken from the front of the dome by means of a 3" diameter pipe into a tee-piece from which two external pipes passed around the boiler to a tee-joint underneath the boiler at the centre line of the locomotive. From this point a single pipe passed steam to a valve chest between the cylinders. There were no swivelling joints in the steam transmission train as would be found on a modern articulated locomotive. Turning movement of the power bogie was accommodated solely through the elasticity of the pipes and bends.

The blast pipe was fitted with a petticoat pipe, the lower mouth of which was large enough to permit the bottom portion of the blast pipe to move within it. The locomotive was very steady in motion and could easily negotiate curves of 300 feet radius. The tightest radius was 200 feet, the effective limit of tolerances as the driving wheels almost touched the frames.

In a discussion at the Institute of Civil Engineers in 1873, McDonnell disclosed that No 33 had run 30,977 miles up until then (and No 34 had run 22, 738 miles) with average coal consumption of 19.8 and 21 lb per mile respectively hauling an average load of six 6-wheel coaches. There were no reports of excessive steam leaks and as both engines worked for 20 years they were clearly successful. CE Spooner, engineer of the Festiniog and North Wales Narrow Gauge railways visited the GSWR in September 1869, possibly to view the prototype while under construction. The FR acquired an 0-4-4TSF in 1876 and the NWNGR, a pair of 0-6-4TSFs in 1877.

--- o O o ---

It is not coincidental that an engraving of an 0-4-4T appears on the rear cover of this work. Locomotives of this wheel arrangement were in service continuously between 1869 and 1945, and the family formed an unusual and distinctive element in the company's motive power story. Their antique appearance belied their operational effectiveness and the genre underwent little modification. The most significant change was unwittingly brought by Robert Fairlie whose greed enforced construction of No 31 in 1870 as an outwardly similar machine that concealed an entirely conventional chassis layout.

The change might have been detrimental as the conventional 0-4-4BTs suffered from a certain rear end movement that earned them the nickname of "fantails". McDonnell's chassis and bogie layout seems to have rendered a locomotive of superior riding qualities. Had it been economic to build the additional 25 that McDonnell sought, the presence of the Single Fairlie in these islands might have be significantly greater. Slightly confusingly, GSWR railwaymen referred to the Single Fairlies as "double-bogie engines" and to the conventional 0-4-4BTs that followed as "single-bogie engines".

Opposite page: Type XLV [45] 0-4-4BT (Single Fairlie). *Centre Image Attribution D. Prior*

Tank Locomotives

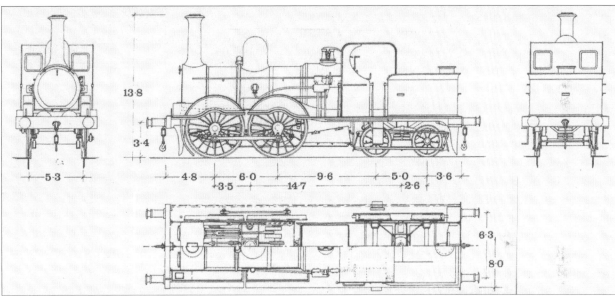

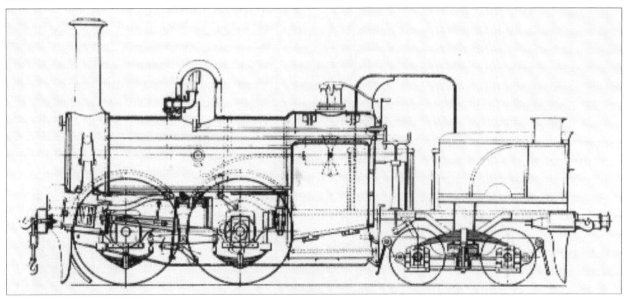

RNC Type: XLVI [46]		0-4-4BT		GSWR Class: n/a
No §	**Introduced**	**Class 47 boiler**	**16" diameter cylinders**	**Withdrawn**
"X" later 27	Jan 1871	1883	1883	1899
"Y" later 30	Mar 1871	1885	1880	1899
"N" later 31	Jun 1870	1884	1884	Apr 1896
"O" later 32	Jun 1870	Jun 1884	1880	Aug 1896
35	Oct 1875	-	1889	Oct 1892
36	Oct 1875	-	1886	Nov 1892
37	Nov 1875	-	-	Mar 1893
38	Dec 1875	-	-	Mar 1893

§ Temporary letter designation replaced by running number on or shortly after entry into service.

Designer: McDonnell **Built at Inchicore**
Nos 27, 30-32:

Boiler pressure – 140 lb/ sq in	Heating surfaces:	Tractive effort – 7,820 lb
Cylinders – 15" x 20"	tubes – 771 sq ft	later – 8,900 lb
later – 16" x 20"	firebox – 74 sq ft	Coal capacity – 1 ton 10 cwt
Driving wheels – 5' 7½"	grate – 15 sq ft	Water capacity – 814 gal
Trailing bogie wheels – 2' 11"		Locomotive weight – 38 tons 2 cwt
Wheelbase – 6' 0" + 9' 6" + 5' 0" (see below)		Adhesive weight – 25 tons 2 cwt
		Max axle loading – 12 tons 13 cwt

Nos 35-38:

Boiler pressure – 150 lb/ sq in	Heating surfaces:	Tractive effort – 8,500 lb
Cylinders – 15" x 20"	tubes – 686 sq ft	later – 9,670 lb
later – 16" x 20"	firebox – 77.5 sq ft	Coal capacity – 1 ton 10 cwt
Driving wheels – 5' 8½"	grate – 15 sq ft	Water capacity – 1180 gal
Trailing bogie wheels – 3' 8"		Locomotive weight – 39 tons 12 cwt
Wheelbase – 6' 0" + 12' 0" + 5' 5"		Adhesive weight – 29 tons 4 cwt
		Max axle loading – 13 tons 2 cwt (compensated)

The date when the royalty dispute with Robert Fairlie was concluded is unknown but the chronology suggests that at commencement of construction, locomotives N, O, X & Y were intended to be Single Fairlies. The orders for main components were exactly as for Type XLV and McDonnell would have sought to maximise the orders in pursuit of unit cost containment. The superstructure was exactly as for the Single Fairlies but there were changes in heating areas, water capacity and wheel diameters. The 1' increase in driving wheel size was probably due to thicker tyres; 5' 8½" was becoming the mixed traffic standard diameter about that time.

There is uncertainty concerning the wheelbase as alternative specifications have been quoted which are considered unreliable.
Bogie technology was in its infancy at this time and it is possible that the sophisticated trailing bogie design that McDonnell had developed for Nos 33 & 34 could not be applied or was judged too expensive in this case. It is significant that in addition to the components supplied, a royalty was paid to Sharp Stewart in respect of the bogies built for Nos 31 and 32. RNC believed that the bogies for Nos 27 and 30 were of pure Inchicore origin. Nos 35 to 38 were fitted with outside-framed swing link trailing bogies.

Tank Locomotives

Type XLVI [46] 0-4-4T.

RNC Type: XLVII [47]   0-4-2T plus bogie for coach unit   **GSWR Class: Sprite**

Name	Built	Withdrawn
Sprite	Jan 1873	1927
Fairy	Dec 1894	1927

NB Although covered by Type 47, there were sufficient details differences for the GSWR to regard the two locomotives as of separate classes. It should be noted that the 1873-built locomotive was the second to carry the name *Sprite* (see Type XLIV [44]).

Sprite:

Boiler pressure – 150 lb/ sq in	Heating surfaces:	Tractive effort – 2,040 lb
Cylinders – 8" x 15"	tubes – 220 sq ft	Coal capacity – 1 ton
Driving wheels – 5' 0"	firebox – 53.5 sq ft	Water capacity – 570 gal
Trailing bogie wheels – 3' 6"	grate – 10.5 sq ft	Locomotive weight – 21 tons 10 cwt
Wheelbase – 5' 6" + 7' 10¼" (engine only)		Adhesive weight – 14 tons 8 cwt
		Max axle loading – 7 tons 4 cwt

This locomotive was built as a combined engine and pay carriage on the same chassis. Originally, it was a back tank with 300 gallon estimated capacity; coal was carried in pocket bunkers next to cab sides. In October 1889, the ensemble was split into locomotive and permanently close-coupled 4-wheel carriage; the latter was lengthened and a rear balcony added.

Also the locomotive was converted to a side tank (capacity 570 gallons) with a bunker containing 37 cu ft of coal. In November 1879, new 9" x 15" cylinders were fitted. In December 1892, it received a new boiler, and another in 1919 when the cab roof was raised by 12" to an interior of 6' 3" and the cab cut-out was reduced by the fitting of additional side sheets.

Fairy:

Boiler pressure – 150 lb/ sq in	Heating surfaces:	Tractive effort – 2,500 lb
Cylinders – 9" x 15"	tubes – 310 sq ft	Coal capacity – 44 cu ft
Driving wheels – 5' 2"	firebox – 52 sq ft	Water capacity – 475 gal
Trailing bogie wheels – 3' 0"	grate – 10 sq ft	Locomotive weight – 21 tons 10 cwt
Wheelbase – 5' 6" + 7' 10¼ (engine only)		Adhesive weight – 14 tons 8 cwt
		Max axle loading – 7 tons 4 cwt

This engine was based on the 1889 rebuild of *Sprite* but had several dimensional differences.

Locomotives of the Great Southern & Western Railway

These units were used as pay carriages, touring the system to distribute wages. Steps on each side allowed the employees to queue; mount from one side, collect their reward and then walk down the steps on the opposite side. The working timetable included a two-week cycle which covered the entire system. In 1901, this was:

Tuesday:	Inchicore-Tullow-Kildare-Charleville-Limerick via Croom
Wednesday:	Limerick-Sligo via Ennis and Tuam
Thursday:	Sligo-Limerick via Tuam and Ennis
Friday:	Limerick-Roscrea-Birr-Maryborough-Waterford (via Abbeyleix)-Kilkenny-Bagenalstown
Saturday:	Bagenalstown-Ballywilliam-Bagenalstown-Inchicore (via Carlow).
Monday:	Inchicore-Tullamore-Bangher-Athlone-Inchicore
Tuesday:	Inchicore-Cork, Cobh and Youghal and back to Cork
Wednesday:	Cork-Waterford (via Dungarvan), back to Fermoy-Mitchelstown-Mallow
Thursday:	Mallow-Kanturk-Headford Junction-Kenmare-Farranfore-Cahirciveen-Tralee
Friday:	Tralee-Listowel-Ballingrane-Foynes-Limerick-Waterford (via Clonmel)
Saturday:	Waterford-Clonmel-Thurles-Inchicore

The pay carriage was on the road from about 7.00 am to about 4-30 pm; Saturdays were half-days. In 1864, the Waterford & Limerick Railway allowed pay train services to run over their metals from Limerick via Killonan to Birdhill.

This method of paying personnel was withdrawn in 1926 and both engines were withdrawn the following year. *Sprite* had covered 1,220,000 miles, possibly a record for such a small engine. It survived for six more years at Inchicore on washout duties. The carriage portions of both survived longer as lineside huts.

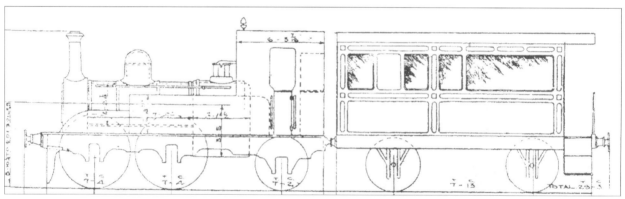

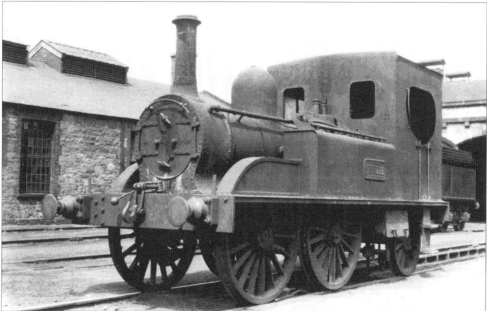

Above: Type XLVII [47] 0-4-2T *Sprite* after the coach section had been detached from the locomotive's chassis and then permanently close-coupled.

Left: Type XLVII [47] *Sprite* after detachment of coach vehicle.

Tank Locomotives

RNC Type: XLVIII [48] **0-6-4T / 0-6-0T** **Classifications:** *see below*

No	Built	GSWR Class	Rebuilt	Withdrawn
C later 90	Sep 1875	90	1915 §	Oct 1959
C2 later 91	Apr 1881	91	1924 *	1930
C3 later 92	Jun 1881	92	-	1945

Designer: McDonnell   **Built at Inchicore**

Boiler pressure – 140 lb/ sq in	Heating surfaces:	Tractive effort – 4,840 lb
Cylinders – 10" x 18"	tubes – 317.5 sq ft	Coal capacity – 10 cwt
Driving wheels – 3' 8¼"	firebox – 51 sq ft	Water capacity – 370 gal
Trailing wheels – 3' 1½"	grate – 10 sq ft	Locomotive weight – 26 tons 7 cwt
Wheelbase – 5' 0" + 5' 11" + 7' 6" + 5' 0" (estimated)		Adhesive weight – 18 tons 10 cwt
		Max axle loading – 6 tons 5 cwt

No 90 was fitted with 10" x 15" cylinders in 1875 which reduced the tractive effort to 4,030 lb; this locomotive's wheelbase was 5' 0" + 5' 11" + 7' 6" + 5' 6".

§ Rebuilt as 0-6-0T with rear carriage section removed

Boiler pressure – 150 lb/ sq in	Tractive effort – 5,190 lb
Driving wheels – 3' 8¼"	Locomotive weight – 23 tons 8 cwt
Wheelbase – 5' 0" + 5' 11"	Max axle loading – 7 tons 15 cwt

* Rebuilt as 0-6-0ST with rear carriage section removed

Boiler pressure – 150 lb/ sq in	Tractive effort – 5,190 lb
Driving wheels – 3' 8¼"	Locomotive weight – 23 tons 8 cwt
Wheelbase – 5' 0" + 5' 11"	Max axle loading – 7 tons 18 cwt

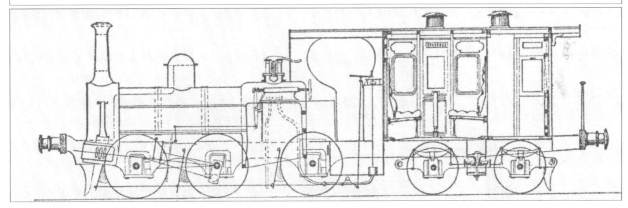

0-6-4T Type XLVIII [48] combined locomotive and coach unit.

C was built for the Castleisland Railway as a combined locomotive and carriage, an exercise that breached the injunction policed by the Locomotive Manufacturers Association against railway companies building motive power for other companies. It was originally a well tank with limited coal capacity carried in pocket bunkers in the cab. A key design limitation was axle loading as the CR used 40 lb rails. It became GSWR property with effect from 31st August 1879 and was renumbered 90.

The design apparently derived from the second *Sprite* (type XLVII [47]), but use of six-coupled driving wheels was intended to produce a more powerful engine capable of hauling one or more coaches, as was proven in service. Following use on the CR section, No 90 worked on the Mitchelstown branch, still in railmotor form, but poor fuel capacity and limited driver visibility impeded its usefulness. In 1915, the carriage portion was removed and side tanks were added. It thereafter worked as a conventional locomotive. In GSR days, No 90 plus No 100 of Type LIV [54] were allocated to Cork Albert Quay to work the restricted Timoleague-Courtmacsherry section, maximum 8 tons axle loading limit. No 90 survives in preservation.

In 1878 Two more of the same basic design were authorised as Nos C2 and C3 (apparently No 91 and 92 on entering service) but intended to have a van section in place of passenger accommodation. However on completion in 1881, No 91 had a passenger section similar to No 90, possibly to act as spare for Castleisland services. No 92 was built with a single passenger compartment with seats all around the sides and is believed to have gone straight to work as the Inchicore "cab", shuttling staff between Kingsbridge and the works.

0-6-4T Type XLVIII [48] combined locomotive and coach unit No 91.

0-6-4T Type XLVIII [48] Class 92 combined locomotive and coach unit.

RNC Type: XLIX [49]		0-6-4BT / 0-6-0T		GSWR Class: Jumbo
No	Built	Rebuilt	Named (1897)	Withdrawn
201	Sep 1876		*Negro*	May 1910
202	Sep 1876	1897 §	*Jumbo*	Mar 1957

Tank Locomotives

Designer: McDonnell   **Built at Inchicore**

Boiler pressure – 140 lb/ sq in	Heating surfaces:	Tractive effort – 16,980 lb
Cylinders – 18" x 24"	tubes – 900 sq ft	Coal capacity – 2 tons 10 cwt
Driving wheels – 4' 6½"	firebox – 84.5 sq ft	Water capacity – 1320 gal
Trailing bogie wheels – 3' 8½"	grate – 18.8 sq ft	Locomotive weight –46 tons 16
Wheelbase – 7' 3" + 6' 0" + 6' 1½" + 5' 5"		Adhesive weight – 34 tons 8 cwt
Locomotive length – 35' 4"		Max axle loading - 11 tons 18 cwt

§ Rebuilt as 0-6-0T, with a Class 60 boiler.

Boiler pressure – 150 lb/ sq in	Heating surfaces:	Tractive effort – 18,190 lb
Driving wheels – 4' 6½"	tubes – 938 sq ft	Locomotive weight – 37 tons 3 cwt
Wheelbase – 7' 3" + 6' 0"	firebox – 112 sq ft.	Max axle loading – 13 tons 16 cwt
Length 28' 8¾"	grate – 19 sq ft	

These, the first 0-6-4Ts in these islands, were initially used as bankers to goods trains over the new North Wall line (from Islandbridge Junction to Glasnevin Junction) and out of Kingsbridge. Built as back tanks with a capacity of 950 gallons, their capacity was increased to 1320 gallons with the fitting of side tanks in 1883, which improved their adhesive capacity. They became departmental locomotives in 1895 and lost their numbers in favour of names only two years later. *Negro* reverted to a back tank in December 1896. *Jumbo* apparently retained its departmental status despite spending 60 years as a yard shunter at Waterford where generations of railway men gained their first footplate experience. Inexperienced fireman who allowed the safety valve to blow off soon learned that the boiler would rapidly empty, reducing pressure to about 75 lbs /sq in. The numbers 201 and 202 were re-allocated to 0-6-0Ts of Type LVIII [58].

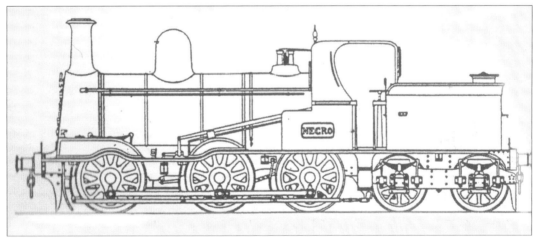

0-6-4T Type XLIX [49] *Negro* (originally No 201) following reversion to back tank.

0-6-4T Type XLIX [49] No 202 as built. *Locomotive Publishing Co*

0-6-0T Type XLIX [49] *Jumbo* as converted from 0-6-4T No 202.

RNC Type: L [50]		0-4-4BT	GSWR Class 28
No	Introduced	Rebuilt	Withdrawn
28	May 1879	-	1906
29	May 1879	Apr 1903	1907
39	Jun 1879	May 1904	1916
40	Jul 1879	c. 1897	1936

No 40 was temporarily renumbered 100 in June 1879 to mark the 100th locomotive built at Inchicore since McDonnell's appointment but not carried in service.

Designer: McDonnell   **Built at Inchicore**

Boiler pressure – 140 lb/ sq in
Cylinders – 16" x 20"
Driving wheels – 5' 8½"
Trailing bogie wheels – 3' 8½"
cwtWheelbase – 6' 0" + 12' 0" + 5' 5"
Locomotive length – 33' 7"

Heating surfaces:
tubes – 677 sq ft
firebox – 78.5 sq ft
grate – 15.2 sq ft

Tractive effort – 8,900 lb
Coal capacity – 2 tons 10 cwt
Water capacity – 1200 gal
Locomotive weight – 41 tons 0
Adhesive weight – 23 tons 8 cwt

The rebuilding process involved the fitting of Class 47 type boilers that were dimensionally almost identical to the originals. Whether this was justified in the case of No 29 must be questionable. No 28 was reported as standing derelict as early as 1904.

Another modification involved the fitting of a well tank that added about 185 gallons to bring the capacity up to the reported 1200 gal. The date when this was carried out is unknown and it is not certain where the additional tank was fitted.

No 40 seems to have gained quasi-celebrity status which might account for its late survival. Around 1925, it was absorbed into Class 47 Type LII [52].

Tank Locomotives

0-4-4T Type L [50] Class 28 No 40.

RNC Type: LI [51] **0-6-4BT/ 0-6-0T** **GSWR Class 203/ 204**

No	Introduced	Rebuilt	Withdrawn
203	Dec 1879	-	1940
204	Dec 1879	1914 §	1952
205	Apr 1880	1914 *	1928
206	May 1880	-	1928

Designer: McDonnell   **Built at Inchicore**

Boiler pressure – 150 lb/ sq in	Heating surfaces:	Tractive effort – 18,190 lb
Cylinders – 18" x 24"	tubes – 903 sq ft	Coal capacity – 2 tons 10 cwt
Driving wheels – 4' 6½"	firebox – 103.5 sq ft	Water capacity – 1540 gal
Trailing bogie wheels – 3' 8½"	grate – 18.8 sq ft	Locomotive weight – 51 tons 6 cwt
Wheelbase – 7' 3" + 8' 3" + 4' 10½" + 5' 5"		Adhesive weight – 35 tons 13 cwt
Locomotive length over buffer beams – 36' 4"		Max axle loading – 12 tons 13 cwt

§ Rebuilt as 0-6-0T with Class 60 boiler; re-classified 204

Boiler pressure – 160 lb/ sq in	Heating surfaces:	Tractive effort – 19,400 lb
Driving wheels – 4' 6½"	tubes – 823.1 sq ft	Coal capacity – 1 tons 10 cwt
Wheelbase – 7' 3" + 8' 3"	firebox – 112.5 sq ft	Water capacity – 1130 gal
Length - 29' 4"	grate – 18.8 sq ft	Locomotive weight – 48 tons 10 cwt
		Max axle loading – 17 tons 19 cwt

* Rebuilt with Class 60 boiler

Boiler pressure – 150 lb/ sq in	Heating surfaces:	Tractive effort – 18,190 lb
	tubes – 823.1 sq ft	Coal capacity – 2 tons 10 cwt
	firebox – 112.5 sq ft	Water capacity – 1540 gal
	grate – 18.8 sq ft	Locomotive weight – 49 tons 11 cwt
		Adhesive weight – 36 tons 19 cwt
		Max axle loading – 17 tons 12 cwt

They were built specifically for banking and shunting in Dublin and Cork and were known as the "North Wall Class". They were capable of hauling 20 wagons from Cork to Rathpeacon as opposed to the 10 wagon maximum for a four-coupled engine. Nos 205/ 6 were armour-plated during the Civil war, 1922-3.

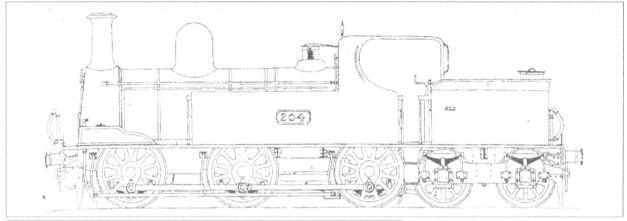

Top and left:
0-6-4T Type LI [51] Class 203 as built
Image H Fayle

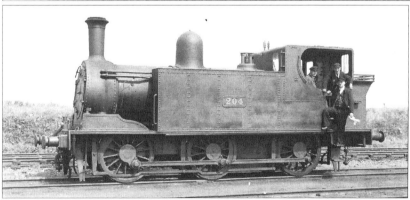

Above: Type LI [51] No 204 before 1914.
LGRP

Bottom: 0-6-0T Type LI [51] Class 204 No 204 as rebuilt from 0-6-4T.

Tank Locomotives

RNC Type: LII [52] **0-4-4BT** **GSWR Class 47**

No	Built	Rebuilt	Withdrawn	No	Built	Rebuilt	Withdrawn
"A" *	May 1883	Sep 1906/ 1925	1945 §	75	Sep 1887	Aug 1912	1931 §
"B" *	Jul 1883	Nov 1917	1930	76	Sep 1887	1907	1931
"C" *	Aug 1883	Nov 1909	1945	77	Sep 1886	Feb 1916	1931
"D" *	Sep 1883	-	1911	78	Sep 1886	Dec 1913	1945
51	Apr 1884	1905	1934	79	Oct 1886	Dec 1906/ 1920	1923 ±
70	Jun 1884	Jun 1904	1934/ 1940 #	80	Oct 1886	Jan 1905	1931
71	Dec 1884	-	1907	81	Aug 1884	1917	1934
72	Dec 1884	Jul 1906	1940	82	Sep 1884	-	1906
73	Jun 1887	-	1928	83	Sep 1884	-	1928 §
74	Jun 1887	Jan 1919	1930	84	Dec 1884	-	1908

* Later Nos 47 to 50 respectively
§ Damaged in the Civil War
# Sources conflict
± Withdrawn and scrapped following an incident at Durrow in the Civil War

NB 0-4-4T No 40 (1879-1936) was the sole survivor of Type [50] Class 28 after 1916 and being dimensionally similar, it was assimilated into Class 47 from around 1925.

Designer: Aspinall **Built at Inchicore**

Boiler pressure – 150 lb/ sq in
    – later 160 lb/ sq in
Cylinders – 16" x 20"
Driving wheels – 5' 8½"
Trailing bogie wheels – 3' 9"
Wheelbase – 6' 0" + 10' 11½" + 5' 5"
Locomotive length – 33' 6"
	Heating surfaces:
	tubes – 677 sq ft
	firebox – 78.5 sq ft
	grate – 15.2 sq ft
		Tractive effort – 9,530 lb
		    – 10165 lb
		Coal capacity – 2 tons 15 cwt
		Water capacity – 1044 gal
		Locomotive weight – 41 tons 16 cwt
		Adhesive weight – 23 tons 6 cwt
		Max axle loading – 11 tons 12 cwt
		It is believed side tanks of aggregate
		capacity 135 gallons were also fitted

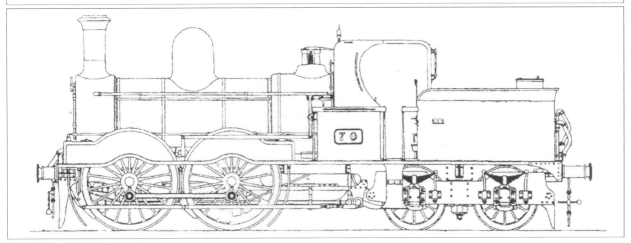

0-4-4T Type LII [52] Class 47.

This class was built with boilers pressed to 140 lb/ sq in (yielding tractive effort at 8,900 lb); rebuilding involved installation of new boilers with boiler pressures of 150 or 160 lb/ sq in. No further information is available on which engines received the higher of the new pressures. No 49 was unique in having a window in the cabside.

There were reports that four larger boilers were built about 1924 for this class but they seem to have been fitted to members of classes 2, 33 and 37. They were used on services such as Cork to Cobh, and to Youghal At the 1925 Amalgamation, the ex-DSER section was short of motive power and Nos 47, 48, 72, 73, 75, 80 were drafted in to help. They also appeared on the Castleisland and Cashel branches; the north Kerry line workings from Limerick to Newcastle West/ Abbeyfeale; and local trains in the Wexford area.

RN Clements recorded information about the construction of Nos 73 and 74 that illustrates Inchicore's thoroughness in recovery and recycling of spare parts. Sharp Stewart 2-2-2 Type I [1] Nos 9 and 16 were built in August 1846 and December 1847 respectively. They were rebuilt as 2-4-0s Type VIII [8] in October 1866/ April 1866, and again in that form in October 1874/ January 1873. The two 2-4-0s (ex-2-2-2s) were finally withdrawn in May 1884/ November 1885. Parts recovered and used in construction of 0-4-4Ts Nos 73 and 74 included:- coupled wheel centres, slide bars, eccentric rod ends, reversing levers & pins, reversing screws, washers and wheels, 3 x expansion links, 4 x expansion link brackets, 4 x lifting brackets, 2 x pulling links, 2 x swing links, 4 x swing brackets.

0-4-4T Type LII [52] Class 47.

RNC Type: LIII [53]/ LVIII [58]/ LX [60]   **0-6-0T**   **GSWR Class 201/ 207/ 217**

No	Introduced	Type	Withdrawn	No	Introduced	Type	Withdrawn
201	Dec 1895 §	LVIII [58]	1963	210	Dec 1887	LIII [53]	Oct 1959
202	Dec 1895 §	LVIII [58]	Nov 1955	217	1901	LX [60]	Mar 1961
207	Dec 1887	LIII [53]	Oct 1959	218	1901	LX [60]	Oct 1959
208	Dec 1887	LIII [53]	Oct 1959	219	1901	LX [60]	Aug 1955
209	Dec 1887	LIII [53]	Mar 1949	220	1901	LX [60]	Oct 1959

NB The GSWR treated these ten locomotives as one class but RN Clements sub-divided them into separate Types in recognition of their differing dimensions.

Tank Locomotives

Designer: Ivatt **Built at Inchicore**
1887 Batch Nos 207-210:

Boiler pressure – 150 lb/ sq in	*Heating surfaces:*	*Tractive effort – 18,190 lb*
later – 140 lb/ sq in	*tubes – 938 sq ft*	*later – 16,980 lb*
Cylinders – 18" x 24"	*firebox – 112.5 sq ft*	*Coal capacity – 2 tons 0 cwt*
Driving wheels – 4' 6½"	*grate – 18.8 sq ft*	*Water capacity – 945 gal*
Wheelbase – 7' 3" + 8' 3"		*Locomotive weight – 40 tons 4 cwt*
Locomotive length over buffers – 29' 4"		*Max axle loading – 15 tons 0 cwt*

1895 Batch Nos 201, 202:

§ Numbers re-used following their transfer from Type XLIX [49] *Negro* & *Jumbo*

Boiler pressure – 160 lb/ sq in	*Heating surfaces:*	*Tractive effort – 19,400 lb*
later – 150 lb/ sq in	*tubes – 823.1 sq ft*	*later – 18,190 lb*
Locomotive length over buffers – 28' 9"	*firebox – 112.5 sq ft*	*Coal capacity – 1 ton 10 cwt*
	grate – 18.8 sq ft	*Water capacity – 730 gal*
		Locomotive weight – 42 tons 15 cwt
		Max axle loading – 15 tons 0 cwt

1901 Batch Nos 217-220:

Boiler pressure – 160 lb/ sq in	*Heating surfaces:*	*Tractive effort – 19,400 lb*
later – 150 lb/ sq in	*tubes – 934 sq ft*	*later – 18,190 lb*
Locomotive length over buffers – 28' 9"	*firebox – 105 sq ft*	*Coal capacity – 1 ton 10 cwt*
	grate – 19.3 sq ft	*Water capacity – 730 gal*
		Locomotive weight – 43 tons 16 cwt
		Max axle loading – 15 tons 10 cwt

Their duties included banking goods trains from Cork; hauling goods trains ("runs of goods" in the Working Timetable) from Cork to Rathpeacon; working the Cork City Railway; and some services on the West Cork lines. Nos 201, 207 and 209 later had steam heating equipment fitted and may have worked passenger trains in West Cork. Nos 208, 210, 217 and 220 were also Cork-based. No 207 retained its traditional GSWR sloped double-door smokebox until withdrawal. Nos 218/ 9 were fitted with stove pipe chimneys at Limerick *circa.* 1919.

0-6-0T Type LIII [53] Class 201 No 207.

Locomotives of the Great Southern & Western Railway

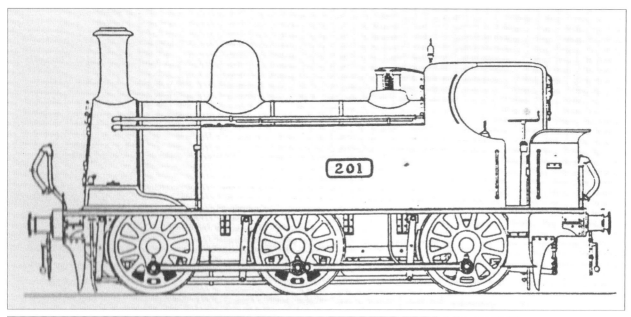

Top: 0-6-0T Type LVIII [58] Class 201 as built.

Left: 0-6-0T Type LVIII [58] Class 201 No 201.

Bottom: Type LX [60] Class 201 No 218 with non-standard chimney at Limerick in 1931. *LGRP*

Tank Locomotives

RNC Type: LIV [54]   **0-6-0T**   **GSWR Class 99**

No	Introduced	Rebuilt	Withdrawn
99	Dec 1890	Feb 1901	1930
100	Jan 1891	1905	Oct 1959

Designer: Ivatt   **Built at Inchicore**

Boiler pressure – 150 lb/ sq in *Heating surfaces:* *Tractive effort – 5,160 lb*
Cylinders – 10" x 18" *tubes – 310 sq ft* *later – 7,430 lb*
later – 12" x 18" *firebox – 52 sq ft* *Coal capacity – 10 cwt*
Driving wheels – 3' 8½" *grate – 10 sq ft* *Water capacity – 434 gal*
Wheelbase – 5' 0" + 5' 11"   *Locomotive weight – 23 tons 8 cwt*
Length over buffers – 22' 3½"   *Max axle loading – 7 tons 18 cwt*

Precise rebuilding details have not been traced except that both appear to have been fitted with 12" x 18" cylinders. They were built specifically for the 12-mile Fermoy to Mitchelstown branch. The design was a derivation of Type XLVIII [48] No 90.

0-6-0T Type LIV [54] Class 99 No 99.

0-6-0T Type LIV [54] Class 99 No 100. *Real Photographs*

Locomotives of the Great Southern & Western Railway

RNC Type: LV/ LVI [55/ 56] **2-4-2T** **GSWR Class 33/ 35**

No	Introduced	Type	Rebuilt	Withdrawn	No	Introduced	Type	Rebuilt	Withdrawn
33	Dec 1892	LV [55]	-	Aug 1957	36	Apr 1894	LVI [56]	1921	Dec 1957
34	Dec 1892	LV [55]	-	Dec 1957	41	Dec 1892	LV [55]	-	Dec 1957
35	Feb 1894	LVI [56]	1924	Oct 1959	42	Mar 1893	LV [55]	May 1907	1964

Designer: Ivatt **Built at Inchicore**

Nos 33, 34, 41, 42:

Boiler pressure – 150 lb/ sq in Cylinders – 16" x 20" Pony wheels – 3' 9" Driving wheels – 5' 8½" Trailing wheels – 3' 9" Wheelbase – 6' 0" + 7' 11" + 6' 0" Locomotive length - 31' 0"	Heating surfaces: tubes – 770 sq ft firebox – 83.8 sq ft grate – 16 sq ft	Tractive effort – 9,530 lb Coal capacity – 2 tons 15 cwt Water capacity – 1250 gal Locomotive weight – 46 tons 12 cwt Adhesive weight – 25 tons 2 cwt Max axle loading – 12 tons 10 cwt

Nos 35, 36:

	Heating surfaces: tubes – 757 sq ft firebox – 83.8 sq ft grate – 16 sq ft	Coal capacity – 3 tons 0 cwt Water capacity – 1130 gal Locomotive weight – 46 tons 2 cwt Adhesive weight – 24 tons 6 cwt Max axle loading – 12 tons 12 cwt
Boiler was originally 160 lb/ sq in yielding tractive effort at 10,170 lb but all had been reduced to 150 lb/ sq by 1923		

To cope with the sharp curves on the Kenmare and Valencia lines, these locos were built with radial axles and a system (designed by Stroudley) of water jets to cool the flanges, on the leading and trailing wheels. They were later found on Cork suburban services and on branches such as Birr and Castleisland. Nos 33 and 42 at one time had bells fitted for working the Cork City Railway; Nos 33, 34, and 36 also worked on the West Cork lines.

2-4-2T Type LV [55]
Class 33 No 33.
W *A Camwell*

Tank Locomotives

2-4-2T Type LVI [56] Class 33 No 35. The reduced water capacity was achieved by removing the forward upper sections of the side tanks. *D Donaldson*

RNC Type: LVII & LXI [57 & 61]   4-4-2T   GSWR Class 37/ 317

No	Introduced	Type	Withdrawn	No	Introduced	Type	Withdrawn
37	Jul 1894	LVII [57]	Dec 1954	318	Jun 1901	LXI [61]	May 1953
38	Oct 1894	LVII [57]	Aug 1950	319	Jun 1901	LXI [61]	1950
317	Jun 1901	LXI [61]	Apr 1955	320	Jun 1901	LXI [61]	Dec 1954

Designer: Ivatt/ Coey **Built at Inchicore**

Boiler pressure – 160 lb/ sq in	*Heating surfaces:*	*Tractive effort – 10,160 lb*
later – 150 lb/ sq in	*tubes – 757.1 sq ft.*	*later – 9,530 lb*
Cylinders – 16" x 20"	*firebox – 83.8 sq ft*	*Coal capacity – 3 tons 0 cwt.*
Pony wheels – 3' 0"	*grate – 16 sq ft*	*Water capacity – 1130 gal*
Driving wheels – 5' 8½"		*Locomotive weight – 49 tons 10 cwt*
Trailing wheels – 3' 9"		*Adhesive weight – 25 tons 4 cwt*
Wheelbase – 5' 3" + 5' 5" + 7' 11" + 6' 6"		*Max axle loading – 12 tons 12 cwt*
Locomotive length – 31' 0"		

1901/ 2 Batch Nos 317-320:

Water capacity – 1245 gal
Locomotive weight – 49 tons 12 cwt
Adhesive weight – 25 tons 4 cwt
Max axle loading – 12 tons 14 cwt

Nos 317-320 were regarded as an improvement on the original design. No 320 was temporarily named *Inchicore* for display at the Cork Exhibition in 1902. They were used principally on trains from Cork to Youghal and Cobh. Nos 317 and 320 were drafted in to help on the ex-DSER section immediately after the Amalgamation. No 317 was armour-plated during the Civil War.

4-4-2T Type LVII [57] Class 37 No 37.

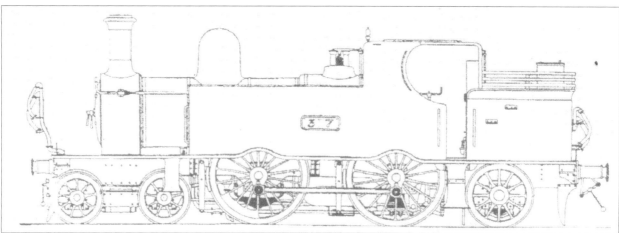

Above and left: 4-4-2T Type LXI [61] differed from Type LVII [57] in the full depth side tanks that added over 100 gallons to the capacity.

Tank Locomotives

RNC Type: LIX [59] **4-4-2T** **GSWR Class 27**

No	Introduced	Withdrawn
27	Nov 1900	Mar 1953
30	Dec 1900	May 1950
31	Dec 1900	May 1953
32	Jun 1901	Mar 1951

Designer: Coey **Built at Inchicore**

Boiler pressure – 160 lb/ sq in
    later – 150 lb/ sq in
Cylinders – 17" x 22"
Pony wheels – 3' 0"
Driving wheels – 5' 8½"
Trailing wheels – 3' 9"
Wheelbase – 5' 3" + 6' 5" + 7' 9" + 6' 0"
Length over buffers – 35' 11"

Heating surfaces:
tubes – 753.9 sq ft
firebox – 97.1 sq ft
grate – 17.5 sq ft

Tractive effort – 12,620 lb
    later – 11,830 lb
Coal capacity – 3 tons 0 cwt
Water capacity – 1425 gal
Locomotive weight – 54 tons 15 cwt
Adhesive weight – 30 tons 18 cwt
Max axle loading – 15 tons 10 cwt

These locomotives were mainly Cork based; No 31 was noted as the Mallow shunter in 1917. No 27 was armour- plated during the Civil War from Dec 1922 until Aug 1923.

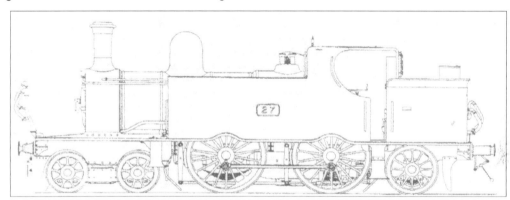

4-4-2T Type LIX [59] Class 27 as built.

4-4-2T Type LIX [59] Class 27 No 31.
Ken Nunn

RNC Type: LXII [62] **0-6-2T** **GSWR Class 211/ 213**

No	Built	Makers No	Rebuilt	Withdrawn
211	Dec 1903	16021	1907 §	-
212	Dec 1903	16022	1907 §	-
213	Dec 1903	16023	-	Jan 1953
214	Dec 1903	16024	-	1949

§ Rebuilt as 0-6-0 Type XL [40] Class 211 (see Chapter 5) retaining same running numbers; remaining pair were re-classified 213.

Designer: Coey **Built by North British**

Boiler pressure – 160 lb/ sq in
Cylinders – 18" x 26"
Driving wheels – 4' 6½"
Trailing wheels – 3' 9"
Wheelbase – 7' 7" + 8' 6" + 6' 0"
Locomotive length – 35' 2"

Heating surfaces:
tubes – 1129 sq ft
firebox – 118 sq ft
grate – 20.4 sq ft

Tractive effort – 21,020 lb
Coal capacity – 2 tons 5 cwt
Water capacity – 1050 gal
Locomotive weight – 58 tons 0 cwt
Adhesive weight – 47 tons 7 cwt
Max axle loading – 17 tons 3 cwt

Builder's records indicate that the original water capacity was 1500 gallons but on entering service, the recorded capacities were 725 gallons (back tank) and 307 gallons (each side tank). This suggests that these engines never actually worked with the original water capacity, the problem having been identified at Inchicore following weighing in full working order. GA drawing indicates original boiler pressure at 175 lbs/ sq in but apparently reduced to 160 lb/ sq in before entering service.

Sources differ on the reported overall weight and maximum axle loading; those quoted above seem to be the most probable. As built, these locomotives were found to be overweight for their intended duties: - shunting and banking in the Dublin area, and haulage of heavy freight trains over the North Wall branch. Accordingly Nos 211/ 2 were rebuilt as tender locomotives to ease the weight issue and to broaden the range of duties. They were known colloquially as the "Scotch Engines".

0-6-2T Type LXII [62] Class 211 later Class 213.

Tank Locomotives

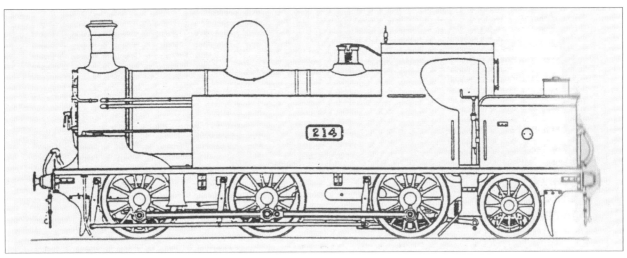

0-6-2T Type LXII [62] Class 211 later Class 213.

RNC Type: LXIII [63]   0-2-2VBT   **GSWR Class: n/a**

No	Built	Withdrawn
Rail motor No 1	Aug 1904	Taken out of service in 1912; coach section converted to tri-composite brake No 1118 but scrapped 1914; locomotive section scrapped 1915 which is recorded as official withdrawal date

Designer: Coey   **Built at Inchicore**

Engine Unit:

Boiler pressure – 130 lb/ sq in *Cylinders – 9" x 12" (later 8" x 12")* *Driving wheels – 2' 9"* *Trailing wheels – 2' 9"* *Wheelbase (engine unit) – 8' 0"*	*Heating surfaces:* *multi-tubular vertical* *boiler – 367.7 sq ft* *firebox – 41.4 sq ft* *grate – 8.4 sq ft*	*Tractive effort – 3,250 lb* *– later 2,570 lb* *Coal capacity – 10 cwt* *Water capacity – 430 gal*

Cylinder diameter was sleeved down to 8½" and then 8" which modifications have baffled observers. The reason probably was that the engine was originally over-cylindered. Elsewhere, it was found to be virtually impossible to fire the vertical boilers of rail motors while on the move; this unit was reputed to have a voracious appetite. Problems might have also stemmed from the valve motion, this being the first outside cylindered standard gauge engine in Ireland and the first on the GSWR to be fitted with (minuscule) Walschaerts gear.

Coach Unit:

Frame length – 50' 1". Access was by means of an open platform at the non-engine end, protected by "collapsible swing gates". A 5' 11" long first class compartment seated six which third class passengers by-passed by means of a side corridor to reach a 26' long saloon that seated 40. There was a small luggage compartment between that saloon and the engine unit, accessed by side doors. Overall width was 9' 10"; total weight, engine and coach units combined – 32 tons 10 cwt. Trailing bogie wheelbase was also 8' 0".

Livery:

The engine unit was black lined red and white. The coach section had crimson lake lower panels and waist while the upper panels were cream and white, lined gold and vermilion.

--- o O o ---

Steam-driven rail cars or rail motors were tried by several railways in the 1900s to counter competition from tramcars on suburban routes or to reduce operating expenses on lightly-trafficked rural lines. This unit closely followed Drummond's design for the London & South Western Railway. The concept suffered from several drawbacks including modest haulage and hill-climbing capacity, inability to handle unexpected surges in traffic levels, and difficulty in keeping the coach section internally and externally clean while the engine was serviced in a motive power depot. RM No 1 was used at first on the newly opened 5¾ miles Goold's Cross-Cashel branch where it worked five daily return trips but suffered several breakdowns. It also proved incapable of hauling a trailer. It was then moved to the poorly patronised Amiens Street-Glasnevin-Kingsbridge suburban service which was withdrawn in 1907 as unable to compete with the tramways. Its later duties are unknown. Following its conversion to hauled stock, the coach was in the Birdhill accident that involved ex-WLWR 0-4-0ST No 229 on 8th January 1914. Damage sustained was apparently moderate but sufficient to warrant its withdrawal that year.

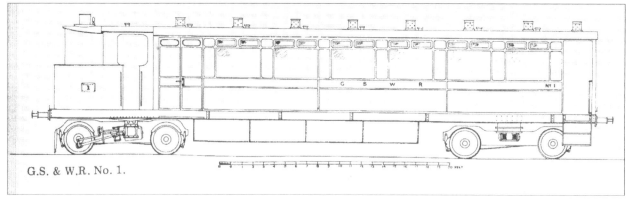

0-2-2VBT Type LXIII [63] Rail motor No 1. *Image LGRP*

RNC Type: LXIV [64]	0-4-2ST	GSWR Class Sambo
Name	**Introduced**	**Withdrawn**
Sambo	Jun 1914	1962

NB This locomotive replaced Type XXVII 0-4-2T (ex-0-4-2), the first *Sambo* withdrawn c 1913.

Designer: Maunsell **Built at Inchicore**

Boiler pressure – 150 lb/ sq in	*Heating surfaces:*	*Tractive effort – 11,980 lb*
Cylinders – 16" x 20"	*tubes – 685 sq ft*	*Coal capacity – 1 ton 10 cwt*
Driving wheels – 4' 6½"	*firebox – 83.8 sq ft*	*Water capacity – 467 gal*
Radial wheels – 3' 9"	*grate – 16 sq ft*	*Locomotive weight – 34 tons 13 cwt*
Wheelbase – 6' 0" + 7' 11"		*Adhesive weight – 23 tons 4 cwt*
Locomotive length – 25' 7"		*Max axle loading – 11 tons 12 cwt*

Possibly assembled from spare parts, this locomotive spent most of its life as Inchicore works shunter where it was known as the "Premises Pilot". When steam working ceased there, it led a more adventurous life, going to Broadstone wagon works and finally a spell of shunting at Amiens Street.

Tank Locomotives

0-4-2ST Type LXIV [64]
Sambo.

RNC Type: LXV [65]		4-8-0T	GSWR Class 900
No	**Built**	**Withdrawn**	
900	Sep 1915	1928	
[901	Dec 1924	1931] §	

Designer: Watson **Built at Inchicore**

§ With minor modifications, No 901 was constructed on the instructions of Bazin; it was almost complete when the GSWR ceased to exist as an independent entity, and was the only new locomotive introduced by the short-lived Great Southern Railway (note not "Railways").

Locomotives of the Great Southern & Western Railway

Boiler pressure – 175 lb/ sq in
Cylinders – 19¼" x 26"
Bogie wheels – 3' 0"
Driving wheels – 4' 6½"
Wheelbase – 6' 4" + 7' 6¼" + 5' 1" + 5' 1" + 5' 1"
Locomotive length – 37' 10¾"

Heating surfaces:
tubes – 1426.5 sq ft
firebox – 138.5 sq ft
grate – 24.8 sq ft

Tractive effort – 26,300 lb
Coal capacity – 3 tons 10 cwt
Water capacity – 1500 gal
Locomotive weight – 80 tons 15 cwt
Adhesive weight – 62 tons 9 cwt
Max axle loading – 17 tons 4 cwt

At the time he left Inchicore for Ashford, Richard Maunsell was working on a 3-cylinder 0-8-2T heavy shunter for use at Dublin North Wall yards. The design appears to have been inspired by the remarkable 3-cylinder 0-8-4Ts (the "Daisies") built by JG Robinson to work the new Great Central hump marshalling yards at Wath-upon-Dearne, Yorkshire. At the point of his departure, the outstanding issue was to sort out the layout for the three sets of inside valve motion.

Maunsell's successor iconoclastically scrapped these plans and substituted his own 2-cylinder 4-8-0T design. This was a simpler machine that had the merit of making extensive use of existing components, a practice very much in the Inchicore tradition. Cylinders were common with Class 362 while the boiler, valve motion, connecting rods, crank and coupled axles, and axles boxes were all interchangeable with Class 368. An unusual feature was that the inside cylinders drove the leading coupled axle which gave the font end and ungainly appearance. Outside cylinders with connecting rods driving the second or third axles might have been a preferable solution but it is possible that such a layout was precluded by the loading gauge.

No 900 was prone to derailment and banned from certain sharply curved sidings, a problem that was commonly attributed to the length of the coupled wheel base. However, this explanation seems untenable as this dimension was 3" shorter than the coupled wheelbase of the later version of 0-6-0 Class 101. In November 1927 the coupling rods between the third and fourth driving wheels were removed thereby converting the engine into a 4-6-2T which did not resolve this issue. The more likely cause was the combination of poor weight distribution (the loading on the leading driving axle was two tons more than that borne by the second axle), the overall weight at over 80 tons, and poor quality trackwork at certain yard locations. A widely circulated weight diagram decribes the distribution as 15 tons 10 cwt on the bogie and 16 tons 5 cwt on each coupled axle which is obviously impossible. With cylinders and all motion forward of and connecting with the leading coupled axle, the load carried at the front end was invariably disproportionate. When weighed in November 1915, the recorded axle loadings were bogie - 18 tons 6 cwt; driving axles: first -17 tons 4 cwt; second - 15 tons 4 cwt; third - 15 tons 1 cwt; fourth - 15 tons 0cwt. No 900 was not regarded as a success so why No 901, incorporating only minor changes, was built nine years later has never been adequately explained.

Both locomotives spent their entire careers in the Dublin area engaged in heavy shunting and banking goods trains as far as Clondalkin.

4-8-0T Type LXV [65] Class 900 No 900. *Locomotive Publishing Co*

Tank Locomotives

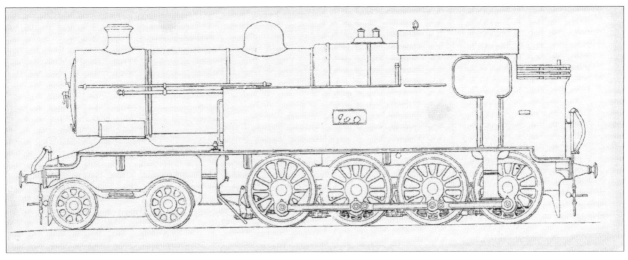

4-8-0T Type LXV [65] Class 900 No 900.

RNC Type: LXVI [66]   0-6-0ST   **GSWR Class 299**

For information on No 299 *Shamrock* refer to **Chapter 7** Acquired companies' locomotives, Page 190

--- o O o ---

RNC Type: LXVII [67]   0-6-0ST   **GSWR Class Erin nominally 300**

For information on No [300] *Erin* refer to **Chapter 7** Acquired companies' locomotives, Page 179

--- o O o ---

RNC Type: LXVIII [68]   0-4-0ST   **GSWR Class Cambria**

For information on No 609 *Cambria* refer to **Chapter 7** Acquired companies' locomotives, Page 180

--- o O o ---

RNC Type: LXIX [69]   0-4-0T   **GSWR Class: Imp**

For information on *Imp* refer to **Chapter 7** Acquired companies' locomotives, Page 192

--- o O o ---

RNC Type: NONE		0-2-2T	**GSWR plant: Pat**
Name	**Built**		**Withdrawn**
Pat	1884		1963
Designer Aspinall (possibly)			**Built at Inchicore**

Boiler pressure – 80 lb/ sq in
Cylinders – 6½" x 7½" (twin, vertical)
Driving & trailing wheels – 3' 7½"
Wheelbase – 8' 0"
Length over buffers – 13' 4"

Heating surfaces: not stated; vertical cross tube boiler

Tractive effort – 495 lb

The two vertical cylinders worked a light crankshaft on which was mounted a geared pinion that engaged with a large toothed gear fitted on the inner face of the two drive wheels. How the reverse gear was engaged is not recorded but the presence of two gear wheels on the driving axle suggests some form of dog clutch. Technically this machine was self-propelled plant that was built to work over the 5' 3" gauge track laid on the overhead gantry from Penrose Quay on the River Lee to the coal bunkers at Cork, Glanmire shed, a distance of 1,140 feet. It was capable of hauling five laden hopper coal wagons with an aggregate weight of about 120 tons. It was last steamed on 24th June 1963 and was broken up the following November.

0-2-2T Plant named "Pat"

Top left: Original front end;

Top right: Boiler end;

Bottom left: Modernised front end in 1938.

Bottom right: In charge of hopper wagons. *Real Photographs*

Chapter 7
Acquired companies' locomotives

In the 19th Century, a major element of the GSWR's system expansion was achieved through organic growth i.e. the raising of capital through the stock market or by harnessing public funds to construct directly-owned lines of route. However, as outlined in Chapter 1 some new lines were funded and developed through third party ventures that were later absorbed into GSWR ownership and control. Several enterprises advanced no further than railway construction with services provided by GSWR-owned locomotives and rolling stock under specific operator agreements. In a few cases as outlined below, these smaller companies acquired their own mobile assets but generally this independence was short-lived. Proprietors often under-estimated the legal costs of gaining parliamentary sanction and the necessary capital expenditure in civil works, and over-estimated the realisable net operating receipts. Motive power added to the GSWR fleet in this fashion varied in effectiveness and condition.

Another source of acquired locomotives could be through the activities of railway construction contractors. There may have also been occasions on which contractors' locomotives were borrowed or hired to undertake revenue-earning work but there were few cases of direct purchase for service with the GSWR. Some other engines passed through contractor's hands as result of proprietors' misjudgement and resultant procurement of the wrong category of motive power. The 5' 3" gauge limited the trading of second-hand locomotives to the island of Ireland. Local contractors were active in this market with Dargen playing a prominent role, no doubt to his personal benefit.

Locomotives thus acquired tended to be non-standard types, of obsolete design, and in a condition that reflected the vicissitudes of chequered working careers. They received comparatively unsympathetic treatment from the GSWR and several did not survive long enough to carry their newly allocated numbers. The small Hunslet tanks found niches in the larger fleet while one company-acquired locomotive (the Castleisland engine) was actually a GSWR design that worked until 1959 and which survives in preservation. All the other absorbed engines had gone by 1914. For completeness, this chapter covers all the locomotives of the companies listed, including those withdrawn before absorption. (The only locomotive-owning company acquired during the 20th Century was the Waterford Limerick & Western Railway which is surveyed in Chapter 8).

Company	Absorbed into GSWR	Locomotive type	Wheel arrangement	Previous identity
Cork & Youghal	1st January 1866	LXX [70]	2-4-0ST	1-5, 9, 10
		LXXI [71]	2-2-2ST/ 2-4-0ST	6-8
Castleisland	31st August 1879	XLVIII [48]	0-6-4T (combination)	C
Waterford, Dungarvan & Lismore	1st November 1898	LXXII [72]	0-4-2	1-4
		LXXIII [73]	0-4-2	6-7
		LXX [70]	2-4-0ST	5
Waterford & Wexford/ F&RR&HC §	1st November 1898	LXVII [67]	0-6-0ST	*Erin*
		LXVIII [68]	0-4-0ST	*Cambria*
Waterford & Central Ireland (formerly Waterford & Kilkenny)	1st September 1900	I [1]-WKR	2-2-2-2T	1-3
		II [2]-WKR	2-4-0	4/ 5 later 2/ 3
		III [3]-WKR	2-2-2	6, 7 later 4/ 5
		IV [4]-W	2-4-0	1
		IV [4]-WKR	0-4-2	2
		V [5]-WKR	2-4-0T/ 2-4-0	6, 7
		VI [6]-WKR	2-4-0	8, 9
		VII [7]-WKR	0-4-2	10, 11
		VIII [8]-WKR	0-4-2T	12
		IX [9]-WKR	0-4-2	1
		X [10]-WKR	0-4-2	4
Bought from Tralee & Fenit Pier & Harbour Commissioners	1901	LXVI [66]	0-6-0ST	*Shamrock*
Dublin & Blessington Steam Tram'y	1921	LXIX [69]	0-4-0T	2

§ Fishguard & Rosslare Railways & Harbours Company.

Cork & Youghal Railway

This opened in 1859-62 with a 26-mile mainline to Youghal and a 5½-mile branch to Queenstown (now Cobh) which was to prove the more important route. The company was absorbed into the GSWR on 1st January 1866, but formal possession did not take place until 1st April and included all ten engines it then owned. The CYR's terminus at Cork (Summerhill) above and close to the GSWR, closed to passengers in 1893 when the link to Glanmire Road Station was opened.

RNC Type: LXX [70]   **2-4-0ST**   **GSWR Class n/a**

CYR No & Name	Maker's No.	Built	GSWR No (Jan 1866)	GSWR No (Oct 1870)	Withdrawn
1 Lewis	542	Sept 1859	61	71	Jan 1883 §
2 Roney #	543	Sept 1859	62	72	Dec 1884
3 Carlisle #	544	Sept 1859	63	73	Jun 1885 to creosote works 1886
4 Chambers	599	1860	64	74	Dec 1887
5 Pike	600	1860	65	75	Jun 1887
9 Hartington	885	1862	66	76	Jun 1887
10 Arnott	886	1862	67	77	Dec 1884 (to foundry)

§ Sold for £500 to the Waterford Dungarvan & Lismore Railway to become their No 5. For later career details see Waterford Dungarvan & Lismore Railway section below.
# Some sources state No 2 Carlisle and No 3 Roney.

Built by Neilson

Boiler pressure – 100 lb/sq in assumed	Heating surfaces:	Tractive effort – 6,650 lb
Cylinders – 15" x 24" ±	tubes – 955 sq ft	Coal capacity – not recorded
Leading wheels – 4' 0"	firebox – not recorded	Water capacity – 600 gal
Driving wheels – 5' 9"	grate – not recorded	Locomotive weight – not recorded
Wheelbase – 6' 3" + 8' 0" (Nos 1-5); 6' 8" + 7' 7" (Nos 9,10)		
Locomotive length –25' 5⅛" (Nos 1-5); 24' 9" (Nos 9,10) [GA drawing does not show buffers]		
± RNC records No 9 had 14" x 24" cylinders		

All supplied with dome-less boilers and weather board but no cabs; they were later fitted with simple wrap-over cabs without side sheets. No 10 was added specifically for opening of the Queenstown branch on 10th March 1862.

Cork & Youghal Railway Type LXX [70] 2-4-0ST No 5 Pike. RH Inness. Darlington

Acquired companies' locomotives

RNC Type: LXXI [71]   **2-2-2ST/ 2-4-0ST**   **GSWR Class: n/a**

CYR No & Name	Makers No	Built	GSWR No (Jan 1866)	GSWR No (Oct 1870)	Rebuilt	Withdrawn
6 Fermoy	689	1861	68	78	1879	Jun 1885
7 Stuart de Decies	690	1861	69	79	1879	Dec 1884
8 -	691	1861	70	80	1879	Jun 1886

Built by Neilson

Boiler pressure – 100 lb/ sq in assumed *Heating surfaces:* *Tractive effort – 5.840 lb*
Cylinders – 15" x 22" *tubes – 937 sq ft* *Coal capacity – not recorded*
Leading wheels – 4' 0" *firebox – not recorded* *Water capacity – 600 gal*
Driving wheels – 6' 0" *grate – 12.4 sq ft* *Locomotive weight – not recorded*
Trailing wheels – 4' 0"
Wheelbase – 6' 8" + 7' 1"
Locomotive length – 23' 10" (over buffers)

RNC notes that Neilson records indicate that one engine had 16" x 22" and two had 15" x 24" cylinders. Other sources state dimensions of 15" x 22" (and also 15½" x 22", possibly due to re-boring later in career).

There is also uncertainty regarding the initial wheel arrangement. Some sources, including McDonnell (proceedings of Institute of Civil Engineers Vol 48.7), state that they were originally 2-2-2 tender engines, and were delivered in this state. RNC cites Neilson records as confirming this, stating that they were converted to 2-2-2STs prior to takeover by the GSWR. However, the authors' investigations have failed to confirm RNC's interpretation of these records. With a total mileage of 31½, use of tender locomotives by the CYR was hardly justified, unless intended for planned route expansion.

As rebuilt:

Boiler pressure – 100 lb/ sq in assumed *Heating surfaces:* *Tractive effort – 6,900 lb*
Cylinders – 15" x 22" *tubes – 937 sq ft* *Coal capacity – not recorded*
Leading wheels – 3' 8" *firebox – not recorded* *Water capacity – 600 gal*
Driving wheels – 5' 1" *grate – 12.4 sq ft* *Locomotive weight – not recorded*
Wheelbase – 6' 8" + 7' 1"
Locomotive length – 23' 10" (over buffers)

McDonnell's may have recycled parts from Types V [5] Nos 77-9 and XXIX [29] Nos 119-121 in rebuilding these engines.

The Neilson GA drawing confirms the cylinder dimensions and the 2-2-2ST configuration. They were supplied with short saddle tanks, with the dome between saddle tank and smokebox on first ring of the boiler. McDonnell was authorised to rebuild these engines in January 1876 as 2-4-0STs, although Nos 78 and 79 were apparently available for sale the following year. Nevertheless, conversion of all three to 2-4-0ST was completed in 1879, although their subsequent careers were short.

Castleisland Railway

The 4¼-mile line of this independent company from Gortatlea (on the Mallow to Tralee route) opened in August 1875. Its only powered unit was a combined locomotive and carriage, which was built at Inchicore at a cost of £1,585 and identified as "C". On absorption of the CR on 31st August 1879, it was taken into GSWR stock and apparently numbered 90 from then. Further details are recorded under GSWR Type XLVIII [48] Class 90 in Chapter 6.

Waterford, Dungarvan & Lismore Railway

This company opened between the towns in its title, a distance of 43 miles, on 12th Aug 1878. To the west, the 16-mile Fermoy & Lismore Railway (FLR) opened on 1st October 1872 and continued to an end-on junction with the GSWR's 17-mile branch from Mallow. This link provided the company with its only connection to the rest of the Irish railway network.

The GSWR worked the FLR from opening until 1893, when the WDLR took over running that line. At Waterford South, it was separated from the WLR/ WKR station by the River Suir, which it lacked the resources to bridge. The WDLR was built on the cheap, with sharp curves and steep banks to save on earthworks, which caused problems in later years for the heavy Cork-Rosslare boat trains that used this route.

Like the WLR and WCIR, it depended on financial support from the GWR until that company looked elsewhere for preferential trading relationships. The WDLR then became part of the Fishguard & Rosslare Railways & Harbours Company (F&RR&HC) in July 1898, and services continued to be worked by the WDLR for a short time. The GSWR took over the working of the former WDLR line on 1st November 1898, absorbing its seven locomotives and all rolling stock. The new concern could afford not only the missing Waterford-Wexford link, but also a bridge across the River Suir both of which were opened in August 1906. Thus Dungavan passenger trains finally achieved a cross-platform connection at Waterford, some 60 years after a direct Cork-Waterford link was first proposed.

In 1877 the WDLR ordered four six-coupled engines from Avonside for delivery by April 1878 but refused them because of late completion; the MGWR (a company with ever an eye for bargains) then bought them. As built, they were delicate-looking machines but following rebuild, they became powerful goods engines and three ran until 1949. While awaiting replacement engines from Sharp Stewart, the WDLR borrowed engines from the Dublin Wicklow & Wexford Railway and the GSWR. Like the Waterford & Central Ireland Railway it could only afford to buy engines in small batches, but it did at least rely on a standard design. This was a Sharp Stewart small wheeled mixed traffic 0-4-2 (of which there were eventually six), and which were similar to locomotives supplied to the DWWR. The only other acquisition was a 2-4-0ST from the GSWR, which had started life as Cork & Youghal Railway No 1.

The WDLR locomotive livery was red (exact shade unrecorded) with numbers on the smokebox door. Other than re-building ex-WDLR No 3 as a saddle tank, the GSWR took little interest in the WDLR locos: all were scrapped by 1914 and they had no influence on Inchicore practice.

RNC Type: LXXII [72]		0-4-2			GSWR Class: 244/ 246
WDLR No	Makers No	Built	GSWR No (1898)	GSWR No (1901)	Withdrawn
1	2818	1878	211	244	1909
2	2819	1878	212	245	1906
3	2820	1878	213	246 §	July 1914
4	2821	1878	214	247 §	1905

WDLR Type LXXII [72] No 3 following conversion to 0-4-2T and running as GSWR No 246. *LPC*

Built by Sharp Stewart

Boiler pressure – 120 lb/ sq in assumed	Heating surfaces:	Tractive effort – 12,200 lb
Cylinders – 17" x 24"	tubes – 1037 sq ft	Coal capacity – unknown
Driving wheels – 4' 10"	firebox – 81.4 sq ft	Water capacity – 1560 gal
Trailing wheels – 3' 7"	grate – not recorded	Locomotive weight – 35 tons 10 cwt
Wheelbase – 6' 11" + 7' 4"		
Locomotive length over buffers – 24' 1½"		

§ No 3 was converted by the GSWR into an 0-4-2ST, probably in 1898, becoming the sole member of Class 246. As a tank locomotive its carrying capacities were 540 gallons and 18 cwt of coal. Sources indicate that No 247 might have been rebuilt as an 0-4-2ST after 1901 but this is unconfirmed. Otherwise, they were little altered by GSWR except for shorter chimneys.

Waterford, Dungarvan & Lismore Railway Type LXXII [72] 0-4-2 No 1 running as GSWR No 211. *Ken Nunn*

RNC Type: LXXIII [73]		0-4-2			GSWR Class: 248
WDLR No	Makers No	Built	GSWR No (1898)	GSWR No (1901)	Withdrawn
6	3665	1891	216 §	248	1913
7	3813	1892	217	249	1910

Built by Sharp Stewart

Boiler pressure – 120 lb/ sq in assumed	Heating surfaces:	Tractive effort – 12,200 lb
Cylinders – 17" x 24"	tubes – 1037 sq ft	Coal capacity – unknown
Driving wheels – 4' 10"	firebox – 81.4 sq ft	Water capacity – 1500 gal
Trailing wheels – 3' 7"	grate – unknown	Locomotive weight – 35 tons 10 cwt
Wheelbase – 6' 11" + 7' 4"		
Locomotive length over buffers – 24' 1½" [No 6]; 25' 1½" [No 7]		

§ No 216 was rebuilt in 1899 as a saddle tank for shunting at Limerick. Apart from conversion of No 248 to saddle tank, they were little altered by GSWR except for shorter chimneys. A note on the Sharp Stewart GA drawing adds that No 7 (1892) was to be supplied fitted with vacuum brakes, a longer cab, and the overhang from rear axle to rear of footplate extended from 2' 3" to 3' 3".

It is not clear why RNC drew a distinction between these two locomotives and the four under Type LXXII [72] as they seem to have been very similar when built.

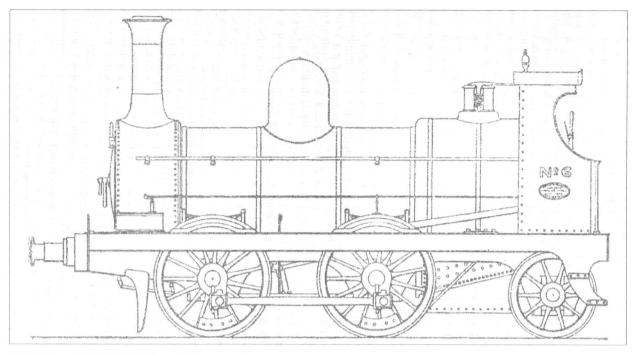

WDLR Type LXXIII [73] 0-4-2 No 6. *The Locomotive*

RNC Type: LXX [70] 2-4-0ST GSWR Class: n/a

This locomotive started life as CYR No 1 Lewis in 1859 and was renumbered 61 on takeover by the GSWR in 1866, and renumbered a second time as 71 in 1870. It was sold by the GSWR to the WDLR in 1883 who applied the number 5 in that company's list. With acquisition of the WDLR in 1898, it was allocated its third GSWR identity (No 215) but this was not applied before the locomotive was withdrawn the same year.

Waterford & Wexford Railway/ Fishguard & Rosslare Railways & Harbours Company

The WWR was 9½ miles long and opened on 24th June 1882 to connect Wexford with Rosslare. The route connected with the Dublin, Wicklow & Wexford Railway by means of an end-on junction at Wexford north. Pending full development of the harbour and with little local traffic, the WWR was unremunerative and closed in May 1889.

The Fishguard & Rosslare Railways & Harbours Company took over the line in August 1894, and acquired the WWR's two tank locomotives. The route was partially re-opened that month and the GSWR assumed operational control in 1898. The F&RR&HC had sufficient resources to complete the connection and an Act passed in August 1898 granted the company authority to: (a) build a new line from Waterford to Rosslare Strand (b) to acquire the Waterford, Dungarvan & Lismore and the Fermoy & Lismore railways (c) to build a branch from Fermoy to Dunkettle on the route from Cork City to Youghal/ Queenstown. Branch (c) was not built and this project was abandoned in 1903 although the GSWR chose to levy fares and rates calculated *via* the non-existent Fermoy-Dunkettle section. A further Act passed in 1903 permitted the bridging of the River Suir at Waterford and closure of Waterford South station. The new bridge enabled creation of a through route from Rosslare to Cork *via* Waterford, Lismore and Mallow, thereby avoiding the journey *via* Waterford, Clonmel and Limerick Junction, a distance of 164 miles. The new route via Dungarvan was 147 miles although had the Fermoy-Dunkettle branch been incorporated, the mileage would have been reduced to 123.

The new route was ceremonially opened on 21st July 1906 and to the general public 30th August 1906; from its inception, the F&RR&HC leased the line to the GSWR and it was worked jointly with the Great Western Railway. Following the closure in 2010 of the South Wexford Line (from Waterford to Rosslare Strand), the Wexford-Rosslare section remains the last operational section of the F&RR&HC's Irish railway system. The two original WWR locomotives entered the GSWR fold by way of the F&RR&HC in 1898.

Acquired companies' locomotives

RNC type: LXVII [67]   **0-6-0ST**   **GSWR Class Erin**

No	Name	Built	Makers No	Absorbed into GSWR stock	Withdrawn
(300)	Erin	1894	610	1898	1930

Built by Hunslet Engine Co

Boiler pressure – 130 lb/ sq in	Heating surfaces:	Tractive effort – 9,280 lbs
Cylinders – 14" x 18"	tubes – 520 sq ft	Coal capacity – 44 cu ft
Driving wheels – 3' 6"	firebox – 54 sq ft	Water capacity – 580 gal
Wheelbase – 5' 4" + 5' 5"	grate – 8.25 sq ft	Locomotive weight – 25 tons 18 cwt
		Max axle loading 9 tons 1 cwt

This locomotive together with *Cambria* (Type LXVIII [68]) was supplied to Messrs Rowlands and Cartland, business men involved in the development of the F&RR&HC. *Erin* and *Cambria* were used to re-open the line to Kilrane in August 1894 by which time the F&RR&HC had absorbed the WWR plus the two engines. They carried the initials R&WR (for Rosslare & Wexford Railway) on their buffer beams which was a geographically more accurate summary of what the WWR had achieved thus far. Both may have been employed in construction of the pier at Rosslare which opened in 1895. In 1898, the GSWR took over operation of the Irish railways owned by the F&RR&HC including both engines. *Erin*, which never carried its allotted number, was latterly used in the Tralee area and occasionally at Fenit Pier.

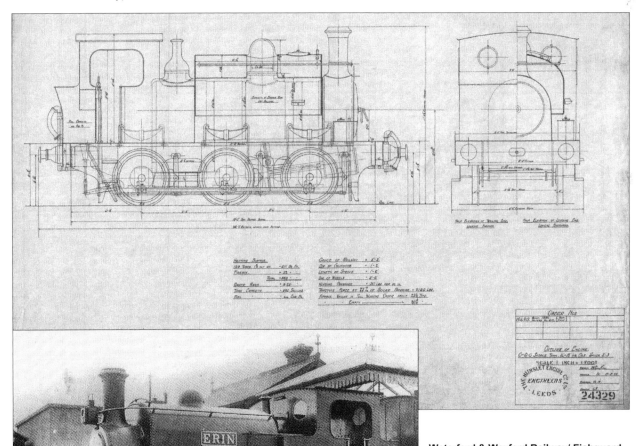

Waterford & Wexford Railway/ Fishguard & Rosslare Railways & Harbours Company 0-6-0ST Type LXVII [67] *Erin* (nominally GSWR No 300 at Wexford North).

Drawing – *Hunslet Archive, Statfold Barn Railway*

Locomotives of the Great Southern & Western Railway

RNC type: LXVIII [68]   0-4-0ST   **GSWR Class: Cambria**

Name	Built	Makers No.	Absorbed into GSWR stock	Withdrawn
Cambria	1894	609	1898	1921

Built by Hunslet Engine Co

Boiler pressure – 130lb/ sq in	Heating surfaces:	Tractive effort – 4,870 lbs
Cylinders – 10" x 15"	tubes – 262 sq ft	Coal capacity – 22 cu ft
Driving wheels – 2' 10"	firebox – 31 sq ft	Water capacity – 300 gal
Wheelbase – 4' 9"	grate – 5.5 sq ft	Locomotive weight – 16 tons

This locomotive was supplied new to the F&RR&HC for the re-opening of the WWR and passed into GSWR ownership in 1898; cross-reference entry appears on Page 171.

It never received a GSWR number, continuing to be identified by name only. In late 1921, it was transferred to the Dublin & Blessington Steam Tramway in return for the locomotive from ex-DSER rail-motor 0-4-0T No 70. This engine had been bought from the DSER in 1918 but its stay was brief as it was soon found to be too heavy. *Cambria* was lighter on the poorly maintained tramway trackwork and became D&BST No 5, retaining the name. It was withdrawn in 1928. For later history of ex-DSER No 70, refer to RNC Type LXIX [69] *Imp* in this chapter.

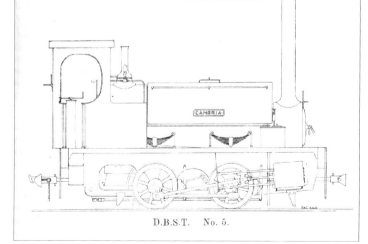

WWR/ FRRHC 0-4-0ST Type LXVIII [68] *Cambria* as Dublin & Blessington Steam Tramway No 5 (This drawing dates refers to its DBST condition; the extraordinary chimney was necessary so that exhaust would clear the towed double-deck tram vehicles). *IRRS*

Acquired companies' locomotives

Waterford & Central Ireland Railway (previously Waterford & Kilkenny Railway)

In its early days, this railway seems to have been quite experimental. It toyed with, but did not use, Prosser's system of wooden rails and introduced the side tank type to these islands. These three engines proved to be its most numerous "class". Two Jenny Lind type 2-2-2s came later from Kitson, but the rest were all small wheeled four-coupled designs. The WKR had an uneasy and occasionally violent cohabitation with the Waterford & Limerick Railway at its southern terminus. Nevertheless, on 28th January 1861 the company entered a working agreement with the WLR, which absorbed the WKR engines into its own fleet. When that agreement was dissolved in 1867, the WKR received back seven engines of which five were understood to have been in working condition. Between 1848 and 1900, it possessed a total of eighteen locomotives of which eleven passed into GSWR ownership in 1900. Financial constraints enforced purchase in ones and twos resulting in a fleet of small, varied and in some cases elderly, machines. Not surprisingly, the GSWR took little notice of them and scrapped the last in 1909. In WCIR days, the livery was:

Locomotives: dark green with black bands and light green lines with red inner lines on cab and tender. Frames brown with black border and red lines. Engine number in gold on buffer beam and rear of tender

Coaches: dark lake with vermillion lines; gold lettering, shaded red and black

Wagons: dark slate grey lettered white.

Despite the signing of the WKR/ WLR working agreement in January 1861, there is evidence of the WLR taking over the smaller company's trains the previous July. This contract was due to last for five years, but by mutual consent (unusual between these two lines) was extended to 1st June 1867, when the WKR resumed responsibility for its own services and motive power.

Surviving records of the WCIR are incomplete, but a set of guards' journals from 1st August 1900 has allowed re-construction of the working timetable. This required four engines in steam, plus presumably a station pilot (probably 0-4-2T No 12) at Waterford:

Locomotive	Departure	Departure	Mileage
Vulcan 0-4-2 No 4	7.00 am	Waterford-Maryborough Passenger	
	10.08 am	Mayborough-Kilkenny Goods	
	1.20 pm	Kilkenny-Maryborough Goods	
	4.25 pm	Maryborough-Waterford Mixed	175
Avonside 0-4-2 No 11	7.40 am	Kilkenny-Waterford Mixed	
	10.45 am	Waterford-Kilkenny Mixed	
	2.45 pm	Kilkenny-Waterford Mixed	
	6.30 pm	Waterford-Kilkenny Goods	124
Vulcan 2-4-0 No 8	8.05 am	Maryborough-Waterford Passenger	
	3.40 pm	Waterford-Mountmellick Passenger	
	6.55 pm	Mountmellick-Maryborough Passenger	134
Avonside 0-4-2 No 10	8.20 am	Maryborough-Mountmellick	
	9.20 am	Mountmellick-Waterford Mixed	
	4.50 pm	Waterford-Maryborough Mixed	134

WKR locomotives, first period (1848-1861):

For much of this period, the company was at loggerheads with its neighbour, the Waterford & Limerick Railway but some form of rapprochement must have been established to enable conclusion of the working agreement of 28th January 1861.

A deciding factor in the arrangement was probably the WKR's persistently precarious financial condition that necessitated help from the WLR.

In other circumstances purchase of its financially troubled neighbour might have been the obvious next step but the WLR itself was never a prosperous concern and probably lacked the requisite financial resources.

The terms of the working agreement have been lost but commercial logic suggests that:

[1] The WKR passed all its mobile assets into the care of the WLR, regardless of condition, to strengthen its apparently poor bargaining position (i.e. to avoid discounting the value of their "contribution").

[2] The agreement granted possession but crucially not ownership of the mobile assets to the WLR.

[3] The WLR warranted to return all assets to the WKR at termination of the agreement in unchanged or better condition than that in which they had been acquired.

From its inception, the WKR had acquired nine locomotives comprising three 2-2-2-2Ts by Charles Tayleur, two 2-4-0s by Stothert & Slaughter, two 2-2-2s by Kitson, one 2-4-0 by Fairbairn, and one 0-4-2 by EB Wilson. All locomotives and rolling stock had suffered from poor maintenance when the WLR assumed control.

The first of the 2-2-2-2Ts had been sold sometime between 1859 and 1861, but if the foregoing assessment is accurate, then the WLR took possession of the remaining eight locomotives. All were then overhauled except for the remaining pair of 2-2-2-2Ts whose condition and/ or unsuitable design did not justify their receiving further workshop attention. However, as possessors rather than owners the WLR would not have been legally entitled to break them up. At conclusion of the working agreement in 1867 and return to their owners, these two curiosities were reportedly immediately dismantled. Other sources proffer alternative accounts but the authors maintain that this is the most probable explanation.

RNC Type: I[1]-WKR 2-2-2-2T **GSWR Class n/a**

First WKR No	Maker's No	Built	WLR No.	Second WKR No	Withdrawn
1	241	1846	-	8 (1857)	1859
2	242	1846	[22] §	-	by 1867
3	243	1846	[23] §	-	by 1867

Built by Charles Tayleur

Boiler pressure – 80 lb/ sq in assumed *Cylinders – 14" x 20"* *Leading wheels – 3' 6"* *Driving wheels – 5' 6"* *Trailing wheels – 3' 6"* *Wheelbase – 4' 10" + 5' 6" + 5' 6"* *Locomotive length – 24' 9"*	*Heating surfaces:* *not recorded*	*Tractive effort – 4,040 lb* *Coal/ water capacities – not recorded* *Locomotive weight – not recorded*

§ Some sources attribute these numbers but they are considered unreliable, especially as No 23 was carried by a 2-4-0 described in the next section; and No 22 may have been carried by the Wilson 0-4-2 (Type VII [7]-W). For this reason, 2-2-2-2T Nos 22 and 23 are NOT included in the WLR/ WLWR Locomotive number Key. As they were apparently not in operable condition prior to 1861, no practical purpose would have been served by giving them WLR running numbers.

Completed in 1846, these unusual and historically significant locomotives were not delivered until 1848, making their first trial trip on 1st May. They were the first side tanks built in these islands and might have been among the first of this type built anywhere. The long, deep side tanks, necessitated the extra pair of wheels for weight distribution, at a time when most new engines were six-wheeled. They are sometimes mis-described as 4-2-2Ts whereas all wheels were set within a rigid frame resulting in a long fixed wheelbase, which must have caused excessive wear on curves. As supplied, they were very heavy on fuel, burning 32-34 lb of coke per mile but by 1852, overhaul had reduced this to 15-16 lb per mile.

Fairbairn-built 2-4-0 No 1 (later WLR No 26) was added to the WKR fleet in 1855 which suggests that 2-2-2-2T No 1 was by then out of service although it was resuscitated and renumbered 8 about 1857. It was sold to Messrs Carlisle & Hutchings (contractors) in 1859 who apparently went bankrupt shortly afterwards. It is possible that the WKR was never paid for the engine; its history thereafter is unknown. It appears that under the operating agreement, 2-2-2-2T Nos 2 and 3 joined the WLR's ranks but probably did no further work. On return to WKR control/ ownership they were promptly scrapped.

This section is cross-referenced with Type VIII [8]-W in Chapter 8.

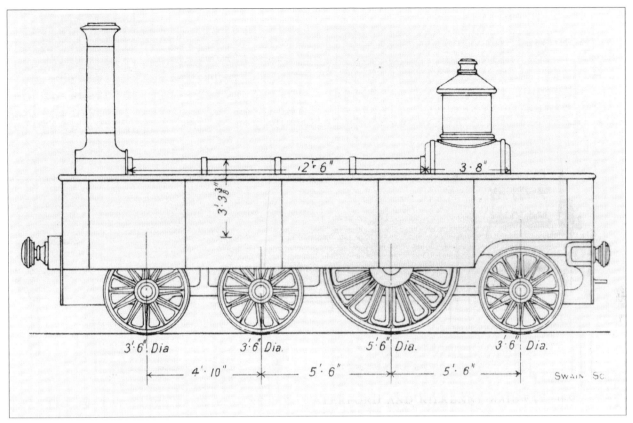

Waterford & Kilkenny Railway 2-2-2-2T Type I[1]-WKR Nos 1 to 3, as built by Charles Tayleur in 1846. *The Locomotive*

RNC Type: II [2]-WKR			2-4-0		GSWR Class n/a	
First WKR No	**Built**	**WLR No**	**Second WKR No**	**Rebuilt**	**GSWR No**	**Withdrawn**
4	July 1852	23	2	-	[251]	1901
5	July 1852	24	3	1875	-	1900

Built by Stothert & Slaughter

Boiler pressure – 120 lb/ sq in	Heating surfaces:	Tractive effort – 8,280 lb
Cylinders – 15" x 22"	not recorded	Coal capacity – not recorded
Leading wheels – 3' 6"		Water capacity – 1300 gal
Driving wheels – 5' 1"		Locomotive weight – 24 tons
Wheelbase – 14' 6"		

Second WKR No 3, as rebuilt:

Boiler pressure – 140 lb/ sq in	Tractive effort – 9,350 lb
Cylinders – 15" x 22"	
Driving wheels – 5' 3"	

Following rebuilding of No 3, Fayle quotes cylinders for No 2 as 15' x 24" but RNC does not agree with these dimensions.

No 3 appears to have been out of service following an accident at Ballyhale on 26th March 1895 when a connecting rod pierced the boiler (see Appendix C). Despite the serious nature of this damage, it was reportedly repaired in 1898 but only worked until 1900. When taken into GSWR ownership, the only brakes for both locomotives were hand-operated with wooden blocks on the 4-wheel tenders. Refer to Appendix C for summary details of this accident.

This section is cross-referenced with Type IX [9]-W in Chapter 8.

Locomotives of the Great Southern & Western Railway

WKR Type II [2]-WKR 2-4-0 First No 4 or 5 (later Waterford & Limerick Railway Nos 23 & 24, then Waterford & Central Ireland Railway Nos 2 & 3).

RNC Reference: Type III [3] - WKR		2-2-2		GSWR Class - n/a	
First WKR No	**Built**	**Maker's No**	**WLR No**	**Second WKR No**	**Withdrawn**
6	May 1853	320	25	4	1892
7	May 1853	321	27	5	1892

Built by Kitson & Co

Boiler pressure – 120 lb/ sq in assumed *Heating surfaces:* *Tractive effort – 7,320 lb*
Cylinders – 15" x 22" *tubes – 800 sq ft* *Coal/ water capacities – not recorded*
Leading wheels – 4' 0" *firebox – 93 sq ft* *Locomotive weight – not recorded*
Driving wheels – 5' 9" *grate – 14.6 sq ft*
Trailing wheels – 4' 0"
Wheelbase – 7' 10" +7' 2"
Length over frames but excluding front buffer beam and rear drag beam – 21' 3"

These were of the Jenny Lind type i.e. outside bearings on the leading and trailing wheels; inside bearings on the drivers.

This section is cross-referenced with Type X [10]-W in Chapter 8.

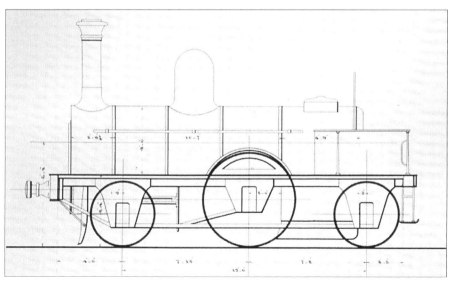

WKR 2-2-2 Type III [3]-WKR First Nos 6, 7 built 1853 (later Waterford & Limerick Railway Nos 25 & 27, then Waterford & Central Ireland Railway Nos 4 & 5).

Stephenson Locomotive Society

RNC Type IV [4]-W (No WKR Type allocated) 2-4-0 **GSWR Class n/a**

WKR No	Built	WLR No
1	1855	26

For dimensional and other information, refer to Chapter 8 Type IV [4]-W. This locomotive was retained by the WLR in 1867.

RNC Type: VII [7]-W (also Type IV [4]-WKR) 0-4-2 **GSWR Class n/a**

WKR (1st) No	Built	WLR No	WKR (2nd) No	Makers No	Withdrawn
2	1857	22 §	1	578	1892

Built by EB Wilson

Boiler pressure – 140 lb/ sq in reduced Nov 1861 – 110 lb/ sq in Cylinders – 16" x 24" Driving wheels – 4' 9" Trailing wheels – not recorded Wheelbase – not recorded	Heating surfaces: – not recorded	Tractive effort – 12,830 lb – 10,080 lb Coal/ water capacities – not recorded Locomotive weight – not recorded

§ There is ambiguity about the identity of this locomotive on its inclusion in the WLR stock list. RN Clements stated that it was numbered 19 but other sources claim that it was No 22. After exhaustive investigation, the authors opine that No 22 was the more likely. However, the locomotive is believed to have carried the following additional identities during its mysterious and inadequately recorded career:- WKR No 2; WCIR (i.e. second WKR) No 1.

There is also doubt about the wheel arrangement as some sources state it was a 2-4-0, but this is considered unlikely. By 1857 Wilson had virtually given up construction of 0-4-2s although it did build some 5' 6" gauge locomotives of this type for service in India and No 22 might have been a modification of this design. This locomotive was supplied new to the Waterford & Kilkenny Railway becoming that company's No 2. When operation of the WKR was taken over by the WLR in 1861, it was one of six locomotives added to the WLR stock list, duly numbered 22 in the latter's series. In 1867, the WKR reverted to independent ownership and control; this locomotive became WKR No 1. It apparently later underwent another identity change at an unrecorded date, becoming No 13. It may have been out of service for some years prior to withdrawal. There were concerns about it being overweight for passenger work and it was mainly confined to slow speed goods duties.

RNC noted that in April 1861, the boiler pressure was 110 lb/ sq in which would suggest 14" diameter cylinders. At that time, it bore the number 2 but less than a month later there was a board reference that stated "large Kilkenny engine now number 22 will be out of shops this weekend". The locomotive (at which time it was carrying the number 1) was involved in an accident at Ballylowra on 6th September 1867 (See Appendix C). As a result, it was entirely rebuilt in 1869 which might have included an increase in boiler pressure to 140 lb/ sq in, although details are not available. In summary, recorded information about this locomotive should be treated with caution.

Working arrangement with the Waterford & Limerick Railway (1861-67)

During this period, the WLR renumbered six of the WLR locomotives in its own list. On dissolution of the arrangement, the five serviceable locomotives that returned to the WKR were apparently insufficient for the latter's needs so three new engines were purchased immediately, and a fourth the following year. Five further engines were later obtained in piecemeal manner. For clarity, the WKR/ Waterford & Central Ireland Railway locomotives are summarised below:

RNC Type	W.A.	Builder	Built	First WKR No	WLR No	Post-1867 No	Withdrawn
I[1]-WKR	2-2-2-2T	Tayleur	1846	1 (later 8)	-	-	1859
I[1]-WKR	2-2-2-2T	Tayleur	1846	2	-	-	by 1867
I[1]-WKR	2-2-2-2T	Tayleur	1846	3	-	-	by 1867
II[2]-WKR	2-4-0	Stothert & Slaughter	1852	4	23	2 §	1901
II[2]-WKR	2-4-0	Stothert & Slaughter	1852	5	24	3	1900
III[3]-WKR	2-2-2	Kitson	1853	6	25	4	1892
III[3]-WKR	2-2-2	Kitson	1853	7	27	5	1892
IV[4]-W	2-4-0	Fairbairn	1855	1	26	-	1875
VII[7]-W	0-4-2	EB Wilson	1857	2	22	1	1892

§ GSWR No 251 allocated but not carried

New WCIR locomotives, second period (1867-1900):-

RNC Type	W.A.	Builder	Built	WCIR No	GSWR no	Withdrawn
V[5]-WKR	2-4-0T	Fowler	1866	6	[253]	1901
V[5]-WKR	2-4-0T	Fowler	1866	7	[254]	1901
VI[6]-WKR	2-4-0	Vulcan Foundry	1867	8	[255]	1902
VI[6]-WKR	2-4-0	Vulcan Foundry	1868	9	[256]	1902
VII[7]-WKR	0-4-2	Avonside	1873	10	257	1906
VII[7]-WKR	0-4-2	Avonside	1873	11	258	1907
VIII[8]-WKR	0-4-2T	Avonside	1876	12	[259]	1902
IX[9]-WKR	0-4-2	Sharp Stewart	1884	1 §	[250]	1905
X[10]-WKR	0-4-2	Vulcan Foundry	1897	4	252	1909

§ Possibly originally No 13

RNC Type: V[5]-WKR		2-4-0T/ 2-4-0			GSWR Class n/a
WCIR No	Built	Maker's No	GSWR No	Rebuilt as 2-4-0	Withdrawn
6	1866	706-9 (see below)	[253]	April 1872	1901
7	1866		[254]	October 1869	1901

Built by J Fowler

Boiler pressure – 140 lb/ sq in
Cylinders – 15" x 22"
Leading wheels – 3' 6'
Driving wheels – 5' 0"
Wheelbase – 14' 6"

Heating surfaces:
not recorded

Tractive effort – 9,820 lb
Coal capacity – not recorded
Water capacity – 1300 gal
Locomotive weight – 24 tons

In 1866, the Belfast, Hollywood & Bangor Railway (BHBR) ordered four 2-4-0Ts (works Nos, 706-9), from Fowler, but only took delivery of one. The BHBR apparently encountered difficulties in paying (not uncommon for Irish railways), in this case exacerbated by the collapse of the company's bankers (Overend & Gurney) in 1866. The Belfast & Co Down Railway (associated with the BHBR) bought one of the remainder and the WKR acquired the other two the following year. It is no longer possible to identify the relevant works numbers. As tank engines, they were too heavy for the WKR track leading to their rebuild as 2-4-0s with four-wheel 1300-gallon tenders from Avonside. Each conversion cost £355 and the work included addition of a heavy balance weight at the rear to compensate for removal of the bunker.

By 1900, like all WCIR locos (except Nos 2 and 3), they had been fitted with steam and automatic vacuum brakes. Equipped originally with weather boards only, at its second rebuilding in 1897 No 7 was fitted with a cab and square base to its chimney, the latter being carried until shortly before the GSWR takeover.

Waterford & Central Ireland Railway 2-4-0 Type V [5]-WKR following conversion to tender locomotives, No 6 (GSWR allocated but not carried No 253) with No 7 (GSWR allocated but not carried No 254) behind.
Ken Nunn

Acquired companies' locomotives

RNC type:	VI[6]-WKR		2-4-0		GSWR Class n/a
WKR No	**Maker's No**	**Built**		**GSWR No**	**Withdrawn**
8	591	1867		[255]	1902
9	592	1868		[256]	1902

Built by Vulcan Foundry

Boiler pressure – 140 lb/ sq in	Heating surfaces:	Tractive effort – 9,350 lbs
Cylinders – 15" x 22"	tubes – 950 sq ft	Coal capacity – 46 cu ft
Leading wheels – 3' 3"	firebox – 70 sq ft	Water capacity – 1400 gal
Driving wheels – 5' 3"	grate – 13.7 sq ft	Locomotive weight – 26 tons
Wheelbase – 6' 7" + 7' 5"		
Length over frames, engine only – 21" 7"		
NB the leading wheel diameter is based on Vulcan company records; RNC states 3' 6"		

Originally these had dome-less boilers; later they had brass domes and square bases to chimney. Tender wheel base was 5' 6" + 5' 6" with 3' 6" diameter wheels; inside bearings. In 1871, Sir Daniel Gooch arbitrated in a dispute between builders and the WCIR, and awarded £655 to Vulcan.

WCIR 2-4-0 Type VI[6]-WKR No 8 or 9 built by Vulcan Foundry in 1867/ 8. Later allocated GSWR Nos 255/ 6 but not carried.
Ken Nunn

RNC type: VII[7]-WKR			0-4-2		GSWR Class 257
WCIR No	**Built**	**Maker's No**		**GSWR No**	**Withdrawn**
10	1873	965		257	1906
11	1873	966		258	1907

Built by Avonside Engine Co

Boiler pressure – 140 lb/ sq in	Heating surfaces:	Tractive effort – 11,600 lb
Cylinders – 16" x 24"	not recorded	Coal capacity – not recorded
Driving wheels – 5' 3"		Water capacity – 1600 gal
Trailing wheels – 4' 0"		
Wheelbase – 7' 6" + 7' 0"		

They were equipped with Naylor safety valves and supplied with six-wheel tenders. These were the first engines on WCIR fitted with cabs.

WCIR 0-4-2 Type VII[7]-WKR No 11 running as GSWR Class 257 No 258.

WCIR 0-4-2T Type VIII[8]-WKR No 12, allocated GSWR No 259 but not carried. *Statfold Barn Railway*

Acquired companies' locomotives

RNC type: VIII[8]-WKR   0-4-2T   **GSWR Class n/a**

WCIR No	Built	Maker's No	GSWR No	Withdrawn
12	1876	1169	[259]	1902

Built by Avonside Engine Co

Boiler pressure – 140 lb/ sq in	Heating surfaces:	Tractive effort – 6,980 or 9,500 lb
Cylinders – 12" x 22" or 14" x 22"	not recorded	Coal capacity – 10 cwt
Driving wheels – 4' 6"		Water capacity – not recorded
Trailing wheels – 3' 6"		Locomotive weight – not recorded

Supplied with copper-capped chimney and polished brass dome, this locomotive was sometimes referred to as "The Geashill", on the grounds that it might have been built for the Central Ireland Railway, which at one stage had aspirations to reach that town. It may have been used by the contractors on the Mountmellick branch, but it spent the rest of its working life shunting at Waterford.

RNC type: IX[9]-WKR   0-4-2   **GSWR Class n/a**

WCIR No	Built	Maker's No	GSWR No	Withdrawn
1	1884	3233	[250]	1905

Built by Sharp, Stewart

Boiler pressure – 140 lb/ sq in	Heating surfaces:	Tractive effort – 11,890 lb
Cylinders – 16" x 24"	tubes – 1007 sq ft	Coal capacity – 4 tons
Driving wheels – 5' 1½"	firebox – 88.5 sq ft	Water capacity – 1600 gal
Trailing wheels – 3' 7½"	grate – sq ft	Locomotive weight – not recorded
Wheelbase – 7' 2" + 6' 10"		
Locomotive length over buffers – 23' 5½"		

NB These dimensions are based on Maker's GA drawing; RNC states boiler pressure – 130 lb/ sq in; cylinders – 17" x 24"; driving wheels – 5' 3"; trailing wheels 3' 6".

This engine was almost identical to Sharp Stewart order No E729 dated 1876 (Builder's No 2656) which became DWWR No 37. The two locomotives used the same GA drawing. This drawing has a number of amendments in red ink, which is assumed to apply to the later WCIR order. It came with raised round-top firebox casing, Ramsbottom safety valves and a six-wheel tender. This locomotive was possibly numbered 13 until 1892.

WCIR 0-4-2 Type IX[9]-WKR No 1, allocated GSWR No 250 but not carried.

RNC Reference: X[10]-WKR		0-4-2		GSWR Class 252
WCIR No	**Built**	**Maker's No**	**GSWR No**	**Withdrawn**
4	1897	1558	252	1909

Built by Vulcan Foundry

Boiler pressure – 140 lb/ sq in *Heating surfaces:* *Tractive effort – 11,420 lb*
Cylinders – 16" x 24" *total – 1036 sq ft* *Coal capacity – 4 tons*
Driving wheels – 5' 4" *grate – not recorded* *Water capacity – 1600 gal*
Trailing wheels – 4' 1" *Locomotive weight – 32 tons 15 cwt*
Wheelbase – 8' 0" + 7' 4" (other records state total 15' 0")

This was the last 0-4-2 tender engine built for any railway in these islands. Supplied with six-wheel tender.

WCIR 0-4-2 Type X[10]-WKR No 4, running as GSWR Class 252 No 252.

Ex-contractor's locomotive

RNC type: LXVI [66]		0-6-0ST		GSWR Class 299
GSWR No.	**Built**	**Name**	**Makers' No**	**Withdrawn**
299	1892	"Shamrock"	557	1957

Built by Hunslet Engine Co

Boiler pressure – 130 lb/ sq in *Heating surfaces:* *Tractive effort – 7,740 lb*
Cylinders – 12" x 18" *tubes – 356 sq ft* *Coal capacity – 47 cu ft.*
Driving wheels – 3' 1" *firebox – 45 sq ft* *Water capacity – 500 gal*
Wheelbase – 5' 4" + 5' 2" *grate – 7.4 sq ft* *Locomotive weight – 23 tons 5 cwt*
Length over buffer – 22' 5" *Max axle loading – 7 tons 9 cwt*
Boiler pressure later reduced to 120 b/ sq in.

This locomotive was supplied to TH Falkiner for construction of the Kenmare and Clifden branches, and then sold to the Tralee & Fenit Pier & Harbour Commissioners in 1899. It became GSWR No 299 in 1901, and remained shunting at Fenit until 1941, when wartime conditions had reduced traffic to almost zero. It moved to Limerick and finally Cork (Rocksavage) for use on the Courtmacsherry branch beet trains.

Acquired companies' locomotives

Ex-contractor's locomotive 0-6-0ST Type LXVI [66] GSWR No 299 [Shamrock].
Drawing - *Hunslet Archive, Statfold Barn Railway*

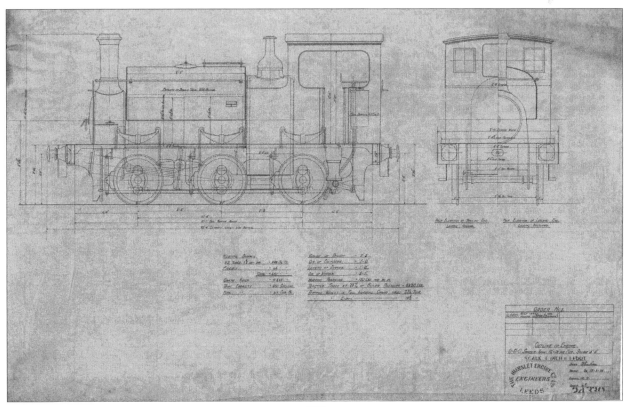

Ex-railmotor locomotive

RNC Type: LXIX [69] 0-4-0T **GSWR Class: Imp**

Name	Makers No	Built	Purchased	Withdrawn
Imp	1693	Aug 1906	1921	1928

Built by Manning Wardle

Boiler pressure – 175 lb/ sq in	Heating surfaces:	Tractive effort – 7,970 lb
later – 160 lb/ sq in		– 7,300 lb
Cylinders – 12" x 16" + Marshall valve gear	tubes – 441 sq ft	Coal capacity – 1 ton 5 cwt
Driving wheels – 3' 7"	firebox – 45 sq ft	Water capacity – 540 gal
Wheelbase – 8' 0"	grate – 9.5 sq ft	Locomotive weight – 26 tons 14 cwt
Locomotive length – 20' 6" (over buffers as 0-4-0T)		Max axle loading – 13 tons 7 cwt

NB The Manning Wardle catalogue quotes the engine portion as weighing 23 tons 10 cwt; weight above would include bunker, drawgear etc added on conversion to a tank locomotive.

The Dublin & South Eastern Railway in 1906 obtained two railmotors from Manning Wardle which it numbered 1 and 2. They were built as a small 0-4-0T power unit and a saloon coach body on a single frame. Proving unsuccessful with poor riding qualities, they were withdrawn in 1907-8. The units were split with the power sections becoming small 0-4-0Ts Nos 69 and 70 while the coach portions became locomotive-hauled 44' long saloons that lasted until 1959. The locomotives then worked with the erstwhile railmotor coaches plus one or two 6-wheel coaches but without any push-pull facility. Other than the need to run round, this configuration proved reasonably successful on Westland Row-Kingstown services.

No 70 was sold to the Dublin & Blessington Steam Tramway in 1918 becoming their No 2 but it proved too heavy. It was swapped with No 609 *Cambria* from the GSWR in 1921, who named it *Imp* but gave it no number.

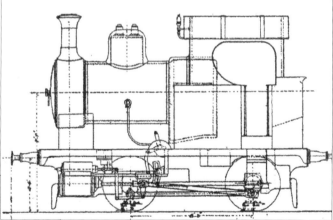

Drawing and official builder's photographer of railmotor engine unit as originally supplied to DESR; later 0-4-0T Type LXIX [69] *Imp*.
Manning Wardle, Statfold Barn Rail

Chapter 8
Locomotives of the Waterford, Limerick & Western Railway

A total of ninety-eight locomotives were owned and operated by the Waterford & Limerick Railway, and by its successor from 1st January 1896, the Waterford, Limerick & Western Railway. Fifty-eight remained on the books at the takeover on 1st January 1901, making the WLWR the GSWR's largest corporate purchase in terms of fleet size and route mileage. For most of its existence the WLR had survived in an impecunious condition which apart from its original Waterford-Limerick section largely served remote, impoverished and thinly-populated areas. With capital perennially in short supply, new locomotives were obtained in small batches from English and Scottish manufacturers. The numerically largest group was ten 2-4-0s (Type XIX [19]-W supplied by Vulcan Foundry between 1874 and 1882.

Further diversity resulted from locomotives which emerged from the workshops at Limerick whose progeny was uncertain i.e. either earlier machines rebuilt or "new" locomotives created from spare parts on hand or other sources. WLR locomotive history is further complicated by the acquisition of second hand engines, some of obscure origins. Also, from 1861-7, it operated the Waterford & Kilkenny Railway, taking six engines from that company into its stock and returning five when the WKR resumed working its own line. The origins of the fleet being varied, every locomotive associated with the WLR has been included despite some never having passed into the hands of the GSWR.

The WLR's locomotive history is more clear following recruitment in 1884 of JG Robinson as Assistant Locomotive Superintendent. He took charge of the company's Limerick works four years later and proceeded to modernise the fleet. By 1901, the WLWR owned 58 locomotives of which exactly half were to his designs plus six earlier machines rebuilt under his direction.

The WLR/ WLWR fleet is segmented into thirty-five Type categories using the Roman-numeric system devised by RN Clements. This methodology was an effective means of distinguishing locomotive groups from an era when the notion of "Class" in the now accepted sense did not exist. However, in certain obscure cases distinctions may have become blurred and RNC's allocations appear to contain anomalies. These are explained in the relative histories: - Type V [5]-W; Type XIV [14]-W; Type XVII [17]-W; Type XXX [30]-W.

In addition, three locomotives in two RNC Types were acquired by the WLR from other companies and taken out of service well before takeover by the GSWR. Relevant details are recorded at the end of this chapter; they are referenced by the RNC's Roman-numeric system:

Type I[1]-MGWR: 2-2-2 WLR Nos 30 & 31

Type XXIII [23]-GSWR: 0-4-2 WLR No 25

RNC's system remains the core means of identification as it is important to maintain continuity between his archives and this survey. It also stands as appropriate recognition of his invaluable pioneering research into a complex and confusing segment of motive power history.

View of Limerick works on the occasion of the visit by the Duke and Duchess of York on 31 August 1897. The locomotive at the head of the train is No 55 *Bernard*. The carriage workshops are to the left with those for locomotives in the centre background. The offices of the locomotive superintendent are to the right.

New construction, rebuilding and dimensions

The comments in Chapter 3 concerning access to commercial manufacturers' records are particularly relevant to the WLR/ WLWR. All the locomotives reviewed in this chapter can trace their origins in whole or in part back to British manufacturers. Builders' records occasionally conflict with dimensions recorded by RNC and other sources. Some inconsistencies can be reconciled by the cycle of repair, renewal or more extensive rebuilding (e.g. thicker tyres, re-bored cylinders, changed tube plates and tube dimensions) while others are less easy to justify.

Up to six engines that emerged from Limerick workshops have been recorded by some sources as new builds. In practical terms it is difficult to distinguish between the products of rebuilding and those that blended new components from commercial manufacturers with parts recovered from withdrawn machines. Further complication might have arisen from alternative definitions to support variations in accounting treatment. At this distance, there is little purpose in refining definitions other than to note that certain engines within the following Types could be interpreted as the result of either new construction or extensive rebuilding: XIVA [14A]-W/ XVIIA [17A]-WW/ XXA [20A]-W; XXX [30]-W. Details are provided in the relevant Type histories.

Variations in dimensions have been noted and reconciliation of the differences is complicated by the manner in which the WLR managed its business. Prior to 1884 the company suffered from poor maintenance, erratic time-keeping, low staff morale and an unacceptable level of operating incidents and accidents. A succession of Locomotive Superintendents failed to tackle a parlous situation or were prevented from so doing. Under these conditions, the company's records, where such survive, should be regarded as unreliable.

Of the fifty-eight locomotives passed to the GSWR, thirty-six were scrapped between 1901 and 1919. Nine never carried their allotted GSWR numbers and probably did little or no work for their new owners. All but one of the 21 engines that survived to pass into Great Southern Railways' ownership in 1925 had been introduced by Robinson. His designs were notably more modern-looking than contemporary GSWR locomotives, displaying the characteristic elegance that in part contributed to his later fame. No further locomotives based on WLWR designs were built and Robinson exerted no direct influence on Inchicore policy. Sixteen ex-WLWR locomotives worked into Corás Iompair Eireann days. 2-4-0 No 291 (ex-No 44 *Nephin*) remaining in service until 1959.

Survey by Great Western Railway

In 1874, William Dean of the GWR surveyed the WLR's motive power and rolling stock and his signed report survives, duly stamped "GWR Loco and Carriage Engineer's Office, Swindon" (Kew PRO File Rail 1057). This document is clearly for asset valuation purposes as part of a due diligence exercise, preparatory to considering a takeover bid. The basis for the GWR's interest would have been the LNWR's competing relationship with the GSWR and the possible consolidation of an Irish presence through capital investment. However, the English banking crisis of 1866 had brought the GWR uncomfortably close to bankruptcy. Chairman Sir Daniel Gooch in his rigorous financial husbandry would have given short shrift to spending scarce cash on purchase of a marginal operation.

Dean's report provides a useful overview of the WLR's locomotive fleet and has also enabled re-construction of the WLR timetable and locomotive allocation. No station pilot was provided at Limerick, but links Nos 3, 7 and 10 allowed for sufficient time for shunting there. The basic service required 18 engines in steam:

Depot	Link	Services	Elapsed journey time	Distance (nearest mile)
Limerick	1	2.30 am Mixed Limerick-Tuam Arr 2.45 pm	12 hr 15 min	76
		3.45 pm Mixed Tuam-Limerick Arr 9.40 pm	5 hr 55 min	76
Ennis	2	7.45 am Pass Ennis-Limerick Arr 9.10 am	1 hr 25 min	25
		9.55 am Pass Limerick-Tuam Arr 5.25 pm	7 hrs 30 mn	76
Tuam	3	6.15 am Passenger Tuam-Limerick Arr 11.20 am	5 hr 5 min	76
		3.20 pm Pass Limerick-Tuam Arr 7.40 pm	4 hrs 20 min	76
Tuam	4	8.45 am Pass Tuam-Athenry Arr 9.25 am	40 min	16
		10.00 am Pass Athenry-Tuam Arr 10.35 am	35 min	16
		11.15 am Pass Tuam-Limerick Arr 6.15 pm	7 hr	76
		6.55 pm Pass Limerick-Ennis Arr 8.20 pm	1 hr 25 min	25
Limerick	5	6.00 am Pass Limerick-Waterford Arr 10.25 am	4 hr 25 min	77
		2.45 pm Pass Waterford-Limerick Arr 6.50 pm	4 hr 5 min	77
Waterford	6	5.40 am Pass Waterford-Limerick Arr 9.45 am	4 hr 5 min	77

Locomotives of the Waterford, Limerick & Western Railway

		11.20 am Mail Limerick-Waterford Arr 2.45 pm	3 hr 25 min	77
Limerick	7	1.35 pm Pass Limerick-Tipperary Arr 3.30 pm	1 hr 55 min	25
		6.30 pm Goods Tipperary-Limerick Arr 9.00 pm	2 hr 30 min	25
Waterford	8	11.45 am Mail Waterford-Limerick Arr 3.15 pm	3 hr 30 min	77
		4.00 pm Pass Limerick-Waterford Arr 8.15 pm	4 hr 15 min	77
Waterford	9	8.30 pm Mail Waterford-Limerick Arr 1.30 am	5 hrs	77
Limerick	10	10.40 am Mail Limerick-Waterford Arr 3.45 pm	5 hrs 5 min	77
Limerick	11, 12	Each locomotive working one Goods Limerick-Waterford	-	77
Waterford	13, 14	Each locomotive working one Goods Waterford-Limerick	-	77
Limerick	15, 16	Foynes and Newcastle branches	-	§
Limerick	17	Killaloe branch	-	69 #
Waterford	18	Station pilot	-	-

§ The operation of these branches was quite complex and It seems that they were worked by two locomotives, one allocated to each terminus. The public timetable for 1875 suggests that between them, the two locomotives covered around 240 miles in a working day.

The public timetable for 1875 indicates three return workings per day.

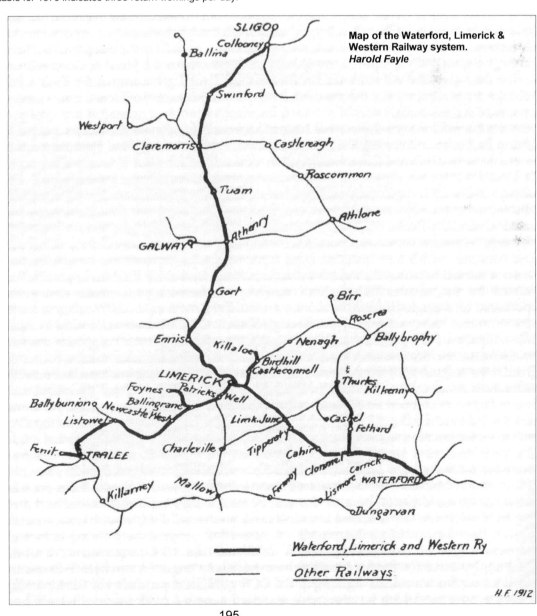

Map of the Waterford, Limerick & Western Railway system. *Harold Fayle*

The leisurely timings were largely the product of the WLR's unique geographic character. Its route crossed a succession of other companies' trunk lines and off-shoots that radiated from Dublin. The timetable was thus structured to maximise traffic opportunities by co-ordinating with the schedules of others. Waiting time to make connections could be lengthy. In the case of Athenry, timetabled pauses by WLR trains in 1874 could vary between ten minutes and two hours. Also, even trains described as passenger were expected to "work the road" (i.e. become mixed) for parts of their journeys; in 1891 there were no separate goods trains on the northern line. Goods trains between Waterford and Limerick Junction (55½ miles) took between four and six and a half hours, with around half that time spent on station work or while side-lined to allow passenger train movements. With the completion of the route from Waterford to Sligo, there were probably very few passengers who actually travelled end-to-end by the WLWR between those two points. A dog-leg journey that included changing termini at Dublin possibly consumed less elapsed time and would certainly be less frustrating.

Working southwards, the WLWR timetable tried to achieve practicable connections at:

Sligo with the Midland Great Western and Sligo, Leitrim & Northern Counties railways.

Claremorris with the MGWR services to Dublin, Westport, and Ballina.

Athenry with trains on the MGWR Dublin-Galway line.

Limerick City with services to Limerick Junction, Cork, Dublin, north Kerry.

Clonmel for Thurles.

Waterford with services to Kilkenny.

The GWR's report opined that the fleet of 32 engines was inadequate to cover the 18 links as only 15 were in good or fair mechanical order including two singles (an old Bury and the newer Kitson engine) which were of limited value. Four locomotives were judged in poor condition; although at work, three were rated dangerous; and twelve were under or awaiting repair or (like Sharp 0-4-2 No 27) not considered worth repairing. There was nothing in reserve for excursions, fair specials, ballast trains and to provide cover for breakdowns.

Names and liveries

The early WLR livery was mid-green but this was changed to brown, lined light blue and edged in yellow in the 1870s. By 1889 there had been a reversion to mid-green. About 1896, Robinson introduced crimson lake for passenger and tank engines, lined either yellow or gold and black. Goods locomotive were black, with French grey panels, lined gold but soon changed to red. The domes of some tank locomotives and 2-4-0s were polished brass but those on the 4-4-0s were painted. Selected engines displayed the company crest on cab or tender sides. This combined the coats of arms of Waterford, Clonmel and Limerick, with an archaic 2-2-2 in the centre, but to celebrate completion of the Sligo extension and the new company name, the 2-2-2 was replaced with 4-4-0 *Jubilee* in green livery. With copper chimney caps, varying degrees of brass-work, colourful liveries and names applied to all fleet additions after 1886, the WLWR locomotives were among the most attractive in Ireland. The need to keep the GWR happy meant smart work on the mainline, especially the boat trains for the New Milford steamers. GSWR ownership brought more sombre colours and removal of the names.

Dramatis Personae

Reflecting the chaotic affairs for much of the company's history, the position of Locomotive Superintendent was held by thirteen individuals between 1847 and 1900, of whom only three are worthy of note. The competent Martin Atock was in charge at Limerick from 1861 until 1872 before moving to the Midland Great Western Railway. There followed a confused period under indifferent leadership before Henry Appleby moved from the Great Western Railway to take over in 1882. Appleby was capable but faced a myriad of issues in an organisation that had been badly led by a faction-ridden directorate bent on meddling in management-level issues. While these problems were largely resolved around the time of his arrival, the company's motive power deficiencies were exacerbated by poor quality staff, low morale, and inadequate workshops. Appleby, overwhelmed by the burden, gained approval in 1884 to recruit JG Robinson from the GWR as his assistant. Appleby's health deteriorated under the pressure and was made worse by serious injury sustained in a road accident in 1888 from which he never fully recovered. The directors were reluctant to let him retire, but eventually relented. He returned to England in March 1889, dying later that year aged 52.

When John George Robinson (1856-1943) succeeded Appleby in 1889, operating standards were well short of Board of Trade requirements. Locomotive renewal and improved repair facilities were major priorities and demands would soon increase through completion of the WLR's extension from Tuam to Sligo. Although the tradition of motive power additions in small batches continued,

Robinson introduced dimensional standardisation in cylinders, Stephenson valve gear, motion, boilers and other components. Steam and vacuum brakes were fitted, arranged so the steam brake could be applied at the same time as the vacuum via the ejector handle, or independently. An inconvenience for the GSWR was that all Robinson's engines had right-hand drive.

Robinson's modernisation programme remained incomplete at the GSWR's takeover. There was no place for him in the GSWR hierarchy but in the summer of 1900 SW Johnson, Locomotive Superintendent of the Midland Railway while holidaying in the Limerick area had been much impressed by the motive power fleet. He sought out the man responsible and in the ensuing discussion mentioned that Harry Pollitt, Locomotive Superintendent of the Great Central Railway would shortly retire. This information led to Robinson's departure from Ireland.

Above: GSR/ GSWR No 298 (previously WLWR Type XXXIV [34]-W No 55 *Bernard* under repair in Limerick workshops on 13 July 1932. *Real Photographs*

Right; GSR/ GSWR No 237 (previously WLWR Type XXXV [35] – W) 0-6-0 No 56 *Thunderer* on a lengthy passenger service, bogie coach leading and the remainder apparently 6-wheelers. *Stephenson Locomotive Society*

Locomotives of the Great Southern & Western Railway

WLR/ WLWR Locomotive Number Key

WLWR/ WLR No	GSWR No	RNC Type	Built	W.A.	Withdrawn
1		I [1] - W	1846	2-2-2	Nov 1861
		XI [11] - W	Aug 1859	0-4-2	1883
		XXIII [23] - W	1879	0-6-0	1899
	221	XXIII [23] - W	1899	0-6-0ST	1909
2		I [1] - W	1846	2-2-2	Jul 1862
		XII [12] - W	1854 or 1856	0-4-2	1900
	222	XXXV [35] - W	Mar 1900	0-6-0	1949
3		I [1] - W	1846	2-2-2	Nov 1861
		XIII [13] - W	1845 (See No 27)	0-4-2	Dec 1874
		XVII [17] - W	Feb 1872	0-4-2	1892
	260	XXX [30] - W	1892	0-4-2T	1912
4		I [1] - W	1846	2-2-2	Nov 1861
	[223]	XIV [14] - W	Jun 1862	0-4-2	1901
5		I [1] - W	1846	2-2-2	Jul 1862
		XIV [14] - W	Jun 1862	0-4-2	1893
	224	XIVA [14A] - W	1893	0-6-0	1909
6		I [1] - W	1846	2-2-2	Jul 1862
		XIV [14] - W	Aug 1864	0-4-2	Oct 1890
	225	XIVA [14A] - W	1890	0-6-0	1907
7		II [2] - W	1848 or 1851	2-2-2	1867 ?
		XVII [17] - W	Feb 1872	0-4-2	Jul 1888
	226	XVIIA [17A] – W	Jul 1888	0-6-0	1905
8		III [3] - W	May 1849	2-2-2	1880
	[261]	XIX [19] - W	Mar 1881	2-4-0	1902
9		III [3] - W	Apr 1848	2-2-2	Mar 1885
	262	XXV [25] - W	1886	4-4-0	1912
10		III [3] - W	Apr 1848	2-2-2	1888
	263	XXVIII [28] - W	May 1889	2-4-0	1907
11	[264]	IV [4] - W	Jan or Apr 1853	2-4-0	1901
12		IV [4] - W	Feb or May 1853	2-4-0	1885
		XXVI [26] - W	1886	4-4-0	1894
	265	XXVI [26] - W	1894	2-4-0	1907
13		V [5] - W	Aug 1853	0-4-2	1891
	266	XXIX [29] - W	1891	2-4-2T	1934

WLR/ WLWR Locomotive Number Key (continued)

WLWR/ WLR No	GSWR No	RNC Type	Built	W.A.	Withdrawn
14		V [5] - W	Aug 1853	0-4-2	1891
	267	XXIX [29] - W	1891	2-4-2T	1935
15		V [5] - W	Sep 1853	0-4-2	1894
	268	XXX [30] - W	1894	0-4-4T	Nov 1912
16		V [5] - W	Jan 1854	0-4-2	1896
	269	XXXIII [33] - W	Feb 1896	4-4-2T	Mar 1957
17		IV [4] - W	Jan or Feb 1854	2-4-0	1896
	270	XXXIII [33] - W	Feb 1896	4-4-2T	1949
18		IV [4] - W	Jan or Feb 1854	2-4-0	1897
	271	XXXIII [33] - W	1897	4-4-2T	1949
19		IV [4] - W §	Apr 1854	2-4-0	1875
		VI [6] - W	1855	2-2-2WT	1874
	[272]	XX [20] - W	1876	0-4-2	1901
20		IV [4] - W	Apr 1854	2-4-0	1892
	273	XXVIII [28] - W	Mar 1892	2-4-0	1909
21		IV [4] - W	Dec 1855	2-4-0	1897
	274	XXXIII [33] - W	1897	4-4-2T	1949
22		VII[7]-W	1857	0-4-2	1892
		XVIII [18] - W	1862	0-4-2	Oct 1890
	275	XXVIII [28] - W	1890	2-4-0	Mar 1913
23		XVIII [18] - W	1862	0-4-2	1892
	276	XXVIII [28] - W	Mar 1892	2-4-0	1949
24		XVIII [18] - W	1862	0-4-2	1886
	227	XXVII [27] - W	1886	0-6-0	Nov 1910
25		XXIII [23] - GSWR	Sep 1847	0-4-2	c.1874
	[277]	XIX [19] - W	May 1874	2-4-0	1902
26		IV [4] -W	Oct 1855	2-4-0	1875
	278	XX [20] -W	1876	0-4-2	Mar 1910
27		XIII[13]-W	1845 (ex No 3)	0-4-2	Dec 1874
		XX [20] - W	1876	0-4-2	1899
	279	XXa [20A] - W	1899	0-4-4T	Aug 1953

§ Records re No 19 (Types IV[4]-W and VI[6]-W) are ambiguous; refer to Histories for best explanation.

WLR/ WLWR Locomotive Number Key (continued)

WLWR/ WLR No	GSWR No	RNC Type	Built	W.A.	Withdrawn
28	[280]	XV [15] - W	1864	2-2-2	1902
29	228	XVI [16] - W	Dec 1865	0-4-0ST	1925
30		I [1] – MGWR	1847	2-2-2	1873
	281	XIX [19] - W	May 1874	2-4-0	1903 or 1904
31		I [1] – MGWR	1847	2-2-2	1873
	282	XIX [19] - W	May 1874	2-4-0	Nov 1910
32	283	XIX [19] - W	May 1874	2-4-0	Nov 1910
33	[284]	XX [20] - W	1876	0-4-2	1901 or 1902
34	[229]	XXI [21] - W	1877	0-6-0T	1901
35	285	XIX [19] - W	Mar 1881	2-4-0	Feb 1911
36	286	XIX [19] - W	Apr 1881	2-4-0	1903
37	287	XIX [19] - W	Apr 1881	2-4-0	1909
38	288	XIX [19] - W	Nov 1882	2-4-0	1907
39	289	XIX [19] - W	Dec 1882	2-4-0	May 1905
40	230	XXII [22] - W	1883	0-6-0	1909
41	231	XXII [22] - W	1883	0-6-0	Sep 1910
42	[232]	XXIV [24] - W	Jun 1862	0-6-0WT / 0-4-2WT	1901
43	290	XXVIII [28] - W	Jun 1893	2-4-0	Oct 1951
44	291	XXVIII [28] - W	Jun 1893	2-4-0	Aug 1959
45	233	XXXI [31] - W	1893	0-6-0	Jun 1919
46	234	XXXI [31] - W	1893	0-6-0	Apr 1911
47	292	XXVIII [28] - W	Apr 1894	2-4-0	Jun 1915
48	293	XXVIII [28] - W	Apr 1894	2-4-0	Feb 1954
49	235	XXXI [31] - W	1895	0-6-0	1927 or 1928
50	236	XXXI [31] - W	1895	0-6-0	1951
51	294	XXXII [32] - W	1895	0-4-4T	Nov 1910
52	295	XXXII [32] - W	Jun 1895	0-4-4T	Aug 1954
53	296	XXXIV [34] - W	Mar 1896	4-4-0	1949
54	297	XXXIV [34] - W	Apr 1896	4-4-0	May 1928
55	298	XXXIV [34] - W	May 1897	4-4-0	1949
56	237	XXXV [35] - W	Mar 1897	0-6-0	1951
57	238	XXXV [35] - W	Mar 1897	0-6-0	1934
58	239	XXXV [35] - W	Mar 1897	0-6-0	1949

Notes:

(1) For long it was uncertain whether 0-4-2 Locomotive No 22 of WLR Type VII [7]-W was part of the fleet of the Waterford & Limerick Railway or the Waterford & Kilkenny. Detailed investigation has confirmed this was never a WLR locomotive; allocation of Type VII [7]-W was erroneous. Although included in the Key above, refer to Chapter 7 Page 185 for details.

(2) The following WKR locomotives were allocated WLR Types in respect of the 1861-7 working agreement. These Types are not recorded in the WLR Key. Their details appear in Chapter 7 Pages 182 to 184 as follows:

Original WKR No	WLR Temporary No	WCIR No	WKR Type	WLR (notional) Type
2, 3	n/a	n/a	I [1]-WKR	VIII [8]-W
4, 5	23, 24	2, 3	II [2]-WKR	IX [9]-W
6, 7	25, 27	4, 5	III [3]-WKR	X [10]-W

Great Western Railway.

Locomotive and Carriage Department,
ENGINEER'S OFFICE.
Swindon, 18th December, 1874.

Report of Inspection of Rolling Stock, and Locomotive & Carriage Department appliances in use on the Waterford & Limerick Railway & Branches.

Locomotives.

The number of Locomotive Engines is stated in the Rolling Stock Return published with the Waterford & Limerick Railway Co's accounts for the half year ending June 30th 1874, to be 31 Engines & Tenders and 1 Tank Engine. These I found in the following condition at the date of my inspection, 7th to 11th Nov.;

Engines at work	New Engines Nº 25. 30. 31. 32.	Total	4
	In good order – 3. 4. 5. 7. 8. 10. 13. 14. 28. 29		10
	Will shortly require ordinary repairs Nº 15. 23		2
	Will shortly require heavy repairs (new boilers & cylinders) . 1. 2. 17.		3
	Must soon be condemned . 20. 21.		2
			21
Engines not at work	Condemned Nº 19. 26. 27.		3
	Waiting new boilers . 11. 18.		2
	Repairs will be completed in 2 weeks 12. 16.		2
	Waiting general ordinary repairs 6. 9. 22. 24.		4
			11
		Total	32

Diagrams giving the principal outline dimensions of the Engines & Tenders are enclosed herewith, and in statement Nº 6 will

Locomotives of the Great Southern & Western Railway

RNC Type: I [1]-W   2-2-2   GSWR Class n/a

WLR No & Name	Built	Withdrawn	WLR No & Name	Built	Withdrawn
1 *Glengall*	1846	Nov 1861	4 *Limerick*	1846	Nov 1861
2 *Bessborough*	1846	Jul 1862	5 *Suir*	1846	Jul 1862
3 *Waterford*	1846	Nov 1861	6 *Shannon*	1846	Jul 1862

Built by Stothert & Slaughter

Boiler pressure – 80 lb/ sq in	*Heating surfaces:*	*Tractive effort – 4,880 lbs*
Cylinders – 15" x 22 "	*not recorded*	*Coal capacity – 2 tons [coke]*
Leading wheels – 3' 6"		*Water capacity – 3 tons*
Driving wheels – 5' 9"		*Locomotive weight – 21 tons 0 cwt*
Trailing wheels – 3' 6"		*Tender weight – 11 tons*
Wheelbase – 7' 6" + 8' 6"		
Locomotive length – 25' estimated		

All were delivered in March 1847, and one was used to help in construction of the line. They were unusual in having outside cylinders and an accident near Kilsheelan on 31 Nov 1853 was attributed to this feature. (Fayle suggested that the type was similar to the Eastern Counties Railway Class 51 but this cannot be verified). All were removed from main line duties by 1854 and Atock authorised scrapping in 1861-2. Number 6 was possibly rebuilt as a 2-2-2T in 1857 but this is unconfirmed. Board minute of 3rd October 1849 records that locomotives between Limerick and Tipperary burned turf in preference to coal/ coke and that a cottage near Pallas was burned by "flakes of fire" from a passing engine.

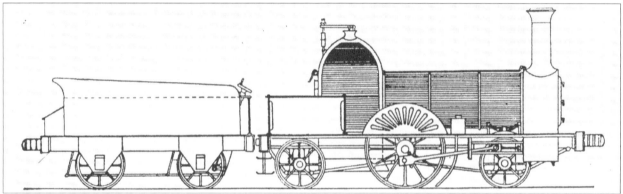

The first locomotive type for the WLR was unusual for its time in having outside cylinders. *The Locomotive*

RNC Type: II [2]-W   2-2-2   GSWR Class n/a

WLR No	Built	Withdrawn
7	1848 or 1851	1867? or converted to 2-4-0

Built by Grendon

Boiler pressure – 80 lb/ sq in	*Heating surfaces:*	*Tractive effort – 3,640 lb*
Cylinders – 14" x 18 "	*not recorded*	*Coal/ water capacities – not recorded*
Driving wheels – 5' 6" or 5' 7"		*Locomotive weight – 19 tons 0 cwt*
Carrying wheels – not recorded		
Wheelbase – not recorded		

This locomotive appears to have been supplied to Dargan and used by him on the WLR 1848-1852. It was possibly lent to the company and then sold to the WLR in Jan 1853, becoming No 7. Recorded information is sparse and inconsistent.

RNC Type: III [3]-W   2-2-2   GSWR Class n/a

WLR No	NWRR No	Built §	Renewed	Withdrawn
8	3	May 1849	1867	1880
9	1 or 2	April 1848	1865	Mar 1885
10	1 or 2	April 1848	1871	1888

§ These dates are unconfirmed

Locomotives of the Waterford, Limerick & Western Railway

Built by Bury, Curtis & Kennedy

Boiler pressure – 80 lb/ sq in *Cylinders – 15" x 20"* *Leading wheels – 4' 1"* *Driving wheels – 5' 8"* *Trailing wheels – 3' 6"* *Wheelbase – 6' 11" + 6' 2"*	*Heating surfaces:* *tubes – not recorded* *firebox – not recorded* *grate – 11.6 sq ft*	*Tractive effort – 4,500 lb* *Coal/ water capacities – not recorded* *Locomotive weight – not recorded*

As renewed, dimensions are believed to have been:

Boiler pressure – 100 lb/ sq in *Cylinders – 15" x 20"* *Leading wheels – 4' 1"* *Driving wheels – 5' 8"* *Trailing wheels – 3' 6"* *Wheelbase – 7' 9" + 7' 1"*	*Heating surfaces:* *tubes – not recorded* *firebox – not recorded* *grate – 14 sq ft*	*Tractive effort – 5,630 lb* *Coal/ water capacities – not recorded* *Locomotive weight – not recorded*

Records indicate that at renewal a stronger boiler was installed with working pressure of 100 lbs/ sq in.

Built for the Newry Warrenpoint & Rostrevor Railway (NWRR), these engines were a typical Bury design with bar frames, D-shaped firebox with low crown and a good deal of decorative brass-work. They cost the NWRR £2,162 each and were apparently similar to other Bury engines built for the Belfast & Ballymena Railway (October 1847), and the GSWR (January 1848). They were externally similar to near-contemporary GSWR Type II [2] but did not accord precisely in leading dimensions with any of the three variants of the latter. A design difference was that the front axle of the NWRR version had a swivel arrangement so that it performed like a pony truck. The Belfast & Ballymena Railway (BBR) also had similar locomotives.

Being considered too heavy and powerful for the NWRR, in conjunction with a 5-year contract to work that railway, Dargan took them over in May 1850 and

This diagram was prepared for the GWR Survey Report of 1874. By this time Bury was well embarked upon design and construction of six-wheeled locomotives.

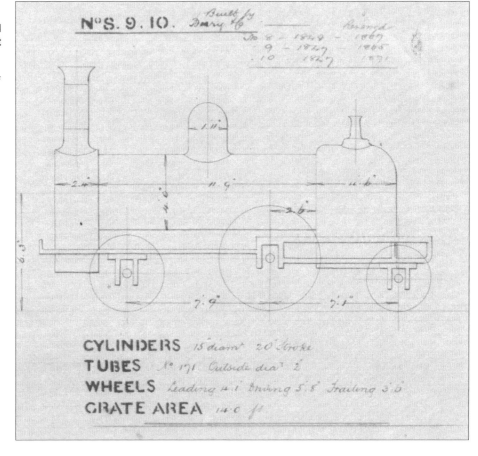

substituted smaller locomotives. He may have used one or all of the ex-NWRR trio in construction of the Tipperary to Dunkitt section before selling them to the WLR in 1852. By February 1861 No 8 was running with a boiler pressure of 95-100 lbs, and rated to haul ten carriages. One or more may have run with a boiler pressure as high as 120 lb/sq in (see below). They were probably supplied with standard Bury 4-wheel tenders but by 1874 were apparently running with 6-wheel tenders built by Slaughter & Co.

GWR survey comments dated 21st September 1874:

No 8: Patches put on bottom of barrel inside; new iron and brass tubes; tyres in fair condition; commenced running in April 1874; engine at work.

No 9: Second boiler now nine years old cannot be in good condition in view of its age; this boiler has never been examined as the tubes were only taken out a few at a time as they failed; advised Mr Mills (foreman at Waterford) to reduce boiler pressure from 120 lb to 95 lb; engine at work. (Supplementary report 10th November 1874: Engine now under repair; a very faulty plate taken out of boiler at smokebox end. Crank axle recently renewed.)

No 10: In good order

Board minute dated March 1888 records that No 10 was not worth further expenditure although it was still shunting at Tuam the following June. It was later used to drive the sawmill in Limerick Works; the cylinders and motion were recorded as still there in 1938.

RNC Type: IV [4]-W			2-4-0		GSWR Class n/a	
WLR No	Built	Renewed	Withdrawn	WLR No	Built	Withdrawn
11	Jan or Apr 1853	before 1874	1901	19	Apr 1854	1875
12	Feb or May 1853	before 1874	1885	20	Apr 1854	1892
17	Jan or Feb 1854	before 1874	1896	21	Dec 1855	1897
18	Jan or Feb 1854	before 1874	1897	26	Oct 1855	1875

(No 11 was allocated GSWR No 264, not carried)

Built by William Fairbairn

RN Clements treated these eight locomotives as a single Type but there were sufficient differences for them effectively to comprise two separate groups of four:

Nos 11, 12, 17, 18 (as rebuilt):

Boiler pressure – 90 lb/ sq in	*Heating surfaces:*	*Tractive effort – 6,850 lbs*
Cylinders – 16" x 21"	*tubes – not recorded*	*Coal/ water capacities – not recorded*
Leading wheels – 3' 6"	*firebox – not recorded*	*Locomotive weight – not recorded*
Driving wheels – 5' 0"	*grate – 14.3 sq ft*	
Wheelbase – 6' 5" + 7' 6½"		
Locomotive length – 25' 9"		

Boiler pitch was 6' 2½" for Nos 11, 17, 18 and 5' 10" for No 12. Diagram carries notation "reconstructed by WLR"; no details have been confirmed.

Nos 19-21, 26:

Boiler pressure – 95 lb/ sq in	*Heating surfaces:*	*Tractive effort – 5,780 lb*
Cylinders – 15" x 21"	*tubes – not recorded*	*Coal/ water capacities – not recorded*
Leading wheels – 3' 9"	*firebox – not recorded*	*Locomotive weight – not recorded*
Driving wheels – 5' 6"	*grate – 14.3 sq ft*	
Wheelbase – 6' 5" + 7' 6½"		
Locomotive length – 25' 9"		

Boiler pitch was 6' 1".

The origins are uncertain as Fairbairn records no longer survive but seemingly eight were built as a single order. Apparently only seven (Nos 11,12, 17-21) were delivered to the WLR while the eighth (No 26) went to the Waterford & Kilkenny Railway. The reason is unknown but it is speculated that the WLR

lacked the ability to pay for the final example. An alternative explanation is that the WKR ordered a single locomotive to the same design for its own needs. On expiry of the WLR/ WKR working agreement, No 26 was retained by the WLR presumably because the company already had seven basically similar locomotives. Nos 19-21, 26 had a bell-mouthed dome on the middle boiler ring.
As built, all eight featured polished brass work, weather boards and were coupled to inside-framed 4-wheel tenders. By withdrawal, No 11 had acquired a Robinson-style chimney and 6-wheel tender. RNC records that Nos 11, 17 and 18 were renewed in 1875, although the GWR 1874 report suggests that all three and plus No 12 had been rebuilt at an earlier date, details unrecorded. Despite their modest driving wheel sizes, all were regarded as passenger engines.

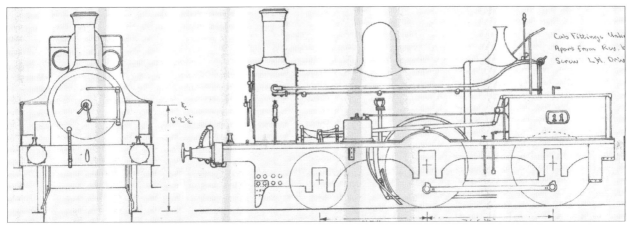

WLWR Type IV [4] – W No 11 (GSWR No 264, allocated but not carried) was a late survivor from the company's early motive power fleet and provides a useful illustration of design and construction from those days. *Richard Chown (by courtesy of Paul Greene) Photograph LGRP.*

The GWR 1874 report shows 11, 12, 17 and 18 as having been "reconstructed" and running with 5' 0" wheels and cylinders 16" x 21" but dates are lacking. All might have been built with 5' 6" wheels and 15" x 21" cylinders but this is speculative in the absence of builder's records. All seem to have been heavily used and by 1874, all were in poor condition.

GWR survey comments dated 21st September 1874; supplementary report 10th November 1874 in brackets [ ]:

No 11: New boiler, tubes and cylinders required; new boiler being made by Avonside Engine Co [Engine not at work].

No 12: Undergoing extensive repairs at Limerick [Very thorough repairs to engine and tender nearly completed; tyres recently renewed].

No 17: New boiler being made by Avonside Engine Co; new driving and trailing tyres May 1874; needs new cylinders; engine still at work [tyre recently renewed].

No 18: Not at work; condemned; new boiler being made by Avonside Engine Co; needs new cylinders [New cylinders ready; tyres middling].

No 19: Condemned; requires new boiler, frames, cylinders frames and leading axle [Boiler sufficiently good to be used for a stationary engine at reduced pressure].

No 20: Required new boiler, cylinders, frames, driving wheels, tyres and leading axle; this engine is still at work although in a dangerous condition [Crank axle recently renewed; tyres good (sic); boiler pressure 80 lb].

No 21: Required new boiler, cylinders, frames, driving wheels, tyres and leading axle; engine is still at work although in a dangerous condition [Tyres good (sic); boiler pressure 80 lb].

No 26: Condemned; wants new boiler, cylinders, frames, crank and leading axle [Not at work; tender in good condition].

Nos 19 and 26 were scrapped the following year. However repairs to Nos 20 and 21 extended their working careers by 18 and 23 years respectively. Fairbairn supplied a similar engine with smaller cylinders to the Dublin & Wicklow Railway (DWR, their No 3) in 1853 and near identical 2-4-0s to the MGWR (1852-4), DWR (1860) and the Dublin & Drogheda Railway (1855).

RNC Type: V [5]-W   0-4-2   **GSWR Class n/a**

Note: Some 0-4-2s were divided by RNC into different types: Sharp Nos 13-16 of 1853-4 (Type V [5]-W); Sharp Nos 4-6 of 1862-4 (Type XIV [14]-W); and Kitson Nos 3 & 7 of 1871-2 (Type XVII [17]-W). However, their leading dimensions were identical and the 1874 GWR Report (see below) combines them as a single group of engines.

WLR No	Makers' No	Built	Renewed	Withdrawn
13	736	Aug 1853	1869	1891
14	737	Aug 1853	1871	1891
15	740	Sept 1853	June 1868	1894 §
16	764	Jan 1854	1867	1896

§ Rebuilt as/ parts used for 0-4-4T Type XXX [30]-W No 15 (GSWR No 268).

Built by Sharp Stewart and Company

Boiler pressure – 95 lb/ sq in	*Heating surfaces:*	*Tractive effort – 9,190 lb*
Cylinders – 16" x 24"	*tubes – 1102 sq ft*	*Coal capacity – not recorded*
Driving wheels – 4' 6"	*firebox – 82 sq ft*	*Water capacity – 1000 gal*
Trailing wheels – 3' 6"	*grate – 13 sq ft*	*Locomotive weight – not recorded*
Wheelbase – 7' 11" + 6' 11½ "		
Locomotive length – 27' 2½"		

Nine locomotives of this type were supplied by Sharp Stewart to the following companies: WLR [four]; Dublin & Belfast Junction Railway [two]; Ulster Railway [three], as follows:

Order No	Builder's Nos	Built	Supplied to:	Running Nos
E259	736/ 737/ 740	1853	WLR	13 to 15
E274	764	1854	WLR	16
E268/ E325	738/ 992	1853/ 1857	DBJR	9/ 14
E319/ 366/ 398	975/ 1156/ 1274	1856/ 1860/ 1861	UR	16/ 3/ 4

Locomotives of the Waterford, Limerick & Western Railway

The WLR ordered four of this type but on completion, builder's No 738 was diverted to the DBJR to become their No 9 because either their need was more urgent or the WLR wished to defer delivery for financial reasons. Builder's No 764 was delivered to the WLR in substitution the following year to become their No 16.

When renewed in 1867-71, they received 1864-vintage boilers, with 180 two-inch diameter tubes, similar to Type XIV [14]. RNC records that four tenders were ordered with these engines, two for delivery by Dec 1852, two by March 1853 at £400 each. No 15 was derailed on 3rd March 1861 near Kilkenny while working the 11.40 am train, breaking 1000 rail chairs. The civil engineer attached blame to wheel flats and requested that locomotives in such a state should not work this line as it had light rails. The WLR was then working the WKR and that the mechanical engineer was willing to use locomotives in such condition on other lines suggests that the WLR loco department was struggling to find adequate motive power for both systems.

The conclusions of the September 1874 Survey; supplementary report dated November 1874 in brackets [ ]:

No 13: This engine is in fair condition (sic); one cylinder split and patched; engine at work

No 14: In good order; tyres new (Bessemer metal) 10th November 1873

No 15: This engine wants new tubes and probably some repairs to the boiler when examined; one cylinder split; engine still at work; [Crank axle recently renewed; leading and driving wheels good; trailing middling]

No 16: This engine requires a new set of tubes and one new cylinder; left one split; new tyres January 1874; the barrel of the boiler will probably require patching when the tubes are taken out; engine still at work; [Crank axle recently renewed; engine now under repair and boiler re-tubing; a new cylinder is ready for the left-hand side; tyres recently renewed]

The General Arrangement drawing by Sharp is in very poor state but clearly shows the dome immediately behind chimney. Three more very similar Sharp 0-4-2s (type XIV [14]-W) followed in 1862-4, but with the dome in the centre of a three-ring boiler.

RNC Type: VI [6]-W			2-2-2WT	GSWR Class n/a
WLR No	**Built**	**Withdrawn**		
19	1855	Believed scrapped by 1874		

Built by William Fairbairn or Stothert & Slaughter

Boiler pressure – 95 lb/ sq in	Heating surfaces:	Tractive effort – 2,930 lb
Cylinders – 11" x 18 "	not recorded	Coal/ water capacities – not recorded
Leading wheels – 3' 4"		Locomotive weight – not recorded
Driving wheels – 5' 0"		
Trailing wheels – 3' 4"		
Wheelbase – not recorded		

The origins of this locomotive are a mystery as the incomplete existing records conflict. It might have been built by Fairbairn but positive identification is prevented by the destruction of that company's records. Alternatively, No 19 might have been the Stothert & Slaughter 2-2-2 (Type: I [1]-W) which may have been rebuilt as a 2-2-2T or 2-2-2WT in about 1857. As the WLR did not use the number 6 again until 1864, it is not clear why it should have been renumbered from 6 to 19. RN Clements suggests the cylinders for the WLR Fairbairn 2-2-2WT at only 11" x 18" which would have rendered it a feeble machine. With a mainline then of 77 miles and with little local traffic, the WLR would have had little use for this type of engine.

Also, although the WLR recycled spare engine numbers, rather than keeping "class" members together, it did not (usually) have more than one loco in service with the same number at the same time, unless one was scheduled for early withdrawal.

A new Fairbairn locomotive (Type IV [4] – W) entered service as No 19 in 1854, and it seems unlikely that there was another No 19 in service concurrently. Byrom's list (dated 2015) does include a 2-2-2WT for the WLR in 1855 but omits the 2-4-0s of 1854-5. In 1855, Fairbairn did produce a number of 2-2-2WTs for other railways:

Three were supplied to the Ballymena, Ballymoney, Coleraine & Portrush Junction Railway, probably their Nos 5, 6, 7 one of which was later sold to the Londonderry & Coleraine Railway. All later passed to the Belfast & Northern Counties Railway. These were small engines, with 13" x 18" cylinders and 5' 0" driving wheels. Byrom (2015) also includes a fourth Fairbairn, a 2-2-2 supplied to the same railway via Dargan in 1855, but this cannot be reconciled with Scott's history of BNCR locomotives.

Two similar locomotives were supplied to the Waterford & Tramore Railway in 1855 as Nos 1 and 2.

Type VII [7]-W			0-4-2	**GSWR Class n/a**
First WKR No	**Built**	**Temporary WLR No**	**Second WKR No**	
2	1857	22	1	

This section is cross-referenced with Type IV [4], refer Chapter 7 Page 185.

RNC Type: VIII [8]-W			2-2-2-2T	**GSWR Class n/a**
First WKR No	**Maker's No**	**Built**		
1	241	1846		
2	242	1846		
3	243	1846		

This section is cross-referenced with Type I [1]-WKR, refer Chapter 7 Page 182/3.

RNC Type: IX [9]-W	2-4-0	**GSWR Class n/a**
First WKR No		
4		
5		

This entry is cross-referenced with Type II [2]-WKR, refer Chapter 7 Page 183.

RNC Type: X[10]-W	2-2-2	**GSWR Class n/a**
First WKR No		
6		
7		

This entry is cross-referenced to Type III [3]-WKR, refer Chapter 7 Page 184.

RNC Type: XI [11]-W	0-4-2	**GSWR Class n/a**
WLR No	**Built**	**Withdrawn**
1 (previously Limerick & Ennis Railway No 1)	Aug 1859	1883

Built by William Fairbairn

Boiler pressure – 90 lb/ sq in assumed	Heating surfaces:	Tractive effort – 7,180 lb
Cylinders – 16" x 22 "	tubes – not recorded	Coal capacity – not recorded
Driving wheels – 5' 0"	firebox – not recorded	Water capacity – 1250 gal
Trailing wheels – 3' 9"	grate – 15 sq ft	Locomotive weight – not recorded
Wheelbase – 6' 11½" + 7' 2"		

(Dimensions based on GWR 1874 survey; a nother source quotes: driving wheels – 4' 9"; grate 13 sq ft).

Prior to construction starting, the Limerick & Ennis Railway accepted an amended quotation for an improved firebox and a 6-wheel tender in replacement of the originally proposed 4-wheel version (price increased from £2,400 to £2,550). Builders declined an offer of preferential shares in lieu of cash settlement; the debt was eventually cleared in April 1860. This locomotive was added to stock in 1861 when the WLR took over the LER.

GWR Survey report dated September 1874 states: "Firebox patched, both tube plates extra stayed [sic] and old tubes pieced [sic]; tyres new (Bessemer [steel]) commenced running after repairs Aug 5th 1873; from what I saw of this boiler last May, it will require renewing in about 12 months; also wants new cylinders."

WLR 0-4-2 No 1 of 1859.

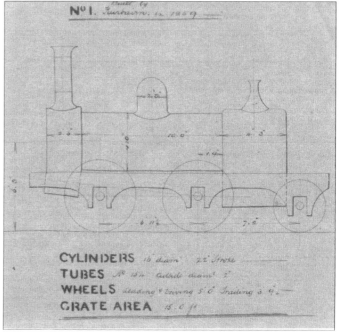

RNC Type: XII [12]-W	0-4-2	GSWR Class n/a
WLR No	**Built**	**Withdrawn**
2 (previously Limerick & Ennis Railway No 2)	1854 or 1856 Purchased from Dargan in 1859	1900

Built by William Fairbairn

Boiler pressure – 90 lb/ sq in assumed *Heating surfaces:* *Tractive effort – 7,180 lb*
Cylinders – 16" x 22" *tubes – not recorded* *Coal capacity – not recorded*
Driving wheels – 5' 0" *firebox – not recorded* *Water capacity – 1550 gal*
Trailing wheels – 3' 9" *grate – 14.46 sq ft* *Locomotive weight – not recorded*
Wheelbase – 7' 6" + 6' 9¼"

This locomotive might have been used initially by Dargan on the Waterford & Tramore Railway (the WTR purchased two 2-2-2WTs from Fairbairn in 1855). It was purchased from Dargan by the LER in 1859; it entered WLR stock in 1861 on take over the LER. GWR Survey report dated September 1874 stated: "Requires new cylinder and boiler, the sooner the better; don't consider it safe; tyres new; engine still at work."

In view of this condition, survival until 1900 must have been the result of extensive repairs but no details have been traced.

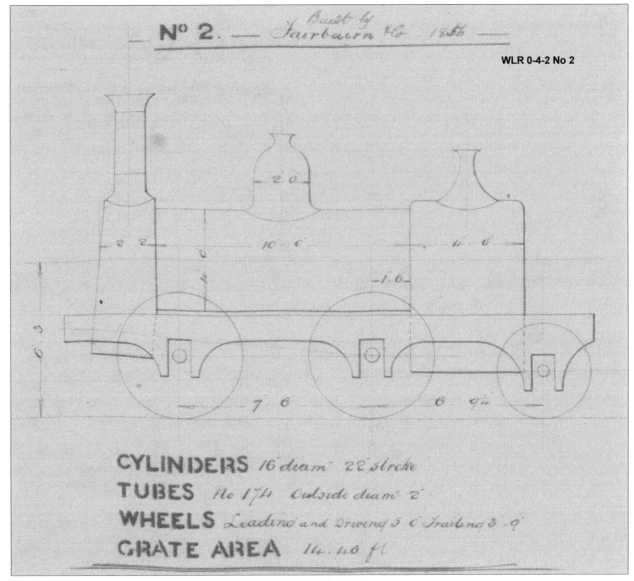

WLR 0-4-2 No 2

Locomotives of the Great Southern & Western Railway

RNC Type: XIII [13]-W 0-4-2 **GSWR Class n/a**

WLR No	Makers' No	Built	Withdrawn
27	279	April 1845	Dec 1874

Built by Sharp Bros

Boiler pressure – 80 lb/ sq in	Heating surfaces:	Tractive effort – 4,590 lb
Cylinders – 13½" x 20"	tubes – not recorded	Coal capacity – not recorded
Driving wheels – 4' 6"	firebox – not recorded	Water capacity – 875 gal
Trailing wheels – 3' 6"	grate – 10.5 sq ft	Locomotive weight – not recorded
Wheelbase – 5' 8" + 5' 4"		

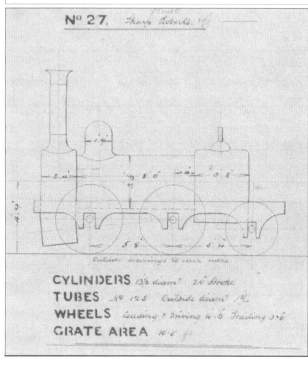

Originally named *Lady MacNeill*, and later *Pioneer*, this engine was built for Dargan and used on various Irish railway contracts. It was involved in an accident between Limerick Junction and Charleville on 8th March 1849 during construction of that line. It was noted in July 1850 at Limerick awaiting transit by canal barge to Athlone for use on construction of the MGWR's Galway route. The Limerick & Ennis Railway purchased this locomotive from Dargan in 1859 and gave it the number 3. It was added to WLR stock in the takeover of 1861, retaining the number 3; it became WLR No 27 in 1872.

The GWR 1874 report states: "No date as to her age; a very old-fashioned type, not worth repairing; not at work." (The drawing with the report shows outside bearings on all three axles).

WLWR 0-4-2 No 27 of 1845. This design copies that of early four-coupled Bury types in the downward inclination of the cylinder to allow for clearance of the motion below the leading axle.

RNC Type: XIV [14]/ XIVA [14A] -W 0-4-2/ 0-6-0 **GSWR Class 224**

Note: Some 0-4-2s were divided by RNC into different types: Sharp Nos 13-6 of 1853-4 (Type V [5]-W); Sharp Nos 4-6 of 1862-4 (Type XIV [14]-W); and Kitson Nos 3 & 7 of 1871-2 (Type XVII [17]-W). However, their leading dimensions were identical and the 1874 GWR Report (see below) combines them as a single group of engines.

GSWR No	WLR No & Name	Makers' No	Built	Rebuilt §	Withdrawn
[223]	4	1345	Jun 1862	-	1901
224	5 *Bee*	1346	Jun 1862	1893	1909
225	6 *Ant*	1529	Aug 1864	Oct 1890	1907

Built by Sharp Stewart

Boiler pressure – 95 lb/ sq in	Heating surfaces:	Tractive effort – 9,190 lb
Cylinders – 16" x 24"	tubes – 1060 sq ft	Coal capacity – not recorded
Driving wheels – 4' 6"	firebox – 76 sq ft	Water capacity – 1200 gal
Trailing wheels – 3' 6"	grate – 13 sq ft	Locomotive weight – not recorded
Wheelbase – 7" 11" + 6' 11½"		
Locomotive length 23' 11"		

§ Rebuilt as 0-6-0. No detail traced but driving wheel diameter might have become 4' 7".

The conclusions of the September 1874 Survey; supplementary report dated November 1874 in brackets [ ]:

No 4: Boiler barrel and tube plates have just been strengthened & new brass tubes tested to 180 lb/ sq inch hydraulic pressure and 120 lb steam pressure on 10 September 1874; tyres new (Bessemer); this engine will be at work in three weeks. [Engine now at work].

No 5: One new plate and three patches put on bottom half of the boiler barrel; also patch on inside of [fire?]-box; one new steel crank, extra stays put in smokebox tube plate; patch on lower part of firebox tube plate; new ends on old tubes; new left cylinder; new tyres Bess[emer] steel; commenced running Feb 1874.

No 6: This engine is in a bad condition and wants new tubes and repairs to boiler; also new tyres; is still at work. Tender in fair condition; trailing tyres fair; new wanted for Ldg and Drg *(presumably leading and driving wheels)*

Robinson confirmed Nos 5 (1893) and 6 (1890) as rebuilds and not new engines; they were classified as Type XIVA [14A]-W by RNC.

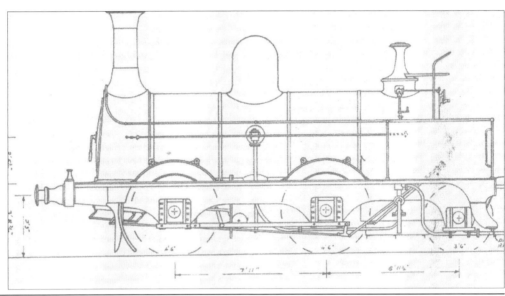

WLWR 0-4-2 (Type XIV [14] – W) in original form. Drawing – *Richard Chown (by courtesy of Paul Greene)*

RNC Type: XV [15]-W		2-2-2			GSWR Class n/a
GSWR No	**WLR No & Name**	**Makers' No**	**Built**	**Rebuilt**	**Withdrawn**
[280]	28 *South of Ireland*	1213	1864		1902

Built by Kitson

The solitary 2-2-2 Type XV [15] – W built by Kitson, No 28 *South of Ireland*. LGRP

(See also drawing overleaf.)

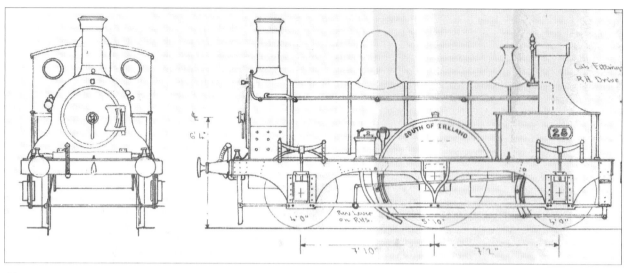

The solitary 2-2-2 Type XV [15] – W built by Kitson, No 28 *South of Ireland. Richard Chown courtesy of Paul Greene*

Boiler pressure – 140 lb/ sq in	Heating surfaces:	Tractive effort – 8,420 lb
Cylinders – 15" x 22"	tubes – 794 sq ft	Coal capacity – not recorded
Leading wheels – 4' 0 "	firebox – 88 sq ft	Water capacity – 1,000 gallons
Driving wheels – 5' 10"	grate – 15 sq ft	Water capacity – not recorded
Trailing wheels – 4' 0 "		Locomotive weight – not recorded
Wheelbase – 7' 10" + 7' 2"		
Locomotive length – 23' 8" [estimated]		

This engine had outside bearings to leading and trailing wheels; inside bearings to driving wheels and was supplied new with a 4-wheel tender. The conclusions of the September 1874 GWR Survey: "Bottom of boiler & inside firebox patched; tubes pierced; new driving tyres and crank shaft [sic] Feb".

Latterly allocated to the Foynes branch, hauling passenger trains.

RNC Type: XVI [16]-W		0-4-0ST		GSWR Class 228
GSWR No	**WLR No**	**Makers' No**	**Built**	**Withdrawn**
228	29 (The) "Darkie"	1653	Dec 1865	1925
Built by Sharp Stewart				

Boiler pressure – 120 lb/ sq in	Heating surfaces:	Tractive effort – 5,200 lb
Cylinders – 12" x 17"	total – 344 sq ft	Coal capacity – not recorded
Driving wheels – 4' 0"	grate – 9 sq ft	Water capacity – 320 gallons
Wheelbase – 7' 4"		Locomotive weight – 20 tons 18 cwt
Locomotive length (over buffers) – 22' 7½ "		

Fayle reports the boiler pressure at 140 lb/ sq in but this is considered unlikely in view of the locomotive's age and the modest nature of its usual duties. As built this loco had a wooden front buffer beam and steel rear one. The Sharp Stewart GA shows 4' driving wheels but the 1874 GWR report records 3' 10".

This was the only pre-Robinson WLWR locomotive to pass to the GSR. It was really little more than a small shunter, first used at Waterford, and later in the Limerick yards. It was unwisely also deployed for a short period on the Killaloe branch where its short wheelbase with front overhang of 5' 3" and 7' 1" at the rear caused severe oscillation at speeds above 20 mph. This proved lethal when the engine de-railed on 8th January 1914 near Birdhill, killing the fireman and seriously injuring a passenger (see Chapter 6 Type LXIII [63]). Although officially withdrawn in 1925 and scrapped in 1928, there were unconfirmed reports of it still shunting in the Limerick area until the early 1930s.

The 1874 GWR report was brief being limited to "Wants a new set of tubes."

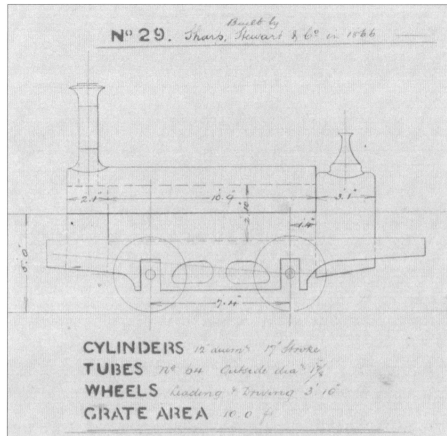

0-4-0T No 29 "The Darkie" (Type XVI [16]) at Limerick. *Photo Ken Nunn*

RNC Type: XVII [17]-W / XVIIA [17A]-W 0-4-2/ 0-6-0   **GSWR Class 224**

Note: Some 0-4-2s were divided by RNC into different types: Sharp Nos 13 to 16 of 1853-4 (Type V [5]-W); Sharp Nos 4 to 6 of 1862-4 (Type XIV [14]-W); and Kitson Nos 3 & 7 of 1871-2 (Type XVII [17]-W). However, their leading dimensions were identical and the 1874 GWR Report (see below) combines them as a single group of engines.

GSWR No	WLR No	Makers' No	Built	Rebuilt	Withdrawn
260	3	1783	Feb 1872	1892 §	-
226	7 *Wasp* ±	1784	Feb 1872	Jul 1888 as an 0-6-0 #	1905

± Named *Progress* until 1893
§ Rebuilt as 0-4-2T; see Type XXX[30]–W for details

Built by Kitson

Boiler pressure – 140 lb/ sq in	*Heating surfaces:*	*Tractive effort – 13,540 lb*
Cylinders – 16" x 24"	*tubes – 925 sq ft*	*Coal capacity – not recorded*
Driving wheels – 4' 6"'	*firebox – 86 sq ft*	*Water capacity – 1200 gal*
Trailing wheels – 3' 6"	*grate – 13 sq ft*	*Locomotive weight – 26 tons 17 cwt*
Wheelbase – 7' 11 " + 6' 11½"		
# Rebuilt 1888: Driving wheels – 4' 7"		

As new engines, the 1874 report stated both to be in good order. They may have been constructed late 1871 before completing trials in February 1872. Kitson had written on 20th Oct 1871 that due to "dissatisfaction of employees", definite delivery dates could not be promised. Sources claim that No 7 later carried a plate: "Built in Limerick.".

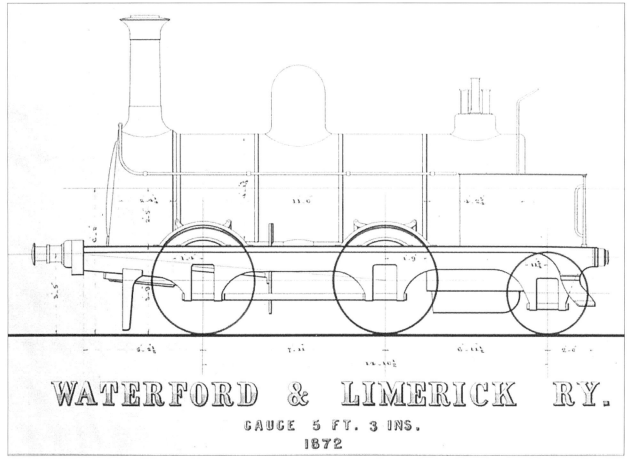

Builder's drawing of 0-4-2 Type XVII [17]-W as built. *Stephenson Locomotive Society*

Locomotives of the Waterford, Limerick & Western Railway

Photograph of 0-6-0 No 7 as rebuilt in 1888.

0-6-0 Type XVIIA [17A] No 226 (previously WLWR No 7). The oval plate on the sandbox appears to state "W.L.R. COMPANY NO 7 JULY 1888 BUILDERS LIMERICK". *Locomotive Publishing Co*

RNC Type: XVIII [18]-W	0-4-2	GSWR Class n/a
WLR No	**Built**	**Withdrawn**
22 (DMR No 1) (ATR No 1, Oct 1870)	1862	Oct 1890
23 (DMR No 6) (ATR No 2, Oct 1870)	1862	1892
24 (DMR No 5) (AEJR No 3, *Gort*, May 1870)	1862	1886

Built by Fossick & Hackworth

Locomotives of the Great Southern & Western Railway

Boiler pressure – 90 lb/ sq in assumed	Heating surfaces:	Tractive effort – 6,040 lb
Cylinders – 15" x 20"	tubes – not recorded	Coal capacity – not recorded
Driving wheels – 4' 9"	firebox – not recorded	Water capacity – 1200 gal
Trailing wheels – 3' 6"	grate – 11.4 sq ft	Locomotive weight – not recorded
Wheelbase – 7' 2" + 6' 3½"		

Note: Sources differ on leading dimensions e.g. cylinder diameters 14" or 15"; driving wheels 4' 8" or 4' 9". Those quoted above are regarded as most likely.

The history of these engines is confused and recognised sources do not agree on details (Clements, 1950; O'Meara, 1957; Mahon, 1972, 1973, 1975; Shepherd, 2006; Rowledge, 1993). Further, it is uncertain who owned them at stages during their careers. The following account is considered the most probable re-construction of their story. In 1862-4, Fossick & Hackworth of Stockton supplied six engines to the Dublin & Meath Railway (DMR):- three 0-4-2s, two 2-2-2s and a 2-4-0. The DMR also acquired a seventh engine of which virtually nothing is known. No Fossick & Hackworth records have been traced and the only illustration of the 0-4-2s believed to survive is the outline diagram in the 1874 GWR report.

In 1869, the MGWR took over the running of the DMR but the only locomotive they were willing to accept into their stock was the most powerful, the 2-4-0 nicknamed the "Drag-All". It is possible that by then the 0-4-2s and 2-2-2s may not have belonged to the DMR. They were stored at Kilmessan engine shed, the inference being that they had been seized through legal process. Fortunately for any party seeking to complete a sale or recover losses, two railways further west were seeking purchase of second-hand engines:

The Athenry & Ennis Junction Railway (AEJR) had opened in 1869 and needed motive power.

The Athenry & Tuam Railway (ATR) had failed in 1870 to gain extension of its 10-year operating agreement with the MGWR.

The two companies commenced running their own services in ramshackle fashion until concluding a more reliable working arrangement with the WLR in 1872. The AEJR may have sought one of the ex-DMR 2-2-2s (Clements 1950, O'Meara 1957 believe it was possibly No 2), although as both Athenry companies operated slow mixed and passenger trains, the 0-4-2s would have been more suitable. In due course all three were obtained by the Athenry companies (who further confused matters by transferring one between themselves) along with three even older second hand engines.

The AEJR paid £750 for their DMR engine, in £50 quarterly instalments. Apparently, there were frequent exchanges of engines between ATR and AEJR which were worked as a contiguous single line. In 1871, AEJR No 3 was repaired at Inchicore and on return was re-labelled ATR No 4 for a period. This was apparently a ploy to hide the engine (i.e. to avoid it being impounded by bailiffs) as Court action had been initiated against the AEJR for the recovery of debt.

In November 1870, the Sheriff of Co Clare had seized a train and only allowed it to continue with bailiffs on the footplate. Later, bailiffs representing the Sheriff of Co Galway also seized the locomotive, fought the Clare bailiffs and successfully evicted them. As locomotives Nos 1 and 2 were AEJR property (at that time) they were seized, auctioned at Ennis, and bought by the only bidder which was the ATR, which moved them to Tuam. The position with No 3 was even less clear-cut as the AEJR was buying the engine by instalments and it may still legally have been DMR property. The inter-bailiff battle was made more complicated by seizure of the coaches in addition but these were later found to be legally owned by a finance house. The passengers' views of these shenanigans are not recorded.

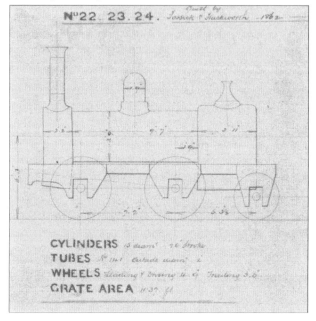

Diagram of Fossick & Hackworth 0-4-2 Type XVIII [18] – W Nos 22-4 of 1862.

Locomotives of the Waterford, Limerick & Western Railway

Mark Wardle, the WLR locomotive superintendent, considered all six AEJR/ ATR engines in poor condition when added to the WLR fleet in November 1872. He valued the ex-DMR locomotives at £350 each; a similar sized locomotive was then worth £200 -220 as scrap metal. However, by 1874 the WLR had two in fairly good order with the third due for overhaul and a more optimistic assessment was made of their value. They continued to work until replacement by Robinson in his modernisation programme.

GWR survey comments dated 21st September 1874; supplementary report 10th November 1874 in brackets [ ]:

No 22: Ex-ATR valuation at takeover £800; now undergoing heavy boiler and other repairs [Boiler repairs completed; new crank axle provided; tyres good]

No 23: Ex-ATR valuation at takeover £725; in bad condition all through, although still at work [Engine at work; crank axle recently renewed; tyres good]

No 24: Ex-AEJR valuation at takeover £825; waiting to come in for very heavy repairs all through; not at work [Tyres good]

Arrival of new 6-coupled engines in the 1880s made them surplus. Estimated repair costs were in the region of £1200 for each as at the following dates: No 22 March 1888; No 23 December 1890; No 24 August 1885. These costs were considered unjustified leading to their withdrawal.

RNC Type: XIX [19]-W   **2-4-0**   **GSWR Class 281**

GSWR No	WLR No & Name	Makers' No	Built	Withdrawn
[261]	8 *Primrose*	910	Mar 1881	1902
[277]	25 *Limerick* (later *Verbena*)	706	May 1874	1902
281	30 *Waterford* (later *Lily*)	707	May 1874	1903 or 1904
282	31 *Ennis* (later *Myrtle*)	708	May 1874	Nov 1910
283	32 *Tuam* (later *Dahlia*)	709	May 1874	Nov 1910
285	35 *Duncannon*	911	Mar 1881	Feb 1911
286	36 *Violet*	912	Apr 1881	1903
287	37 *Camelia*	913	Apr 1881	1909
288	38 *Hyacinth*	990	Nov 1882	1907
289	39 *North Star* (later *Shamrock*)	991	Dec 1882	May 1905

Built by Vulcan Foundry

Boiler pressure – 100 or 140 lb/ sq in
Cylinders – 16" x 24"
Leading wheels – 3' 6"
Driving wheels – 5' 6"
Wheelbase – 7'3" + 7' 6";
Locomotive length over frames – 22' 7½"

Heating surfaces:
tubes – 963 sq ft
firebox – 78 sq ft
grate – 13.7 sq ft

Tractive effort – 7, 910 or 11,080 lb
Coal capacity – 3 tons 5 cwt
Water capacity – 1600 gal
Locomotive weight – 24 tons 9 cwt

Mostly used on Limerick to Sligo and Tralee services. These were listed as mixed traffic engines, supplied with Stephenson link motion, Swan neck regulators, copper fireboxes and mushroom (i.e. poppet) safety valves. The boiler pressure of 100 lbs/ sq in quoted in the Vulcan order book seems very low; by 1904 No 289 (ex-WLR No 39) was running at 140 lbs/ sq in.

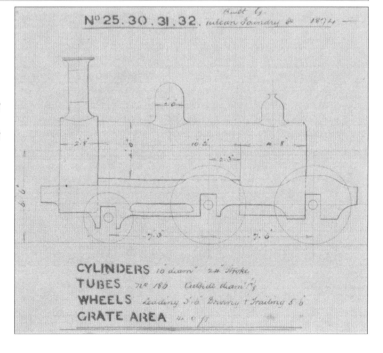

Type XIX [19] – W: diagram as built.

Type XIX [19] No 30 *Lily*. the locomotive's condition, especially the dome, is worthy of note. Taken at Listowel in 1900. *LGRP*

RNC Type: XX [20]-W/ XXA [20A]-W		0-4-2/ 0-4-4T			GSWR Class 279
GSWR No	**WLR No & Name**	**Makers' No**	**Built**	**Rebuilt**	**Withdrawn**
[272]	19 *Kincora*	1126	1876		1901
278	26	1125	1876		Mar 1910
279	27 *Thomond* (after 1899)	1127	1876	1899 §	Aug 1953
[284]	33 *Shamrock* ?	1128	1876		1901 or 1902

Built by Avonside

Note – Little dimensional information has been recorded on these engines as 0-4-2Ts but it seems probable that cylinders and heating surfaces were similar to those recorded for the 0-4-4T rebuild below.

§ As rebuilt by Robinson

Boiler pressure –150 lb/ sq in	*Heating surfaces:*	*Tractive effort – 12,240 lb*
Cylinders – 16" x 24"	*tubes – 808 sq ft*	*Coal capacity – 2 tons 10 cwt*
Driving wheels – 5' 4"'	*firebox – 88 sq ft*	*Water capacity – 1200 gal*
Bogie wheels – 3' 6"	*grate – 15.8 sq ft*	*Locomotive weight – 49 tons 19 cwt*
Wheelbase – 7' 10" + 8' 5" + 5' 6"		*Adhesive weight – 28 tons 12 cwt*
Locomotive length – 34' 7"		*Max axle loading – 15 tons 3 cwt*

RN Clements noted that new boilers were ordered from Kitson for Nos 26/ 27 in January 1896. More material was then ordered for what was officially a "repair" of No 27:-

Kitson: unspecified materials in May 1897 and later two frame plates complete, one bogie complete with wheels, reversing screw, nut and bracket (cost £388 10s) .

Sharp Stewart: two side tanks, coal bunker, coal tank (?) (cost £190).

The later orders were placed in 1896/ 7 so rebuilding (effectively a new construction) proceeded at a leisurely pace but resulted in a modern-looking engine compared with some in the WLWR fleet. On completion, plates stating "Built WLW" were affixed. (The last rebuilding exercise had involved Type V [5]-W No 15 in 1894). As GSWR No 279, it enjoyed a long life for a non-standard design so presumably must have been an effective performer. It received 17" x 24" cylinders and a new boiler in 1927 and apparently spent much of its later career in the Dublin area with a spell at Bagenalstown.

GR Mahon suggested that two of these engines arrived in 1875 and were numbered 7 and 11 (and possibly named *Synnott* and *Suir* respectively). No other sources agree with this and as both numbers were in use in 1875-6 on other locomotives which lasted until 1905 and 1901 respectively these identities seem unlikely.

No 27 in original 0-4-2 form and following its rebuilding by the WLWR to become an 0-4-4T, depicted in later years as CIE No 279. *Upper photograph LGRP*

Locomotives of the Great Southern & Western Railway

RNC Type: XXI [21] -W		0-6-0T		GSWR Class n/a
GSWR No	**WLR No**	**Makers' No**	**Built**	**Withdrawn**
[229]	34	1243	purchased 1877	1901

Maker and origins unknown

Boiler pressure – 100 lb/ sq in assumed *Heating surfaces:* *Tractive effort – 7,170 lb*
Cylinders – 15" x 18"   *– not recorded*   *Coal/ water capacities – not recorded*
Driving wheels – 4 ' 0 "   *Locomotive weight – 24 tons 1 cwt*
Wheelbase – 6' + 6'

This locomotive was purchased second-hand for £1,000 from Avonside which company had been trying to sell it to an Irish railway for some time. Following inspection by an engineer from Limerick, it was delivered by sea from Bristol to Waterford in mid-1878. It reputedly carried (unnamed) builder's number 1243, had been built to 7' ¼" gauge, and had first worked for a Welsh colliery. Exhaustive searches have failed to reconcile this summary with the production records of prominent locomotive builders (Beyer Peacock, Hawthorn, Kitson, Neilson, Robert Stephenson, Sharp Stewart) whose output totals had reached the 1200s by the mid-1860s. Avonside (records later destroyed) would not have reached builder's number 1243 by the estimated construction year. It seems probable that this number was mis-recorded.

Some 7' ¼" gauge engines became stationary boilers in South Wales; a possible link with the Ogmore Valley Railway was proposed, but its engines are fully accounted for. One possibility is that Avonside obtained a second-hand engine of unknown origin and overhauled it to raise funds when its finances were in poor shape. The matter of gauge is also raises questions. It would have been risky to modify a small locomotive in mid-life to suit the smaller Irish market without a firm sales contract.

No 34's photograph suggests it might have been smaller than the quoted dimensions. Lacking vacuum brakes, it apparently spent its Irish life solely as Waterford yard shunter. It was reported as "very tight on the loading gauge" (the WLR was less generous in this respect than other Irish railways). Local alterations might have changed its appearance from that when supplied by Avonside. Finally, the rear wheel spokes differ from the others suggesting possible conversion from an 0-4-2T.

0-6-0T No 34. *LPC*

RNC Type: XXII [22]-W		0-6-0		GSWR Class 230
GSWR No	**WLR No & Name**	**Makers' No**	**Built**	**Withdrawn**
230	40 *Vulcan*	1010	1883	1909
231	41 *Titan*	1011	1883	Sep 1910

Designer: H Appleby **Built by Vulcan Foundry**

Boiler pressure – 100 lb/ sq in	Heating surfaces:	Tractive effort – 11,000 lb
Cylinders – 17½" x 26"	tubes – 935 sq ft	Coal capacity – not recorded
Driving wheels – 5' 1½"	firebox – 91 sq ft	Water capacity – 2000 gal
Wheelbase – 7' 3" + 7' 9"	grate – 19.5 sq ft	Locomotive weight – 38 tons 10 cwt
Locomotive over frames – 24' 10"		

An annotated Vulcan works photo shows the cylinders as 17" x 26"; it seems that Robinson later altered the cylinder diameter to that above. The quoted boiler pressure (and hence tractive effort) appear unduly low for a goods locomotive, but no verifiable alternative pressure has been traced.

Official Vulcan Foundry photograph of No 41 *Titan*.

RNC Type: XXIII [23]-W		0-6-0/ 0-6-0ST			GSWR Class 221
GSWR No	**WLR No**	**Makers' No**	**Built**	**Rebuilt**	**Withdrawn**
221	1	2379	1879	1899	1909

Built by Robert Stephenson

Boiler pressure – 100 lb/ sq in assumed	Heating surfaces:	Tractive effort – 10,920 lb
Cylinders – 17" x 24"	total – 1027 sq ft	Coal/ water capacities – not recorded
Driving wheels – 4' 6"	grate – 19.5 sq ft	Locomotive weight – not recorded
Wheelbase – 7' 0" + 7' 0"		
Locomotive length over frames – 25' 6 "		

This is one of only 34 locomotives built by Robert Stephenson to work in Ireland but the precise details of its origins are uncertain. According to Rowledge (1993) the company received an order for a 5' 0" gauge locomotive which suggests a buyer in Russia, Finland or a Southern state of the USA. The builder's engine record book for the period 1849-1904 (Refence ROB 2/6/1 at Search Engine, York) makes no reference to a locomotive built to that gauge but order No 2379 for 1879 is blank regarding customer identity. Order No 2378 refers to an 0-6-0 sent to Seaton Delaval Colliery, Northumberland in

March 1880; No 2379 was for a 5' 3" gauge 4-4-0 for the Adelaide & Glenelg Railway, South Australia. Known details for No 2379 conform with those for No 2378 which suggests that the pair could have been identical except for the gauge. Stephenson engines were often delivered out of order/ build numerical sequence. No 2379 does not appear in the company's finished record until March 1884, immediately after two engines numbered 2497/ 8 for the Brecon & Merthyr Railway and before two numbered 2547/ 8 for the Great Indian Peninsula Railways.

This chain suggests that the builder had a 5' gauge 0-6-0 on its hands following an unfulfilled order for four to five years with no buyer interest because of the unusual gauge. Narrowing to 4' 8½" would have been uneconomic but broadening to 5' 3" would have been a simpler matter of modifications to axles, hubs and axle boxes. Stephenson's later records merely advise completion and despatch of a 17" six-wheeled engine to the WLR without any reference to its earlier history. In a fire sale situation, a deal could have been struck in November 1883 which included the modification costs. The engine arrived in Limerick in March 1884 and settlement was completed in May, following repairs to cylinder joints and provision of new axle box brasses at builder's expense.

Further problems followed with both Appleby and Robinson complaining to the builders about poor performance; they managed to obtain a new firebox at a £20 discount. The engine was fitted with a device by which the driver could use a steam jet to vary the blast pipe draft, for which Robinson and Appleby jointly took out a patent in 1888. It was rebuilt by the WLR as an 0-6-0ST in 1899 with leading dimensions unchanged. Illustrations in original condition have not been traced; the line drawing as a tank locomotive was prepared by the late Richard Chown.

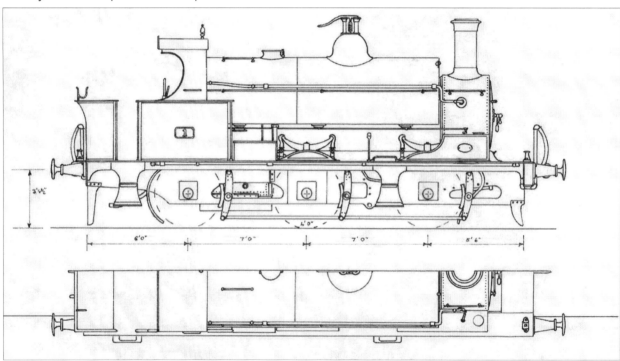

Line drawing of No 1 in its later 0-6-0ST days by the late *Richard Chown*. Note difference in splasher height between photograph and drawing; the latter may be an error. There would be little value in changing the wheel diameter in this rebuild. *Ken Nunn*

RNC Type: XXIV [24] -W		0-6-0WT/ 0-4-2WT		GSWR Class n/a
GSWR No	**WLR No**	**Makers' No**	**Built**	**Withdrawn**
[232]	42	284	Jun 1862	1901
Built by Hawthorn (Leith)				

Boiler pressure – 80 lb/ sq in	Heating surfaces:	Tractive effort – 7,650 lb
Cylinders – 15" x 21"	tubes – 545 sq ft	Coal capacity – not recorded
Driving wheels – 3' 6"	firebox – 67 sq ft	Water capacity – 800 gal
Wheelbase – 5' 9" + 5' 9"	grate – not recorded	Locomotive weight – not recorded
Locomotive length – 23' 6" over buffers		

This locomotive had obscure origins and the following is probably the most accurate historical summary. It was built by Hawthorn to 4' 8½" gauge to the patent of Samuel Dobson Davidson, with Gooch valve gear. After use on the construction of the Anglesey Central Railway, it was moved to the Neath & Brecon Railway (NBR), where it was named *Miers* after Richard Hanbury Miers, a director of the ACR and first chairman of the NBR. It might have spent time on the NBR before going to Anglesey and it may have been owned by John Dickinson & Co (contractors) who were declared bankrupt in 1867. Further confusion results from a postcard of it on the WLR with notation on the rear "bought from Ogmore Railway." No locomotive answering its description can be identified in that company's records, so this is probably an error.

By December 1882, the locomotive was for sale at Neath and was bought by the WLR for £90 plus £98 for repairs and re-gauging to 5' 3". Even for a 20-year old shunting tank, this appears an attractive price at a time when a new Manning Wardle 0-6-0ST cost about £1200. Appleby had earlier been locomotive superintendent with the NBR so was well placed to complete the deal. The price included delivery to Limerick, where it arrived in June 1883. About 1890, Robinson fitted it with a cab and sanding gear, and then sent it to work at Fenit pier. It was then an 0-4-2WT following removal of rear coupling rods to help negotiate tight bends in Limerick yards. Prior to despatch of No 42 to Fenit, an engine had been sent from Limerick as required to cope with periodic surges in mackerel traffic there. The Fenit Harbour Commissioners offered £1,000 for No 42 in 1899 (five times its acquisition cost 16 years earlier) but this was declined.

The GSWR decided to return it to Fenit, but *en route* it was involved in a collision at Abbeyfeale. The accident report for 1st Feb 1901 stated that the 6.10 pm Limerick-Tralee Down ran into the stationary No 42 three quarters of a mile from Abbeyfeale. No 42 had been mis-managed by its driver and had stalled for want of steam; signalling irregularities allowed the following train to enter the same section. The locomotive was scrapped after this mishap.

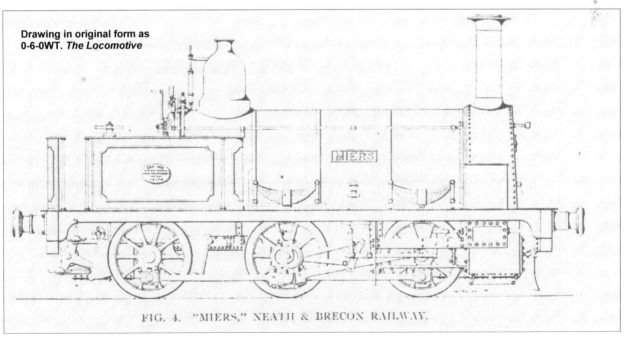

Drawing in original form as 0-6-0WT. *The Locomotive*

FIG. 4. "MIERS," NEATH & BRECON RAILWAY.

Locomotives of the Great Southern & Western Railway

No 42 following conversion to an 0-4-2WT. *LGRP*

RNC Type: XXV [25] - W		4-4-0		GSWR Class 262
GSWR No	**WLR No & Name**	**Makers' No**	**Built**	**Withdrawn**
262	9 Garryowen	2194	1886	1912

Built by Dübs

Boiler pressure – 160 lb/ sq in	*Heating surfaces:*	*Tractive effort – 14,570 lb*
Cylinders – 16½" x 24"	*tubes – 1000 sq ft*	*Coal capacity – 120 cu ft*
Bogie wheels – 3' 0"	*firebox – 98 sq ft*	*Water capacity – 2000 gal*
Driving wheels – 5' 1"	*grate – 15.5 sq ft*	*Locomotive weight – 32 tons 6 cwt*
Wheelbase – total 19' 8½" (rigid 8' 2")		*Adhesive weight – 21 tons 2 cwt*
Length engine and tender over buffers – 48' 2½"		*Max axle loading – 11 tons 3 cwt*

Two 4-4-0s were originally ordered from Dubs in 1885 but at some stage during construction, the second was changed to an 0-6-0. See Type XXVII [27]-W No 24 *Sarsfield*. This 4-4-0 version proved unsuccessful on passenger work and was noted mostly on goods trains.

Official builder's photograph of No 9. *LGRP*

RNC Type: XXVI [26]-W		4-4-0 / 2-4-0			GSWR Class 265
GSWR No	**WLR No & Name**	**Makers' No**	**Built**	**Rebuilt**	**Withdrawn**
265	12 *Earl of Bessborough*	1162	1886	1894	1907
Designer: H Appleby					**Built by Vulcan Foundry**

Boiler pressure – 150 lb/ sq in	Heating surfaces:	Tractive effort – 16,110 lb
Cylinders – 17½" x 26"	total – 1026 sq ft	Coal capacity – not recorded
Bogie wheels – 2' 9"		Water capacity – 2000 gal
Driving wheels – 5' 6"		Locomotive weight – 38 tons 4 cwt
Wheelbase – 20' 6" (locomotive overall)		Adhesive weight – not recorded

This locomotive was prone to derailment, hence its rebuilding as a 2-4-0 in which condition the wheelbase was quoted as 7' 4" + 8' 3". The bogie was recovered for use in the rebuilding of Type XXX [30]-W No 15.

Official builder's photograph of No 12. *LGRP*

RNC Type: XXVII [27]-W		0-6-0		GSWR Class 227
GSWR No	**WLR No & Name**	**Makers' No**	**Built**	**Withdrawn**
227	24 *Sarsfield*	2195	1886	Nov 1910
Manufacturer: Dübs & Co				**Designer: J G Robinson**

Boiler pressure – 160 lb/ sq in	Heating surfaces:	Tractive effort – 17,470 lbs
Cylinders – 17" x 24"	tubes – 1000 sq ft	Coal capacity – 120 cu ft
Driving wheels – 4' 6"	firebox – 98 sq ft	Water capacity – 2000 gal
Wheelbase – total 15' 4"	grate – 15.5 sq ft	Locomotive weight – 33 tons 3 cwt

Boiler pressure may have been later reduced to 150 lb/ sq in. Refer to Type XXV [25]-W on Page 224.

No 24 Sarsfield was originally to have been a 4-4-0 companion to No 9 but the order was changed to that of an 0-6-0 before construction started.

RNC Type: XXVIII [28] W			2-4-0		GSWR Class 263
GSWR No	**WLR No & Name**	**Makers' No**	**Built**	**Rebuilt**	**Withdrawn**
263	10 *Sir James*	2477	May 1889	-	1907
273	20 *Galtee More*	2880	Mar 1892	-	1909
275	22 *Era*	2662	1890	-	Mar 1913
276	23 *Slieve-Na-Mon*	2881	Mar 1892	1925	1949
290	43 *Knockma*	3025	Jun 1893	1926	Oct 1951
291	44 *Nephin*	3026	Jun 1893	1925	Aug 1959
292	47 *Carrick Castle*	3109	Apr 1894	-	Jun 1915
293	48 *Granston*	3110	Apr 1894	1925	Feb 1954

Designer: J G Robinson **Built by Dübs**

Boiler pressure – 150 lb/ sq in	*Heating surfaces:*	*Tractive effort – 13,280 lb*
Cylinders – 17" x 24"	*tubes – 991 sq ft*	*Coal capacity – 3 tons 10 cwt*
Radial wheels – 4' 0"	*firebox – 107 sq ft*	*Water capacity – 2000 gal*
Driving wheels – 6' 0"	*grate – 19.8 sq ft*	*Locomotive weight – 36 tons 9 cwt*
Wheelbase – 7' 4" + 8' 6"		*Adhesive weight – 24 tons 14 cwt*
Locomotive length – 26' 6"		*Max axle loading – 12 tons 10 cwt*

Nos 10 and 22 were supplied with 160 lbs/ sq in boilers yielding tractive effort at 13,100 lbs.

These locomotives were built with traversing axle boxes with inside and outside bearings on the leading axle; the springs on these wheels were of Gooch pattern. Nos 20, 23 and 44 were apparently named after mountains following arrival in Ireland; the remainder were named by Dübs. Robinson's first express passenger design, the late survival of four on branch line duties was remarkable given their large driving wheels. The GSWR used them on secondary passenger duties but the GSR deployed them further afield on such duties as the Loughrea branch. No 291 was the last Robinson engine in service in Ireland. When this class was first introduced the brass caps to the Robinson-style chimney matched the brightly polished brass domes. In GSWR days, the domes were painted over.

No 48 *Granston* running as GSR No 293 at Limerick; theree were eight examples of this type, a major "class" by WLWR standards.

Locomotives of the Waterford, Limerick & Western Railway

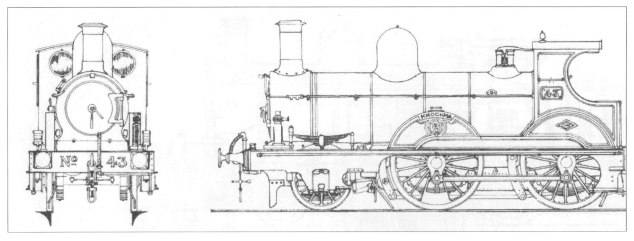

Drawing of GSWR Class 163/ 276 2-4-0. *Stephenson Locomotive Society*

RNC Type: XXIX [29]-W		2-4-2T		GSWR Class 266/ 267
GSWR No	WLR No & Name	Makers' No	Built	Withdrawn
266	13 *Derry Castle*	1315	1891	1934
267	14 *Lough Derg*	1316	1891	1935
Designer: J G Robinson				**Built by Vulcan Foundry**

Boiler pressure – 150 lb/ sq in
Cylinders – 16" x 24"
Pony wheels – 3' 6"
Driving wheels – 5' 6"
Trailing wheels – 3' 6"
Wheelbase – 7' 8" + 7' 6" + 6' 3"
Locomotive length – 34' 0"

Heating surfaces:
tubes – 780 sq ft
firebox – 88 sq ft
grate – 15 sq ft

Tractive effort – 11,870 lb
Coal capacity – 2 tons
Water capacity – 1200 gal
Locomotive weight – 45 tons 0 cwt
Adhesive weight – 24 tons 0 cwt
Max axle loading – 12 tons 10 cwt

Vulcan Foundry official photograph records: total wheelbase – 21' 0"; total heating surfaces – 1170 sq ft; coal capacity – 30 cwt; water capacity – 1230 gallons; locomotive weight – 46 tons 0 cwt

These engines were built with sliding axle boxes on the leading wheels and Webb's radial axle-boxes on the rear. When new, they were shedded at Tralee for working the north Kerry line to Limerick. No 266 was sold in 1914 to the Cork & Macroom Direct Railway as their No 6. After the 1924-5 Amalgamation, despite being identical with No 267, the CMDR engine was treated separately in the GSR renumbering and classification becoming Class 491 (F5) No 491. The GSWR fitted No 267 with an Inchicore built-up chimney and an old-fashioned double-D smokebox door. It was armoured and based at Limerick during the Irish Civil War from August 1922 until August 1923. The GSR later sent it to help out on the DSER section. Despite the recorded withdrawal date of 1935, No 267 ended its days on boiler wash-out duties at the Broadstone from May 1933 until July 1938.

2-4-2T Type XXIX [29] – W. *Stephenson Locomotive Society*

Locomotives of the Great Southern & Western Railway

2-4-2T Type XXIX [29] – W. *LGRP*

RNC Type: XXX [30]-W	**0-4-2T/ 0-4-4T**		**GSWR Classes 260/ 268**
GSWR No	**WLR No & Name**	**Built**	**Withdrawn**
260	3 *Zetland*	1892 0-4-2T	1912
268	15 *Roxborough*	1894 0-4-4T	Nov 1912
Designer: J G Robinson			**Rebuilt at Limerick**

NB No 3 and No 15, after renewal/ rebuilding are included in Type XXX [30]-W, despite one emerging from its metamorphosis as an 0-4-2T; and the other as an 0-4-4T

Boiler pressure – 150 lb/ sq in	Heating surfaces:	Tractive effort – 14,240 lb
Cylinders – 16" x 24"	tubes – 800 sq ft	Coal/ water capacities – not recorded
Driving wheels – 4' 7"	firebox – not recorded	Locomotive weight – 41 tons 6 cwt (No 3)
Trailing wheels – not recorded	grate – 14 sq ft	
Bogie wheels – not recorded		

WLR Type XXX [30] – W 0-4-2T No 3 *Zetland* following its rebuilding from an 0-4-2. *LGRP*

Parts of Type XVII [17]-W No 3 were used in the creation of Type XXX [30]-W No 3 as an 0-4-2T. Parts of Type V [5] -W No 15 were used in construction of Type XXX[30)-W No 15 as an 0-4-4T. Why RN Clements placed them in the same Type is unclear although they did share the same dimensions for driving wheels, cylinders and boiler pressure.

In Oct 1890, a new boiler was ordered from Vulcan Foundry for No 3. Another new boiler, first intended for Type XIV [14]–W No 4 arrived from Kitson (price £575) in March 1893, but this was probably diverted into No 15. The bogie for the latter came from Type: XXVI [26]-W No 12, declared surplus on conversion from 4-4-0 to 2-4-0. No 15 carried plates "Built WLW".

WLR Type XXX [30] – W No 15 *Roxborough* following rebuilding as 0-4-4T. *Locomotive Publishing Co*

RNC Type: XXXI [31]-W   0-6-0   **GSWR Class 233**

GSWR No	WLWR No & Name	Makers' No	Built	Rebuilt	Withdrawn
233	45 *Colleen Bawn*	3042	1893	-	Jun 1919
234	46 *Erin Go Bragh*	3043	1893	-	Apr 1911
235	49 *Dreadnought*	3222	1895	1924	1927 or 1928
236	50 *Hercules*	3223	1895	1925	1951

Designer: J G Robinson   **Built by Dübs**
Nos 45, 46 as built:

Boiler pressure – 150 lb/ sq in	*Heating surfaces:*	*Tractive effort – 14,380 lb*
Cylinders – 17" x 24"	*tubes – 991 sq ft*	*Coal capacity – 3 tons 5 cwt*
Driving wheels – 5' 1½ "	*firebox –107 sq ft*	*Water capacity – 1900 gal*
Wheelbase – 7' 6 " + 8' 3"	*grate – 17.8 sq ft*	*Locomotive weight – 36 tons 13 cwt*
		Max axle loading – 12 tons 13 cwt

Information from Dübs General Arrangement drawing and Order book: *Total wheelbase engine and tender 35' 1"; length of engine over buffers 25' 10 ½; total length engine and tender 42' 10"*

Nos 49, 50 as built:

Boiler pressure – 150 lb/ sq in *Cylinders – 17½" x 24 "* *Driving wheels – 5' 1½"* *Wheelbase – 7' 6" + 8' 3"* *Locomotive length – 26' 7"* *Dübs order book states:*	*Heating surfaces:* *tubes – 877 sq ft* *firebox – 107 sq ft* *grate – 19.8 sq ft*	*Tractive effort – 15,240 lb* *Coal capacity – 3 tons 5 cwt* *Water capacity – 1900 gal* *Locomotive weight – 37 tons 0 cwt* *Max axle loading – 12 tons 16 cwt* *Locomotive weight – 36 tons 13 cwt* *Max axle loading – 12 tons 13 cwt*

GSWR Nos 235, 236 as rebuilt 1924-5:

	Heating surfaces: *tubes – 918 sq ft* *firebox – 99 sq ft* *grate – 19.8 sq ft*	*Locomotive weight – 39 tons 16 cwt* *Max axle loading – 13 tons 14 cwt*

These locomotives were fitted with special springing on the leading axles (sliding blocks) giving ¾" side play, allowing them to run on the secondary lines including the haulage of fish specials from Fenit to Waterford. Processed mackerel packed in ice was despatched to the English markets via Waterford by special fast goods trains taking just over six hours from Fenit. Other trains went to Limerick Junction for forwarding by the GSWR to the North Wall at Dublin.

For comparison, a journey from Fenit to Waterford via Clonmel would have taken a passenger just over ten hours, including a one hour and forty minutes wait at Limerick.

Vacuum brakes allowed their use on heavier passenger excursions. The WLWR apparently considered the first pair to be in a different class from the later two whereas the GSWR grouped them as the same class.

WLWR Type XXXI [31] -W No 50 *Hercules* running as GSR No 236. It is believed that the cut-out section of the tender side was to accommodate staff exchange apparatus.

RNC Type: XXXII [32]-W		**0-4-4T**			**GSWR Class 294/ 295**
GSWR No	**WLWR No & Name**	**Makers' No**	**Built**	**Rebuilt**	**Withdrawn**
294	51 *Castle Hacket*	3587	1895		Nov 1910
295	52 *Brian Boru*	3588	June 1895	Nov 1926	Aug 1954
Designer: J G Robinson					**Built by Kitson**

Locomotives of the Waterford, Limerick & Western Railway

Boiler pressure – 150 lb/ sq in	Heating surfaces:	Tractive effort – 11,870 lb
Cylinders – 16" x 24"	tubes - 780 sq ft	Coal capacity – 1 ton 10 cwt
Driving wheels – 5' 6"	firebox – 88 sq ft	Water capacity – 1000 gal
Bogie wheels – 3' 6"	grate – 15.8 sq ft	Locomotive weight – 43 tons 0 cwt
Wheelbase – 7' 6" + 8' 9" + 5' 6"		Adhesive weight – 26 tons 16 cwt
Locomotive length – 33' 6"		Max axle loading – 13 tons 12 cwt

Kitson records show 140 lbs /sq in boiler; loco weight 46 tons 7 cwt; max axle loading (on bogie) 18 tons 16 cwt; adhesive weight 27 tons 11 cwt; length over frames but excluding buffer beams 29' 8⅛"

These locomotives were ordered for use on the Athenry and Tuam Extension to Claremorris Light Railway Company (A&TECLRC) and specially designed to cope with the sharp curves on that route. In later years, No 295 was Limerick-based, operating Ennis passenger trains plus the Foynes and Birr branches but is thought to have ended its days in Dublin in replacement of No 279. The GSR rebuild gave it slightly larger heating surface and water capacity.

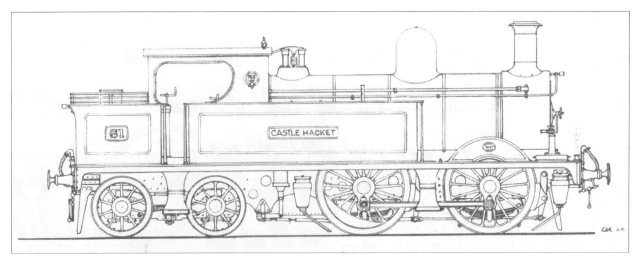

Robinson's programme of fleet modernisation included tank locomotives as expressed in this handsome 0-4-4T design. *Drawing Stephenson Locomotive Society. Image LGRP*

Locomotives of the Great Southern & Western Railway

RNC Type: XXXIII [33]-W   **4-4-2T**   **GSWR Class 269**

GSWR No	WLWR No & Name	Makers' No	Built	Rebuilt	Withdrawn
269	16 *Rocklands*	3616	Feb 1896	June 1925	Mar 1957
270	17 *Faugh-a-Ballagh*	3617	Feb 1896	June 1926	1949
271	18 *Geraldine*	3689	1897	June 1926	1949
274	21 *Blarney Castle*	3690	1897	Dec 1924	1949

Designer: J G Robinson   **Built by Kitson**

Boiler pressure – 150 lb/ sq in
Cylinders – 16" x 24"
Bogie wheels – 3' 6"
Driving wheels – 5' 6"
Trailing wheels – 3' 6"
Wheelbase – 5' 6" + 6' 11" + 7' 6" + 6' 3"
Locomotive length – 36' 0"

Heating surfaces:
tubes – 780 sq ft
firebox – 88 sq ft
grate – 15 sq ft

Tractive effort – 11,870 lb
Coal capacity – 1 ton 15 cwt
Water capacity – 1040 gal
Locomotive weight – 47 tons 10 cwt
Adhesive weight – 26 tons 0 cwt
Max axle loading – 13 tons 15 cwt

Kitson records show: boiler pressure – 140 lbs/sq in; tubes – 769.6 sq ft; wheelbase – 5 ' 6" + 6' 11" +7' 6" +6' 2 ⅜"; length over frames but excluding buffer beams – 32' 4"; locomotive weight – 48 tons 0 cwt; adhesive weight – 26 tons 14 cwt; max axle loading – 13 tons 14 cwt

---

As rebuilt 1924/ 5

Heating surfaces:
tubes – 800 sq ft
firebox – 94 sq ft
grate – 15.8 sq ft

Water capacity – 1200 gal
Coal capacity – 1 ton 15 cwt
Locomotive weight – 50 tons 12 cwt
Adhesive weight – 26 tons 15 cwt
Max axle loading – 13 tons 15 cwt

These engines were considered to be Robinson's first essay into "large engine" design and to some extent foreshadowed 4-4-2T Classes 9K and 9L of the Great Central Railway. They were built with traversing axle boxes on the rear wheels, which gave ⅛' side play. More flexibility was considered necessary for engines on the northern extension, built cheaply with tighter curves than the original mainline. Two were allocated to the Sligo line and two to Tralee-Limerick services. Despite being intended originally for the Sligo extension, in GSR days they were moved away from ex-GSWR territory. By 1927 all were working over the ex-Dublin South Eastern system but they ended their days on the former Cork Bandon & South Coast section. No 269 was the last tank locomotive of Robinson design origin in service in Ireland.

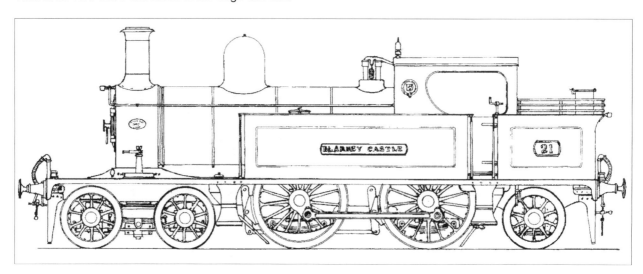

The drawing shows the original-sized side tanks. *Stephenson Locomotive Society*

Locomotives of the Waterford, Limerick & Western Railway

Above: With original-sized side tanks; below, as GSWR No 274 with increased tank capacity.

RNC Type: XXXIV [34]-W		4-4-0			GSWR Class 296
GSWR No	**WLWR No & Name**	**Makers' No**	**Built**	**Rebuilt**	**Withdrawn**
296	53 *Jubilee*	3618	Mar 1896	1923*	1949
297	54 *Killemnee*	3619	Apr 1896		May 1928
298	55 *Bernard*	3694	May 1897	Jun 1927*	1949

Designer: J G Robinson **Built by Kitson**

Boiler pressure – 150 lb/ sq in   Heating surfaces: Tractive effort – 12,280 lb
Cylinders – 17" x 24"   tubes – 887.4 sq ft   Coal capacity – 4 tons
Bogie wheels – 3' 6"   firebox – 107 sq ft   Water capacity – 1940 or 2000 gal
Driving wheels – 6' 0"   grate – 19.8 sq ft   Locomotive weight – 40 tons 0 cwt
Wheelbase – 5' 9" + 6' 8" + 8' 2"   Adhesive weight – 26 tons 10 cwt
Locomotive length – 28' 4½"   Max axle loading – 13 tons 10 cwt
Kitson records: boiler pressure – 140 lb/ sq in; wheelbase 5' 6" + 6' 10" + 8' 3"; grate – 17.8 sq ft; coal capacity – 3 tons; water capacity – 1800 gallons; locomotive weight – 40 tons 12 cwt; length over frames but excluding buffer beams – 26' 9"

* As rebuilt:

	Heating surfaces: tubes – 918 sq ft firebox – 99 sq ft grate – 19.8 sq ft	Locomotive weight – 40 tons 16 cwt Adhesive weight – 26 tons 12 cwt Max axle loading – 13 tons 7 cwt

This was Robinson's last passenger design for the WLWR, intended to work the Waterford-Limerick boat trains that connected with the GWR steam packets on the Waterford-Milford Haven service. At the time of No 53's introduction, a press release indicated that it was to be the first of a class of ten locomotives.

Presumably the takeover by the GSWR quashed plans for construction of the remaining seven. In 1939/40, one of the surviving pair was still working from Limerick while the other was used on secondary duties on the Birr branch.

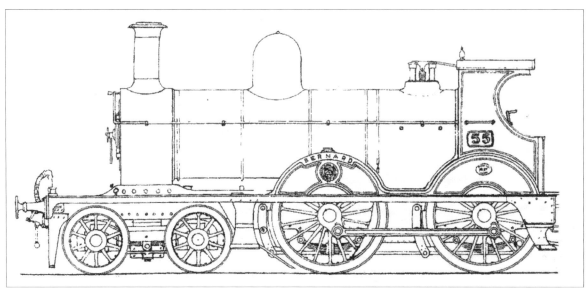

(Type XXXIV [34] – W) with Robinson style chimney and smokebox door design that would be characteristic of a large number of Great Central locomotives he introduced in the 20th Century. Drawing – *Stephenson Locomotive Society*

Locomotives of the Waterford, Limerick & Western Railway

(Type XXXIV [34] – W) No 298.

RNC Type: XXXV [35]-W		0-6-0		GSWR Class 222	
GSWR No	**WLWR No & Name**	**Makers' No**	**Built**	**Rebuilt**	**Withdrawn**
222	2 Shannon	3908	March 1900	1924	1949
237	56 Thunderer	3691	March 1897	1926	1951
238	57 Cyclops	3692	March 1897	1925	1934
239	58 Goliath	3693	March 1897	1925	1949

Designer: Robinson **Built by Kitson**

Nos 237-9 as built:

Boiler pressure – 150 lb/ sq in	Heating surfaces:	Tractive effort – 14,260 lb
Cylinders – 17" x 24"	tubes – 887.36 sq ft	Coal capacity – 4 tons
Driving wheels – 5' 2"	firebox – 107 sq ft	Water capacity – 2000 gal
Wheelbase – 7' 6" + 8' 3"	grate – 17.84 sq ft	Locomotive weight – 38 tons 13 cwt
		Max axle loading – 13 tons 11 cwt

No 222 as built:

Boiler pressure – 150 lb/ sq in	Heating surfaces:	Tractive effort – 14,260 lb
Cylinders – 17" x 24"	tubes – 873 sq ft	Coal capacity – 4 tons
Driving wheels – 5' 2"	firebox – 108 sq ft	Water capacity – 2000 gal
Wheelbase – 7' 6" + 8' 3"	grate – 17.8 sq ft	Locomotive weight – 40 tons 4 cwt
		Max axle loading – 13 tons 19 cwt

A single **Kitson** drawing dated 1897 records: locomotive weight – 40 tons 4 cwt; max axle loading – 13 tons 19 cwt; loco length excluding front buffer beam – 24' 8"

As rebuilt from 1924 onwards:

	Heating surfaces:	Locomotive weight – 39 tons 16 cwt
	tubes – 918 sq ft	Max axle loading – 13 tons 14 cwt
	firebox – 99 sq ft	
	grate – 19.8 sq ft	

Shannon was the first Irish mainline engine to have a Belpaire firebox. Two further 0-6-0s were ordered from Kitson (works Nos 3974-5), but their absorption into the GSWR rendered them surplus to requirements, and the MGWR (a company with a nose for bargains) bought them. Their new identities reflected their origins and they ran as MGWR 141 *Limerick* and 142 *Athenry* (names possibly chosen as a provocation to the GSWR). The GSR recognised their origins by placing them in the ex-WLWR sequence as Nos 233/ 4, but gave them their own identity of Class 234 (J17).

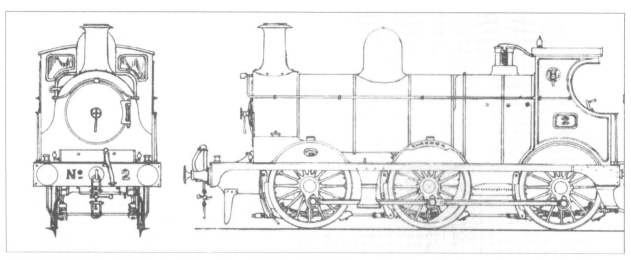

This type was still in production by Kitson at the point of the GSWR takeover. Drawings – *Stephenson Locomotive Society*

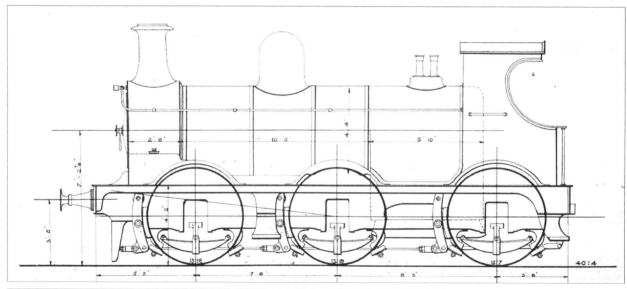

Type XXXV [35]-W No 2 *Shannon* again, on this occasion in normal working condition at Limerick.

Additional Waterford & Limerick locomotives

For completeness, the following three locomotives were acquired by the WLR from other companies and were scrapped well before the GSWR takeover. One of these (No WLR No 25) had commenced its career as GSWR No 43 (1864 No 102). These are cross-referenced in the WLR/ WLWR Locomotive Key above.

RNC Type: I [1]-MGWR 2-2-2 **GSWR Class n/a**

WLR No	Built	Withdrawn by: MGWR	WLR
30 (AEJR No 1 *Drumconora*) (Ex-MGWR 8 *Vesta*)	May 1847	1870	1873
31 (AEJR No 2 *Lough Cutra*) (Ex-MGWR 9 *Venus* or 10 *Luna*)	July or Dec 1847	1869	1873

Built by Grendon

Boiler pressure – 100 lb/ sq in	*Heating surfaces:*	*Tractive effort – 4,430 lb*
Cylinders – 14" x 18"	*tubes – not recorded*	*Coal capacity – not recorded*
Leading wheels – not recorded	*firebox – 62 sq ft*	*Water capacity – 1200 gal*
Driving wheels – 5' 7¾"	*grate – not recorded*	*Locomotive weight – not recorded*
Trailing wheels – not recorded		

These locomotives played a minor role in the AEJR/ ATR saga. They were bought by the AEJR in 1870 but neither was in good order when the WLR took over running the AEJR and they were soon scrapped, apparently doing no work under WLR auspices. Their fuel capacity was interestingly described as "enough coke for 60 miles". An inspection report by the WLR in 1872 described the pair as being "in a queer condition having been cruelly used". They were valued only at £200 each (scrap).

RNC Type: XXIII [23] (GSWR) 0-4-2 **GSWR Class n/a**

WLR No	Built	Withdrawn
25 (ex-ATR No 3) (previously GSWR 102 [1864 number] originally No 43)	Sep 1847	c. 1874

Built by Bury

Boiler pressure – 80 lb/ sq in	*Heating surfaces:*	*Tractive effort – 6,960 lb*
Cylinders – 16" x 24"	*– tubes 1000 sq ft*	*Coal/ water capacities – not recorded*
Driving wheels – 5' 0"	*– firebox 60 sq ft*	*Locomotive weight – 24 tons 1 cwt*
Trailing wheels – 3' 0"	*– grate 12.7 sq ft*	
Wheelbase – 8' 0" + 6' 8"		

For further information see Chapter 5 Type XXIII [23] Page 113/4.

This engine was purchased by the ATR from the GSWR in June 1871. In poor condition when the WLR took over running the ATR, it was soon scrapped (value £220) and so does not appear in the 1874 report. There are varying descriptions of its leading dimensions but those quoted above accord with GSWR Type XXIII [23]. Those reported in *The Railway Magazine* (1899) 5: 482 would appear to be in error.

For completeness, it should be noted that other locomotives were hired by the two Athenry companies. The only known examples were:

GSWR Type II [2] 2-2-2 No 26.

MGWR (Grendon) 2-2-2 No 30 *Pallas* and Fairbairn) 2-2-2 No 13 *Condor*.

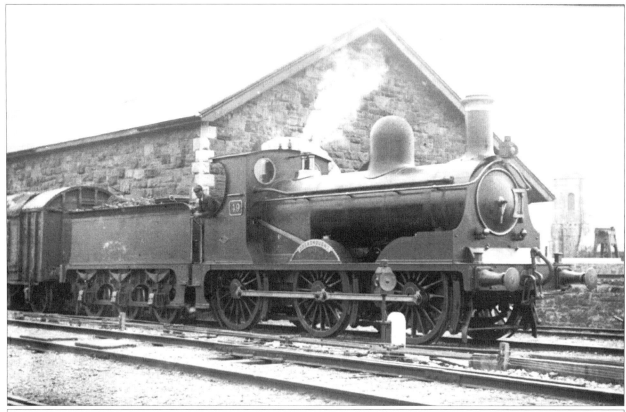

Opposite top: 0-6-0 No 49 Dreadnought (Type XXXI [32]-W) on a goods working at Tralee. *LGRP*

Opposite bottom: On Monday 3 September 1900, Type XXVIII [28] – W No 20 *Galtee More* was entering Limerick with what appears to be a mixed train. Four months later, the WLWR would form part of the GSWR. *Ken Nunn*

This page: The WLWR/ GSWR locomotive that never was. This is the official Kitson photograph of 0-6-0 builder's No 3974 which was completed in January 1901, presented in photographic grey displaying the full glory of the WLWR's lining as that company's No 4 *Shamrock*. This locomotive's companion, builder's number No 3975 intended as WLWR No 11, was completed the same month. There is some mystery concerning what happened next.

As legal successor to the WLWR, the GSWR was contractually obliged to accept delivery and to pay for the pair. For reasons that remain unclear, the GSWR delayed meeting its obligation and in the interim the Midland Great Western Railway took delivery of both. The WLWR already had four of Type XXXV [35] – W in service (No 2 built 1900 and Nos 56-8 built 1897) and perhaps the GSWR was reluctant to take more of what it might have been regarded as unwelcome non-standard additions to its fleet. Whatever the reason, the MGWR stepped in with alacrity and numbered them 141/ 2 respectively. Sources differ on intended WLWR names: No 4 to be *Samson* or *Shamrock* with No 11 to be *Dragon* or *Shamrock*; at least the photograph clears up doubts regarding No 4's planned identity. The MGWR rejected all these options and christened No 141 as *Limerick* and No 142 as *Athenry*. The choice of Limerick was provocative as the city was nowhere near MGWR routes but firmly in GSWR territory.

By the Amalgamation, the six had been subjected to some rebuilding but remained essentially of the same type. Nonetheless they featured in the vagaries of the GSR's re-numbering/ reclassification programme. The ex-GSWR quartet retained their GSWR 222 classification (Nos 222, 237-9) but became J25 under the Inchicore Class system. On the other hand the ex-MGWR pair became J17 but were numbered in the GSWR block as 233/ 4. No 233 never carried its GSR-allocated number so in due course the remaining example became the sole member of GSR Class 234. The locomotive depicted was the first of the six to be withdrawn, in 1929. *L&GRP*

Chapter 9
Tenders

Great Southern & Western Railway

The GSWR's tender supply and construction policy is reviewed under the three chronological divisions applied to the company's locomotives.

Period I

At the time of McDonnell's arrival in 1864, the GSWR's locomotive fleet comprised 55 passenger and 47 goods tender locomotives. The latter figure included engines under construction, delivery of which was completed in 1865. All locomotives were 6-wheelers and their respective builders were:

Builder	Passenger Locomotives	Goods locomotives
Sharp Stewart	20	
Bury	20	10
Inchicore	13	30
Grendon		2
Rothwell		4
Fairbairn	2	1
Total	**55**	**47**

Dimensional data

A contemporary engraving of Sharp Stewart 2-2-2 No 19 (Type I [1]) suggests a well-built 6-wheel tender (capacity 1000 gallons) which would be expected from one of Britain's then leading manufacturers. Bury, Curtis & Kennedy, the other early supplier, reluctantly took up construction of 6-wheeled locomotives around 1845 but all thirty supplied to the GSWR were accompanied by that builder's traditional 4-wheel tender with a capacity of 1344 gallons. This is borne out by the photograph of 0-4-2 No 101 on Page 114 which shows a standard Bury tender, similar to those concurrently being supplied to the London & Birmingham/ London & North Western Railway.

Of the wheel arrangements of the remaining 52 Period I tenders, it is definite that the nine members of 2-2-2 locomotive Type VI [6] built at Inchicore between 1859 and 1863 were equipped with 4-wheel tenders. It is therefore probable that preceding Inchicore-built 2-2-2s of Types IV [4] & V [5] were similar. Fairbairn had a policy of copying the designs of other manufacturers and it seems possible that the 2-4-0s of Type III [3] were coupled to tenders in the Bury style.

This is a standard 6-wheel tender by Sharp Bros & Co. Tenders could be deemed fit for further service when their companion locomotives were either withdrawn or rebuilt. This tender was built for service with locomotive (2-2-2)Type I[1] but is now coupled to Inchicore-built 2-4-0 Type VIII[8], a new locomotive rather than a rebuild. *Locomotive Publishing Co*

Tenders

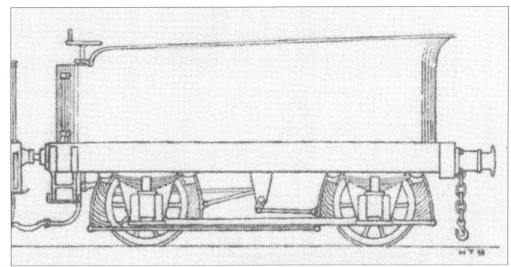

Bury, Curtis & Kennedy Standard 4-wheeled tender: As supplied with 2-2-2 Type II[2] and 0-4-2 Type XXIII[23]. Hand-operated clasp brakes with wooden block. *Image Locomotive Publishing Co*

Regarding goods locomotives, records are opaque for the two tenders supplied by Grendon and the four from Rothwell but the solitary Fairbairn tender (No 75) is known to have been a 1200-gallon capacity 4-wheeler. As the company lacked a qualified Locomotive Superintendent in the period before McDonnell's arrival, it is surmised that design specification was left in the suppliers' hands. If purchase decisions were based on price rather than on optimal technical specification, it seems probable that the Grendon and Rothwell tenders were also four-wheelers.

Under Miller/ Wakefield supervision, 30 goods locomotives were built at Inchicore:

0-4-2 Types:- XXVII [28] – two; XXX [30] – two; XXXI [31] – nine; XXXII [32] - six

2-4-0 Type:- XXIX [29] – three

0-6-0 Types:- XXXIII [33] – two; XXXIV [34] – six

Wakefield is on record as having preferred the 4-wheel tender, despite the greater capacity potential and superior riding qualities of the 6-wheel tender. On this basis, it seems possible that the twenty Sharp Stewart tenders (locomotive Type I [1]) were the only six-wheelers in service prior to McDonnell's arrival.

The Maunsell record referred to elsewhere in this work is a pro forma booklet in which current locomotive data were up-dated annually. The booklet's layout clearly differentiates between 4-wheel and 6-wheel tenders but there is no information recorded for the former. The booklet is dated 1911 which implies that all 4-wheelers had been withdrawn from ordinary service by then.

Inchicore-built 4-wheeled tender: With Inchicore-built 2-2-2 Type VI[6] No 48 (original number 80) introduced December 1859. The 4-wheeled type was favoured by Inchicore pre-1864, apparently based on the standard Bury type but with differences in the superstructure. Note the wooden brake blocks; there was no form of braking on the locomotive. *Locomotive Publishing Co*

No source has been traced that provides additional dimensional information on pre-McDonnell tenders. It appears that they were numbered, probably taking the same identities as the locomotives with which they were paired on entering service. This is interpreted from the manner in which tender numbers were allocated early in Period II where some new Type A tender took low numbers, probably in replacement of withdrawn earlier vehicles.

Period II

There is more clarity regarding tenders built during this period. McDonnell was receptive to advice from experienced locomotive engineers and manufacturers, and this open-mindedness included tender design which appears to have acknowledged the contemporary practice of Beyer Peacock and the LNWR.

At the start of his tenure, McDonnell was beset with numerous organisational and engineering problems that required careful financial husbandry, as reflected in his "make do and mend" approach to locomotive rebuilding and renewal. It would have been logical also to extend the working lives of existing tenders. Rotation and re-use of old tenders is evident in construction statistics for new locomotives and tenders (latter were authors' Type A):

	Locomotives	Tenders
	Class 101	Type A
1866	2	-
1867	7	2
1868	6	5
1869	2	2
1870	-	2
1871	6	6
Total	23	17

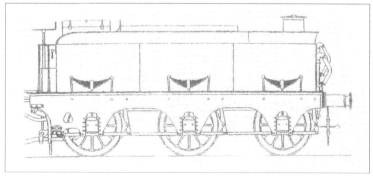

Left and opposite: GSWR Type A: Introduced in 1867, this was McDonnell's first standard tender design with carrying capacities of 1864 gallons and 4 tons, in original condition.

As a tender requires significantly less works attention than a locomotive, universal compatibility and frequent rotation were constants in motive power policy. Tenders from the early singles were re-used with the locomotives that McDonnell rebuilt early in his tenure e.g. Type VIII [8] during their convoluted renewal phase. Practical experience would have emphasised the importance of universality in locomotive/ tender compatibility which became a standard Inchicore practice. This is illustrated with Type XXXV [35] 0-6-0 Class 101 No 186 built 1879 which is paired in preservation with a 3345-gallon tender, a type not introduced until 1899.

McDonnell commenced new construction in 1866, focussed particularly on Type XXXV [35] Class 101 with 37 examples in service by 1873. Of this group, twelve locomotives were built by Beyer Peacock and eight by Sharp Stewart to relieve pressure on Inchicore. The first four from BP were for engines only whereas the remainder came with 6-wheel tenders. The supply of tenders seems to have been influenced by availability of refurbished vehicles retained when their companion locomotives were taken out of service.

It is known that locomotive Nos 151-54 were delivered by Beyer Peacock in 1868 at £2,700 each including tenders whereas four locomotives only were supplied by Sharp Stewart in 1872, priced at £1,917. The quotation for the related tenders was rejected as too expensive. The required vehicles were built at Inchicore for £433 each. This variance reveals price volatility and underlines the wisdom of McDonnell's policy of maximising in-house manufacturing capability.

The central design role played by Beyer Peacock with Type XXXV [35] Class 101 was also evident in the concurrent construction of the first new 6-wheel tenders of McDonnell's tenure. Externally, they resembled those supplied earlier together with 0-6-0s to Australia, Dutch East Indies, India, Sweden plus the Midland and Manchester, Sheffield & Lincolnshire railways. These were the precursors of what became the GSWR's most numerous tender class (designated Type A by the authors), which eventually totalled 117, but subject to the following reservations.

The 12" 4" evenly distributed wheelbase became the GSWR standard for this and successive types until 1922, with the exception of some in the same style but with wheelbase shortened by two feet (authors' Type A1). The tender register shows that ten of Type A1 were built at Inchicore (six in 1873 and four in 1876 for use with 2-4-0 Type X [10] over the Kerry lines (locomotives and tenders Nos 21-6, 65-8). However, the adjacent illustration reveals an A1 type bearing a Beyer Peacock builder's plate. Further research in the archives of the late Joe Lloyd, an acknowledged Gorton Foundry historian, has identified a poor quality photograph of Class 101 No 154 coupled to a Type A1 tender (both bearing BP builder's plates). As this locomotive was built in 1868, it seems probable that the A1 Type was originated by BP with at least four (locomotives and tenders Nos 151-4). The register does not identify these as having the shorter wheelbase or the smaller (1608-gallon) tank capacity so the anomaly remains unexplained.

Beyer Peacock's files confirm supply of the following to the GSWR:

Order No	Date	Works Nos	Running Nos
2045 (locomotives)	1867	747-50	147-150
2102 (locomotives)	1868	780-3	151-4
2179 (tenders)	1868	780-3	151-4
2960 (locomotives)	1873	1251/ 2	177/ 8
2961 (tenders)	1873	1251/ 2	177/ 8
3970 (locomotives)	1881	2029/ 30	189/ 90
3971 (tenders)	1881	2029/ 30	189/ 90

With regard to locomotives and tenders supplied by Sharp Stewart & Co, the following orders have been traced:

Order No:	Date	Works Nos	Running Nos
E588 (locomotives)	1872	2155-2158	163-166
E630 (locomotives)	1873	2310/ 1	175/ 6
T630 (tenders)	1873	Not known	175/ 6
E766 (locomotives)	1879	3837/ 8	185/ 6
T766 (tenders)	1879	Not known	185/ 6

The third variant in Period II was Type B which was a response to faster speeds, heavier loads and longer non-stop distances. The overall chassis dimensions remained unchanged from Type A but removal of the springs from running plate to the outside frames directly above the axle boxes permitted a wider body. Carrying capacities were increased to 5 tons 10 cwt and 2730 gallons, and a later modification was the fitting of extension plates above the flared sides. Twenty-three of this type were built between 1883 and 1895 plus rather strangely four more (Nos 305 to 308) in 1904, although 4-4-0s Nos 305 to 308 were built two years earlier. No reason has been established for this reversion to an older, smaller tender when Type C, introduced in 1899 was under construction, with intervals, until 1922. Type B was known as the "2700 gallon express type"

The tender numbering discipline introduced in Period II requires some explanation. Multiplication of locomotive Class 101 was the main stimulus for construction of Type A and initially numbers below 101 seem to have been taken from pre-McDonnell tenders that were no longer in ordinary service. However, expansion of the class soon outstripped the availability of redundant Period I numbers and in many cases, albeit not all, locomotives and tenders built concurrently were given the same number. This practice, which also applied to other locomotive classes, seems to have had no practical operating purpose but was perhaps an accounting or administrative convenience during the construction phase. Tenders whose numbers and construction dates match those of locomotives are duly annotated on page 250.

The third variant in Period II was Type B which was a response to faster speeds, heavier loads and longer non-stop distances. The overall chassis dimensions remained unchanged from Type A but removal of the springs from running plate to the outside frames directly above the axle boxes permitted a wider body. Carrying capacities were increased to 5 tons 10 cwt and 2730 gallons, and a later modification was the fitting of extension plates above the flared sides. Twenty-three of this type were built between 1883 and 1895 plus rather strangely four more (Nos 305 to 308) in 1904, although 4-4-0s Nos 305 to 308 were

Type A. Modified with side and rear fenders above the side flare to increase coal capacity. *Ken Nunn*

GSWR Type A1: The wheelbase was two feet shorter than that of the standard Type A. It is believed that only ten of this type were built, but as explained in the text, records conflict.

built two years earlier. No reason has been established for this reversion to an older, smaller tender when Type C, introduced in 1899 was under construction, with intervals, until 1922. Type B was known as the "2700 gallon express type."

The tender numbering discipline introduced in Period II requires some explanation. Multiplication of locomotive Class 101 was the main stimulus for construction of Type A and numbers below 101 seem to have been taken from pre-McDonnell tenders that were no longer in ordinary service. However, expansion of the class soon outstripped the availability of redundant Period I numbers and in many cases, albeit not all, locomotives and tenders built concurrently were given the same number. This practice, which also applied to other locomotive classes, seems to have had no practical operating purpose but was perhaps an accounting or administrative convenience during the construction phase. Tenders whose numbers and construction dates match those of locomotives are duly annotated again on page 250.

Period III

Slightly in advance of the new order of 4-4-0 express locomotives, Coey introduced Type C in 1899, colloquially known as the "3300 gallon express tender", although it was equally at home with goods engines. Chassis dimensions remained unchanged from those introduced with Type B but with minor modifications to the braking arrangements. The first examples had side profiles similar to, but taller than, Type B. The first modification, introduced at an unknown date, was the fitting of three or four side coal rails. From about 1911, it became practice to fit plating behind these rails although the official photograph of 4-6-0 No 400 dated 1916 shows its tender still to be the open coal rail version. Later examples had solid side fenders to the same profile fitted from new.

Tenders

Top: GSWR Type B: Removal of springs to the frames above the axleboxes allowed a wider body and greater carrying capacities with modest increase in body height. The disparity between Coey's larger locomotive policy and the size of traditional GSWR tenders is apparent.

Middle: GSWR Type B: Twenty-seven were built between 1883 and 1895, and a further four in 1905.

Bottom: GSWR Type C: The deeper body and increased capacity meant that originally no extensions or side fenders above the side flair were necessary.

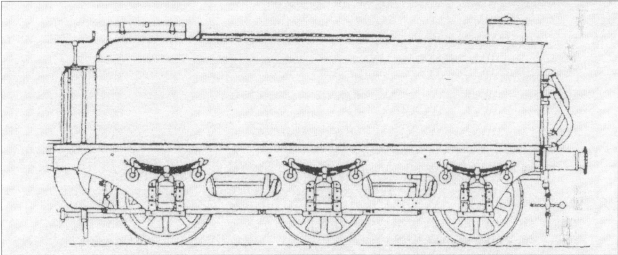

Type C appeared with several GSWR locomotive classes including 0-6-0s, 2-6-0s, the 20th Century 4-4-0s, plus goods and passenger 4-6-0s. There were nine larger tenders available for the ten GSWR-design 4-6-0s in service after 1930 but Type C still made appearances with these engines e.g. with No 407 (the last remaining 4-cylinder 4-6-0) in 1947 and with No 500 in 1950. Rotation should have yielded adequate numbers of the later types, allowing for the periods the relevant locomotives spent in works.

A total of 62 Type C tenders were introduced of which 49 were built at Inchicore. Six numbered 309 to 314 were delivered in 1903 from Neilson Reid & Co together with 4-4-0s Type XVII [17] Class 309. Seven numbered 355 to 361 followed from North British Locomotive Co later the same year as Nos 355 to 361 in company with 0-6-0 Type XXXVIII [38] Class 355.

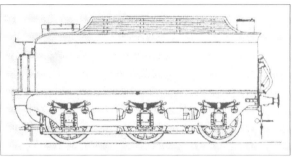

Above: GSWR Type C: The first modification to increase coalcapacity was installation of side coal rails. This version was attached to 4-6-0 No 400 for the official photograph of that locomotive on completion in 1916.

Right: GSWR Type C: Coal rail version with backing plates.

Bottom: GSWR TYPE C: Coupled to Type XXXV [35] Class 101 No 118 at Cork, Glanmire. This photograph illustrates the height disparity between this class and the Type C tender. It also shows the rear tender details and what appears to be a unique combination of *two* coal rails with backing plate.

Right: GSWR Type C: Plain plate side fenders to same profile as for coal rail version.

Above and below: GSWR Type D: Solitary example introduced with 4-6-0 No 500.

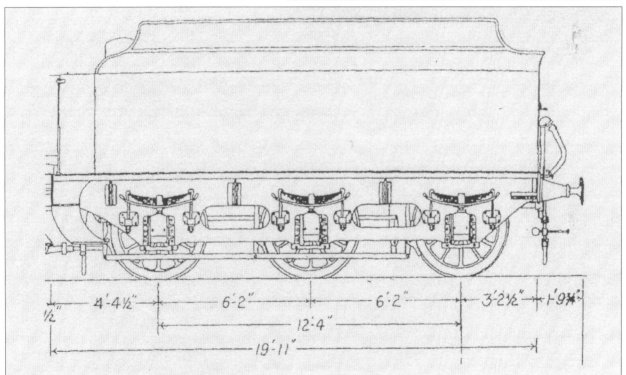

Tender No 406 of Type D was a solitary example constructed in 1924 to complement 4-6-0 No 500. Its styling generally followed that of Type C with solid side fenders but the body was deeper. The sides were extended at the front by an additional panel while the length over buffers was about three inches less than Type C although chassis dimensions remained unchanged. The carrying capacities were eight tons and 3870 gallons.

The four Inchicore-built members of 4-6-0 Type XXI [21] Class 400 were provided from new with Type C tenders, but when the order was placed with Armstrong Whitworth for six more locomotives of this class, it seems that the manufacturers were allowed a free hand in tender design. Designated Type E by the authors, they were completed in 1922 with generally traditional styling. The wheelbase was extended to 15' 2" and the length over buffers was almost four feet more than Type C. Shallower than those of Type D, the side fenders stretched almost the whole length of the body resulting in a more modern appearance. Carrying capacities were 7 tons and 4500 gallons.

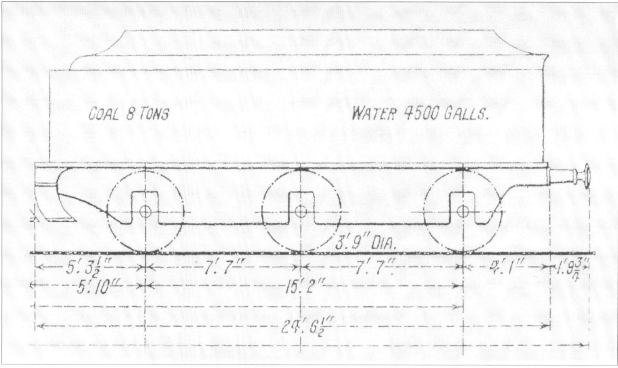

The final two tenders (Type F) were quite different from preceding styles. They were the only tenders of GSWR design-origin to have all-welded body construction and their box-like appearance was distinctly austere. Frame design resembled that of Type E but the wheelbase was reduced to 13 feet. Carrying capacities were 7 tons and 4670 gallons. They were built together with the two members of 4-6-0 Class 500 (Nos 501/ 2) that appeared in 1926 under GSR auspices. They were numbered 407/ 8 by the GSR in continuation of the GSWR's series.

Tenders

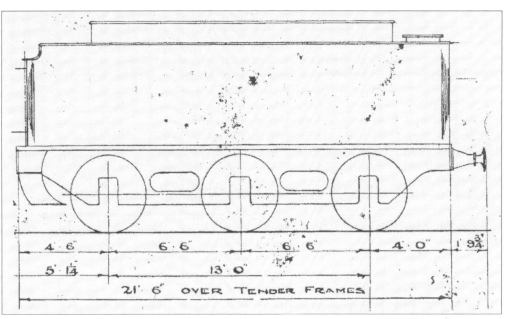

Opposite top and opposite bottom: GSWR Type E: As built by Armstrong Whitworth together with six members of locomotive Type XXI [21] Class 400.

Right: [GSWR] Type F: Final GSWR design of which two were built by the GSR in 1926.

[GSWR] Type F: This modern, functional design was to be ignored by the GSR as the few tenders built by that company reverted to a more traditional styling.

General statistics

The leading dimensions of the standard GSWR tenders were:

Type	Years built	Official weight:		Wheelbase	Water	Coal	Number
		- Empty	- Laden		(gallons)	(tons)	Built
A	1867-1890	11 tons 16 cwt	24 tons	12' 4"	1864	4 tons	117
A1	1873 & 1876	11 tons 11 cwt	22 tons 2 cwt (est)	10' 4"	1608	3 tons 10 cwt (est)	10
B	1883-1904	13 tons 4 cwt	28 tons 5 cwt	12' 4"	2730	5 tons 10 cwt	27
C	1899-1922	14 tons 17 cwt	32 tons 10 cwt	12' 4"	3345	7 tons	62
D	1924	not recorded	42 tons	12' 4"	3870	8 tons	1
E	1922	21 tons 2 cwt	48 tons	15' 2"	4500	7 tons	6
F	1926	not recorded	49 tons	13'	4670	7 tons	2

Wheel diameters were 3' 9" with axles evenly spaced in all types.

Locomotives of the Great Southern & Western Railway

GSWR Tender List

No	Built	Type	Capacity Gallons	No	Built	Type	Capacity Gallons	No	Built	Type	Capacity Gallons
1	1884	B	2730	64	1875	A	1864	127	1882	A [e]	1864
2	1877	A [a]	1864	65	1875	A	1864	128	1882	A [e]	1864
3	1884	B	2730	66#	1876	A1 [b]	1608	129	1890	A [e]	1864
4	1888	A [c]	1864	67	1876	A1 [b]	1608	130	1882	A [e]	1864
5	1877	A [a]	1864	68	1876	A1 [b]	1608	131	1882	A [e]	1864
6	1877	A [a]	1864	69	1876	A1 [b]	1608	132	1888	A [e]	1864
7	1877	A [a]	1864	70-84		Vacant		133	1885	A [e]	1864
8	1880	A [a]	1864	85	1886	B [d]	2730	134	1885	A [e]	1864
9	1884	B	2730	86	1886	B [d]	2730	135	1885	A [e]	1864
10	1880	A [a]	1864	87	1886	B [d]	2730	136	1888	A [e]	1864
11	1888	A [c]	1864	88	1886	B [d]	2730	137	1888	A [e]	1864
12	1884	B	2730	89	1886	B [d]	2730	138	1888	A [e]	1864
13	1880	A [a]	1864	90-92		Vacant		139	1880	A [e]	1864
14	1888	A [c]	1864	93	1885	B [d]	2730	140	1881	A [e]	1864
15	1880	A [a]	1864	94	1885	B [d]	2730	141	1881	A [e]	1864
16	1884	B	2730	95	1885	B [d]	2730	142	1881	A	1864
17	1884	B	2730	96	1885	B [d]	2730	143	1877	A [e]	1864
18	1888	A [c]	1864	97	1895	B	2730	144	1877	A [e]	1864
19	1884	B	2730	98	1895	B	2730	145	1877	A [e]	1864
20	1884	B	2730	99/100		Vacant		146	1877	A [e]	1864
21	1873	A1 [b]	1608	101	1882	A [e]	1864	147	1880	A	1864
22	1873	A1 [b]	1608	102	1873	A [e]	1864	148	1881	A	1864
23#	1873	A1 [b]	1608	103	1881	A	1864	149	1881	A	1864
24	1873	A1 [b]	1608	104	1873	A [e]	1864	150	1882	A	1864
25	1873	A1 [b]	1608	105	1882	A	1864	151§	1868	A [e]	1864
26	1873	A1 [b]	1608	106	1874	A [e]	1864	152§	1868*	A [e]	1864
27-40		Vacant		107	1881	A [e]	1864	153§	1868	A [e]	1864
41	1890	A	1864	108	1875	A [e]	1864	154§	1868	A [e]	1864
42	1890	A	1864	109	1876	A [e]	1864	155	1871	A [e]	1864
43	1878	A [a]	1864	110	1880	A	1864	156	1871	A [e]	1864
44	1878	A [a]	1864	111	1882	A	1864	157	1875	A	1864
45	1878	A [a]	1864	112	1881	A	1864	158	1872	A [e]	1864
46	1878	A [a]	1864	113	1881	A	1864	159	1871	A [e]	1864
47-51		Vacant		114	1869	A [e]	1864	160	1871	A [e]	1864
52	1883	B [c]	2730	115	1869	A [e]	1864	161	1871	A [e]	1864
53	1883	B [c]	2730	116		Vacant		162#	1871	A [e]	1864
54	1883	B [c]	2730	117	1876	A	1864	163	1872	A [e]	1864
55	1883	B [c]	2730	118	1890	A [e]	1864	164	1872	A [e]	1864
56	1868	A	1864	119	1876	A [e]	1864	165	1872	A [e]	1864
57	1868	A	1864	120	1876	A [e]	1864	166	1872	A [e]	1864
58	1872	A	1864	121	1876	A [e]	1864	167	1873	A [e]	1864
59	1876	A	1864	122	1882	A [e]	1864	168		Vacant	
60	1870	A	1864	123	1881	A [e]	1864	169	1873	A [e]	1864
61	1870	A	1864	124	1881	A [e]	1864	170	1874	A [e]	1864
62	1867	A	1864	125	1881	A [e]	1864				
63	1867	A	1864	126	1881	A [e]	1864				

§ Built by Beyer Peacock (Nos 151-4).
* Register records construction year for No 152 as 1873 which appears to be a clerical error; 1868 is more probable.
# Withdrawn by 1923.

Tenders

GSWR Tender List (continued)

No	Built	Type	Capacity Gallons	Previous identity/ builder
171	1874	A [e]	1864	
172	1874	A [e]	1864	
173	1874	A [e]	1864	
174	1874	A [e]	1864	
175	1874 ±	A [e]	1864	
176	1873 ±	A [e]	1864	
177	1873 §	A [e]	1864	
178	1873 §	A [e]	1864	
179	1875	A [e]	1864	
180	1875	A [e]	1864	
181	1879	A [e]	1864	
182	1879	A [e]	1864	
183	1880	A [e]	1864	
184	1880	A [e]	1864	
185	1879 ±	A [e]	1864	
186	1879 ±	A [e]	1864	
187	1882	A [e]	1864	
188	1882	A [e]	1864	
189	1881 §	A [e]	1864	
190	1881 §	A [e]	1864	
191	1885	A [e]	1864	
192		Vacant		
193	1884		2000	WLR No 1 Step'n
194	1899	C [f]	3345	
195	1899	C [f]	3345	
196	1899	C [f]	3345	
197	1899	C [f]	3345	
198	1899	C [f]	3345	
199	1899	C [f]	3345	
200-221		Vacant		
222	1900		2000	WLWR No 2 Kit'n
223-230		Vacant		
231	1883		2000	WLR No 41 Vulcan
232		Vacant		
233	1893		1900	WLR No 45 Dübs
234	1893		1900	WLR No 46 Dübs
235	1895		1900	WLR No 49 Dübs
236	1895		1900	WLR No 50 Dübs
237	1897		1980	WLR No 56 Kitson
238	1897		1980	WLR No 57 Kitson
239	1897		1980	WLR No 58 Kitson
240-246		Vacant		
247	1878		1560	WDLR No 4 Sharp
248	1891		1500	WDLR No 6 Sharp
249-260		Vacant		
261	1881		1585	WLR No 8 Vulcan
262	1886		2000	WLR No 9 Dübs
263	1889		1990	WLR No 10 Dübs
264-271		Vacant		
272	1876		1600	WLR No 19 Avonside
273/ 274		Vacant		
275	1890		1940	WLR No 22 Dübs
276	1892		1940	WLR No 23 Dübs
277-280		Vacant		
281	1874		1630	WLR No 30 Vulcan
282-285		Vacant		
286	1881		1630	WLR No 36 Vulcan
287	1881		1600	WLR No 37 Vulcan
288		Vacant		
289	1882		1630	WLR No 39 Vulcan
290	1893		1900	WLR No 43 Dübs
291	1893		1900	WLR No 44 Dübs
292	1894		1940	WLR No 47 Dübs
293	1894		1940	WLR No 48 Dübs
294-295		Vacant		
296	1896		1940	WLR No 53 Kitson
297	1896		2000	WLR No 54 Kitson
298	1897		2000	WLR No 55 Kitson
299/ 300		Vacant		
301	1903	C	3345	
302	1903	C	3345	
303	1903	C	3345	
304	1903	C	3345	
305	1904	B [g§]	2730	
306	1904	B [g§]	2730	
307	1904	B [g§]	2730	
308	1904	B [g§]	2730	
309	1903	C [g]	3345	Neilson Reid
310	1903	C [g]	3345	Neilson Reid
311	1903	C [g]	3345	Neilson Reid
312	1903	C [g]	3345	Neilson Reid
313	1903	C [g]	3345	Neilson Reid
314	1903	C [g]	3345	Neilson Reid
315-320		Vacant		
321	1904	C [g]	3345	
322	1904	C [g]	3345	
323	1904	C [g]	3345	
324	1904	C [g]	3345	
325	1907	C	3345	
326	1907	C	3345	
327	1907	C	3345	
328	1907	C	3345	

§ Built by Beyer Peacock (Nos 177/ 8, 189/ 90); no construction year in GSWR Register for Nos 177 /8 so year 1873 is based on BP records.

± Built by Sharp Stewart.

GSWR Tender List (continued)

No	Built	Type	Capacity Gallons	Builder	No	Built	Type	Capacity Gallons	Builder
329	1908	C	3345		361	1903	C [h]	3345	North British
330	1908	C	3345		362	1910	C	3345	
331	1908	C	3345		363	1911	C	3345	
332	1908	C	3345		364	1911	C	3345	
333	1908	C	3345		365	1911	C	3345	
334	1908	C	3345		366	1911	C	3345	
335	1908	C	3345		367	1911	C	3345	
336	1908	C	3345		368	1911	C	3345	
337	1909	C	3345		369	1911	C	3345	
338	1909	C	3345		370	1917	C	3345	
339	1909	C	3345		371	1917	C	3345	
340	1909	C	3345		372	1917	C	3345	
341-350		Vacant			373	1917	C	3345	
351	1910	C	3345		374	1922	C	3345	
352	1910	C	3345		375	1922	C	3345	
353	1910	C	3345		376	1922	C	3345	
354	1910	C	3345		400	1922	E	4500	Armstrong Whitworth
355	1903	C [h]	3345	North British	401	1922	E	4500	Armstrong Whitworth
356	1903	C [h]	3345	North British	402	1922	E	4500	Armstrong Whitworth
357	1903	C [h]	3345	North British	403	1922	E	4500	Armstrong Whitworth
358	1903	C [h]	3345	North British	404	1922	E	4500	Armstrong Whitworth
359	1903	C [h]	3345	North British	405	1922	E	4500	Armstrong Whitworth
360	1903	C [h]	3345	North British	406	1924	D	3870	

Where locomotive and tender numbers plus construction dates coincide, following annotations apply:

[a]   4-4-0 Type XII [12] Class 2.
[b]   2-4-0 Type X [10] Class 21.
[c]   4-4-0 Type XIII [13] Class 52; tender Nos 4,11,14,18 were Type A and Nos 52-55 were Type B.
[d]   4-4-0 Type XIV [14] Class 60.
[e]   0-6-0 Type XXXV [35] Class 101.
[f]   0-6-0 Type XXXV [35] Class 101 Nos 194-199 were built between November 1898 and November 1899; the first batch of Type C tenders.
Nos 194-199 were recorded as built 1899; It seems possible that most, if not all, of these 0-6-0s entered service with the first of the new 3345 gallon type.
[g]   4-4-0 Types:- XVII [17] Class 309; XVIII [18] Class 321 No 321.
[g§]   4-4-0 Type XVI Nos 305-8 preceded Tender Nos 305-8 by two years.
[h]   2-6-0 Types XXXVII [37]; XXXVIII [38] Class 355.

Acquired companies (other than WLR/ WLWR)

Information about these tenders is sparse. What is known by way of dimensional information is summarised by railway company as follows:

Cork & Youghal Railway

With a total mileage of 31½, use of tender locomotives on this line was hardly justified. Nevertheless, some sources indicate that 2-2-2ST/ 2-4-0ST Type LXXI [71] Nos 6-8 were built by Neilson and delivered by the makers as 2-2-2s. RN Clements cites Neilson records as confirming this and as states that they were converted to 2-2-2STs prior to the takeover by the GSWR. Investigations into Neilson records during preparation of this work have failed to confirm RNC's interpretation of these records. On this basis, it seems most unlikely that the CYR contributed any tenders to the GSWR's fleet.

Waterford, Dungarvan & Lismore Railway

This company operated a total route mileage of 59 and owned six 0-4-2s in two types. The respective locomotive types were very similar and the tenders were almost identical.

Tenders

RNC Type	LOCO Nos	W.A.	Built	Builder		TENDER No of wheels	Wheelbase	Water gal
LXXII[72]	1-4	0-4-2	1878	Sharp Stewart	>	6	11' 6"	1560
LXXIII[73]	6, 7	0-4-2	1891/2	Sharp Stewart	>	6	11' 6"	1500

These engines were supplied with standard Sharp 6-wheel tenders, with outside springs over the running plate, a design also supplied to the Dublin Wicklow & Wexford, Newry & Armagh and Waterford & Central Ireland railways between 1863 and 1884. The water capacity seems to have increased in this period from 1000 gallons, but it seems probable that these engines ran with tenders similar if not identical to WCIR No 1 (1884, type: IX[9]-WKR).

Waterford & Kilkenny Railway (pre-1861)

A few of the WKR tenders survived into the 1940s in service with the water tender train based at Limerick Junction

RNC Type	LOCO WKR No	W. A.	Built	Builder		TENDER No of Wheels	Wheel-base	Tank (gal)	Coal
II[2]-WKR	4, 5	2-4-0	1852	Stothert & Slaughter	>	4 §	unknown	1300	unknown
III[3]-WKR	6, 7	2-2-2	1853	Kitson	>	unknown	unknown	unknown	unknown
VII [7]-W	2	0-4-2	1857	EB Wilson	>	unknown	unknown	unknown	unknown

§ Fitted with hand brake only; wooden brake blocks

Waterford & Kilkenny Railway (post-1861) [Later Waterford & Central Ireland Railway]

RNC Type	LOCO WKR No	W. A.	Built	Builder		TENDER No of Wheels	Wheel-base	Tank (gal)	Coal
V[5]-WKR	6, 7	2-4-0	1866	Fowler	>	4‡	unknown	1300	unknown
VI[6]-WKR	8, 9	2-4-0	1867/8	Vulcan Foundry	>	6 §	11' 0"	1400	unknown
VII[7]-WKR	10, 11	0-4-2	1873	Avonside	>	6	unknown	1600	unknown
IX[9]-WKR	1	0-4-2	1884	Sharp Stewart	>	6	11' 6"	1600	4 tons
X[10]-WKR	4	0-4-2	1897	Vulcan Foundry	>	6	11' 0"	1600	4 tons

‡ Supplied by Avonside in 1869 and 1872 when these locomotives were converted from 2-4-0Ts to 2-4-0 tender engines.

§ Tenders for Nos 8/9 had 3' 6" wheels, inside bearings throughout and weighed 18 tons in working order (empty 10 tons 11 cwt) and with wooden brake blocks on all wheels.

Waterford Limerick & Western Railway

The motive power fleet of the WLWR and its predecessor predominantly comprised tender locomotives. Recorded data are fragmentary but the asset survey conducted by the GWR in 1874 and the GSWR Locomotive Superintendent's personal locomotive & tender record dated 1911 (as amended to 1924) provides basic information on the profile of the tender fleet at those particular dates. Constant shortage of funds necessitated purchase of locomotives in small batches and while each order would have accorded with the railway's specification, it seems probable that companion tenders were to the manufacturer's standard design to contain cost.

Locomotives of the Great Southern & Western Railway

WLR Tender Fleet: GWR Survey of 1874

It is evident that each tender in 1874 carried the same running number as that of the locomotive with which it was currently paired. The survey, summarised in the table below, reveals that 14 locomotives were working with tenders that had been built by a different manufacturer. This implies that second generation motive power was introduced under locomotive-only orders, old tenders having been recycled for re-use. Modification of couplings fo compatibility with new engines would have been substantially cheaper than new replacement tenders. Unfortunately, tender construction dates were not recorded.

LOCO Nos	W. A.	Built	Builder	TENDER Nos	Builder	No of Wheels	Wheel-Base	Tank (gallons)
8-10	2-2-2	1847/ 8 ±	Bury	8-10	Slaughter	6 §	9' 6"	1120
11, 12	2-4-0	1850 ±	Fairb'n	11, 12	Slaughter	6 §	9' 6"	1120
17	2-4-0	1854	Fairb'n	17	Slaughter	6 §	9' 6"	1120
18	2-4-0	1854	Fairb'n	18	S. Stewart	6	10' 6"	1200
19-21	2-4-0	1854	Fairb'n	19-21	Fairb'n	6	10' 6"	1550
26	2-4-0	1855	Fairb'n	26	Fairb'n	6	10' 6"	1550
2	0-4-2	1856 ±	Fairb'n	2	Fairb'n	6	10' 6"	1550
1	0-4-2	1859 ±	Fairb'n	1	Fairb'n	6	11' 0"	1250
3	0-4-2	1872 ±	Kitson	3	Fairb'n	4	8' 0"	1200
4	0-4-2	1862 ±	S. Stewart	4	Fairb'n	4	9' 0"	1200
5, 6	0-4-2	1862 ±	S. Stewart	5, 6	S. Stewart	6	10' 6"	1200
7	0-4-2	1872 ±	Kitson	7	Fairb'n	4	8' 0"	1200
13	0-4-2	1869 ±	S. Stewart	13	Fairb'n	6	10' 6"	1550
14	0-4-2	1871±	S. Stewart	14	Fairb'n	6	10' 6"	1550
15	0-4-2	1868 ±	S. Stewart	15	Fairb'n	6	10' 6"	1550
16	0-4-2	1867 ±	S. Stewart	16	Fairb'n	4	8' 0"	1200
28	2-2-2	1864 ±	Kitson	28	Kitson	4	8' 0"	1000
22-4	0-4-2	1862	Fos & Hack	22-4	Fos & Hack	6	10' 3"	1200
25, 30-2	2-4-0	1874	Vulcan	25, 30-2	Vulcan	6	10' 6"	1600
27	0-4-2	???	S. Roberts	27	S. Roberts	4	8' 0"	875

± These dates derive from the GWR survey; they do not accord with those quoted in the individual locomotive histories.

§ Denotes 3' 8" wheel diameter; all others were 3' 6".

Fairb'n = Fairbairn; Fos & Hack = Fossick & Hackworth; S. Roberts = Sharp Roberts; S. Stewart = Sharp Stewart.

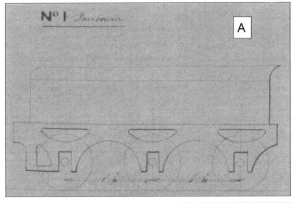
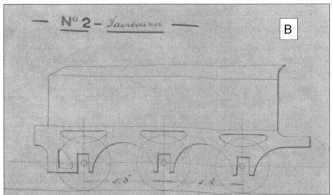
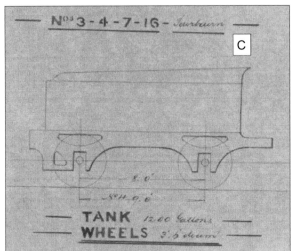
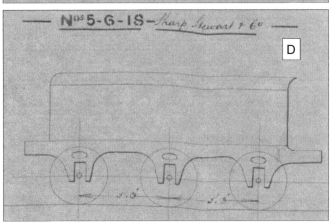
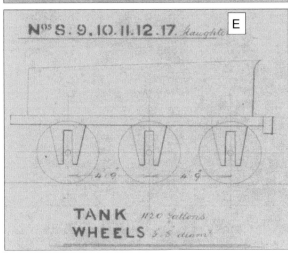
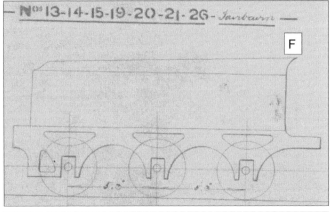
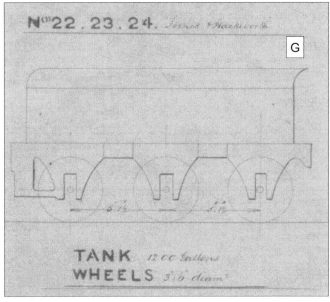

A: WLR No 1: Built by Fairbairn 1859.
B: WLR No 2: Built by Fairbairn 1856.
C: WLR Nos 3, 4, 7, 16: Built by Fairbairn.
D: WLR Nos 5, 6, 18: Built by Sharp Stewart.
E: WLR Nos 8 to 12, 17: Built by Slaughter.
F: WLR Nos 13 to 15, 19 to 21, 26: Built by Fairbairn.
G: WLR Nos 22 to 24: Built by Fossick & Hackworth.

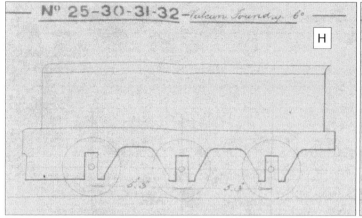
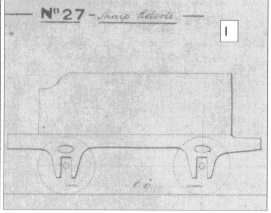
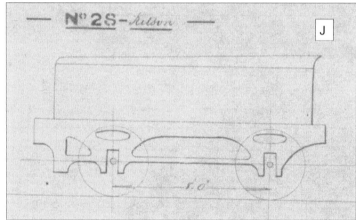

H: Nos 25, 30-32: Built by Vulcan Foundry.

I: WLR No 27: Built by Sharp Roberts.

J: WLR No 28: Built by Kitson.

Bottom left: WLWR tender built by Vulcan Foundry, with 2-4-0 Type XIX[19]-W Nos 8, 25, 30-32, 35-39 (GSWR Class 281).

Bottom centre: WLWR tender built by Vulcan Foundry, with 0-6-0 Type XXII[22]-W Nos 40, 41 (GSWR Class 230).

Bottom right: WLWR tender built by Dübs, with 4-4-0 Type XXV[25]-W Nos 9 (GSWR Class 262).

Period: 1875 to 1910

No official records have been traced on disposition of the WLR/ WLWR tender fleet during this 36-year period; the GSWR Tender Register dated 1911 as amended up to 31st December 1923 is fortunately a reliable record. The pairings detailed in the 1874 report confirm that it had been practice to recycle older tenders for use with new locomotive-only orders placed with manufacturers, a necessary measure given the company's financial condition. However, around about the opening of the Appleby/ Robinson era, there appears to have been a policy change whereby some new orders were for locomotives plus tenders. This might have reduced opportunities for rotation, at least among vehicles of different manufacturing origin and it seems fairly certain that new locomotives delivered in the 1890s remained paired with their original tenders.

Tenders

Reconciliation of such records as are available suggests the following:

WLWR/ WLR Tender No	GSWR Tender No	Built	Builder	Period 1901 > 1910	December 1911	December 1923
1	193	1884	Stephenson		In service	In service
2	222	1900	Kitson		In service	In service
5	Unknown			0-6-0 No 5 withdrawn 1909		
7	Unknown			0-6-0 No 7 withdrawn 1905		
8	261	1881	Vulcan Foundry		In service	In service
9	262	1886	Dübs		In service	Withdrawn
10	263	1889	Dübs		In service	Withdrawn
11	Unknown			2-4-0 No 11 withdrawn 1901		
12	Unknown			2-4-0 No 12 withdrawn 1907		
19	272	1876	Avonside	0-4-2 No 19 withdrawn 1901	In service	In service
20	Unknown			2-4-0 No 20 withdrawn 1909		
22	275	1890	Dübs	[2-4-0 No 22 withdrawn 1913]	In service	In service
23	276	1892	Dübs		In service	In service
24	Unknown			0-6-0 No 24 withdrawn 1910		
25	277			2-4-0 No 25 withdrawn 1902		
26	Unknown			0-4-2 No 26 withdrawn 1910		
28	Unknown			2-2-2 No 28 withdrawn 1902		
30	281	1874	Vulcan Foundry	2-4-0 No 30 withdrawn 1903/ 4	In service	Withdrawn
31	282			2-4-0 No 31 withdrawn 1910		
32	283			2-4-0 No 32 withdrawn 1910		
33	Unknown			0-4-2 No 33 withdrawn 1901/ 2		
35	Unknown			[2-4-0 No 35 withdrawn 1911]		
36	286	1881	Vulcan Foundry	2-4-0 No 36 withdrawn 1903	In service	In service
37	287	1881	Vulcan Foundry	2-4-0 No 37 withdrawn 1909	In service	Withdrawn
38	Unknown			2-4-0 No 38 withdrawn 1907		
39	289	1882	Vulcan Foundry	2-4-0 No 39 withdrawn 1905	In service	In service
40	Unknown			0-6-0 No 40 withdrawn 1909		
41	231	1883	Vulcan Foundry	0-6-0 No 41 withdrawn 1910	In service	Withdrawn
43	290	1893	Dübs		In service	In service
44	291	1893	Dübs		In service	Withdrawn
45	233	1893	Dübs	[0-6-0 No 45 withdrawn 1919]	In service	In service
46	234	1893	Dübs	[0-6-0 No 46 withdrawn 1911]	In service	Withdrawn
47	292	1894	Dübs	[2-4-0 No 47 withdrawn 1915]	In service	In service
48	293	1894	Dübs		In service	In service
49	235	1895	Dübs		In service	In service
50	236	1895	Dübs		In service	In service
53	296	1896	Kitson		In service	In service
54	297	1896	Kitson		In service	In service
55	296	1897	Kitson		In service	In service
56	237	1897	Kitson		In service	In service
57	238	1897	Kitson		In service	In service
58	239	1897	Kitson		In service	In service

Locomotives of the Great Southern & Western Railway

It should be noted that:

a. There is no means of confirming that at withdrawal date each locomotive or tender was paired with its notional numerical partner.

b. Some tenders enjoyed significantly long working lives after withdrawal of their nominal partner locomotive. For example, tender No 1 which was rendered surplus in 1899 by conversion of 0-6-0 No 1 to a saddle tank was still in service in GSR days. Tenders No 19, 22, 30, 36, 37, 39, 41, 45-7 similarly outlived their nominal partners, in some cases for lengthy periods.

c. So far as can be ascertained, there was no mingling of GSWR/ WLWR locomotives/ tenders in the 1901-24 period.

d. A number of tenders withdrawn from ordinary service found further work in the Limerick Junction-based tender train apparently including some 4-wheel types.

Dimensions: Ex-WLWR tenders in service as 31st December 1911

WLWR No	GSWR No	Built	Builder	No of wheels	Wheelbase	Tank (gallons)	Type of Brake
1	193	1884	R. Stephenson	6	10' 6"	2000	Vacuum
2	222	1900	Kitson	6	9' 8"	2000	Steam
8	261	1881	Vulcan Foundry	6	10' 6"	1585	Vacuum
9	262 §	1886	Dübs	6	10' 6"	2000	Vacuum
10	263 §	1889	Dübs	6	10' 6"	1990	Vacuum
19	272	1876	Avonside	6	10' 0"	1600	Vacuum
22	275	1890	Dübs	6	10' 6"	1940	Vacuum
23	276	1892	Dübs	6	10' 6"	1940	Steam
30	281 §	1874	Vulcan Foundry	6	10' 6"	1630	Vacuum
36	286	1881	Vulcan Foundry	6	10' 6"	1630	Vacuum
37	287 §	1881	Vulcan Foundry	6	10' 6"	1600	Steam
39	289	1882	Vulcan Foundry	6	10' 6"	1630	Vacuum
41	231 §	1883	Vulcan Foundry	6	11' 0"	2000	Steam
43	290	1893	Dübs	6	10' 6"	1900	Steam
44	291 §	1893	Dübs	6	10' 6"	1900	Steam
45	233	1893	Dübs	6	10' 6"	1900	Steam
46	234 §	1893	Dübs	6	10' 6"	1900	Steam
47	292	1894	Dübs	6	10' 6"	1940	Hand
48	293	1894	Dübs	6	10' 6"	1940	Steam
49	235	1895	Dübs	6	10' 6"	1900	Steam
50	236	1895	Dübs	6	10' 6"	1900	Steam
53	296	1896	Kitson	6	9' 8"	1940	Steam
54	297	1896	Kitson	6	9' 8"	2000	Steam
55	298	1897	Kitson	6	9' 8"	2000	Steam
56	237	1897	Kitson	6	9' 8"	1980	Steam
57	238	1897	Kitson	6	9' 8"	1980	Steam
58	239	1897	Kitson	6	9' 8"	1980	Steam

§ Withdrawn between 1911 and 1924; actual withdrawal date not recorded.

± The only recorded weights are Nos 2 (17 tons 0 cwt) and 19 (21 tons 6 cwt), both empty.

Tenders

Top left: WLWR tender built by Dübs, with 2-4-0 Type XXVIII[28]-W Nos 10, 20, 22, 23, 43, 44, 47, 48 (GSWR Class 263 later 276).

Top right: WLWR tender built by Dübs, with 0-6-0 Type XXXI[31]-W Nos 45, 46, 49, 50 (GSWR Class 233).

Bottom left: WLWR tender built by Kitson, with 4-4-0 Type XXXIV[34]-W Nos 53-55 (GSWR Class 296).

Bottom right: WLWR tender built by Kitson with 0-6-0 Type XXXV[35]-W Nos 2, 56-58 (GSWR Class 222).

The Tender Train

A constant problem was the poor water quality in many parts of Ireland and columns in areas where supplies had a particularly high lime contact often carried warning signs that they should only be used in emergency. The GSWR installed water softening plants at several points, the best known of which were at Inchicore and Limerick Junction, (the latter beside the stone water tower opposite the scissors crossover at the main platform). Water trains comprising redundant tenders were worked from Inchicore down the mainline to supply depots in need and from Limerick Junction to Limerick City. These did not appear in the Working Timetables and seemed to operate as block trains on an "as required" basis. Old 4-wheel tenders were reportedly used on these duties but these may have been confused with larger tenders where the centre axle had been removed.

Locomotives of the Great Southern & Western Railway

Top: Type XII [12] 4-4-0 Class 2 No 2 is shunting Composite Dining Car No 2092 or 2093 (seating for 12 First Class and 24 Second Class passengers, built 1915) in the Gas Siding (where vehicle gas tanks were recharged) at Limerick Junction. The water softening plant (the tank had a capacity of 26, 686 gallons!) can be partly seen behind the carriage. This view also provides useful rear three quarter information on locomotive cab details and also on an unmodified early McDonnell era tender. The angle makes confirmation difficult but the tender seems to be one of the Type A1 variety, of which few remained in service at the date of this view which is 1933. *LGRP*

Bottom: An unidentified member of Type XXII [22] Class 500 stands at Limerick Junction with its Down train. The tender train is in the background.

Tenders

The tender train was being reversed out of Limerick Junction on 4th August 1953 by Type LXI [61] Class 37 No 317. *RM Arnold*

Another view of the same train on 4th August 1953, standing beside the Limerick Junction water tower and softening plant. *RM Arnold*

Chapter 10
Amalgamation

The Great War of 1914-1918 profoundly changed the railway industry in both Ireland and Britain. In the case of the latter, the companies were significantly more involved through closer proximity to the continental European battlefields, and through the obligation to provide locomotives, rolling stock, materials and manpower in support of the armed effort. While British railways suffered very little infrastructural damage, the cost of war took more the form of unprecedented loss of life plus severe backlogs in repairs and maintenance. Nonetheless, the impact was sufficient to make fundamental re-adjustment of industry ownership inevitable. Even before the Armistice of November 1918, recognition that companies had limited independent life expectancy in the post-war world engendered serious consideration of nationalisation. Eventually, these plans were modified taking physical form in the Big Four through the Grouping of 1923.

Irish railways played their part in the Great War but insulation by gauge and geography had left them in better shape than their British counterparts. A far greater measure of disruption was wrought on the system by the Civil War that followed the signing of the Treaty on 6th December 1921 that established the Irish Free State under a Provisional Government. JC Conroy in his seminal work *History of Railways in Ireland* (Longmans Green Publishing 1928) provides a detailed contemporary account of the situation confronting the industry consequent upon achievement of independence. Most pressing was railwaymen's remuneration with employer-worker negotiations in hand on a pan-Ireland scale. On 15th February 1922 an agreement was reached whereby the Ministers for Labour in the Free State and Northern Ireland would deal in consort with workers' representatives but this soon foundered through south-north political differences, an early indicator of practical issues that partition would raise.

In April 1922 the Provisional Government appointed a Railways Commission to review and report on (i) the industry's current position, (ii) the best method of administration in the collegiate interests of shareholders, employees and general public (iii) relations between employees and the railway companies. The Commission's findings provide an informative statistical snapshot of the industry's situation which underlines its significance for the new state. The year 1913 had been the best trading-wise in the industry's history with net revenue of £4.9 million against operating expenses of £3.1 million. The railways were regarded as having been well managed despite persistent complaints of practices that hampered economic development, and of excessive tariffs. Railway companies had been considered a sound investment with a good dividend record, albeit at the expense of employee remuneration. Control had been vested in the Irish Railways Executive Committee from 1916 and then on a *de facto* basis by the Provisional Government. The Commission provocatively stated that Government control had "definitely, and we believe, permanently worsened the position of the Irish Railway Stockholders".

The report concluded with a recommendation that the industry be fully nationalised but with administration resting in the hands of an "independent board". The report was received with hostility by the national press which expressed several reservations, particularly concerning the implicit basis for conflict between theoretically independent directors and a single shareholder. The government rejected the report on the pragmatic grounds that the industry's equity and debt capital aggregated £46.9 million and due compensation would be a heavy imposition on the new state's finances. Despite this reluctance, a nationalisation Bill based on the Commission's recommendations was introduced into the Dáil in November 1923. It was decisively defeated in the absence of governmental support.

During this period the railway companies seemed to become a political football as indicated by two official reports presented the following year. That of the Agricultural Commission demanded fundamental changes in the manner by which railway charges were set i.e. to achieve significant tariff reductions. However, the 1924 Report to the Fiscal Inquiry Commission noted that in the preceding three years "many orders for express type locomotives, tenders, goods waggons and locomotive boilers had been sent to England" and continuation of these practices would lead to complete closure of Dublin's workshops except for repairs. Normally 1700 personnel were employed at Inchicore but the GSWR reported that fewer were currently engaged as coaches could be built in England and delivered to Ireland at £300 less per unit than could be supplied locally. Given that debate over the industry's re-configuration had started with pressure to increase remuneration levels, there is an impression of attempts to square the circle.

Inchicore's reported inability to compete on price was more the result of spare production capacity in Britain than its supposed manufacturing inefficiency. The Great War had engendered massive expansion in industrial capacity and now there was an acute shortage of custom, especially among munitions

The final locomotive introduced by the GSWR was 2-cylinder 4-6-0 No 500 which had been shortly preceded by the final three of 4-cylinder 4-6-0 Class 400. No 407, the first of this batch, had been built by Armstrong Whitworth (builder's No 185) and delivered in October 1922. The circumstances of the Civil War presented difficulties in accumulating the contracted test mileage prior to final settlement with the builders. This delay coupled with the GSWR's precarious financial condition is believed to have caused Armstrong Whitworth some anxiety over whether they would see their money but the balance due was probably paid in the second half of 1923.

It is uncertain who was responsible for the decision to build Nos 407-9 with saturated boilers. At time of order, Locomotive Superintendent Watson with his eyes set on his new job with Beyer Peacock had probably lost interest in the matter. Bazin, his successor might have opted for lack of superheating and higher boiler pressure at 225 lb/ sq in as a combination that might improve the class's lacklustre performance. The issue was quickly resolved once the trio was put to work; superheating was installed in Nos 408 & 409 in 1924, and in No 407 the following year. This is an early but undated view of the engine in externally as-built condition, and possibly still in saturated state.

manufacturers (in the Irish context particularly Armstrong Whitworth and the Woolwich Arsenal, both of which took up locomotive manufacture). Of more immediate concern was the operational condition to which the GSWR had been reduced by national developments. The Civil War which started in June 1922 resulted in the railways becoming a major strategic target. By January 1923, five minor railways in the south had been rendered completely inoperative while the GSWR was working at a substantially diminished level.

Much of the system was crippled and with concerns about serious food shortages threatening inland towns, the Railway Protection, Repair and Maintenance Corps was created to ensure operational continuity through emergency repairs to infrastructure. In this period, the GSWR sustained damage to permanent way at 375 locations; 255 bridges were damaged and 96 buildings including 71 signal cabins were destroyed or severely damaged. There were over 200 cases of stations and trains raided with goods stolen. The biggest single infrastructural challenge was replacement of the viaduct over the River Blackwater near Mallow which had been blown up during the Civil War, severing the Dublin-Cork main line. Mobile assets had fared no better and 468 locomotive, coach and wagon units had been destroyed or damaged. Such was the number of pending claims under the Malicious Injuries Act that a composite agreement was reached through the Damage to Property Compensation Act 1923 to distribute governmental compensation for war damage.

Meanwhile the GSWR was engaged in disputes arising from there being insufficient traffic to justify the minimum three days' work per week for much of the labour force, in breach of pre-existing agreements. Government compensation to cover shortfalls was provided in August and September but was inadequate to arrest the GSWR's deteriorating financial condition. Accordingly, the company served notice of intent to close down with effect from 8th January 1923. In response, the Minister for Industry and Commerce announced that the government would meet the difference between income and expenditure but, controversially, would not cover interest due on debenture stock. Complex structures were then established for labour representation and remuneration. However desirable, these measures could not disguise the fact that the January announcements amounted to admission by the company that it was no longer viable, which was tacitly confirmed by the government's response.

Since 1922 there had been general, albeit not total, acceptance that corporate unification was central to the industry's future. With nationalisation a proven non-starter, a merger agreement was reached in principle in April 1922 between the GSWR and the Cork, Bandon & South Coast Railway. This was not enacted pending resolution of broader ownership issues confronting the industry but the understanding was regarded as a model for the future. During 1923, general acceptance was reached by all but two of the 5' 3" gauge companies. (The situation regarding the narrow gauge companies was complex and required separate treatment which is not material to this account).

Negotiations were held between the major railway companies and the government with intention that agreement on unification should be achieved by 1st March 1923. It was first proposed to form two groups. The MGWR and GNR(I) would merge to form a northern group while in the south there would be a marriage between the GSWR, DSER and CBSCR. The two groups would then absorb the smaller companies within their respective regions. The Northern Ireland government supported this proposal in the expectation that significant additional British-Irish traffic would be directed through Belfast/ Enniskillen/ Cavan but it ultimately failed through the inability of the MGWR and the GNR(I) to agree merger terms.

Debate then focussed on unification only of those companies that operated solely within the Free State. Following intense bargaining, the GSWR/ MGWR/ CBSCR had agreed by May 1923 to merge in a single grouping to be entitled "The Great Southern & Midland Railway Company". However, the Dublin & South Eastern Railway and the Cork & Macroom Direct Railway strenuously resisted these plans, vigorously expressing their intent to remain independent. The latter was a well-run and prosperous concern that genuinely believed retention of the *status quo* to be in its best interests but eventually acceptable compensation terms were agreed. The position concerning the DSER was significantly more complex.

Of the larger Irish companies, the DSER was probably the weakest and most in need of absorption into a larger organisation. Its suburban business had suffered badly from tramway competition and it was saddled with a long-standing operating agreement with the Dublin & Kingstown Railway (DKR) under which it paid an unduly generous rent that significantly exceeded traffic receipts. (Incidentally, this burdensome contract rendered the DKR the wealthiest of all Irish railway companies). Hostility from local landowners had forced the DSER line south from Dublin to be closer to the seashore than was prudent and defensive maintenance against depredation by the sea was very costly. Expensive re-alignment inland of parts of the route was considered inevitable. The sum of these issues had reduced the company to a fragile financial condition before considering the grievous damage wrought during the Civil War.

The dominant force behind the DSER's opposition was HG Burgess, the company's Deputy Chairman. Born in Co Tipperary in 1859, his career had started with the Dublin, Wicklow & Wexford Railway in 1873 before joining the London & North Western Railway's Irish operations. His career rise had been meteoric, holding important positions with the Ministry of Transport during the war before appointment as General Manager of the LNWR in 1920. He was then actively engaged in supervising the formation of the London Midland & Scottish Railway before becoming that company's General Manager in 1924, while retaining his DSER board seat.

Burgess had played a significant behind-the-scenes role in the Treaty negotiations that ended the Anglo-Irish War, despite his Unionist sympathies. His attitude towards railway unification was driven more by protection of LMS interests in a newly partitioned Ireland than by concern for the future of the Irish system at large. The LMS dominated traffic across the Irish Sea and Burgess feared that amalgamation would lead to GSWR-based influence favouring diversion of traffic through the southerly route in partnership with the Great Western Railway. For Irish interests, there was a concern that the LMS would secure a stranglehold which would be strengthened should the alternative idea of a merger between the DSER and GNR(I) proceed. This offered logical north-south operational integration along the eastern seaboard although the GNR(I) did not appear overly keen.

Contentious negotiations too complex to describe in detail here followed between the Free State

During the short interregnum (12th November-31st December 1924) of the Great Southern Railway (note, not Railways), only one locomotive was completed at Inchicore. This was 4-8-0T No 901 which apart from minor variations was to the same design as GSWR Type LXV [65] Class 900. The first locomotive had not proved very successful so why Bazin chose to build another is unclear. No 900 had been a synthesis of existing parts and components from Coey-era designs. It is possible that with the company chronically bereft of funds and Inchicore works on short time, this locomotive was created to provide work using surplus material already to hand. No 900 worked from 1915 to 1928 while No 901's career was even shorter, being withdrawn in 1931.

government, the Railways Commission and the companies. With the DSER situation still unresolved, the government proceeded with the Railways Act 1924, closely based on the Railways Act 1921 under which the British Grouping of 1923 had been achieved. The Act, which became law on 23rd July, embraced all the major companies plus most of the minor concerns that operated solely within the boundaries of the Irish Free State. A tribunal was established to oversee practical aspects of the amalgamation process, to handle the myriad of related legal issues, and to tackle the DSER matter. The interests of the acquiescent companies were vested in the newly formed Great Southern Railway with effect from 12th November 1924 and the tribunal then proceeded to monitor negotiations between the GSR and the DSER.

The LMS sought to drive a hard bargain with the DSER as the negotiating tool. Proposed terms were (i) repayment of a £100,000 loan extended by the LNWR to the DWWR in 1905 to finance the Waterford Extension (ii) GSR to purchase £87,000 (nominal value) 4% Stock in the New Ross & Waterford Extension Railway (iii) GSR to purchase at par £126,800 of stock held in the GSWR's North Wall Extension (iv) LMS to nominate a member of the GSR board. While proposals (i) to (iii) were flatly rejected, it was recognised that compromise was desirable in the interest of future Anglo-Irish political and trade relations.

During November/ December 1924 with governmental agreement, compensation terms were finally settled whereby the GSR paid £47 10s for every £100 of DSER stock. This was a substantial increase over both the nominal market valuation of £15 and the £20 that had been offered sometime earlier by the GSWR, and quite excessive in view of the DSER's near bankrupt condition. Directors and shareholders did well out of the transaction while, to the fury of the GSR board, £25,000 of the proceeds were set aside for "exceptional payments" at the discretion of the DSER directors and £5,000 were distributed among office personnel. Ordinary DSER workers received nothing despite union protestations and of course none of the largesse was deployed in improvement of the company's run-down assets. Burgess declined any compensation for loss of office but did accept a seat on the GSR board. In summary, the DSER saga turned out to be a shabby affair.

Differences having been resolved in December 1924, the newly styled Great Southern Railways which included the DSER's undertaking commenced operations with effect from 1st January 1925. The ex-GSWR element predominated in the new company by way of senior management:

	GSWR	GSR
Chairman	Sir William Goulding	Sir William Goulding
General Manager	EA Neale	MF Keogh (ex-MGWR)
Secretary	R Crawford	CE Riley (ex-GSWR)
Superintendent of the Line	PJ Floyd	PJ Floyd
Civil Engineer	JF Sides	JF Sides
Chief Mechanical Engineer	JR Bazin	JR Bazin

At the time of the Amalgamation, the constituent companies were operating the following route mileages, including worked or leased lines that were nominally independent until taken over the GSR. The GSWR figure also includes the Irish lines of the Fishguard & Rosslare Railways & Harbours Company:

Great Southern & Western Railway 1150 miles
Midland Great Western Railway 538 miles
Dublin & South Eastern Railway 156 miles
Cork Bandon & South Coast Railway 95 miles

Completion of the GSWR's motive power story lies in the early history of the Great Southern Railways where responsibility for the new company's locomotives was vested in two Englishmen. JR Bazin had joined the GSWR as Running Superintendent in 1919 from the (English) Great Northern Railway where he had been a contemporary and colleague of Gresley, and had succeeded Watson as Chief Mechanical Engineer in November 1921. His deputy was WH Morton who had joined the MGWR as Chief Draughtsman (No 4 in the hierarchy) from Kitson in 1900, rising to become Locomotive Superintendent in 1915. Bazin's seniority derived from his being the elder of the pair, and through his being already in post in the larger, better-equipped Inchicore facility.

Bazin's 4-6-0 No 500 was an excellent design. Its multiplication was planned but the reason for curtailment beyond two more of the type was charged with irony. Not long before the Amalgamation, at Morton's instigation the MGWR had ordered from the Woolwich Arsenal twelve 2-6-0s in kit form based on the South Eastern & Chatham Railway's Class N and several factors favoured more Woolwich moguls at the expense of Class 500. They were a more effective interpretation of the Swindon design school than had been achieved with Class 400; they enjoyed wider route availability and thus greater utility than any GSWR 4-6-0; they were acquired in kit form at bargain basement unit prices, far lower than the comparative cost of new construction. The design was attributed to Maunsell, who had wearied of Watson's enthusiasm while in charge at Inchicore but later became a disciple of Swindon's principles. The combination of low cost and performance led to the GSR's purchase of fifteen more kits in 1927 which effectively closed the book on further GSWR-sourced initiatives.

Bazin retired in 1929 and was succeeded by Morton. The former was reputed to be sceptical about the benefits of superheating although the curiosity of 4-6-0 Nos 407-9 in saturated form probably had more to do with exploration of all possible alternatives to improve the type in its original 4-cylinder form. Bazin was nevertheless reluctant to superheat second-string motive power in marked contrast to Morton's enthusiasm for the measure.

Morton was the only CME of the GSR not to have worked for the GSWR but his three-year tenure was notable in pursuit of Inchicore's cause, prior to his elevation to the position of General Manager (1932-1942). He introduced no new designs and refrained from further effort to improve the remaining un-rebuilt members of Class 400. Instead, he focussed on upgrading the operational performance of the fleet as a whole through a programme of superheating in contrast to Bazin's reticence. GSWR classes 52, 60, 301, 305, 309, 321, 333, 351, 355, 368 benefitted as a result but the biggest impact was upon Class 101 of which 67 were eventually treated. For a cash-strapped organisation, this policy was ideal for extending the working lives of ageing locomotives and for extracting more value from them. The dividend lay in ex-GSWR locomotives playing an active and valuable role almost to the end of Irish steam.

It was an exercise of which McDonnell, no stranger to financial stringency and to eking out the working lives of old engines, would surely have approved.

Amalgamation

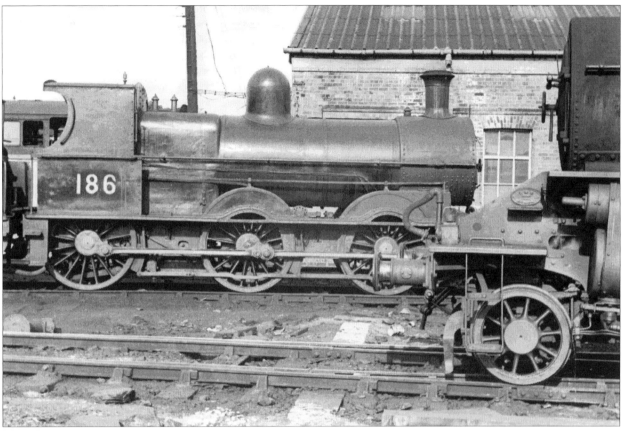

WH Morton (ex-Locomotive Superintendent with the Midland Great Western Railway) was Chief Mechanical Engineer of the Great Southern Railways from 1929 until 1932, before becoming General Manager of the company. He introduced no new designs but concentrated on improving the performance, and thus extending the viable working lives, of ageing locomotives. Probably the most significant element of this programme was the fitting of Type Z superheated boilers to ex-GSWR Class 101. No 186 which had been completed by Sharp Stewart (builder's No 2838) in November 1879, was fitted with a 4' 4" boiler by 1910, with a Type Z boiler in 1932, and with new frames in 1935. This view, taken in 1967, shows the final development of this venerable class with the 1930s-vintage boiler and modernised cab where the side cut-out has been reduced to improve crew protection. The location is Belfast York Road in Northern Ireland in company with an LMS Northern Counties Committee 2-6-4T "Jeep" to the right and another behind. No 186 had embarked upon its career in preservation. *EM Patterson via Charles Friel*

The last locomotive built to a GSWR design was delivered under the auspices of the Great Southern Railways in March 1926 as Type XXII [22] Class 500 No 502. All three locomotives of this class were excellent performers that gave trouble-free service. No 502 was the last at work being withdrawn in August 1957. It is at Cork Glanmire shed, coupled to one of the two Type F tenders introduced concurrently with Nos 501/2.

Appendix A: Influences on locomotive design policy

A.1 Boiler Pressure (BP)

No record has been traced of the BP for several of the earlier locomotive Types although in the pre-McDonnell period, 80 to 100 lb/ sq in was the norm. Progressive increases were possible as improvements in boiler materials and engineering standards eased safety concerns. Nevertheless, it would be unwise to impute modern standards of accuracy to records from the early days. For example, on 15th September 1872 the boiler of Dublin Wicklow & Wexford Railway 2-2-2T No 4 exploded at Bray killing the crew. The boiler had been built in 1855 and at the time of the accident, its two safety valves had been set at 105 lb/ sq in. These were of poor design and might have been subjected to some illicit tampering but most significantly, the railway's engineers apparently had no record of the safety valve setting on construction of the locomotive.
The BP for 0-6-0 Type XXXV/ Class 101 was 140 lb/ sq in when introduced. Increase in BP was probably the simplest means of extracting better performance and there were numerous instances of it being raised during a locomotive's career (plus unofficial increases through interfering with the safety valve mechanism). By the turn of the century, new 4-4-0s were being pressed to 160 lb/ sq in and the last of this wheel arrangement eventually worked at 175 lb/ sq in. Superheated members of Type XXI Class 400 worked at 175 lb/ sq in but it was notable that the short-lived saturated experiment saw boiler pressures of 225 lb/ sq in without any other modification to the vessel. This indicates that there was a significant in-built safety margin at both pressures. In the same vein, retention of safety margins seems to have been material to some reductions in working pressures for ageing boilers with limited residual life expectancy.

Poor water quality endemic to many areas was clearly a factor in boiler design. Comparatively modest working pressures compared with some other railways would seem to have formed part of pragmatic measures to contain maintenance costs. A scientific survey conducted system-wide by British Railways during the 1950s confirmed what the GSWR would seem to have established years earlier on a practical working plane i.e. increased BP can exponentially advance boiler wear. The GSWR's devotion to tender locomotives to minimise use of water sourced in poor quality areas, installation of water softening plants at Inchicore and Limerick Junction, soft water distribution by means of the tender trains, adherence to a regular boiler wash-out regime, and modest working pressures reflect a holistic devotion to cost minimisation. This culture probably had it roots in policies established in Period II (1864 to 1895).

A.2 Tractive Effort (TE)

Boiler pressure is a key determinant in the calculation of tractive effort which in this work is expressed to the nearest 10 lb. For two-cylinder locomotives, it is calculated by the standard formula:

$$TE = \frac{D^2 \times S \times P \times 85}{W \times 100}$$

Where: D = cylinder diameter in inches

S = cylinder stroke in inches

P = maximum boiler pressure in lb/ sq in, assumed to be working at 85% of this level

W = driving wheel diameter in inches

The sum is multiplied by two for four-cylinder locomotives.

TE is a superficial and inaccurate measure of power output that is probably most useful in comparing the potential haulage capacity of different classes. In practical terms, other less common measurement criteria made TE more informative. Comparison of the relationship between aggregate cylinder volumes and aggregate heating surfaces can help determine whether a design is over-cylindered (or alternatively under-boilered). Another useful indicator is factor of adhesion (total adhesive weight in pounds divided by the TE in pounds); the optimal median factor in Irish/ British practice is regarded as 4. Factors significantly less than this level increase the propensity to wheel slip i.e. inability to apply effectively at the rail the power generated by the boiler.

A.3 Superheaters

Superheating in its modern form was first developed through experimental work undertaken by Wilhelm Schmidt in the late nineteenth century. A Prussian State Railways 4-4-0 Class S3 (of which 1027 were in service) was the world's first superheated locomotive and once teething problems had been overcome, the equipment was proven sufficiently effective for all 104 members of the following PSR 4-4-0 Class S4 to be so fitted.

In the opening years of the 20th Century, some British engineers investigated compound steam to improve thermal efficiency as had become the practice with marine engines. However, in May 1906 GJ Churchward of the Great Western fitted 4-6-0 Saint Class No 2901 *Lady Superior* with a Schmidt superheater. The results encouraged further development, culminating by 1909 in the Swindon No 3 superheater which was fitted extensively to that company's fleet. The GWR abandoned further thought of compound propulsion, its experience remaining limited to the three De Glehn Atlantics that had purchased from France. As related in Chapter 2, the GSWR's experience with compound steam was

Appendix A

fleeting with experimentation ending in 1901; over a decade later the company cautiously adopted superheating.

A superheater avoids an embedded problem where water and steam are in direct contact within a closed vessel. The boiling point of water rises in relation to the pressure exerted upon it, thus:

Pressure	Boiling point
Atmospheric	212° F
85 lb/ sq in	327° F
225 lb/ sq in	397° F
250 lb/ sq in	405° F

It follows that a stronger, heavier and more expensive boiler would be required to accommodate a higher steam temperature at the regulator valve. However, once steam has passed this point, its temperature can be raised further by re-directing it back though the hottest part of the boiler which is in the immediate vicinity of the top and front of the firebox. This is achieved by steam passing from the regulator valve through the main steam pipe into a header mounted on the front tube plate in the smokebox. From the header, the superheater tubes take the steam back to the firebox throatplate, through a U-bend, and then forward to the main steam pipes and on to the steam chest. Installation of enlarged flues and insertion of the superheater tubes therein is only possible by reduction in the number ordinary boiler tubes and thus the related heating area. However, the impact of this reduction is more than off-set by the higher temperature of the superheated steam at the admission valve. Steam processed in this fashion can be safely subjected to more heat at normal working pressures, making possible temperatures as high as 600° F to 750° F.

Three advantages result:

[1] Any water that has passed through the regulator valve and header is converted into more steam.
[2] Condensation within the cylinder is eliminated.
[3] The volume of steam increases as compared with its saturated condition. The volume increase depends upon the boiler working pressure e.g. at 225 lb/ sq it is approximately 30%.

The third factor reduces demand upon the firebox and thus fuel consumption. Passage of steam through the superheater tubes (elements) helps keep temperatures in reasonable equilibrium, although a hot fire when running with closed regulator (i.e. while coasting) risks their exposure to excessive heat and thus melting.

Installation of a superheater was cheaper than conversion from simple to compound propulsion but the GSWR was reticent about its application.

Saturated steam's moisture content imparted a lubricating effect upon valves and cylinders that was denied by ultra-dry superheated steam. The resultant increased wear required better oil lubrication which was easier to apply with a piston valve than with the traditional slide valve. Although some conversions to piston valves were effected, in most cases slide valves were retained with locomotives that received superheaters in mid-life. This was probably a marginal decision based on relatively relaxed operating schedules (except for high speed expresses) where inadequate lubrication was less of a problem.

The Watson superheater seems to have been a variant of that developed by Robinson. The latter had personally registered the first patent on his superheater in 1911 and the following year it was announced that the system would be adopted as the Great Central Railway's standard. Further, Robinson formed the Superheater Corporation of London to exploit the commercial potential. In the meantime, Schmidt's patents had been acquired by the Schmidt Superheating Company (SSC), an American organisation formed in 1910 for that purpose. SSC perceived a breach of intellectual property rights and the matter was raised during Robinson's visit to the USA in 1913. Samuel Vauclain of Baldwin Locomotive Works (and inventor of the eponymous compound system) arranged a meeting with SSC representatives who proposed purchase of the Robinson patents for use in north America. Lengthy but inconclusive discussions were held, with Robinson apparently believing that further negotiations would follow. Early the following year, Robinson's system received widespread exposure through the forum of the Institution of Civil Engineers. Almost concurrently, SSC announced commencement of legal proceedings against Robinson personally, the Great Central and the Superheater Corporation. Robinson again met SSC representatives but there was no resolution to the dispute.

SSC's case was weakened by the Germanic connotations of its product and the outbreak of World War I delayed any proceedings. With public sentiment on Robinson's side through emphasis on the "Britishness" of his design, negotiations recommenced post-war on more amicable terms leading to the merging of the two parties' commercial interests.

GSWR superheater policy

The first attempt to improve the quality of steam on admission to the valves was the experimental fitting of a steam drier to 4-4-0 No 62 in 1896. This locomotive was otherwise unmodified and the trial does not appear to have lasted long before the locomotive reverted to normal.

Coey demonstrated awareness of current developments in authorising the fitting of tapered boilers to some of his 4-4-0s and it is believed that he first considered adoption of superheating in about 1909. The decision to proceed with a trial was taken in 1911 with procurement and installation becoming Maunsell's responsibility. The selected locomotive was 4-4-0 No 326 and the fitting of a Schmidt superheater was undertaken in 1912 as part of an extensive rebuilding exercise. The locomotive received 8" diameter piston vales in replacement of the original slide type, new 20" x 26" cylinders (previously 18½" x 26"), and a smokebox extension to accommodate the header. As was usual in the early days of superheating, a mercury pyrometer was fitted to register the degree of superheat. Also a damper was fitted, operated by a cylinder on the side of the smokebox, automatically to close the ends of the superheater flues when steam was shut off. Boiler pressure remained unchanged at 160 lb/ sq in while the tractive effort was raised from 15,320 lb to 17,900 lb; the overall weight was increased by a modest 1 ton 1 cwt. No 326's success in service confirmed the potential of superheating for large engines but its career in this condition was short-lived. A cylinder block fracture in late 1915 led to reversion to original form although the extended smokebox was retained.

Coey favoured the tapered boiler for his 4-4-0s but not together with a Belpaire firebox, a combination proven by Swindon to be very effective but costly to manufacture. The 2-6-0s of Class 368 of 1909 introduced the Belpaire firebox to the GSWR and these engines had parallel boilers. This format was adopted with 4-4-0 No 341, a locomotive that embraced so many modern features that despite its Coey/ Maunsell attribution, it seems to have been largely a creation of the latter. Full details are included in Chapter 4 but it is worth noting that No 341 combined Walschaerts inside valve gear, Belpaire firebox, and a 31% increase in aggregate heating surface over No 340, the last Coey 4-4-0. Dimensional comparison shows how much more Maunsell was able to extract from what was still a moderately-sized machine.

No 341's effectiveness was due in no small part to its Schmidt superheater. Maunsell's unequivocal commitment to superheating became evident with his 0-6-0 Class 257, the first four of which entered service in 1913 just after his departure to Ashford. These engines were fitted with Schmidt superheaters but the second batch of four introduced the following year carried what was known as the "Maunsell-Hutchinson" superheater. This had been developed by Maunsell in collaboration with his personal assistant, George Hutchinson, and the pair duly patented the header design. This was adopted in later GSWR locomotives (with one possible exception discussed below) and by the South Eastern & Chatham/ (English) Southern railways.

No 400, Watson's first 4-6-0, encountered problems from its introduction in August 1916 including fractured piping and steam leaks. It is speculated that Watson might have re-used the Schmidt superheater rendered spare through reversion of 4-4-0 No 326 to saturated condition. Longer elements would have been necessary but it is feasible that the original header might have been resuscitated.

It is believed that the Maunsell-Hutchinson superheater was fitted to Nos 401-406, and after a short interval to Nos 407-409. The anachronistic construction of the latter batch in saturated form has been much debated. It has been cited as an early expression of Bazin's reservations about the value of superheating but the authors believe it was more in the spirit of a radical attempt by Watson to rectify the class's shortcomings. The speed with which superheaters were applied to the saturated trio seems to have rapidly allayed concerns in that respect.

Bazin was nevertheless reluctant to apply superheating on a broad scale, and practice elsewhere showed that while effective for locomotives engaged on longer distance and heavier duties that imposed continuous demands upon the boiler, it was not necessarily a panacea. For example, 4-8-0T No 900 would not have benefitted as shunting duties made only intermittent demands upon the boiler with time to recover while coasting or stationary. This was evident in London & South Western Railway 4-8-0T Class G16 which was

Locomotive No:	340	341
Boiler pressure lb/ sq in	160	160
- later	-	175
Cylinders	18" x 26"	20" x 26"
- later	-	19" x 26"
Driving wheels	5' 8½"	6' 7"
Tractive effort	16,730 lb	17,900 lb
- later	-	17,670 lb
Heating surfaces (sq ft)		
- firebox	128	156
- tubes	1284	1365
- superheater	-	335
Total	1412	1856
Grate	21	24.8
Overall weight	50 tons 6 cwt	60 tons 3 cwt
Max axle loading	16 tons 5 cwt	19 tons 2 cwt

Appendix A

GSWR superheated locomotives:

Class	321	341	257	400	400	400	500
Wheel arrangement	**4-4-0**	4-4-0	0-6-0	4-6-0	4-6-0	4-6-0	4-6-0
Running No	326	341	257-264	400	401/ 2/ 6	403-5	500-2
Number superheated	1	1	8	1	3	3	3
Superheater type	Schmidt	Schmidt	Schmidt	Schmidt (?)	Maunsell	Maunsell	Maunsell
Heating areas (sq ft)							
- firebox	145	156	118	158	158	158	158
- tubes	1153	1365	844	1614	1590	1614	1590
-superheater	345	335	224	440	350	366	350
Total	1643	1856	1186	**2212**	**2098**	**2138**	**2098**
Dimensions:							
Tubes	177 x 1 5/8"	205 x 1 3/8"	122 x 1¾"	173 x 1¾"	168 x 1¾"	170 x 1¾"	168 x 1¾"
Flues	24 x 5¼"	24 x 5¼"	18 x 5"	24 x 5"	24 x 5 1/8"	24 x 5 1/8"	24 x 5 1/8"

always superheated but in its hump shunting work is estimated to have consumed much more fuel than it would have in saturated form, to no measurable advantage.

Another factor was cost. A superheater unit was comparatively simple to manufacturer and install but to extract maximum benefit, installation of piston valves and improved lubrication was desirable. These measures added to the all up-cost which might be hard to justify with a locomotive in mid-life.

Post-Amalgamation

Bazin as the first Chief Mechanical Engineer of the Great Southern Railways remained reticent over the superheating of second-string motive power. However Morton, his deputy and successor who had been his opposite number at the Midland Great Western Railway, was unreservedly enthusiastic. He had superheated 32 MGWR engines in eight different classes prior to the Amalgamation. Following Bazin's retirement, the measure was key to motive power policy at a time when the GSR's finances were hard-pressed. As a cost-effective means of improving performance, 131 locomotives drawn from eleven ex-GSWR classes (52/ 60/ 101/ 301/ 305/ 309/ 321/ 333/ 351/ 355/ 368) were superheated.

Appendix A.4 Continuous brakes

In 1876 McDonnell fitted a locomotive and eight passenger coaches with the Smith continuous brake but the board was reluctant to sanction more expenditure on this equipment. Nevertheless two years later, it was reported that this form of brake had been fitted to 39 locomotives, 50 carriages and 23 other passenger train vehicles. There had been twelve occasions when couplings had parted while on the move which, for reasons explained below, rendered the Smith brake inoperative. The limitations of the system were officially acknowledged by standing instructions that trains were to be halted by use of the locomotive handbrake in the traditional manner and that the Smith brake was not to be fully engaged except in emergency.

Further installations were approved which led to the curiosity of a number of goods locomotives being so fitted. Use of the Smith system discrete to locomotive and tender certainly improved its braking power, which was at least acknowledgement of previously inadequate stopping capacity, but did not meet the need for continuous brakes throughout a complete passenger train. McDonnell persisted and by 1881 all passenger locomotives had been fitted with the Smith brake while the remainder of the goods locomotive fleet was converted in the period 1884-7.

Even so, Aspinall doubted the wisdom of reliance on the simple but flawed Smith system. It was worked by admission of steam to the locomotive's large ejector thereby drawing air from the brake pipes to create a vacuum in an enclosed concertina rubber cylinder mounted below the solebar. The lower cylinder face was mechanically linked with the brake blocks. The rising piston thus engaged the brakes, but there were drawbacks:-

1. If for any reason the vacuum was destroyed (e.g. by the train parting or a leak in the pipe), the brake ceased to function entirely.

2. There was a delay between engagement of the ejector and evacuation of sufficient air for all the brake cylinders to be activated. This problem was exacerbated as trains became longer (and thus heavier) where the greater inertia demanded prompt delivery of brake power throughout the train.

3. The delay before the train brake became fully

engaged extended emergency stopping distances and thus necessitated greater headroom between services. This was not an immediate problem on the lightly trafficked GSWR but the implicit erosion of safety margins was unwelcome.

In considering these drawbacks, Aspinall recognised that brake power could be improved by substituting a double-acting closed cylinder where the piston's rise drawn by the vacuum could be assisted by admission of air below. After numerous experiments, he proceeded to modify the Hardy cylinder (which itself was an improvement on the Smith type) whereby the small ejector created a vacuum above and below a flexible diaphragm. To apply the brake the driver opened the valve that admitted air to the lower part of the cylinder thus forcing the diaphragm upwards. To release the brake, vacuum was restored to the lower section of the cylinder and the diaphragm sank to its original position, forcing the brake into the off position. The system relied on two pipes connected throughout the train. A 2-inch diameter pipe connected with the bottom of the cylinder while a 1½-inch diameter pipe permanently connected the ejector with the upper brake reservoirs to maintain the vacuum. Aspinall's system was evident in the two brake pipes on carriage stock and on the rear of tenders. For tank locomotives the double pipes were fitted front and rear.

The widely-monitored Newark brake trials of 1875 had proven inconclusive in the cause of continuous brake standardisation but Aspinall's system, which remained unique to the GSWR, crucially embraced the fail-safe principle. The shortcomings of the simple brake system that Aspinall and Ivatt had feared were revealed with dreadful consequences in the Armagh disaster of 12th June 1889 where the Great Northern Railway (Ireland) had failed to match the GSWR's progress in continuous braking systems.

From about 1910, GSWR coaches were converted to the single pipe vacuum system and locomotives had all lost the second pipe from about 1922 although the system remained in place between engines and tenders. A drawback of the Aspinall system was its uniqueness which caused compatibility problems when working with other companies' stock, leading to its eventual replacement. On 20th June 1904, the problem was highlighted in a buffer stop collision at Greenore, which involved a DNGR locomotive hauling four 6-wheel SLNCR coaches, two 6-wheel GSWR coaches and one GNR(I) van where systems incompatibility resulted in the train having no continuous braking capacity when it was most needed.

The Gallant 44 resting in Ballygeary shed. See Appendix E, Page 279.

Appendix B: McDonnell at the North Eastern Railway

McDonnell's short, ill-starred reign at the North Eastern Railway has been traditionally attributed to the workforce's objections to his efforts at re-organisation of workshop facilities and modernisation of production processes. Resistance to change is not unusual but this explanation is unconvincing in an era when management and social conditions took little or no account of the feelings of the rank and file. In particular, the NER had demonstrated an uncompromising policy towards industrial relations. In 1867, footplate personnel who had gone on strike were promptly locked out with summary dismissal following for most. With this management culture, the proposition that discontented personnel could unseat a senior officer is simply untenable.

Several leading commentators (Ahrons, Nock, Tuplin) have presented theories to explain the reasons for McDonnell's departure which appear fanciful, poorly researched or simply misinformed. George Heppell, who had a varied career with commercial engineering companies in the North East before joining the NER in 1883 and who became the company's chief draughtsman in 1906 provided an account of the saga. This is so far apparently the only recorded first-hand account of the affair; his memoirs have been published by the North Eastern Railway Association.

When McDonnell arrived on the NER in November 1882, he discovered that Gateshead had built locomotives in six different classes that year while Darlington delivered locomotives in three different classes, of which only 0-6-0 Class 398 (a variegated type comprising 160 engines) was common to both works. Further, production capacity was limited and in need of overhaul at both locations while the situation at several repair depots also required attention. It was a situation that compared extremely poorly with the conditions obtaining at Inchicore after 17 years of hard work.

There was apparently an entrenched management attitude concerning retention of the *status quo* – particularly at Gateshead. Heppell personally pointed out to McDonnell certain physical deficiencies at the Gateshead site that would complicate improvements. McDonnell responded that Civil Engineer Harrison was prepared to spend a lot of money rather than see the operation relocated. In any event, McDonnell identified that significant savings could be achieved with investment in more modern workshop equipment with resultant advances in productivity. He proceeded to attempt improvements but these had the reverse effect as production rates dropped. How and why this happened is not recorded but there may have been attempts by others to sabotage his efforts. (Railway histories show that conflict between civil and mechanical engineers to the detriment of the collegiate good was not uncommon as witness the case of Smith [Locomotive Superintendent], the River Class 4-6-0s and the Highland Railway's directors).

While working on the Gateshead project, Heppell suggested to McDonnell that there would be room to install a foundry which elicited the response "Young man, do you want the sack? Don't you know that several of our directors have iron foundries?" (In the later years, Darlington obtained its castings from Kitson & Co, controlled by Sir James Kitson who was then chairman of the NER; even in the 1950s, Darlington still did not have a proper foundry). McDonnell would have been familiar with the advantages from his experiences at Inchicore where the facility had proven its worth many times over.

As a first step towards fleet rationalisation, McDonnell initiated construction of 0-6-0 Class 59 (later LNER J22) based on GSWR Class 101, and 4-4-0 Class 38 (GSWR Class 2). Both were enlargements of what had proceeded at Inchicore but Darlington Drawing Office expressed reservations concerning their adequacy. McDonnell's insistence on their suitability seemed to derive from Irish experience rather than recognition of the NER's existing and potential traffic demands. The preceding Class 398 was more powerful than the new 0-6-0 which was regarded as under-powered and too lightly built. Comparison with other railways' construction programmes revealed substantial increases in cylinder sizes which implied a need for larger boilers and stronger frames.

There was also a question over contract authorisation. Because of the problems at Gateshead, it seems that construction was farmed out to a commercial builder without McDonnell having first obtained board authorisation; further details are unavailable. Even then, termination of employment does not appear to have derived from actions in excess of delegated authority. On his departure, McDonnell was granted one year's salary (£1,600) by way of compensation and also received £500 as a farewell gift.

There were clearly contradictory elements to the saga and it seems certain that the full story has not been revealed. What is definite, however, is that McDonnell after leaving the NER had a successful career with William Armstrong on Tyneside, followed by years as an engineering consultant in Australia and South America. He never returned to the British railway sector which in view of his Inchicore achievements was a significant loss for the industry.

Appendix C: Accident Reports

First hand, reliable accounts of operating conditions are scarce but official accident reports provide some insight into how the railway worked in those days long ago. These four summaries, while not typical of recurrent daily events, at least paint a picture of conditions in adversity.

Waterford & Kilkenny Railway: Ballylowra, 6th September 1867

Four months after the WKR took back operating control of its system from the Waterford & Limerick Railway, the 10.25 am Maryborough-Waterford mixed service comprised four wagons and a van, then two passenger coaches and another van, hauled by Kitson Type III [3] -WKR 2-2-2 No 4. At Kilkenny, Type VII [7] -WKR 0-4-2 No 1 built by EB Wilson which was required in Waterford, was added to the consist, coupled between No 4 and the train. Thomastown (milepost 39) was passed six minutes late and at milepost 41½, No 4's driver observed that a permanent way gang was replacing a section of left hand rail. Speed was "not much reduced" by the time the No 4, its tender and locomotive No 1 reached and successfully cleared the missing rail. No 1's tender and the train were less fortunate in being derailed. No 1's tender turned over and the fireman was "thrown underneath and much knocked about".

The Board of Trade's Inspecting officer attributed the accident to the ganger's failure to take proper precautions to warn trains and significantly commented "It certainly seems desirable that gangers should be provided with watches". A timetable had been provided but was of little value without the means of telling the time.

Waterford & Central Ireland Railway: Ballyhale, 26th March 1895

This tragic accident throws light on some of the WCIR's operating practices. Locomotive No 3, one of the Stothert & Slaughter 2-4-0s of 1852 (Type: II [2]-WKR) was hauling the 8.00 am Kilkenny-Waterford goods, which loaded three horseboxes, thirteen wagons and a brake van. At the time of the accident, it had been fitted with 5' 3" coupled wheels and had run 705, 992 miles on the WCIR since its return from the WLR in 1867.

The engine had been in the shops for attention in February-March 1894 so should have been in good mechanical order. A mile south of Ballyhale, the locomotive's right-hand connecting rod broke and pierced the firebox. The rush of water and steam from the boiler blew out the brick arch, and engulfed the footplate in steam, brick fragments and hot coals. The footplatemen were severely scalded and thrown off the engine. The driver died instantly while the fireman survived a week, but never recovered sufficiently to provide a first-hand account .

The Inspecting Officer blamed the accident on the driver's failure to attend to the wicks on the big end brasses. Lack of lubrication caused overheating and thus seizure of the connecting rod bearing. He noted that the rod, although of iron (presumably wrought) and of modest cross-sectional dimensions, was in good condition and if properly lubricated should have been adequate for a small engine like No 3. He also noted that the safety valves had been wedged with a piece of wood, presumably to increase the boiler pressure and thus haulage power, as the engine had just ascended a bank of just over a mile with gradients between 1 in 358 and 1 in 90. The inspecting officer condemned this as a "most dangerous practice." He appears to have held the crew largely responsible for their own deaths due to sins of both omission (inadequate lubrication of the connecting rod bearings) and commission (jamming the safety valves).

Tampering with safety valves to increase working pressure seems to have been a cause of several boiler explosions in the late 19th Century. It must have been a tempting but risky practice for crews trying to coax their charges up inclines or when overloaded.

Great Southern & Western Railway: Carlow, 24th November 1900

This collision occurred at Carlow station at 8.25 am when the stationary 7.24 am Down Kildare-Kilkenny service comprising five coaches hauled by 2-4-2T Type LVI [56] No 36 was struck by the 7.35 am Up train from Kilkenny to Dublin Kingsbridge headed by 2-4-2T Type LV [55] No 34 with seven coaches. The route from Dublin became single track at Carlow and these services were scheduled to cross at Milford, 6 miles further south. Rather than cause the Up service unnecessary delay at Milford, it was allowed to proceed on to Carlow for the crossing to take place there. There had been several such changes to regular traffic arrangements during the previous month without any unusual occurrence. The resulting slow speed collision (estimated 7-8 mph) caused significant equipment damage but fortunately only six or seven passengers sustained minor injuries. No 34 suffered most whereas No 36 was able to limp back to Inchicore under its own steam.

The Enquiry (Lt Col PG von Donop, R.E. presiding) concluded that as the Down train was stationary, the Carlow signalman lowered the Up Home approach signal which until then had properly been kept at danger. The Up train passed this signal at 8.26 am at a speed variously estimated at between 10 and 25 mph. The driver averred that the brakes had been applied and that his train was well under control to stop in the station. About 15 yards short of the points at the start of the passing loop, he saw that they were incorrectly set. He applied emergency braking which proved insufficient to prevent his striking the stationary locomotive and train at 7-8 mph.

The signalman candidly admitted his error in pulling the wrong point lever after the Up train had cleared the home signal. The distance between the signal and the points was 281 yards so the train having passed, there was nothing in the interlocking to prevent the signal being returned to danger thus releasing the point mechanism before the train arrived at the loop. The company stated that the excessive distance between signal and loop was intended to protect shunting movements over a siding serving a cattle bank against approaching Up trains.

It was recommended that the home signal be re-located closer to the points controlling admission to the loop. Also the points for the siding should be locked by a key on the staff of the Carlow-Milford section. This would prevent use of the siding when an Up train was approaching. The signalman was held solely accountable. It was noted that he committed his error a few minutes short of the end of his 12-hour shift. However, as he had only dealt with four goods train prior to the two passenger services, the presiding officer noted that he was hardly overworked.

Great Southern & Western Railway: Felthouse Junction, 19th January 1910

Felthouse Junction was situated 3½ miles from Wexford on the single line branch from that point to Killinick Junction on the Waterford-Rosslare route. The line both sides of Felthouse was double track for a short distance. On this double line portion there was a double junction with its facing connection on the Up line. The right-hand line led to the Killinick branch and the left-hand to a branch direct to Rosslare Strand. These diverging lines were double for about three hundred yards before becoming single again.

The 8.10 pm Up goods train from Wexford South became derailed while negotiating the tight reverse curve that gave access to the Killinick route. 0-4-2 Type XXA [20A] – W No 278 was running tender first with sixteen vehicles in tow comprising thirteen wagons, a 6-wheel brake van, an 8-wheel coach and a 6-wheel coach in that order. There was no continuous brake in operation and there were no passengers on the train. The 6-wheel tender with 10' wheelbase ended up straddling the track sideways, the locomotive was thrown on its side, the leading wagon was destroyed and the next three were slightly damaged.

Lt Col PG von Donop, R.E. presided over the Enquiry at which the only effective witness was Driver Doyle. It was concluded that the trackwork at the junction which had been completely re-laid four years earlier was in excellent condition. There was no evidence of any obstruction on the line. Train speed was estimated at less than 10 mph (as confirmed by the guard), so suspicion fell upon the locomotive.

Tender- and bunker-first running was never common in Ireland and in this case, it was an operating convenience for a return passenger train working. Marks on the track indicated that the rear (i.e. leading in this situation) tender wheels had become derailed while traversing the right section of the reverse curve leading to the single line. Tender and locomotive wheels were examined and found in excellent condition and in gauge, with the tyres almost new.

Doyle expressed the view in evidence that the accident had been caused by defects in the coupling between tender end locomotive. He was the regular driver of No 278 and the engine had de-railed on two or three occasions previously. He had formed the view that the coupling was at fault and reported it as a repair needing attention. The matter was investigated at Inchicore in September 1909, and replacement of the existing rubber springs with the standard pattern of buffer springs had been considered but rejected. The engine had been built in 1876 and as modifications to the footplate would have been necessary, it seems that the work was ruled out as not being not cost justified. Accordingly the rubber springs were replaced following minor attention which left the overall locomotive and tender wheelbase unreasonably rigid.

On the morning prior to the accident, the engine had de-railed in Wexford goods yard while being propelled around a right hand curve as at Felthouse. The poor quality track in the yard might have been a contributory factor but it was concluded that the pressure between the flange of the leading left-hand wheel and the outer left-hand rail would tend to turn the leading end of the tender to the right. When this turning movement took place, the right hand buffer between engine and tender would be compressed or at least restricted. In turn the flange pressure between wheel and rail would be increased, thereby forcing the wheel to mount the rail. The tightness of the coupling could not be measured subsequently as it had to be cut away to part engine and tender. It was nevertheless admitted that the rubber buffer springs allowed insufficient compression. The presiding officer concluded with the remark "The company informs me that this engine is the last of this description now remaining at work on the line, and that it will be forthwith taken out of use." No 278 was officially withdrawn in March 1910.

Appendix D: Locomotive Names

Comparatively few locomotives of GSWR origin were named but the practice was favoured by the WLWR and some of smaller constituent companies. Popular choices included flowering plants, animals, geographic locations and personalities. The meanings of some were familiar but others were less clear being from either parochial or obscure sources.

Name	Original railway	Original No	GSWR No	Description
Ant	WLR	6	225	An insect of the *Formicidae* family, of order *Hymenoptera*
Arnott	CYR	10	67	Sir John Arnott, Mayor of Cork; retail businessman; director of CYR and Cork & Macroom Direct Railway
Antelope	GSWR		Unknown	Of family *Bovidae*; sister group to deer in Eurasia and Africa; affixed for short period but number and type unidentified
Bee	WLR	5	224	A social flying insect within the superfamily *Apoidea*
Bernard	WLWR	55	298	Percy B Bernard of Castle Hacket, Tuam, was chairman of the Athenry & Tuam Railway, WLR director and chairman from 1893
Bessborough	WLR	2	-	Co Waterford home of Earl of Bessborough, WLR director
Blarney Castle	WLWR	21	274	Castle built 1446; home of the famous stone
Brian Boru	WLWR	52	295	King of Munster; (c. 941 - April 1014); died at Battle of Clontarf
Buffalo	GSWR		Unknown	Bovine species in Africa, Asia and north America (bison); affixed for short period but number and type unidentified
Cambria	WWR		-	Latinised version of Cymru, the local language name for Wales
Camel	GSWR		Unknown	Even-toed ungulate in genus *Camelus* native to Asia and Africa; affixed for short period but number and type unidentified
Camelia	WLR	37	287	Species of evergreen shrubs in family *Theaceae*
Carlisle	CYR	3	63	George Howard, 7th Earl of Carlisle, Lord Lieutenant of Ireland 1859-64; railway enthusiast who exclaimed at opening of the CYR that "Europe was behind it and America ahead of it!"
Carrick Castle	WLR	47	292	Alternative for Ormond Castle, built pre-1315; on River Suir
Castle Hacket	WLWR	51	294	Percy Bernard's demense Tuam, Co. Galway (see *Bernard* above)
Chambers	CYR	4	64	Believed to have been the name of a director but not confirmed
Colleen Bawn	WLWR	45	233	"The fair haired lass"
Cyclops	WLWR	57	238	Gigantic stature with single eye in his forehead; according to Greek mythology a son of Cœlus and Terra
Dahlia	WLR	32	283	Herbaceous plant in Central America; formerly named *Tuam*
(the) Darkie	WLWR	29	228	Origin of this locally applied name is unclear; not actually carried but locomotive was universally known by this name; acquired semi-official recognition
Derry Castle	WLR	13	266	Derry Castle is in Co Limerick; home of a WLWR director; also a ruin on Lough Derg
Dreadnought	WLWR	49	235	Means "fear nothing"; associated with warships from Elizabethan times; a type of early 20th Century battleship
Dromedary	GSWR		Unknown	Large even-toed ungulate with one hump; native to Arabia; affixed for short period but number and type unidentified
Drumconora	WLR	30		Country home near Ennis, of O'Loghlen and Culliney families
Duncannon	WLR	35	285	Co Wexford home of Abraham Stevens, ELR Chairman (1883-5)
Earl of Bessborough	WLR	12	265	Chairman of the WLR; (see *Bessborough* above)
Ennis	WLR	31	282	County town of Co Clare; later renamed *Myrtle*
Era	WLR	22	275	A span of time, for example "geological era"
Erin	GSWR		[300]	Derivative in Hiberno-English of Eirinn, the Irish word for Ireland
Erin-go Bragh	WLWR	46	234	A term that expresses allegiance; translates as "Ireland Forever"
Fairy	GSWR		Sprite	Small imaginary being with magical powers
Faugh-a-Ballagh	WLWR	17	270	Irish battle cry "clear the way"; motto of the Royal Irish Fusiliers

Appendix D

Name	Railway	No.		Description
Fermoy	CYR	6	68	A town on the River Blackwater in East Co. Cork
Galtee More	WLR	20	273	Highest peak in Galtee Mountains between Tipperary and Limerick
Garryowen	WLR	9	262	The "Brides of Garryowen"; melodrama by Dion Boucicault
Geraldine	WLWR	18	271	Alternative name for FitzGerald dynasty of Hiberno-Norman or Cambro-Norman origins; Irish peers since the 14th Century
Glengall	WLR	1		Richard Butler, 2nd Earl of Glengall, Chairman of the WLR
Goliath	WLWR	58	239	Son of Gath; the Philistine giant slain by David
Gort	WLR	24		Town in South Co. Galway; railway crossed main street by bridge
Granston	WLR	48	293	Manor house near Abbeyleix
Grouse	GSWR		Unknown	Game bird of order *Galliformes* from the family *Tetraonidae*; affixed for short period but number and type unidentified
Hartington	CYR	9	66	8th Duke of Devonshire (of Lismore Castle);also Marquess of Hartington; involved with several railways in Munster
Hercules	WLWR	50	236	Mythical Greek hero noted for his strength
Hyacinth	WLR	38	288	Small, spring-blooming, perennial, fragrant flowering plant
Imp	GSWR	Imp		Mythological being similar to a fairy or demon
Inchicore	GSWR		320	District of Dublin 8 and location of Inchicore Works
Jubilee	WLWR	53	296	Commemorated WLR's 50th anniversary, 21st July 1895
Jumbo	GSWR		201	Large animal, person or object; a nickname for an elephant
Killemnee	WLWR	54	297	Residence in Co Waterford of a WLR director
Kincora	WLR	19	[272]	Brian Boru's palace at Killaloe; ancient weir across the Shannon
Knockma	WLR	43	290	Mountain between Tuam and Headford in Co. Galway
Lady MacNeill	WLR	3		Wife of Sir John MacNeill, 19th Century engineer; later *Pioneer*
Leopard	GSWR		Unknown	Large cat of species *Panthera*; affixed for short period but number and type unidentified
Lewis	CYR	1	61	Twice bankrupt London financier who partly financed the CYR; his third bankruptcy ended the CYR; Lewis went to prison
Lily	WLR	30	281	Diminutive of *Lilium*, a flowering plant; originally named *Waterford*
Limerick	WLR	4		Major Irish City in Munster, 129 miles from Dublin Kingsbridge
Limerick	WLR	25	[277]	City and county in Munster; later renamed *Verbena*
Lion	GSWR		Unknown	Large cat in the family *Felidae*; affixed for short period nut number and type unidentified
Lord Roberts	GSWR		301	From an Anglo-Irish family in Co Waterford, Lord Roberts of Kandahar; commanded British forces in the Boer War; created Baron 1892; became Earl Roberts 1901
Lough Cutra	WLR	31		A lake in Co Galway near the railway between Gort and Tubber
Lough Derg	WLR	14	267	Southernmost freshwater lake on the River Shannon
Myrtle	WLR	31	282	Flowering plants of family Myrtaceae; formerly named *Ennis*
Negro	GSWR		201	Person of negroid ethnicity; unacceptable term in modern usage
North Star	WLR	39	289	Brightest star in constellation Ursa Minor; renamed *Shamrock*
Nephin	WLR	44	291	Mountain, part of the Nephin Beg range in Co Mayo
Pat	GSWR		No class	Diminutive of "Patrick", machine (technically plant) carried this name; worked the coal gantry at Cork depot
Pheasant	GSWR		Unknown	Bird of family Phasianidae; affixed for a short period but number and type unidentified
Pike	CYR	5	65	Ebenezer Pike, Cork shipowner and CYR Director
Pioneer	WLR	3		Person who abstains from alcohol; formerly *Lady MacNeill*
Primrose	WLR	8	[261]	Small Spring-flowering plant in the genus *primula*
Princess Ena	GSWR		301	Named at Inchicore 25 April 1900 by Princess Victoria Eugenie while accompanying Queen Victoria on a visit to Ireland (Ena is a diminutive of Eugenie); board minute 26 March 1900 records decision to use name *Shamrock* but last-minute change was was made; named while still under construction

Locomotives of the Great Southern & Western Railway

Name	Railway	No.	No.	Description
Progress	WLR	7	226	Implies improvement and advancement; later renamed *Wasp*
Rocklands	WLWR	16	269	Residence of a WLWR Director
Roney	CYR	2	62	Sir Cusack Patrick Roney, secretary of Eastern Counties Railway; appointed Chairman of the CYR in 1859
Roxborough	WLR	15	268	Shaw family home of departmental store fame; area in Limerick City, the Roxborough Road crosses the railway near the station
Saint Patrick	GSWR		301	Anglicised Pátraic or Pádraig, from Latin Patricius (patrician); patron saint of Ireland, thought to have come from come from Wales missionary; who introduced Christianity to Ireland
Sambo	GSWR		Sambo	Traditional name for unnumbered Inchicore works shunter,
Sarsfield	WLR	24	227	Patrick Sarsfield, 1st Earl of Lucan; Irish Jacobite soldier; leader in Williamite War; after Treaty of Limerick (October 1691), led 11,000 soldiers to France; "Flight of the Wild Geese"
Shamrock	WLR	33	[284]	A young sprig, national symbol of Ireland linked with St Patrick
Shamrock	GSWR		299	
Shannon	WLR	6		Ireland's longest river, rises in Fermanagh, enters sea
Shannon	WLWR	2	222	near Limerick
Sir James	WLR	10	263	Sir James Speight was High Sheriff and Mayor of Limerick City; WLR Chairman from 1885 until death in 1892
Sir William Goulding	GSWR		341	Sir William Joshua Goulding Bt. (1856-1925), chairman GSWR (1901-24); GSR (1925); Irish Railway Clearing House (1907-25)
Slieve-na-Mon	WLR	23	276	Mountain north of Carrick-on-Suir and Clonmel
South of Ireland	WLWR	28	[280]	Generic term for the southern part of the island of Ireland
Sprite	GSWR		Spite	Mythical being, usually and elf, fairy or goblin
Stag	GSWR		Unknown	Male hoofed mammal of family *Cervidae*; affixed for short period but number and type unidentified
Stuart de Decies	CYR	7	69	Henry Villiers-Stuart, 1st Baron Stuart de Decies; Lord Lieutenant of Co Waterford (1831-74)
Suir	WLR	5		River Suir rises near Templemore, and joins the River Barrow
Synott	WLR	7?		(Possibly named), Thomas Synott, WLR Chairman 1876-1883
Thunderer	WLWR	56	237	One that thunders; might refer to the British battleship of 1872; nickname for *The Times* newspaper of London
Thomond	WLR	27	279	Anglicised form of Tuamhain, name for most of North Munster; used by present-day establishments in the region
Titan	WLR	41	231	Greek mythology, person of great intellect, strength or importance
Tuam	WLR	32	283	Second largest town in Co Galway; later renamed *Dahlia*
Urus	GSWR		Unknown	Extinct large cattle in Europe, Asia and north America; affixed for short period but number and type unidentified
Verbena	WLWR	25	[277]	A genus of perennial and annual herbaceous plants native to the Americas; formerly named *Limerick*
Violet	WLR	36	286	A member of the *viola* genus of flowering plants
Victoria	GSWR		301	Queen Victoria was the British Monarch when locomotive was built
Vulcan	WLR	40	230	In Roman mythology, god of fire, volcanoes and metal-working
Wasp	WLR	7	226	Insect of the order *Hymenoptera* ; formerly named Progress
Waterford	WLR	3		County City, 106 miles by rail from Dublin Kingsbridge (Heuston)
Waterford	WLR	30	281	Later renamed *Lily*
Zetland	WLR	3	260	Archaic spelling of Shetland; Lawrence Dundas, 3rd Earl of Zetland Lord Lieutenant of Ireland (1889-1892); WLR director

Appendix E: The Gallant 44

The new pier at Rosslare was opened in 1906 by the Fishguard & Rosslare Railways & Harbours Company and the first train to use this facility was driven by Pat Duggan, a native of the area and a railway bard. The local community was essentially a small railway town, set beside the "say" (sea). To cater for the augmented services, in particular the prestigious Cork Express, additional locomotive personnel were posted to Ballygeary shed at Rosslare from Dublin and Waterford. These elite crews looked down on the local men who were retained on goods and shunting duties. Pat Duggan and others regarded themselves as the equal of the "blow-ins", if only given the opportunity to prove it. In the 1920s, Kerry Bogie Type XII [12] No 44 (1878 to 1950) was Ballygeary shed pilot whose most demanding duty was to work trips over the 11 miles to Wexford. However, on one occasion it was called to greater glory to assist the Cork Express.

Come all you engine drivers from Cork unto Tralee,
From there to Dublin and Rosslare, just listen unto me,
The feat that I accomplished was never known before,
With the Ballygeary Pilot, the gallant 44.
'Twas early in the morning, before the break of day,
There came a wire from Fishguard, "a big crowd to you by sea"
If Cotter is upon "the hill", let him at once be called.   (1)
For by him and him only, must this big load be hauled.

I was sleeping like an infant, with my hands across my breast
Dreaming of my childhood days, the days I always blest
Just when in that position, the Call Boy knocked the door,
"Arise" he said "Jack Cotter, you're required for 44".
I arose without a murmur, and strolled down to the shed
But I would have rather, they let me stay in bed
No big loco there was handy, the like not known before   (2)
So I mounted with Pat Lucey, the gallant 44.

I filled the lubricator, to make her pistons as free,
For this big crowd of passengers, that was coming o'er the sea.
I took the damper handle off and ditto off the blower
For I knew I'd require neither, with the gallant 44.
Away I set out from the shed, and steamed off to the Pier
The first to greet me was Pat Smith, and in his eye a tear.   (3)
He said, "Good morning skipper, are you long ashore?"
"Or what port are you bound for, with the gallant 44?"

I stood in silence for a while, not knowing what to say
To my true and trusty friend, on that auspicious day
I stoutly clasped him by the hand, saying "Good Pat ashore
I'm going to take the helm now of the gallant 44".
Now Heffernan was the driver of the express that day,
He walked around my little craft, smiled, and turned away
And said to his mate Kelly "the skipper is no more
He'll rue the day he came in front of me, with gallant 44".

We started off right bravely and passing through the Strand
She registered 60 on the gauge, I had her well in hand
If I had plenty of water here, 'tis I could do the swank
But alas! it was not boiling, 'twas only in the tank.
However, nearing Wellington Bridge, she had 70 or more
"Come up" I cried "for Taylorstown, my gallant 44!"
She responded right bravely, like a steed driven to the fray
And mounted the bank at Taylorstown, how she did I'll not say.
We passed through famed Ballycullane, the buffers nearly wore,
And myself and Lucey gasping on the gallant 44.

Locomotives of the Great Southern & Western Railway

Going down Campile I held what steam I had
The reason I did this was the brake had gone down bad,
The vacuum had long since gone by, like the spirits of the dead
That hover round Dunbrody, a-past which we now sped. (4)
And as I passed that grand old pile, my thoughts fondly strayed
To the men and times long past and gone, ere railways first were made
For they were the men that had the times, when no Call Boy knocked the door
And woke you to the tune of, "You're required for 44!"

We sped through Kilmannock, skipped the Barrow Bridge. (5)
Went through Snowhill tunnel, driven like a wedge
She got a twist going round the curve, like an eel on a hook
That twist will never leave her, of that I'll kiss the book.
Now all this time the needle of the gauge was going round
And passing Abbey Junction, it was pointed to the ground. (6)
We had water left at Waterford, that was never known before
And 'twas then it began boiling, in the gallant 44.

I made my way to the turntable, by strategy, of course
Thinking of the trip I'd had and how the story could be worse
I coupled up the damper handle, put the handle on the blower,
For I knew, I'd want them going back with the gallant 44.
I'd brought her back unsullied, to her station at Rosslare
After making the record run, since the opening of the Pier
I handed her to Linskey, saying "lend her Bill no more
"For a credit to the neighbourhood, is the gallant 44!"

When Linskey in the morning to his duty he came down
And heard of how Jack Cotter had taken her to town
He got into a passion and on me cursed and swore
For stealing in his absence the gallant 44.
Since then I have learned with sad regret, they've taken her away
Far, far from Ballygeary that old shed by the "say"
And given her a rest, at a place called Inchicore
And left him sad and lonely, for his Gallant 44.

Notes:

(1)   Rosslare locomotive men frequently used nautical terms. Driver Jack Cotter had worked in his teens on coastal vessels serving English ports. He referred to the footplate as the quarter deck and his fireman was the first mate. He was nicknamed "the skipper".
(2)   The non-available "big engine" would probably have been a 2-6-0 Type XLI [41] Class 368 which was favoured as the pilot for heavy trains to Waterford.
(3)   Pat Smith was a trawlerman who had been at sea with Jack Cotter.
(4)   Dunbrody Abbey is a 13th Century ruin beside the railway.
(5)   Barrow Bridge was Ireland's longest at the time of writing.
(6)   Abbey Junction for the New Ross line was site of one of four signal cabins that served the Waterford station area.

It was normal practice for the Great Western Railway to send word from Landore advising the number of passengers that would be making the crossing to Rosslare and thus whether an assisting engine would be needed. There was usually adequate time to prepare the spare express engine but on that particular day the message was delayed, arriving shortly before the steamer berthed at Rosslare. Sufficient steam could not be raised on the spare engine and the only other candidate was No 44 with around 60 lb/ sq in on the clock.

Heffernan reputedly covered the 39 miles to Waterford in 43 minutes start to stop, hauling the train and pushing No 44 which was still chronically shy of steam. Firing was only possible on the few straight stretches of that twisting route and for most of the journey, No 44's crew just hung on for dear life. Cotter so frequently boasted afterwards of having assisted Heffernan on this important service that Duggan recorded the event in this poem.

Bibliography

Author	Title	Publisher & date
Ahrons, E	Locomotive and Train Working in the Latter Part of the Nineteenth Century, Vols 5 & 6	Heffer 1953/ 4
Bulleid, HAV	The Aspinall Era	Ian Allan 1967
Byrom, R	William Fairbairn - experimental engineer and mill-builder	University of Huddersfield 2015
Carter, E	Britain's Railway Liveries	Burke 1952
Clements, Jeremy & McMahon, Michael	Locomotives of the GSR	Colourpoint Books 2008
Conroy, J C	History of Railways in Ireland	Longmans Green Publishing 1928
"DC"	Irish Industrial and Contractors Locomotives	Union Publications 1962 & 1969
Dean, William	Report on Waterford & Limerick Railway PRO ref 1057/3176	Great Western Railway 1874
Fryer, C	The Waterford & Limerick Railway	Oakwood 2000
Flanagan, PJ	The 101 Class Locomotives of the GSWR	Irish Railway Record Society 1966
Hancox, A	The Harmonious Blacksmith Robinson Cramlington	Stephenson Locomotive Society 1995
Haresnape, Brian & Rowledge, Peter	Robinson Locomotives – a Pictorial History	Ian Allan 1982
Heppell, George	North Eastern Locomotives, a draughtsman's life	NE Railway Association 2012
Jackson, D	JG Robinson – a lifetime's work	Oakwood 1996
Johnson, S	Johnson's Atlas & Gazetteer of the Railways of Ireland	Midland Publishing 1997
Johnston, N	Locomotives of the GNR(I)	Colourpoint Books 1999
Joynt, EE	Modern Locomotives of the GSWR	The Locomotive Railway & Carriage Review
Joynt, EE	Reminiscences of an Irish Locomotive Works	The Locomotive Railway & Carriage Review
Loyd, Joe	List of Beyer Peacock Locomotives (2nd Edition)	Self-published, Manchester 2003
Lowe, J	British Steam Locomotive Builders	Goose & Son 1975
Mansfield, Dermot	Express Steam. Dublin to Cork	Unpublished work, 1999
McCutcheon, A	Railway History in Pictures: Ireland Vol 1	David & Charles 1969
Murray K, & McNeill, D	The Great Southern & Western Railway	Irish Railway Record Society 1976
O'Neill, Jack	Engines & Men, Irish Railways - A view from the footplate	Rectory Press 2005
O'Rourke, A	The Locomotives of the Waterford & Tramore Railway	Historical Model Railway Society, Journal
O'Rourke, A	The wreck of the Darkie	Irish Railway Record Society, Journal
Prior, Alan	19th Century Railway Drawings in 4mm scale	David & Charles 1983
Redman, R	The Railway Foundry Leeds 1839-1969	Goose & Son 1972
Rowledge, JWP	Irish Steam Loco Register	Irish Traction Group 1993
Rowledge, JWP	The Turf Burner	Irish Railway Record Society 1972
Russell, P	Steam in Camera 1898-1960: photographs from the LCGB Nunn Collection (2nd series)	Ian Allan 1981
Ryan, Gregg	The Works, Celebrating 150 Years of Inchicore	Self-published, 1996
Scott, W	Locomotives of the LMS NCC and its predecessors	Colourpoint Books 2008
Shepherd, Ernie	Bulleid and the Turf Burner	KRB Publications 2004
Shepherd, E	The Waterford, Limerick & Western Railway	Ian Allan 2006
Shepherd, E	Fishguard & Rosslare Railways & Harbours Company	Colourpoint Books 2015
Archival Material	Bazin's Annual Register (December 1923)	Author's collection
	Beyer Peacock & Co	Manchester Museum of Science & Industry
	Clements, RN - Papers	IRRS, Dublin
	Great Southern & Western Railway Timetables	Author's collection
	GSWR Appendix to the Working Timetable	Author's collection
	Hunslet Engine Co and Manning Wardle & Co,	Statfold Narrow Gauge Museum Trust
	John Fowler & Co,	Museum of English Rural Life, Reading
	Kitson & Co	Stephenson Locomotive Society
	Mahon, GR - Papers	IRRS, Dublin
	North British Locomotive Company	National Railway Museum, York
	Riley's Register (December 1877)	Author's collection
	Vulcan Foundry	Merseyside Maritime Museum
Periodicals:		
	Fayle's Bulletins	railwayarchive.co.uk
	Five Foot Three	Railway Engineer, The
	Industrial Locomotive, The	Railway Magazine, The
	Irish Railway Record Society, Journal	Scientific American
	Locomotive Railway & Carriage Review, The	steamindex.com

Index

Canal transport	23, 27-8

Companies (except GSWR):-

Athenry & Ennis Junction	76, 215-7, 237-8
Athenry & Tuam	113, 215-7, 231, 237-8
Castleisland	29, 47, 151, 173, 175
Cork, Bandon & South Coast	76, 113, 115, 264
Cork & Limerick Direct	26, 29, 30
Cork & Macroom Direct	227, 264
Danube & Black Sea	36, 123
Dublin & Blessington St. T'way	20, 173, 180,192
Dublin & Drogheda	23, 33, 76-8, 113
Dublin & Kingstown	23, 264
Dublin & Meath	215-7
Dublin, Wicklow & Wexford/ Dublin & South Eastern	22, 29, 176-8, 192, 264-6
Fermoy & Mitchelstown	29, 82, 161
Great Central	54, 57, 107,170, 232
Great Leinster & Munster	24, 27
Great Northern (Ireland)	29, 100, 264
Great Southern	18, 32, 265-6
Great Western	4, 8, 24-7, 31-2, 39, 57, 106-7, 176, 193-6, 253
Irish Great Western	27
Irish South Eastern	27
Killarney Junction	28/ 29
Limerick & Ennis	208-10
Limerick & Foynes	26
London & Birmingham	23-4, 27, 77-8, 240
London & North Western	4, 30, 33, 39, 40, 83, 107, 123, 264
London, Midland & Scottish	264-5
Midland Great Western	22, 27-8, 30-3, 35, 176, 193, 216, 236-9, 264
Newry Warrenpoint & Rostrevor	202-4, 220
North Eastern	273
Tralee & Killarney	29
Waterford & Tramore	207, 209
Waterford & Wexford	173, 178-80
Wexford, Carlow & Dublin	26-27

Locomotive builders:-

Armstrong, Whitworth	60, 61-2, 105-9, 247, 263
Avonside Engine Co	4, 62-3, 187-9, 218-21, 253, 258
Beyer, Peacock & Co	4, 8, 33, 40, 42, 60, 63, 112, 123-4, 128, 243
Bury, Curtis & Kennedy	4, 34-5, 60, 63, 73, 76-81, 112-5, 202-4, 240-1, 254
Dübs & Co	63, 224-7, 229-30, 256-8
William Fairbairn & Sons	4, 33, 35, 64, 73, 81, 112, 116-7,204-9, 241,254-5
Fossick & Hackworth	64, 215-7, 254-5
Fowler, John & Co	64-5, 186, 253
Grendon, Thomas & Co	33, 35, 65, 115, 202, 241
Hawthorns (Leith)	65-6, 223-4
Hunslet Engine Co	66-7, 179-80, 190-1
Inchicore Works	4, 6, 35-6, 46-7, 58-60, 152
Kitson & Co	66, 184, 211-5, 230-6, 253-8
Limerick Works	194, 210-1, 214-5, 218-9, 228-9
Manning, Wardle & Co	68, 192
Neilson, Reid & Co	68, 73, 99, 174-5, 246
North British Locomotive Co	53, 60, 68, 113, 136-7, 140, 143, 166-7
Robert Stephenson & Co	70, 221-2, 258
Rothwell & Co	35, 70, 112, 116, 241
Sharp, Stewart & Co	4, 6, 34-5, 60, 70, 73-6, 128, 176-8, 189, 206-7, 210-3, 240, 243, 253-6
Stothert & Slaughter	62-3, 183-4, 202, 207, 253-5
Vulcan Foundry	70-1, 182-3, 187, 190, 217-8, 221, 225-8, 253-4, 256-8
Wilson, EB & Co	72, 185, 221, 253

Personalities:-

Ahrons, EL	37, 49, 83, 89, 117, 273
Appleby, Henry	196, 221-3, 225
Aspinall, John	36, 45-7, 50, 92-5, 156-8, 171, 271-2
Atock, Martin	47, 55, 196
Bazin, JR	8, 21, 50, 110-11, 266, 271

Index (continued)

Personalities (cont):-

Bianconi, Carlo	24-5;
Burgess, HG	264
Bury, Edward	26, 59, 77
Churchward, George	52, 97, 106-7
Clements, RN	4-8, 106, 124, 125, 163-8
Coey, Robert	50, 52-3, 96-105, 134-1, 244-6
Dargan, William	24, 25, 29, 203-4, 209-10
Dean, William	193-6, 201
Dewrance, John	33
Goulding, Sir William	266
Fairlie, Robert	145-6
Ivatt, Henry	8, 36, 46-8, 50, 143, 158-63
McDonnell, Alexander	4, 6-8, 18-9, 36-50, 85-92, 121-4, 145-56, 242-4, 271-3
Maunsell, Richard	50, 53-4, 104-5, 142, 168-9
Miller, George	33-4, 82-5, 117-23, 144, 241
Morton, Walter	55, 266, 271
Park, JC	38, 45
Ramsbottom, John	40, 45
Riley, CE	266
Robinson, JG	54, 57, 170, 193-7, 218, 222-3. 225-36
Rowledge, JWP	5
Wakefield, John	33-4, 82-5, 117-23, 241
Watson, EA	50, 54-5, 105-9, 169-71
Webb, Francis	45, 47-8, 227

Railway: GSWR:-

Absorbed companies	29
Accidents	29, 168, 212, 223, 274-5
Amalgamation into GSR	264-6

Railway: GSWR (cont.) :-

Construction	24-32
Livery	55-7, 167
Permanent way	37
Relations with other companies	28, 30-1

Political factors:-

First World War	262-3
Grouping, UK	262
Irish Railway Executive Com'tee	32, 262
Railways Commission (1922)	32, 262
Royal Commission (1837-8)	23, 27
War of Independence & Civil War	32, 163, 165, 227, 262-4

Technical issues:-

Belpaire fireboxes	53, 97-8
Bogies	52, 103, 148
Boiler design & pressure	47, 52-3, 97-8, 268
Brakes	29-30, 50, 271-2
Compound steam	48-9, 95
Fairlie design	42, 143, 145-7
Iron and steel	37-8, 47
Locomotive classes & numbers	5, 6-21, 193
Locomotive fuel	42-5
Locomotive liveries	55-7, 176, 181, 196
Locomotive rebuilding	6, 7, 38-9, 123-5, 158, 194
Railmotors	167-8, 192
Superheater	95, 268-71
Valve gear	98, 223
Water	42, 259-61
Wheels	37-8

283

4-4-0 Type XX [20] No 341 *Sir William Goulding* is crossing Kilnap Viaduct with the 9.30 am Dublin Kingsbridge-Cork, coasting down the 1 in 60 descent to Cork, Glanmire Road with scheduled arrival at 2.15 pm. This service stopped at Maryborough (now Portlaoise), Ballybrophy, Thurles, Limerick Junction and Mallow. This was the second Dublin-Cork train of the day, following the Mail which departed Kingsbridge at 7.00 am, having started out from Kingstown (now Dun Laoghaire) at 6.10 am. Views of No 341 at work are rare; this image was discovered on the eve of manuscript delivery to the printers! *By courtesy of CP Friel*

4-6-0 No 500 (Type XXII [22]) climbs away from Cork with the 4.00 pm Up mail bound for Dublin Kingsbridge and Kingstown (now Dun Laoghaire). This train was advertised as being made up with "Corridor Dining Cars". The station stops were as for the 9.30 am Down from Kingsbridge with the 51 miles from Maryborough to Kingsbridge timed at 58 minutes. Standing time at Kingsbridge was ten minutes during which the 4-6-0 was detached and a pilot locomotive coupled on to the rear to drag the train back to Islandbridge Junction (which faced the Up line). There a smaller locomotive would be coupled at the front to work forward to Kingstown by way of Amiens Street (over which route the 4-6-0 was prohibited on grounds of axle loading). Arrival at Kingstown to connect with the Holyhead boat was scheduled for 8.35 pm. *By courtesy of CP Friel*